SPECIAL COMMEMORATIVE EDITION

THE BIONIC BOOK

THE SIX MILLION DOLLAR MAN & THE BIONIC WOMAN

RECONSTRUCTED

HERBIE J PILATO

FOREWORD BY RICHARD ANDERSON
INTRODUCTION BY TERRENCE MCDONNELL

Published in the USA by:
BearManor Media
P O Box 1129
Duncan, OK 73534-1129
www.bearmanormedia.com

ISBN 979-8-88771-256-7

Printed in the United States of America.
Text and content edited by Brendan Slattery.
Cover design by Matt Hankinson and Elaine Byers. Interior photo selection, editing, and layout by Matt Hankinson. Book design by Brian Pearce (Red Jacket Press), and Sarah Joseph.

DEDICATED TO THE TRUE INNER STRENGTH
OF HUMANITY, AND IN MEMORY OF RICHARD
ANDERSON, MARTIN E. BROOKS, HARVE BENNETT,
AND ALL THE OTHER GOOD *BIONIC* SOULS WHO
ARE NO LONGER WITH US IN THIS WORLD.

BIONIC Buzz

"Herbie J Pilato has (re)built it! He has the technology. Now, his how-to-guide to the adventures of pop culture's most beloved bionic heroes is truly definitive."

—**David McDonnell**, legendary Editor,
STARLOG Magazine

"I don't think anyone ever thought that the [Martin Caidin] novel *Cyborg* would generate so much activity in the TV world. For the first time, the behind-the-scenes stories of *Cyborg*, *The Six Million Dollar Man*, and *The Bionic Woman* are revealed. Pilato exposes the connection between science fiction author Martin Caidin and the two shows. He talks about the problems of finding the right actors to play the roles, the many directors and writers involved with both shows and there are episode guides for the series and three movies. The author also shows how modern science has used bionic parts to save many lives. One thing unique is that the Six Million Dollar franchise holds a record for being one of the few series to have played on three major networks. For any fan of these series, this is a must-have book."

—**Midwest Book Review**

"**THE *BIONIC* BOOK** is the ideal read for fans of *The Six Million Dollar Man* and *The Bionic Woman*. Herbie J Pilato delves deep into every facet of the shows and the subsequent reunion movies, from their creation to their casting to their production, and everything in between. A fun but also frank look at what went so right and, at times, so wrong, and at the show's legacy, this book is Bionic nirvana."

 —**Ian Spelling**, entertainment journalist and author

"The fun for me in **THE *BIONIC* BOOK** is in the memories it invokes of those more innocent days when a slow-motion run with sound effects constituted super-speed and we all accepted that…That's where Herbie J Pilato's ***BIONIC* BOOK** hit me: right in the nostalgia. As TV show books go, the author has demonstrated previously that he knows how to write them.

 —**Steve Thompson**, Book Steves Library.com

"Stunning in both depth and attention to detail, **THE *BIONIC* BOOK** is yet another grand slam for Herbie J Pilato, whose work in print and on the small screen is uniformly fantastic and much sought after."

 – **Ian Lowell**, author (*Son of Sam was My Catcher and Other Bronx Tales*)

Herbie J Pilato's **THE *BIONIC* BOOK** is an exhaustively-researched, remarkable volume that is also one of my all-time favorite pop-culture remembrances. Whether you are a fan of all things Bionic, or simply curious as to the inner-workings of television, this book is a marvel."

 – **Joel Eisenberg**, author/producer/screenwriter (*The Chronicles of Ara, Joe Lewis biopic*)

TABLE OF CONTENTS

FOREWORD BY
RICHARD ANDERSON

The success of *The Six Million Dollar Man* and *The Bionic Woman*, more than thirty years after their debut (in America and sixty other countries), is based on a number of factors. Beyond the ideal casting of Lee Majors and Lindsay Wagner as Steve Austin and Jaime Sommers, the shows remain workable, due to a solid combination of drama, action-adventure, fiction, humor, education, communication, entertainment, science and realism.

The *Bionic* shows were the first to bring back heroes to television after the tumultuous 1960s, which was burdened with wars, race rioting and various other hostilities. They retain a sci-fi element bound to a medical message of hope that, as the 20th Century comes to a close, is delivered on many levels. Steve and Jaime's influence has not gone away, and they are proving to have a life of their own.

Herbie J Pilato now retells the story of how it all began and what it's all become, and the results are both stoic and sensitive, as if to signify the very essence of Steve and Jaime themselves.

As my TV namesake, Oscar Goldman, might say, *Good job, pal.*

RICHARD ANDERSON WITH THE ORIGINAL EDITION OF THE BIONIC BOOK AT THE BIONIC FANSOURCE WEEKEND IN 2007. [CREDIT: PHOTOGRAPHY BY MATT HANKINSON]

INTRODUCTION
BY TERRENCE MCDONNELL

After my last final exam at Ohio University in 1969, I drove to Los Angeles to break into the entertainment industry. And like nearly everyone else who ever came here to follow their dream, just getting my foot in the door was a long, tough struggle. I knew I wanted to work in television in some capacity, but exactly where I might fit was the Big Question. Although writing was something that I seemed to have a knack for, actually being *hired* to write prime-time television seemed elusive and unattainable and after many failed attempts, I was *this* close to living on the street. At one point, when I found myself near rock bottom and in desperate need of money, I tried out for and became a contestant on a short-lived ABC prime-time quiz show from Jack Barry Productions called *The Reel Game*. With Jack as its host, it used old newsreel footage in the asking of the questions and they put me on the very first show. I played against a teacher and a young actor named Rod Haase, and though I lost – because I couldn't afford to bet a lot of money on the final question - I left with $800 that managed to keep me afloat for several more months. FADE OUT.

FADE IN: It's now the early 1970s. I'd finally managed to get a few television jobs and by this time was writing questions *for* Jack Barry on the original version of *The Joker's Wild*, a successful daytime CBS game show. Across the hall from me in our Century City offices was Justin 'Lefty' Edgerton, easily one of the most interesting people I ever met. At one time he'd been a carny, now he was the producer of our show. Additionally, he and another guy had just sold a story to *The Six Million Dollar Man*, which I thought was the coolest thing ever. He and his partner wrote the script and later wrote others for *The Bionic Woman* and even *The Incredible Hulk*. In 1973, Jack sold another game show to CBS called *Hollywood's Talking* and he brought in Lefty's writing partner to produce it; he'd worked for Jack in the past on several shows and even served as the producer of my television debut on *The Reel Game*.

His name was Ken Johnson and he changed my life.

Ken was the kind of guy who I liked immediately. Just a few years older than me, I looked up to him and admired how far he'd come and how much he'd accomplished. The two of us had great conversations about some of his earlier jobs, one of them being *The Mike Douglas Show* in Philadelphia and he regaled me with hilarious stories of some of the pranks he and his co-workers pulled. One afternoon Ken came back to the office from a meeting and when I saw his face, I sensed that something had happened; his expression was one of shock and awe and excitement. I asked him if he was all right and he told me, "I think they're going to make me the producer of *The Six Million Dollar Man*!" I was thrilled for him and knew what a tremendous moment this was. After repeatedly congratulating him. I said, "Oh, my god! If you get the job, can I come in and pitch stories?" He gave me an immediate yes and hurried back to his office.

After Ken moved to Universal Studios to produce *The Six Million Dollar Man*, he was as good as his word. On our very first pitch meeting, my new writing partner Jim Carlson and I sold a story and later wrote the script for what became the episode entitled "Divided Loyalty." And in a stupendously serendipitous twist of cosmic fate, one of the actors on that show was Rod Haase, who had played against me on *The Reel Game*. Over the course of four years, Jim and I contributed a half-dozen shows to both *The Six Million Dollar Man* and *The Bionic Woman* and wrote many, many others during our two decades together as a team. He was a dear friend and mentor and one of the best men I ever knew. I miss him every day.

So, here I am, fifty years later, still working in the television industry. And I find it somehow fitting that I'm writing the Introduction to a book celebrating two of the most iconic shows of the '70s, shows that I worked on and loved. For anyone growing up back then, for anyone who remembers them as fondly as I do, and for anyone who liked the original version of this book, you're going to love this revised "Special Commemorative Edition." It not only explores each episode of both shows, it dives deep behind the scenes with countless stories that even I didn't know about.

One last thing, on a purely personal level. As I turned the pages, memories and emotions from a half century ago swept over me with the warmest of feelings that I was lucky enough to collaborate with people like Lee Majors, Lindsay Wagner, Richard Anderson, Harve Bennett, and the entire cast and creative team that brought *The Six Million Dollar Man* and *The Bionic Woman* to life.

Six Million thank you's to all of them - especially to Jim and Ken – and also to Herbie J for writing this book.

Terrence McDonnell
Emmy-winning Writer-Producer
June 2023

TERRENCE MCDONNELL [CREDIT: COURTESY OF TERRENCE MCDONNELL]

MAN, WOMAN, BOOK AND MACHINE

Steve Austin, The Six Million Dollar Man, and Jaime Sommers, The Bionic Woman, are not your average superheroes. As portrayed by Lee Majors and Lindsay Wagner, they're heroes first, *super,* second. Through various incarnations, from the 1970s (on ABC and NBC) to the present (reruns of original episodes and reunion movies on cable's Lifetime and Sci-Fi channels), this atomic-powered, romantically-entangled couple continues to inhabit the television airwaves.

In the initial 1973 ABC pilot film, Steve was the first cyborg (half-human/half machine), rebuilt (made *better...stronger...faster*) by the American-based OSO (Office of Strategic Operations) after a freak accident. When the movie became a monthly, then weekly, series, he rekindled a romance with once-lost love Jaime. They planned to wed. She, too, was injured in a serious accident. Steve pleaded with his superiors to rebuild her, just like him. She, too, was given a hit series.

Millions of *Bionic* fans, general observers and those new to the genre, continue to perceive these programs beyond the contretemps of science fiction. Viewers the world over recognize and respect the unique covenant imparted by and between Steve and Jaime. Be it in France, Germany, Australia, or any number of disparate destinations, the devotion people have for this dynamic couple is evident. They hit a chord in the 1970s.

As children, today's thirty- and forty-somethings once aspired to run in bionic slow motion like Steve and Jaime; mimicked sound effects which accompanied his long-distanced-angled left eye; her sonar powered right ear. Viewers of all ages now continue the bionic legacy, as they still keep on liking and believing in bionic people, because the Austin/Sommers powers of persuasion continue to make bionic people likable and believable.

All these years later, one thing remains indelibly true: these shows were *fun.* It should be *fun* to be bionic, and it was. Waiting for the next episode to air was often sheer agony for younger viewers, who would eagerly break down the previous night's broadcast at school the next day. Fantastical and far-out plots and premises were played with a totally straight face, and we loved every minute of it. Rarities among the science fiction superhero hall of fame, The Six Million Dollar Man and The Bionic Woman prevail as *real*. Superman and Wonder Woman need never fear a rivalry, as they don't *really* exist.

Steve and Jaime are tangible. They care for one another, based upon their pre-cybernetic history, subsequent bionic transformation and distinct, yet combined, destinies. The home onlooker is encouraged (subconsciously or not) to seek sincerity at every turn; to stretch their reality, as well as their imagination; to see past contrarieties, and to focus on the common thread of humanity. TV viewers have sensed all along that these two were fundamentally human. Home observers continue to watch these programs not to laugh at camp, but to be entertained and moved.

As fictional government agents of decades-gone-by, the bionic duo was sent on special assignments, but their most important mission lingers into the present day. They introduced to the general public the bona fide possibility of workable prosthetics. A bionic bond was forged between fantasy and fact; between a farfetched TV concept and the medical visionaries who made good on the promise and potential of bionics.

Clearly, with SM and BW, the extraordinary communicative device known as television has been efficiently engaged. Steve and Jaime prove to be emphatic role models from whom we may ascertain *strength*. The real kind. The kind that lives inside us. The kind that allows us compassion and discretion; forgiveness and endurance. The human kind, motivated by the human spirit.

Through TV's majestic mechanics, and by observing the lives of a uniquely-created pair, struggling for personal identity while acclimating to their new physiology, the pressure to learn is off. We're charmed, and walk away with an inspirational thought and positive reinforcement in the process.

In keeping with the real-to-reel theme, the late, revered writer Martin Caidin (who passed away on March 24, 1997) was, well, a realist. His novel, Cyborg, first published in 1972, was the springboard for *The Six Million Dollar Man*, a tale of one man's triumph over spiritual ruin and Caidin's prognostication on bionic erudition.

Born Martin Karl von Strasser, on September 14, 1927 in New York City, Caidin himself was somewhat of a superior individual.

A commercial and professional US Air Force pilot, teacher and lecturer (at Santa Fe College and the Institute of Advanced Studies, Nebraska), he had studied Atomic-Radiological-Biological-Chemical Warfare, and became a researcher and developer in bionics and telekinetics. He was also a radio and TV talk show host, a war correspondent, stunt pilot, an actor, a consultant to many publications and business firms (including the Air Force Missile Test Center and the FAA), a special agent for several law agencies, an Operative in the US Air Commandos, a parachutist, a military vehicle test driver, and a researcher with the Office of Paranormal Research.

Besides *Cyborg*, Caidin published nearly 200 books (including *Samurai* in 1957, *Marooned* in 1964 — which inspired an Oscar-winning movie in 1969, *Devil Take All* in 1966, *The God Machine* in 1968, *The Saga of Iron Annie* in 1979, and *The Messiah Stone* in 1986). He contributed thousands of articles, short fiction and newspaper stories to a myriad of international publications, earning him many honors (i.e., The James J. Strebig Memorial Trophy from the Aviation/Space Writers Association — many from 1958 on), and awards from various Air Force, Army, Navy, NASA and government agencies and organizations.

The Bionic Book: The Six Million Dollar Man and the Bionic Woman Reconstructed merely expands on what has become Caidin's most successful crafted visions.

In the process, this book explores certain strengths.

The strength in appeal of two of television's top classic shows and their stars. The strength in stamina that was summoned by the cast and crew getting the programs on the air. The made-for-TV *bionic strength* that became legendary due to the twin series.

With text and rare photographs, this book attempts to decipher Steve and Jaime's universal affinity. As a study of both SM and BW, this double TV tome offers everything from personality profiles and complete episode summaries (with anecdotes), to a delineation of the *hows* and *whys* these adventures remain coupled to the psyche of television viewers across continents. Hopefully, it delivers a worthy and constructive chronicle which connects the best of all bionic worlds, officially returning the realm of *bionics* to book form, where it so bountifully began with Martin Caidin's critically-acclaimed, top-selling novel, *Cyborg*.

So let your left eye be your guide, feel free to flip back those dangling hairs from your right ear and, to make certain that you grasp every *better, stronger, faster* word, pace yourself, take your time, and read on...in slow motion.

LEE MAJORS, AS STEVE AUSTIN, INSPECTS A CIRCUIT BOARD
WITH HIS BIONIC LEFT EYE. AUSTIN WAS ALSO FITTED WITH BIONIC
REPLACEMENTS FOR HIS RIGHT ARM AND BOTH LEGS AFTER A
HORRIFYING PLANE CRASH. LINDSAY WAGNER, AS JAIME SOMMERS,
RECEIVED A BIONIC RIGHT ARM, LEGS, AND IMPLANT IN HER RIGHT
EAR AFTER A SERIOUS SKYDIVING ACCIDENT. HER BIONIC HEARING
FREQUENTLY CAME IN HANDY WHEN CRACKING SAFES.

"WE HAVE THE TECHNOLOGY..."
Oscar Goldman

CHAPTER 1

PROGRAMMING

"I USED TO THINK ABOUT WHAT IT WOULD HAVE FELT LIKE TO HAVE BIONIC STRENGTH, PARTLY BECAUSE OF THE RATIONAL APPROACH WE HAD TAKEN WITH THE SHOW. WE TRIED TO CREATE A SENSE OF LOGIC WITHIN THE CONFINES OF THE PREMISE."

LEE MAJORS

Martin Caidin brought his sense of reality to *Cyborg*:

The manned space shuttle program was diminished. Col. Steve Austin, the youngest astronaut to have moonwalked, was demoted in rank to experimental flier with the US Air Force. Highly educated, Col. Austin was considered a genius by his fellow astronauts. He maintained five academic degrees in all, including a masters in aerodynamics, astronautical engineering and, surprisingly enough, history. Physically fit, Austin enjoyed wrestling, boxing and fencing, while achieving a black belt in judo and Aikido. He speaks conversational Russian and fluent Spanish. Before joining the Air Force, Steve had a tour of duty with the Army in Vietnam, where he was a chopper pilot.

In 1973, at 6'1" and 32 years old, his trial-run aircraft, the *M3F5* (the *HL-10* in the series; the *M2-F2* in reality) was annihilated in a horrific mishap, and Austin was nearly killed. Left a multiple amputee, his left arm, both legs, and his left eye were gone (in the series, his right arm was severed). Critically injured, he was remade as The Six Million Dollar Man.

Now bionic, Steve has superhuman strength in both legs, his right arm, and his left eye offers him supersight. He can also run 60 miles an hour. Yet, he's human.

"What happened to Steve in that crash, is what happens to pilots all the time," professed Martin Caidin. In fact, the footage used in SM's opening credit sequence is that of an authentic aircraft accident.

On May 10, 1967, NASA lifting body pilot Bruce Peterson, 33, crashed his M2-F2 while attempting to land at Edwards Air Force Base (California),

WHAT TRANSPIRED ON MAY 10, 1967 WAS NO WORK OF FICTION. ON
THAT DAY, NASA TEST PILOT BRUCE PETERSON LOST CONTROL OF
HIS EXPERIMENTAL M2-F2 AIRCRAFT, RESULTING IN A DEVASTATING
CRASH AND GRUESOME INJURIES. SIX YEARS LATER, LEE MAJORS
WOULD RELIVE PETERSON'S NIGHTMARE IN THE *SIX MILLION DOLLAR
MAN* PILOT FILM.

then commanded by Dave Edwards. Distracted by a rescue helicopter, and blown off course by crosswinds, his flying machine hit the ground at 250 MPH and rolled over six times, bouncing along from wing tip to wing tip, before coming to rest on its flat back, minus its canopy, main gear, and right vertical fin. The crash wreaked terrible facial injuries on the pilot, whose skull was fractured and whose torso was battered by fragmenting sections of the aircraft's nose. Each time the vehicle rolled, a stream of high-velocity lakebed clay assaulted Peterson's face. Apparently, if he had just had a second more, he would have landed the aircraft safely.

"About what is seen on the TV screens every week is what I remember," said Peterson, in a 1975 Associated Press interview. "That partial footage was taken by the cockpit cameras. I blacked out about the same time the cameras stopped working. I was landing, fighting a crosswind which had sprung up, when I saw a helicopter in my way. I tried to avoid it, and the landing gear caught in the dry lakebed — and right there I thought that was it. The next thing I vaguely remember is being trapped in the vehicle upside down."

Severely injured, Peterson was promptly flown to the hospital at Edwards. He underwent restorative surgery on his face during the ensuing months; however, he later lost the vision in his injured right eye from a staphylococcus infection. Following a lengthy rehabilitation, Peterson continued at NASA's Dryden Flight Research Center as the Research Project Engineer on the Digital Fly-By-Wire program of the late 1960s and early 1970s, and later assumed responsibility for Safety and Quality Assurance for Dryden. The film of his crash, meanwhile, would be employed some seven years later for the opening of the weekly, Harve Bennett-produced version of SM. "Our show," explained Bennett, "begins with that piece of incredible stock footage that blew me away when I saw it in the original pilot."

The lifting bodies were a family of small research craft similar to wingless re-entry vehicles thought appropriate for flying down through the atmosphere from space. Designed to be launched from under the wing of a B-52 bomber, they provided aerodynamicists with data on low speed handling characteristics. Peterson's doomed M2-F2, built by the Northrop Corporation, was one of many-such craft built for NASA to test various body designs, one of which would eventually end up as the Space Shuttle. Caidin said Peterson had a "particular distaste" for reliving the accident, week after week, upon viewing Six's opening. But he lived through the terrible crash, and that was no special effect. "The man was absolutely shredded in that cockpit," Caidin reported. "A year later, he took off in a jet fighter."

The M2-F2 was eventually reconstructed as the M2-F3, which is currently on display at the National Air & Space Museum in Washington, D.C.

Though Bruce Peterson and other real-life navigators were never fortunate enough to undergo cybernetic reconstruction, the Bionic scribe set out

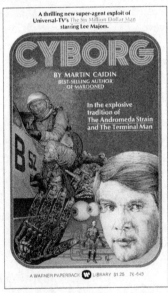

CYBORG CREATOR AND SCI-FI NOVEL ICON MARTIN CAIDIN WAS A
STRAIGHT-SHOOTING CHARACTER HIMSELF, WHO TOLD IT LIKE IT WAS.
BOTTOM RIGHT: THE 1974 PAPERBACK EDITION OF CAIDIN'S *CYBORG*
NOVEL — THE FIRST TO FEATURE LEE MAJORS' LIKENESS.

to explore the emotional impact of their experiences, against a backboard of science fiction.

As with *The Bionic Woman*, Jaime went skydiving. Her parachute failed. Severe damage to her form was the result of an uncontrollable descent into a patch of trees. Upon violent contact with the surface, Jaime lost the use of both legs, a right arm, and hearing in her right ear. (When Caidin was younger, he used to skydive, and the exact same injuries were likely to prevail.)

"We just didn't pick these ideas out of thin air," said Caidin, who had been writing about bionics since 1957. The notions selected were based on actual experiences, as the writer firmly believed in "going with what's real."

For Steve Austin, his accident was real. Disabled, emotionally, as well as physically, he was alone. Jaime was not there for him, like he would be for her during her traumatic human-to-cyborg transformation. The central support system of having a mutual half-human/half-machine counterpart was missing. Steve would help Jaime through the emotional anguish, the physical pain, and the countless hours of therapy for the mind and body.

Who would help him? Austin was without the cybernetic kindred spirit to literally keep him from falling apart. (At least, for now.) Steve awakened in the hospital, where he found himself following his nightmarish accident, and would attempt suicide. The cybernetic physicians were given little options: they were forced to keep him anesthetized. While Steve was comatose (and incapable of judgment), the OSI decided for him that he would become the first to test the newest methods in artificial limb connection.

Steve gave his blessing to the OSI to move forward with the experimental operation. But afterwards, he was still somewhat surprised with the results.

Cognizant, and highly restrained, he was told of his new capabilities. He soon felt intensely isolated and very different. He became unaffected, disagreeable, and entirely unresponsive, even to the allure of his very attractive nurse. Though physically capable, he may have believed his sexual ability to be less than perfect. Or maybe he was thinking of Jaime? (No, she was not yet in the picture; not for the viewer, anyway.)

Eventually, Steve stopped feeling sorry for himself. With his superior engineer's acumen in full stride, he offered assistance to the surrounding bionic medical community, formulating cybernetic limb procedures that had never before been fathomed. In due time, Steve responded to the nurse's sincere affection. They became sexually involved. To his employers, albeit, those responsible for saving his life, he evolved into the super government operative recognized as Steve Austin.

Like Caidin's novel, *The Six Million Dollar Man* pilot was first entitled *Cyborg*, but it was changed days before the film aired. "They may have simply felt it was a better title," the author proposed, "in terms of dramatics."

Though he did say that the *six million dollar* sum-title was created with
some assistance from the Air Force. It was estimated that bionic modifications would total that amount, as every aspect of producing *The Six Million
Dollar Man* was carefully considered. Such facts included the scientific goal
of bionics: to procure particular biological information, then attenuate that
knowledge to mathematical concessions that would prove substantial to an
engineer, who would then generate perfunctory devices that could execute
a biological service.

Now logged in the dictionary, the term, *bionic*, Caidin reported, "is biology applied to electronic engineering systems." The word was constructed
from the Greek term, *bios*, meaning *life*, and the suffix, *ics*, translated as
resembling. He did some prudent investigation and discovered its roots and
the term's inventor: Major Jack E. Steele, a research psychiatrist at the
Aerospace Research Library in Ohio.

Caidin defined the word, *cyborg*, as "one organism...a marriage between
bionics and cybernetics," the latter of which deals with the shared constitu-
ents amid computers and the human nervous system. It's an expression that
was around years before the writer wrote the novel.

"Most people are not aware that the U.S. Air Force maintained a huge,
but secret, bionics program," he said. "At the time that the term [cyborg]
was first used, it was still kept from the general public. Questions were
raised among Congressional leaders from the very beginning of the program, and the more I looked into it, the more likely it seemed that it was real.
Could a cyborg be built? Could a cyborg be trained to act as a weapon? The
answer on both counts was a loud and distinct 'yes!'"

As to the name, Steve Austin, Caidin invented it in piece-meal fashion. He said he always liked the first name, because it's "basically a strong,
healthy name. But I couldn't figure out his last name to save my ass, until,
one day, I flew the *missus* and me across the country, back from California.
I landed to refuel at an airport in *Austin*, Texas, and the name was born. It
was just one of those great wonderful coincidences," he relayed.

While penning *Cyborg*, Martin Caidin said there were special studies
conducted by Congress to investigate the possibilities of attaching an average man to mechanical devices that would catapult him into space — mechanisms that would allow such individuals to adapt to alien atmospheres. The
results proved it was more beneficial for a man to be placed in a suit, than to
actually mold his physical body.

In the novel, the author had a character that stayed a man. Modified,
physically, to save his life. He was fitted with artificial limbs and an eye to
assist with his return to the mainstream of his personal and professional
existence as a pilot. It was not Caidin's intent to create a superhero for the
government, "but to improve upon a man scientifically," he said. "Steve
Austin became that man. Our superhero was actually *supernormal*, which

was a very critical element of the story. After Steve's accident, he was in a completely vulnerable position. He was used to being in control. But it was that vulnerability which kept him on a level playing-field with the rest of us."

Like the rest of us, Steve — and Jaime — (from birth) were not endowed with the anatomical advantages of a *Captain Marvel* or *Supergirl*. Unlike the rest of us, their acquired abilities, supplied by Dr. Rudy Wells, were superior to those granted, biologically — though not as flexible.

In the novel, Dr. Wells (played by Martin Balsam in the pilot; Alan Oppenheimer and Martin E. Brooks, respectively, in the series) informs Steve that his mechanical upper limb will never equal the wondrous pliability of its natural counterpart.

As to the manipulation of the automated appendages, Rudy draws for Steve a stimulating comparison: When a steersman is guiding an aircraft, he and the ramjet, concurrently, are one bionic assemblage. The median point or *interface* between them is the spot where the flier's foot eases toward the rudder pedals and his hands are at the command. With Steve and Jaime, these intersections are positioned where the mechanical components are connected to their human halves. The brain cues that previously controlled their limb muscles were magnified electronically and adjusted to employ their automated parts.

The *Six Million Dollar* pilot (first broadcast on March 7, 1973) was a fitting adaptation of Caidin's Steve and Rudy characters, and general concept, but it differed in small, yet significant ways.

For one thing, Steve's bionic eye was not the same. In the original story, his visual organ was not endowed with functional viewing. Even Caidin's illusory scientists were unqualified to conjoin a manufactured instrument to the optic nerve. The eye was a clandestine camera, created to appear genuine, and to develop microfilm.

Minor alterations to the *Cyborg* story were necessitated by television's "ocular platform," meaning that minimal descriptions work best. Steve's telescopic, infrared *television-vision* sanctioned immediate classification, minus the dawdling and narrative requirements demanded by the development of his *photographic memory*.

The story of *Cyborg's* transmutation from literary to audio/visual form is almost as intricate.

Martin Caidin was determined to convert his novel into a television movie-of-the-week, and followed the accepted Hollywood rules of thumb (readied an outline, sample script and so forth). He left his home (appropriately located near Cape Kennedy), and headed for the West Coast. He had earlier recycled one book, *Marooned*, into a successful Hollywood production (the 1969 theatrical film starring Gregory Peck), and had incentive to conclude that Hollywood would be enthusiastic about another of his *far out* ideas.

LEE MAJORS, SHOWN HERE FROM HIS PRE-*SM* DAYS AS A REGULAR ON TV'S *THE BIG VALLEY*, WAS THE PERFECT CHOICE TO PLAY ALL-AMERICAN HERO STEVE AUSTIN.

The author marketed his wares to Warner Bros., who failed to garner the interest of the only three big webs in town at the time: ABC, CBS, or NBC. Along came Universal Studios, who convinced ABC to produce *Cyborg* as a one-shot television film. "Richard Irving, who was vice-president of Universal, flipped over it," Caidin recalled. "But no one [at the time] was expecting to make a series out of it." Howard Rodman was hired to write the teleplay, which was ghost-written by a then-unknown Steven Bochco, who went on to create and produce *Hill Street Blues*, *L.A. Law*, and the controversial hit, *NYPD Blue* (Emmy-winners, all).

Enter Lee Majors. Before SM, and his post-*Bionic*, popular *Fall Guy* adventure series (ABC, 1981 to 1986), Lee's personal and professional plates were already full. Born Harvey Lee Yeary II, on April 23, 1939, in Wyandotte, Michigan, he grew up in Middlesboro, Kentucky. Like his TV counter-part, Lee's biological father died when he was an infant. By the time he was 3, he lost his biological mother as well, and was adopted (which he didn't discover until he was 12). As an adult, he arrived in Los Angeles with his mind set on becoming a high school football coach. In Middlesboro, he was a star athlete in high school and a member of the Kentucky All-State Football team. His excellence at the game won him an athletic scholarship to the University of Indiana.

Shortly after his arrival at Indiana, Lee sustained a serious injury and was kept out of competition for the next three years. He moved closer to home, to Eastern Kentucky State, for his senior year, where he resumed his football training in earnest. That's where the St. Louis Cardinals spotted him and made an offer.

All that changed when he became a Hollywood film extra, and his interest in acting increased. Among the auditions that beckoned was a chance to play Heath Barkley, the illegitimate son of Barbara Stanwyck, head of a good-sized Old Western TV family in *The Big Valley* (ABC, 1965 to 1969). Lee not only won the role, he beat out 400 other aspirants. He had the soft-spoken sound, the good looks, the confident manner and the melancholy eyes needed for the part.

While performing in *Valley*, Lee made his (credited) feature film debut in 1968's minor classic, *Will Penny*, starring Charlton Heston and Joan Hackett. In 1970, ABC reworked the premise of a tired NBC show, *The Virginian*, and transformed it into *The Men from Shiloh*, on which Lee was hired as a regular. After *Shiloh* survived for only one season, the actor was quickly placed into a new kind of role, Jess Brandon, a lawyer, on ABC's 1971 to 1974 series, *Owen Marshall, Counselor At Law* (a cross-over legal cousin to the network's top medicine man, *Marcus Welby, M.D.*), where he remained until the *Six Million Dollar Man* movies achieved series status.

When he appeared in the first SM film, Majors inherently knew he was making more than just a motion picture for television. When the pilot was broadcast, "It seemed like it would become a regular show, and that felt great," he intones. "I was excited. I had been in a lot of other shows as a supporting player. Finally, I had the lead, which is every actor's fantasy, whether they admit that or not." With the modesty Majors is known for, he adds, "My dream came true."

The film attained knockout ratings. "There was an incredible reaction to the show," said Caidin. "Mail, calls, telegrams, and an avalanche of favorable reviews. The director, Dick Irving, wanted as much reality as possible, and he was a very tough taskmaster."

Glen Larson's abilities as producer have long been synonymous with victory. With some twenty-six multi-season TV series to his name, few can rival his across-the schedule success from the 7:00 PM, Sunday night, youth-and-action shows like *The Hardy Boys* and *Knight Rider*, through the sophisticated later night fare of solid hits like *Quincy* and *Magnum P.I.*

He began his career at Universal, where, in one short season, he went from free-lance writer to producer of *It Takes a Thief* (starring Robert Wagner). Continuing that fast-paced start he went on to develop, create, write and produce the pilots for several successful shows, including *McCloud* (NBC, 1970 to 1977, starring Dennis Weaver).

Larson, however, was not around for the initial *Six* pilot. "That was Richard Irving's project," he said. "But [Universal executive] Frank Price believed there was a hit in that concept and asked me to take over the project and see if I could bring a perspective to it that might make it either more commercial or salable."

Throwing himself into this new project, Glen retreated to his cabin in the mountains the week of July 4, 1973, brainstormed a number of ideas on his portable typewriter, and returned with a *Six* pilot script. On the basis of this new material, ABC timidly commissioned two more 90-minute movies that would be screened in the *Suspense Movie* weekly time-slot the following September. And, in collaboration with Price, he permanently changed the title from *Cyborg* to *The Six Million Dollar Man*.

"Frank actually gave me a page with some thoughts of his, which I combined with mine," Larson explained, "and that was what spurred the initial couple of movies." After completing the first 90-minute film-episode, *Wine, Women and War*, they started discussing a one-hour series. By the time they finished the second movie-episode, *The Solid Gold Kidnapping*, they already had him working on 60-minute scripts. At that point, Larson lobbied against a third 90-minute movie-episode, and suggested a concentration on the one-hour format. He developed a number of *Six* stories that were later incorporated into the one-hour versions, such as the island-crashing premise employed in SM's "Survival of the Fittest." "We probably put a dozen stories into work," he explained, "and I think they shot most of them."

Meanwhile, Larson's closing musical theme to SM's first 90-minute

movie-episode, *Wine, Women and War,* was snappy, very *I-Spy*, and sung by
Dusty Springfield. "We received a lot of mail on that," he said, "which was
kind of a neat thing."

Larson (who went on to guide Lee Majors in *The Fall Guy*) believes pilot
films or episodes that kick off a series should have flashy, ear-catching opening credits, with a "movie feel" and other larger scale attributes. "That was
pretty much my perspective on it," he said. "I didn't take the same approach
to the one-hours we drafted. Basically, on one-hour series, you have to be
careful not to try to have someone save the world every week, like you'd see
in a James Bond movie."

Yet he, in accordance with instructions from ABC, wanted the first few
Six 90-minute movie episodes to have a look that warranted their extra
screen time. "You have to remember the era in which we made them," he
said. "We were not that far from the James Bond heyday. Trying to do
that on television was never a very practical thing because you'd be compet-
ing with the James Bond world. But to have the type of toys and tools that
Steve Austin had, you could capture some of that audience. In fact, the chief
adversary in *Wine, Women and War* was sort of a Bondian bad guy."

Larson was more comfortable with longer forms of programming, like
Quincy and *McCloud*, both of which initially aired as two-hour segments. "I
was a little spoiled by that," he admits. "I did, however, do a number of *Six*
stories that were used in the one-hour format. But we got into bickering
wars into how much they were going to cost. In retrospect, I might have
been wiser to stay with it a little longer. But I accomplished what I set out
to do."

Larson's two commissioned *Million Dollar* telefilms, however, failed to
do *stronger* or *better* in the ratings. They were screened, and the results were
atomic, as in "bombs." The reasons why were plenty.

Though ABC specifically requested the continued escapades of Steve
Austin to be braided with the accouterments of a *James Bond* film (tons of
innuendo, beautiful women; all very Sean-Connery-like), there was a problem: Martin Caidin's bionic hero would never have referred to himself as
Austin, Steve Austin. As such, the early proto-type of *The Six Million Dollar
Man* malfunctioned. The *Six* mix was shaken and too stirred. Caidin was
rattled.

The author may have diligently offered his support as technical consultant for these initial Austin assignments, but he became extremely dissatis-
fied with the show's direction. He refused to be associated with the project
that he so passionately brought to life. "I wanted my name off the credits,"
he relayed. "Creatively, they were grasping at straws. I was embarrassed."
Not one to mince words, Caidin blasted, "They didn't need that *Bond* shit.
Those first few shows were pure crap. They were ridiculous from a technical standpoint, and had nothing to do with reality. Larson is a very success-

AUSTIN. STEVE AUSTIN. ABC HAD INSISTED STEVE AUSTIN BE
A JAMES BOND-LIKE CHARACTER FOR *SM*'S SECOND AND THIRD
MOVIES. THANKFULLY, THIS CHARACTERIZATION WASN'T WELL-
RECEIVED AND LEE MAJORS WAS THEN ABLE TO MAKE THE ROLE HIS
OWN.

ful producer, but we didn't get along. When he turned it into James Bond, I raised holy hell with Dick Irving. I said, 'Dick, you're gonna kill the damn thing. We've got a great thing going here and you're gonna blow it completely with this bullshit!'"

Glen Larson professes not to remember Caidin's *name-erase* request. But he does recall Caidin's larger-than-life persona. "Martin was an off-the-wall character," he said. "He came in from Florida and was sort of a CIA groupie. He sat down one day and told me 12 ways to kill someone without anyone ever finding out it was a murder. He was a fascinating character who was down the hall from me during this thing."

According to Larson, Caidin was a little *too* attached to his prose. "He was a bigger–than-life person, but he didn't know television very well," he said. "A number of authors will sometimes cling to those words and not realize that they have to be translated in a way that you could do it week-to-week or whatever. It happens. He had consultation rights, but we weren't buying scripts from him because that was not his venue. He was very inventive, however. To this day, I'm very thankful for some of those killing techniques because they served me well in my stories."

Adding fuel to the fire, ABC programmed the *Six* films to run on Saturday nights, opposite *The Mary Tyler Moore Show* on CBS, and other of the eye network's 1970s comedy blockbusters (*The Bob Newhart Show*, *The Carol Burnett Show*). The cybernetic wind had been knocked out of Caidin's bionic vision.

When SM did become a weekly, 60-minute series, Larson left due to time management, or lack thereof, and agreed to hand over producing chores to Harve Bennett who, he said, "brought a very pragmatic approach" to the show. Looking back on his departure, he has only one lamentation: financial compensation. "I never once asked for participation," he said, "which I probably would have been entitled to based on my development of it. That's my only regret. Those were tough episodes to produce, and I always thought that Harve, and in time, Ken Johnson, did a really good job."

While Harve Bennett, like Glen Larson, had nothing to do with the creation of the original 90-minute SM pilot, the prolific producer (who would go on to restructure, albeit, rescue, the *Star Trek* film series after the disappointing virgin flight of 1979's *Star Trek: The Motion Picture*) was intrinsically involved with *Million's* metamorphosis into weekly series form. Also, like Larson, his ties to the entertainment industry are solid.

Born and raised in Chicago, the young Harve Bennett Fischman appeared 212 times (a record number) on the network radio show, *Quiz Kids*. He graduated from UCLA's Theatre Arts Department with a major in motion pictures (he's currently the President of the Film Alumni Group) and tried, he said, to become a director and a maker of documentaries, "in that order."

LEE MAJORS, AS STEVE AUSTIN, IN TWO PUBLICITY SHOTS FOR THE
SM PILOT. *BOTTOM RIGHT: SM* SERIES PRODUCER HARVE BENNETT.

Neither position materialized. After Army service in Korea, he ventured to New York and joined CBS, soon becoming their youngest producer, specializing in variety shows and remote specials, including the *Miss America Pageant* and the *Pillsbury Bake-Off*. Following a stint as Johnny Carson's first talk show producer, he joined ABC in 1962 as a Director of Program Development, rising to become Vice-President in Charge of Programming.

After helping to develop *The Fugitive, Peyton Place, Batman, Bewitched* and *The Mod Squad* (among others), Bennett left the alphabet network to become *Squad's* producer/writer for Danny Thomas-Aaron Spelling Productions. During three of *Mod's* five years (1968 to 1973), he was twice nominated by the Writers Guild of America (for best hour script), while the hip-cop drama received seven Emmy nominations.

In 1971, he began a seven-year association with Universal that resulted in a string of TV network successes, including *The Six Million Dollar Man* and *The Bionic Woman*. He later developed and produced *The Invisible Man, Gemini Man* (both NBC) *Rich Man, Poor Man* — the first miniseries (ABC), fifteen *Movies-of-the Week* (ABC), and the three-hour special, *Guilty or Innocent: The Sam Sheppard Story* (NBC). His early presence at Universal was on a long-term contract, based upon his success with ABC's *Mod Squad*.

He became a well-known commodity to studio executives, particularly Sidney Scheinberg, who was then-head of Universal TV development. (Frank Price would succeed Scheinberg, first, as Director of Development and later, Vice-President in charge of programming for the West Coast.)

Bennett said he evolved into the only person at ABC who knew what the terms "frame" and "splice" meant, and who had "some general knowledge of how to actually make a film." He became renowned as the "person who could tackle almost anything."

As *Squad's* third season arrived, the man also became exhausted. After writing nearly the entire show, he gave Spelling his notice. Recovering from Bronchial Pneumonia, Bennett had "coughed" his way through his last episode. He next arrived at Universal with a no-series clause. Around the same time, ABC's *Movie-of-the-Week* entries were enjoying a strong success in the ratings. From a fiscal standpoint, they were yet to register well with the studio, not as much as a series did.

The Six Million Dollar Man leapt out from the pack. The Glen Larson monthly secret-agent-type episodes were aired and, aside from the integrity behind them, they failed to work. Frank Price at Universal wondered what would, and to the surprise of all those involved, ABC decided to give the show a second chance. A distress signal was issued. Despite Bennett's strict no-series clause with Universal, he answered the call.

Could he resolve Austin's bound *Bondism?*

Frank Price asked Bennett to watch the pilot and see what he could do.

The most poignant scene in *The Six Million Dollar Man* pilot, Bennett told Price, was when Austin, in a red khaki shirt, walks back to Edwards Air Force Base (with a matchstick in his mouth) to meditate before he takes that destined flight which, unknowing to him, would nearly cost him his life. That's the image Bennett envisioned.

A *Six Million Dollar Man* weekly series suddenly became one of the *almost anything*s he could tackle. He screened the *Six* pilot, and its two monthly sequels, and conferred with Price, telling him, "The original movie is awfully interesting." Bennett was "turned-on by the writing," unaware that his good friend Steven Bochco was involved.

"We were kind of contemporaries," Bennett said of Bochco. "He told me he was doing a rewrite, but he never quite explained what it was. He was doing a lot of *shadow* rewriting at the time. Howard Rodman was no slouch, either. I just don't think this was his kind of material. He didn't tune into the playful side of Steve Austin."

"With all due respect to Glen Larson," Bennett adds, "who was and remains, without question, a very successful television producer, you cannot take Lee Majors and put him into tuxedo shirts. It just doesn't work. Lee is Gary Cooper, the good ol' American Cowboy. He's [like] James Dean and Paul Newman, *The American Myth, No. 16*. Lee Majors is not *James Bond*."

If Roger Moore wasn't an appropriate model, John Wayne was. "We returned Lee to that monosyllabic, shy-with-the-ladies, aw-shucks kind of hero," he concludes. "That, to me, is what made it work. He was a modest, kind of Western man amidst all of this technology, which he used well. I've worked with the military on films, and I admire military people who keep their cool when worlds collide around them. Lee portrayed that wonderfully."

Though not responsible for discovering Lee Majors, Harve Bennett was in the room representing ABC, as the network's Director of Development when, at the eleventh hour, the blond and blue-eyed actor was cast as Heath Barkley in *The Big Valley*. "Knocked out" by Lee's screen test, he had to call New York, which housed ABC's central office. "In those days," he said, "you didn't make decisions in the West Coast office, without contacting the East Coast, even if you were the Director of Development."

Bennett eventually spoke with Tom Moore, then-President of ABC. "Tom," he presented, "I've found Heath, and he's terrific."

"Yeah?" Moore questioned. "What does he look like?"

"Elvis Presley," Bennett replied.

"That's good enough for me," Moore concluded. "Sign him up."

Years later, *The Six Million Dollar Man* ran into the picture. Once again, Bennett found himself studying the actor whom he instinctively felt possessed star quality. "Lee Majors was the secret ingredient in *The Big Valley*," he said. "Whatever success that show had, was the chemistry that was built around his kind of *lost boy* character." He believed the same quality that Majors brought to Heath Barkley could supplant a *Bionic James Bond*, and transfer to the "real" *Six Million Dollar Man*.

Yet there wasn't much time. The weekly version of *Six Million* was slated to air January 18, 1974. It was already November. Frank Price needed an answer to a very important question: Could he, in a very short period of network (prime) time, reconstruct *The Six Million Dollar Man*, create a *Bionic rebel* with *a cause*, and institute a success for ABC? The only reassembled vision that Bennett saw feasible, and not nearly as positive, was one of recontracting Bronchial Pneumonia. "You have to be out of your mind," he squealed to Price.

The Universal executive did not yield, and instead sweetened the pie. "If you can make *The Six Million Dollar Man* a hit," Price promised, "the brass ring will be yours."

"I remember him saying precisely those words," Bennett said, "because later on, I sued for my brass ring when the show was $162 million dollars into profit, and there were claims of no net return."

The issue was settled out of court, and Bennett is not allowed to discuss the details but, because of the settlement, he has a house and a tennis court. He also has no bitterness about it. "But at the time," he said, "it was a traumatic experience. I would never enter a lawsuit again. Under the circumstances, and because of all of the extraordinarily hard work that I invested into *The Six Million Dollar Man*, it was ethically necessary for me to pursue what was rightfully mine."

Beyond the ensuing legal battles, his self-stated no-series clause, and shades of Bronchial Pneumonia, *The Six Million Dollar Man* held a great appeal for Bennett, who claims he's "really not a sci-fi person." "It spoke to a certain side of me," he clarifies. "What binds me together is my love for heroes, which I think comes from being a child of World War II, when heroes on the screen, in the field and in the White House were gigantic. *The American Hero* was preeminent, and I've never lost that idealism. So for me, Steve Austin was a unique kind of hero, with a marvelous twist of science fiction. But he was first and foremost a human being."

After all was said and *not* done, and Bennett was approached about remodeling *The Six Million Dollar Man*, he ultimately agreed to offer his services. "I could hardly refuse," he said. "It was an irresistible challenge." The remade *Man*, in weekly formation, debuted on schedule in January 1974 as a Friday night action show and immediately rocketed into the top ten. Even previously despondent Martin Caidin breathed a sigh of relief, and requested that his name be returned to the screen crawl. "Harve Bennett did a fabulous job with the show," Caidin said. "He brought it back down to Earth, into the realm of believability."

Actor Monte Markham had known Bennett from guest work on *The*

Mod Squad, and would go on to play The Seven Million Dollar Man in two *Six* episodes. As he recalls, Bennett's *Man* maneuvers became legendary in and around Hollywood.

When he did *Six*, it garnered such high ratings, that Markham said, "Every producer in town took Harve's name in vain." Apparently, each time a producer pitched an idea, they would hear, "Harve Bennett did it in eight weeks. Why can't you?"

It was Monte Markham who was first tagged by Martin Caidin (who did not know Lee Majors at the time), to play the lead in the *Million Dollar* pilot. Caidin was with Richard Irving, then-vice-president of Universal, who was casting the Austin role. When asked for his opinion, Caidin recommended Markham, who he thought, "would have been outstanding in the role." From his perspective, Markham was "always one of the better actors in the business."

The writer first saw the actor in the 1971 TV-remake of *Death Takes a Holiday*, based on the 1934 theatrical film with Fredric March. "It one of the finest things he ever did," Caidin said of Markham. "His performance was incredible."

In 1973, Monte was *The New Perry Mason* on CBS, right about the time Caidin had him in mind for the *Six Million Dollar* pilot. When SM began filming, the actor was unavailable. "We had no mutual friends," Markham explained of his miscommunication with Caidin. "But he had known my brother, Jess [a pilot, like Caidin], who flew Air-America [a CIA airline] in Laos and Vietnam for eight years. He did a lot of black bag jobs. At some point, they started to talk about *Cyborg*." It was then that Martin told Jess that he had Monte in mind for Steve.

"Lee Majors is a very laid back kind of guy," the actor assessed. "His whole demeanor and style is very gentle. I'm much more intense. I would have needed different types of storylines. I don't know if I would have made a good *Six Million Dollar Man*. I would have taken the show in another direction."

Glen Larson agrees with Markham, whom the producer employed in a number of projects. "I like Monte," he said, "but Monte Markham's a little cold. When I came on board, Lee was pretty much a *fait accompli*. I doubt if anybody else was ever considered. Lee and Frank Price were friends. They mixed socially. The property came to me with Lee included, and I certainly had no problem with that."

ABC, on the other hand, took it to Majors, and eventually, Harve Bennett.

The network also had a side agenda in bringing SM to the screen: *Adam's Rib* (with Ken Howard and Blythe Danner, based upon the 1949 Spencer Tracy/Katharine Hepburn film of the same name) and *Room 222* (which, along with *The Courtship of Eddie's Father*, was one of TV's first dramedies), were on the demise. The network was frantic for a fresh Friday night schedule. Coupled with shows like *Happy Days* and *Kung Fu*, *The Six Million Dollar Man* catapulted ABC into a ratings bonanza for the first time in its history.

"I really sensed we had succeeded," said Bennett, "when my five-year-old son, Christopher, began running around the house saying things like 'We have a blowout in the No. 3 damper' and calling himself 'The Six Dollar Man.' To Christopher, six dollars was a lot of money."

The once vulnerable, detached Steve Austin had become invincible.

THE CHEMISTRY BETWEEN STEVE AND JAIME WAS EVIDENT RIGHT
FROM THE START. VIEWERS TRULY BELIEVED THAT STEVE AUSTIN
HAD FOUND HIS TRUE LOVE.

CHAPTER 2
SPARKS

"THE BIONIC WOMAN WAS OBVIOUSLY THE THING GOD SENT TO ME TO DO, TO TOUGHEN ME UP, TO HELP ME DEVELOP AS A HUMAN BEING."

LINDSAY WAGNER

ABC was content with *The Six Million Dollar Man's* performance in the ratings. That is, until the 1974-75 season kicked off. NBC's *Chico and the Man* was hammering *Six* in the Nielsen's. For the first time in TV history, ABC suspended its Friday night lineup and substituted old movies until the schedule could be reworked. "We were close to being canceled," said SM/ BW producer Lionel Siegel. "But the power of Universal and ABC's lack of enthusiasm for their new pilots granted us a reprieve. New story editors were hired, more promotion in the markets was scheduled and bigger budgets were allotted for guest stars."

Yet toward the end of the show's second season the web wanted more flies for the spider. *Six,* now airing on Sunday nights, was okay for kids to watch, but the network and the studio wanted more adults to tune in. As Lee Majors recalls, "I was tired of only looking at *hardware* on the show. It was time for Steve to fall in love, and I was the one who suggested to have him find the love of his life."

In steps a very young Kenneth Johnson, then known to Hollywood as a producer and director of the extremely popular Mike Douglas TV talk show. A prolific writer, director, and actor as well, Johnson became responsible for a wealth of sci-fi TV and screen product, including *The Incredible Hulk* (creator/executive producer) and *V* (the original 4-hour mini-series and subsequent 6-hour mini-series). He also directed the last four *Alien Nation* TV-films: *Millennium* (1996; which he wrote and executive produced), *Body and Soul* (1995; executive produced), *Dark Horizon* (1994), and *Alien Nation* (1989; also wrote).

Johnson's inspiration for going into the entertainment industry, specifically sci-fi entertainment, was the famous radio broadcast of War of the

SM PRODUCER KENNETH JOHNSON, SHOWN WITH LEE MAJORS AND
LINDSAY WAGNER ON THE SET OF *SM*'S "THE RETURN OF THE BIONIC
WOMAN." *BOTTOM LEFT:* ON THE SET OF THE MAJORS-DIRECTED *SM*
EPISODE "ONE OF OUR RUNNING BACKS IS MISSING." JOHNSON
EVENTUALLY LEFT *SM* TO OVERSEE THE *BW* SERIES AS PRODUCER/
WRITER/DIRECTOR.

Worlds, which he heard while he was in junior high school. Playing the lead (as Scrooge) in A Christmas Carol in tenth grade also led him to pursue a career in the entertainment industry. Upon entering Bionic-time, he was encouraged by producer Steven Bochco to try his hand at writing. Soon after, Bochco introduced him to their mutual friend Harve Bennett, who was searching for a way to give Six Million a bionic boost. "*The Six Million Dollar Man* was sort of flagging," Johnson said. "They were desperate for new scripts." From there, "Harve and I hit it off," he said, "and I suggested we do *The Bride of Frankenstein.*"

Come again?

"You have this male cyborg," Johnson told those in power. "Shouldn't the logical extension of that concept be a female counterpart?"

Bennett was quite taken with the idea, as was Frank Price, and Johnson was assigned to write the script, which he completed within one week's time. The plot had Steve relinking with Jaime Sommers, his hometown love, and we came to understand more about Steve's background and his relationships, previous to his joining the Air Force and eventual bionic reconstruction. Johnson delivered the script, and was told, "This is a good story, but it's too dense. It has *too much* story. Go home, take another week, and make it a two-parter."

Though the revised, divided version took a trifle longer than an additional seven days, Johnson completed the new script in advance of schedule. He found that considerable more detail was required for more intricacies:

Jaime had not been a part of Steve's life during the first two seasons of the show. They had to have known each before that period. The two had been high-school sweethearts long before Steve's career in the Air Force, his accident and climb back to physical and mental health. His life was now somewhat together. The time was right for love. The time was right for Jaime to come back into his world.

Her name, meanwhile, was plucked from the real-life experiences of Ken Johnson. "A year or so before I wrote *The Bionic Woman* script," he explained, "I was involved in staging the killer whale shows for Sea World in their San Diego and Ohio parks, and I also put together a water ski extravaganza called *The Roaring Twenties Water Frolics.* One of the skiers was named Jaime Sommers, and I thought, *Wow. What a great name.* So when I was sitting down to write *The Bionic Woman*, it popped into my head and I said, *Oh yeah, perfect name. Nice soft feel. Summery. Kind of a warmth to it.* So that's where it came from."

Once a vital pair, Steve and Jaime gingerly reunited. By the end of the first segment, they were intensely in love once more, and a mechanical marriage was in the making. Perspicacious watchers may have surmised an approaching calamity.

Certainly, Steve, the ex-astronaut-turned-special-agent-for-the-OSI,

LINDSAY WAGNER WAS CAST AS JAIME SOMMERS WHILE SERVING AS
A CONTRACT PLAYER FOR UNIVERSAL STUDIOS IN SUCH TV SHOWS
AS *OWEN MARSHALL, COUNSELOR AT LAW, ADAM-12, MARCUS
WELBY, M.D.*, AND *NIGHT GALLERY*.

could never marry. Such men are not destined for family affairs. Jaime, the small-town girl whose athletic prowess catapulted her to fame, could never find time to have children. The two would have to break apart. Their union was too complete. Too picturesque. Too unreal. Consequently, the continental duo ventured out on an inevitable, life-changing, skydiving excursion near the end of "The Bionic Woman, Part I."

Jaime plunged downward. Steve discovered her crushed frame. She was still alive. He frantically did what no one else would have been in a position to do. He implicitly bribed Oscar Goldman into remaking her. He refused to lose forever the love of which he was once deprived. Jaime must be rebuilt, he demanded. Whatever the price. [Although no exact figure was ever given, when Jaime later asks Oscar if she cost as much as Steve in the SM segment, "Welcome Home, Jaime, Part I," Oscar grins and said, "Oh, not quite six million. After all, your parts are smaller."]

"The Bionic Woman, Part II," was a grave tale of Jaime's various surgeries on the chancy, new portions of her body. Previously concocted as a positive move to save her life, her bionic reconstruction was only beginning to prolong the nightmare. Her physical form was rejecting her automated additions. She was losing command of her body, and she wasn't telling Steve or Rudy Wells.

At first, everything seemed okay. Jaime ran at regularly *Bionic* incredible speeds, just like Steve, and her new arm was nuclear by nature. The hearing she had lost in her right ear had been significantly expanded.

Also, like Steve, she experienced moments of intense self-doubt. She was at once alarmed at — and fascinated by — her newly-acquired skills. With a wedding looming on the horizon, she coyly kept her malfunctions a secret. In the end, Jaime was forced to reveal the truth. Incredibly, the situation got worse. A blood clot was developing in her brain. Nothing could save her.

Any kind of peace she would find with her new life, however, would not transpire until after Jaime experienced much emotional and physical trauma, due to her accident, subsequent reconstruction, and death. Steve lost her again, after finding her years after they first fell in love. When she died, as far as he was concerned, his life had ended as well.

Meanwhile, the viewers were ready to kill.

The rebuttal to Jaime's death, more specifically, Lindsay Wagner's absence, was overpowering. Universal and ABC received thousands of letters, commending Jaime's episodes, but declaring fury at her demise.

As Ken Johnson recalls, "Everyone loved Jaime. Harve [Bennett] even received a letter of outrage from the department head of psychology at Boston University," which read, in part, "How dare you create such a brilliant archetype for women to admire and pattern themselves after and then so brutally kill her!"

"The public reacted to Lindsay and took her to their bosom, period," affirmed Martin Caidin. "The emotional link between she and the viewers was astounding. Even I was getting hell for her death. People were taking it personally, as though Jaime was a real person. They wanted her back. They weren't willing to settle for anyone else in the role. They wanted Jaime and Lindsay. As far as the viewers were concerned, Lindsay Wagner became a part of their family."

Daughter Wagner, however, was estranged from her parent company. Universal contacted their acting offspring for more *Woman* adventures, and found she no longer was under contract. Yet there was clearly a remunerative trade out there for more Jaime Sommers tales. A family reunion (the first of many to follow) not only had to be planned, it became a necessity. ABC ordered Universal to bring back their super female. The studio wanted to conciliate the network's desire, but they were at a standstill. Atomic-powered or not, Jaime Sommers was no more. She was not merely departed. She ceased to exist. She was no longer around. She was out of there. Dead. What was next? *The Bionic Angel?* A second coming?

A resurrection of sorts did occur.

The first two-part *Woman* segment was rerun on August 31 and September 7, 1975. The second episode ended. An announcer said that she would appear again the following week. *The Six Million Dollar Man*'s third season began with another two-part episode, "The Return of the Bionic Woman." Jaime was indeed back, along with Ken Johnson, who "always thought it was kind of strange that Jaime died of a cerebral brain hemorrhage in the midst of the most advanced medical facility in the United States."

Yet when Johnson initially completed the first *Woman* two-parter, that's not what happened. He very carefully kept Jaime alive, but in a cryogenic coma or deep-freeze. A select group of network executives told him to "kill her off." "We don't want a lot of bionic people lying around," they said. They sought to do an allegory like *Love Story* (1970), in which the central character (played by Ryan O'Neal) loses the one true love of his life (Ali McGraw).

"Guys," he replied, "this is a big mistake. Jaime is a great character. You may want to bring her back. So I don't think you should kill her off."

No matter. The writer was repeatedly instructed otherwise. "No, no, no," said the *suits*. "We want her dead, dead, dead."

When Jaime became a hit, they of course sang a different tune. Johnson heard things like, "Hey, whose idea was it to kill her off, anyway?" Bemused, it took Johnson less than two weeks to actualize Jaime's restoration, with a return to what he reported was his original idea of cryogenics.

In 1986, Martin Caidin gave *Starlog* magazine this detailed account of Jaime's resurrection: "For two years, these guys [Universal] paid me $1,000.00 a week as a consultant, and for two years, no one asked me a single question. Then, they ran a two-part episode with the *Bionic Woman* and killed her off at the end. Universal got more than 200,000 letters and phone calls demanding they bring her back. My phone rang at 2 a.m., and they said, *You're on a speaker phone. We're taping this call. There are six writers listening. We're starting production in a few hours on The Return of the Bionic Woman. How do we revive her? We need an absolutely justifiable, acceptable, scientific-medical method.* I worked out a way to keep her alive through cryogenics — putting her on ice."

Johnson's response? "Never in my life have I had a conversation with Mr. Caidin. Since I was executive producer of *Six* at the time, and the one who wrote it, I should know. It all came out of my little pea brain. Nobody else gave me the idea. It was my idea from the beginning."

One-time SM/BW writer/producer Jim Parriott is a tad less diplomatic. "I think Caidin's full of crap," he said. "Not from personal knowledge of the incident, but from him saying that the writers were a few hours away from shooting the episode. These things are written and planned *weeks* ahead of production. Maybe Harve was flattering Caidin with a courtesy call, looking for confirmation of the idea — but I'm sure the cryogenics angle was already in the script."

By the time of *Woman's* re-liberation, Universal retained Caidin as a consultant, and Harve Bennett requested Johnson's presence as producer of *The Six Million Dollar Man*, something he "really didn't want to do." "Producing was a pain in the ass," he told Bennett. "Just let me write and direct episodes, and I'll be a much happier guy."

Bennett convinced Johnson that it was the producer who ultimately shaped the medium of television, the one who controls a project from beginning to end, and hires the writer and the director; all of which meant Johnson could have hired himself in the capacity of his choosing. He did just that and, as he said, "They had their man."

After all the commotion, Jaime was no longer done-in. Miraculously, she was back, breathing again, played by Lindsay Wagner, and a hit once more with the watchers.

In SM's "The Return of the Bionic Woman," Rudy's aide, the youthful Dr. Michael Marchetti (played by Richard Lenz) had, on circumspection, positioned Jaime in cryogenic freeze just prior to her allegedly final heartbeat.

In a suspended state, Jaime's form did not decompose. Apparently, she was dead, but her biological functions had not yet failed entirely. During which time, Rudy and his team labored non-stop to create enhanced cybernetic components; to concoct a procedure of brain surgery that would be accomplished the moment that Jaime began to decongeal.

The vivisection maneuvers were seemingly triumphant. Jaime's heart was reinitiated with electrical currents, as when cardiac confinement takes place during real-life surgeries. She stayed unconscious for a lengthy interval, while the picture was somewhat more focused for Steve, who was initially not told the whole truth of Jaime's death and subsequent second chance.

Austin's heart and emotional stability needed protection, and Oscar and Rudy knew it. For even though Jaime was indeed not gone, her memory of cybernetic love was dead and buried.

She could not recall the time-well-spent with her bionic soul mate. What's more, she was falling hard for Dr. Marchetti, the man who literally gave her a new life.

All the while, Steve still loved Jaime.

Yet any minor recollection of Steve would cause her pain. He had to stand back and watch her love for Dr. Marchetti grow. Her very life depended on Steve's absence. Through it all, Michael was torn as well. He was the interloper, and he knew it. He also knew the intensity level of love that Jaime and Steve had once shared. Where there's a spark, there's fire. She may not have recalled her life with Steve, but Jaime took to him immediately, the second time around. Her heart belonged to Michael, but it also understood how, at one time, she was in love with Steve. She let him help her regain bionic agility. With his assistance and new familiarity, she asserted herself, and sanctioned this current, though different, proposal.

On the other side of the camera, in order for Lindsay Wagner to reprise her *Bionic* role in this second two-part segment, she had to reestablish her relationship with Universal. The studio had unknowingly not renewed their option after Jaime's debut, the season before. The frenzy of her reacquisition became a melodrama. Studio heads traded empty glances. *Lindsay Wagner* was now *gone*.

"What about Stefanie Powers [*The Girl from U.N.C.L.E.*] or maybe Sally Field [*The Girl with Something Extra*]?" someone stammered. ABC, then ruled with a vengeance by a brilliant young programmer named Fred Silverman, said "No way. It's Lindsay Wagner or nothing."

Martin Caidin agreed. "I'm sure Stefanie Powers, Sally Field, or whomever else the studio had in mind for the role would have done a very acceptable job as *The Bionic Woman*," he said. "They just would never have brought to the role what Lindsay did. And everyone inherently knew that. All the wheeling and dealing that was going on to get her back after she left the studio [twice], was just wasted energy. All anyone had to do, who ever saw Lindsay act in anything, was sign her up immediately for whatever part they had mind. And never let her go."

The chore of baiting Lindsay into returning for two more follow-up episodes was assigned to Monique James, the studio vice-president who had been Lindsay's supporter during her previous tenure with Universal. She connected with Lindsay's new manager, Ron Samuels, an eclectic negotiator who, ironically, was married to TV's other super female, *Wonder Woman*'s

Lynda Carter.

James relayed to Samuels that Universal needed Wagner for an additional two episodes. They offered a hefty dollar sum, and the agreement would cover the one performance they required. Samuels conferred with Lindsay, who declined. Universal came back with a stronger offer. He agreed, granting his client an exuberant salary for a mere 21 days of work.

As Samuels told *TV Guide* in 1976, "I felt the studio had treated [Lindsay] shabbily, and I quoted an impossible figure to turn them off. As far as I was concerned, Lindsay had put television behind her and I was concentrating on movie deals." He was "shocked" when Monique tracked him down a few days later, and told him, via the telephone: "Okay. Lindsay gets her $25,000 for the two segments." For most of her career, *TV Guide* noted, that was more than Lindsay had made in two years. The fee was too tempting to resist.

After filming *Second Wind* in Canada, Lindsay returned to Universal to make the second *Million Dollar Man* double-header. "The Return of the Bionic Woman, Parts I and II" became a reality.

Upon completing her finite treaty that included only those two episodes, Lindsay left the studio a second time, and went on to hold conversation with Samuels regarding potential theatrical film roles. September 14, 1975 arrived. *The Six Million Dollar Man*, with the first of another two-part *Bionic Woman* segment, was pitted against *The Cher Show* on CBS, and NBC's *The Family Holvak*, a *Walton's*-like family drama starring Glenn Ford.

That climactic evening, the Lindsay/Jaime return that the fans demanded, toppled the competition. That segment, coupled with its second part the subsequent Sunday, propelled *The Six Million Dollar Man* into the dynamic Top Ten.

The Bionic Woman, in a series of her own, was a sure thing to come. It was Fred Silverman who suggested to Harve Bennett the concept of *a regular Jaime Sommers series*. Years free of Bronchial Pneumonia, et al, Bennett was delighted.

Once again, however, there were obstacles. First, Lindsay Wagner was receiving rave reviews for her work in big-screen movies like *Two People* and *The Paper Chase* (both released in 1973). She wanted to continue her film work. Secondly, Universal had not picked up her option.

Again.

During a very negative experience of deja'vu, the team in Bennett's office began to clatter off their list of different accessible thespians. Once more, "Get me Lindsay Wagner," was the battle cry for ratings. Lindsay surmised that Universal would merely duplicate her previous agreement. She did not yet know what *Wonder Manager* (a.k.a. Ron Samuels) had in mind. He demanded a multi-thousand-dollar annual salary, over a five-year-period, that would include a yearly TV-movie option, and a percentage of all *Bionic*

LEE MAJORS AND LINDSAY WAGNER ON THE SET OF *SM*'S "THE
RETURN OF THE BIONIC WOMAN, PART II." THEIR PAIRING IN THIS
EPISODE WAS ONE OF FIVE ADVENTURES THE DUO WOULD EMBARK
UPON DURING THE SHOWS' ORIGINAL RUN.

Woman memorabilia.

There was an additional issue: Universal had requested ABC to star Lindsay in a pre-*Bionic* series, when she was somewhat more financially obtainable. The network, in their infinite non-wisdom, decided that she was not adequately established with the TV audience.

The offer was declined, which didn't matter to Lindsay. "*The Bionic Woman* came into my life strictly as a business decision," she explained. "I didn't see any real value in it, admittedly, in the beginning. When I left the studio, the character kind of took on a life of her own. The public responded and wanted her so. All I wanted to do was act in films."

Lindsay said she initially began to act "as a form of therapy," when she was very young. "It began to help me understand how important it is to express one's true feelings to another human being," she said. "I couldn't do that as *Lindsay*, but I could do it as a fictional character."

She never envisioned acting as her professional career, especially on television. "I hardly even watched it, for one thing," she reveals. "And I certainly wasn't interested in science fiction. I was more interested in *reality-based* material. I did the first [*Six Million*] episodes only out of a business obligation to the studio."

The actress had no concept of *The Bionic Woman* as a separate series, and the decision to play Jaime on a regular basis became "the most difficult time" in her entire career. "First of all," she explained, "it was tough work. And secondly, I was young. I didn't know how to deal with the tough part. So it became this relentless three-year vigil, but I didn't have the kind of stamina then, that I do now."

While filming *The Bionic Woman*, Lindsay was engaged in various efforts of self-healing, including her involvement with the Church of Religious Science, and her work with under-privileged schools, which were incapable of providing extracurricular activities. She was volunteering her time with children, doing drama exercises and, as she said, "kind of passing along the knowledge that was given to me." She felt torn as an actress, and that the entertainment industry was self-serving.

In her prayers, every day, she would ask for a way to work with children, to do something that she would enjoy, that would be worthwhile to her fellow human beings. All of which eventually equaled her original objective, which was to act. Not for the money. Not for the applause, but because it presented a way for her to communicate.

"That began to work for me," she said. "I had the ability to make choices as an actress and other people had noticed that, which was a real source of joy."

When Lindsay was continually approached to play *The Bionic Woman*, she was bewildered. "Don't you get it?" she would tell the big wigs. "I just don't want to do the show. It's not the type of thing with which I want to be associated."

A close friend of hers wondered why, and thought Lindsay was "missing the point." Jaime Sommers was the exact answer to her prayers. "If you play her," the friend told Lindsay, "you'll be able to communicate with the children of the world, make a living, and act."

"Yes, I know," Lindsay mused, "but running 60-miles an hour and jumping off buildings is not what I had in mind."

"I know your feelings about science fiction," the friend pressed, "that it's usually presented in a way that doesn't mean anything. But so is a lot of drama. But now, you can make this mean something, because of the way you think."

Lindsay analyzed her chum's perceptive words. "This *would* be perfect for me," she remembers telling herself. "First of all, it isn't totally science fiction. Jaime is, in fact, a human being, who ends up with super-human powers." Like Jaime, Lindsay was struggling to maintain her identity. Jaime's experiences were very much metaphors for Lindsay's personal and professional life.

In the end, both Lindsay and Universal conceded, and *The Bionic Woman* and *The Six Million Dollar Man* became separate weekly items on ABC, with Lindsay and Lee Majors crossing over as guest stars on one another's shows (as they do today with *Buffy the Vampire Slayer* and *Angel*, or as with *Hercules* and *Xena*).

Why didn't Jaime appear, simultaneously, with Steve on SM, as maybe Batgirl (played by Yvonne Craig) did on Adam West's classic *Batman* series? When it came to realism and character development, Austin was a different hero than Batman, said Harve Bennett, who worked on the 1960s TV version of the caped crusader (before Bruce Wayne's big-screen *Dark-Knight* persona, with Tim Burton directing Michael Keaton).

It was also extremely profitable for both ABC and Universal to have two different bionic shows. Bennett said *The American Cowboy* (Steve Austin) could not have a steady girl (Jaime Sommers), and then "plop into bed with some other love every week, like Captain Kirk did on *Star Trek*."

There had to be a compromise. Steve and Jaime's mutual love had to remain only slightly ignited, just enough to keep them involved with each other, just enough not to become too much involved with other people. "If not," Bennett said, "we would have lost our audience."

Ken Johnson feels it was important that Jaime had suffered just enough brain damage, that there would be no romantic link to Steve. Otherwise, there would be the big question of why she did not play a more prominent role on SM, and then later, vice versa.

"When I created Jaime I wanted to connect her to Steve as much as possible," he said, "so that it wouldn't be a whirlwind romance where they saw each other for the first time but rather a revisitation of an old relationship.

So it seemed natural to couch it in terms of home and family. It also gave her an ongoing connection to Steve when we spun off the show into a separate series. It kept Steve alive in her life even when he wasn't appearing in the *BW* episodes."

With particular regard to *Six*, he said Jaime's memory loss allowed Lee to play with a wider range of emotions because, even though Jaime forgot, Steve did not. "I loved that pathos," Johnson relays. "Bringing her back to life actually worked to my advantage. In the process of being revived, she had lost her memory of her love for Steve. You felt sympathy for Steve ever after because of his unrequited love for her. It also gave the characters an opportunity to strike sparks and start over again."

Steve and Jaime remained disengaged until *Return of The Six Million Dollar Man and The Bionic Woman* reunion film in 1987 (on NBC), and its sequel, *Bionic Showdown* in 1989 (also NBC), when — to the content of fans everywhere, there was a bionic proposal. Finally, in 1994's *Bionic Ever After?* (this time on CBS), they became cybernetically hitched, sealing the eternal *spring* of their appeal.

CHAPTER 3

POWER

"NEW GENERATIONS OF FANS ARE DISCOVERING THE SHOWS EVERY DAY, WHILE THE DIE-HARDS REMAIN INCREDIBLY LOYAL."

RICHARD ANDERSON

Without a doubt, *The Six Million Dollar Man* and *The Bionic Woman* enjoyed a type of prime-time run that competitors dared only dream of. Top-Ten ratings, an Emmy Award and multiple nominations, Golden Globe nominations (Majors in 1977; Wagner in 1977 and '78), prodigious storylines and multiple endearing reunion movies testify to their prior and latter-day appeal. All this, combined with the passing of time, might lead one to suspect that SM and BW were warmly received from the moment they bolted ABC's stable.

Yet, like Steve and Jaime themselves, *Man* and *Woman* had to crawl before they could run. Call it "the Spielberg Syndrome," but pop culture success does not automatically translate into respect. Despite the intercontinental network of fans, *Six* and *Woman* have for years suffered from somewhat of an image problem. Typical put-downs have ranged from "silly" and "juvenile" to "cartoon-like." Compared to other incendiary reviews that were to follow, one 1973 *Los Angeles Times'* synopsis of the original *Six* pilot was relatively flattering. "*The Six Million Dollar Man* begins ghoulishly, then verges on the amusingly preposterous but is solidly anchored to reality from start to finish," wrote *Times* scribe Kevin Thomas.

Already, however, Thomas saw the makings of a weekly serial. "*The Six Million Dollar Man*," he said, "does not deal with the possibility of Majors' superhuman strength being put to evil uses or what happens to him when he begins to age. But should this film lead to a series, then these and many other questions could be raised."

Clear across the pond, our British cousins were stingier with the praise. A reviewer for *The London Sunday Times*, contemplating a man such as Austin at the disposal of the US Government, wrote, "If Nixon were still in business, this would make me break into a cold sweat. It reeks of a generation which came to believe in the fabricated man as national hero. It has also that confusing quality of putting ultra-modern scientific know-how at the service of people with a preference for primitive rough-house situations." The Brit dressing-down soon took on a mocking tone: "The Doc tries to reassure the hero that his new limbs are indistinguishable from the old. *You'll be able to walk up to a girl and, if that's what you want, ask her to dance!* Their Senior Script Consultant does not seem to realize you don't nowadays hold girls when dancing."

Another *Times* columnist, Alan Corey, was more gracious, describing Austin as "an amalgam of Thomas Jefferson and Pat Boone."

Though the *Six* concept improved by bionic leaps and bounds when it graduated into a weekly serial, the reviews did not. The ever-influential *TV Guide*, courtesy of company hatchet man Cleveland Amory, wasted little time in attacking *Six*. "This show started out at 90 minutes and now is down to one hour," he wrote. "Well, they're getting there, but they haven't gone far enough. We're thinking about Saturday morning — for about a minute and a half."

Less grumpy was Mary Wood of the *Cincinnati Post & Times Star*, who hailed Steve Austin as a man "worth every penny of the taxpayers' investment. His new legs run with the speed of a bullet. He has X-ray vision with his new eye, and his artificial arm beats any battering ram you ever saw. Thank heaven he's on our side."

By the time BW debuted in January of 1976, most of the bionic kinks that had ill-served SM had been ironed out. The way was paved for a slightly smoother transition with Cleveland Amory and other caustic TV scribes. Though he couldn't resist BW's charms, Amory was still sour on the bionic enterprise in general, and displayed a firm grasp of the art of sarcasm. "Her bionic parts give her long-distance hearing and terrific strength," he reported. "Isn't that what you've always wanted — a girlfriend who can break your arm and hear what you whisper a mile away?"

The New York Times' Aleene Macminn mused that viewer enjoyment of *Woman* would require a certain suspension of disbelief: "It's a two-part story in which series star Lindsay Wagner gets to leap tall buildings in a single bound, crumble locks and cages, tear a door from a car, even open a can of tuna with her fingernail. If it sounds like it's stretching credibility too far, remember the stunts Elizabeth Montgomery pulled off all those years with just the twitch of a witch's nose on *Bewitched*. That's really the bottom line here: Either you go along with the bionic, superhuman gimmick, or forget it."

Time Magazine appreciated BW's subtler tone compared to its parent show. "Unlike Steve Austin, who regularly uses his brawn to brain villains, Jaime seldom uses her strength to do more than defensively trip or trick her opponents," they wrote. "The typical show seems to be a collection of ... episodes mainly to display Jaime's powers: She stops a rampaging elephant by tugging on its chain; uses her foot to brake an out-of-control car; leaps onto a second-story fire escape to avoid danger."

Though camp was not considered an integral part of SM or BW's appeal, the shows were not afraid to lure viewers with other lines, sometimes musical lines. As when Jaime sang and played the piano for Helen Hunt's Aura character on *The Bionic Woman* in "Sanctuary Earth," and earlier, when she sang about "Feelings" in BW's "Bionic Beauty." Then, of course, Steve sang "Gotta Get Loose" and "Sweet Jaime" in Jaime's first two-part appearance on SM. Steve sang "Sweet" again in "The Return of the Bionic Woman" episodes of *Six*. The music for the latter two songs was composed by Oliver Nelson, with lyrics by producer Lionel Siegel.

The "Loose" and "Sweet" songs were generated by Lee's desire to have Steve involved within a love story. As Siegel recalls, Majors "had a song-writer friend he was going to have do the songs, which was fine with us and our music composer." Then, certain legalities prevented further development and, as Siegel states, Lee's pal "took a hike." "Meanwhile," he continues, "we were doing a script [the *Six* episode, titled, and introducing, 'The Bionic Woman'] and we had to have some material. So, I wrote the lyrics for both songs in about two days and Oliver Nelson put them to music, and Lee sang them. Personally, I always thought that Nelson's theme music made the *slo-mo*, as we used to call it, work and fly."

All the while, the beginning and closing themes for both *The Bionic Woman* and *The Six Million Dollar Man* became popular, with some changes over the years. For SM, there was a variety of opening music from the pilot, to the monthly series, and again when the show went weekly. The pilot's music was penned by Gil Melle, the weekly versions then were composed by Oliver Nelson, and the monthly James Bond edition of the show, specifically from the telefilm called *The Solid Gold Kidnapping*, had a theme written by Dusty Springfield. Nelson, a talented musician, writer and composer, provided music for *Six* up until the day of his death from a heart attack, October 27, 1975. He was 43. In addition to *Six*, he penned well-known music for series such as *Columbo*, *Ironside*, *Night Gallery*, and *Longstreet*.

With BW, beginning with some trial musical background for the "Bionic Beauty" episode, Ken Johnson explained, "I finally talked Harve Bennett into letting me bring in a composer named Joe Harnell, whom I had been lobbying for the longest time, and who had been my director on *The Mike Douglas Show*. The composers they had been using on the show were okay, but I wanted someone with more sparkle. And Joe came in and really did a great score, and began to create some of the light motifs that would find their way in the rest of *The Bionic Woman*, like the *ting, ting, ting* sound made by the triangle instrument. And Jim and I created the rolling tympanic

THE SIX MILLION DOLLAR MAN.

**All The Excitement!
All The Realism!
All The Bionic™ Action!**

BIONIC™ EYE   Look through real wide angle lens in left eye of figure.

BIONIC™ POWER ARM   Demonstrate super lifting power with Engine Block included with figure.

BIONIC™ ARM MODULES   Roll back skin to reveal modules that can be removed for Bionic™ surgery.

FULLY ARTICULATED 13" Action Figure.

Set contains Six Million Dollar Man™ Action Figure dressed in red NASA-style jumpsuit and sneakers. Includes engine block Ages 5 and up.

NO. 65000
PKD. 6 WT. 7 LBS.

THE BIONIC WOMAN

Beauty and Fashion plus Bionic Action!

12½" beautiful fully articulated figure modeled after Lindsay Wagner, the star of the Bionic Woman TV show.

Silky fully rooted hair.

Bionic modules in ears, right arm and both legs just like the real Jaime Sommers.

Turn her head from side to side and actually hear a Bionic™ pinging noise when Jaime Sommers uses her Bionic ears.

Dressed in official stylish jogging outfit and tennis shoes.

Ages 5 and up.

NO. 65800
PKD. 6 WT. 7 LBS.

TOP: LEE MAJORS AND A YOUNG ADMIRER PLAY THE *SM* BOARD GAME AS PARKER BROTHERS EXECUTIVES LOOK ON. BOTTOM: DEALER PROMOTIONAL ADS FOR KENNER'S *SM* AND *BW* TOY LINE.

AN ASSORTMENT OF OFFICIAL *SM* MERCHANDISE.

AN ASSORTMENT OF OFFICIAL *BW* MERCHANDISE.

A SAMPLING OF COVERS FROM *SM/BW* BOOKS, COMICS, AND MAGAZINES.

theme that she used whenever Jaime was on roll. You know the one that goes, *Bum, bum ba da bum bum bum ba da bum bump bum.*"

While another song, "Friends," can be heard during "The Bionic Dog, Part II" episode of BW, one of Lindsay Wagner's favorite BW-related musical numbers was entitled, "Woman Bionic," concocted by an assistant cameraman.

One aspect of *Bionic* history that stands alone in understanding the popularity of both SM and BW is the ample line of memorabilia and action-figures associated with the shows.

While Universal has recently reissued a new *Bionic* licensing for tee-shirts, caps, DVDs, and trading cards, Steve and Jaime playthings originally surfaced in many shapes and sizes, from waste paper baskets, raincoats and comic books to pillow cases and motorized toothbrushes. It all began in 1970 when the late Bernard Loomis, a rising star at Mattel who gave the world Hot Wheels cars, defected to rival Kenner Toys, which was owned by a division of General Mills. Kenner, based in Cincinnati, Ohio, was foundering. It desperately needed a hot new product.

"When I first saw *The Six Million Dollar Man* in the early seventies, I thought it was *toyetic* as hell," Loomis said. "*Toyetic* means 'the property of being expressible in playable figures and hardware.' What convinced us was that opening bit—it was the very idea that we could make an artificial man with parts, and strength, and things like that."

Without delay, Loomis booked a flight to Los Angeles. "The show was already on the air, which was probably the last kid-oriented show that did not have a toy deal already in place before it was broadcast," he said. "I went out to Universal, located a young man named Steve Adler, who was Universal's Vice President of Merchandising at the time, and said 'I want a world-wide toy exclusive on *The Six Million Dollar Man.*' I made the deal for the General Mills Group and we were off and running. It changed the licensing business forever. Within a year, we had the leading boys' toy in the world."

Although this meeting occurred in early 1974, the first *Six* toys didn't appear on store shelves until fall 1975 at the earliest. "The normal gestation period from start to production is somewhere in the 12- to 18-month range — particularly for the kind of toys we were making," said Loomis, who, ironically, never had any toys as a child.

With Loomis at the helm, General Mills' toy group surpassed Mattel as the world's largest and most profitable toy company. In a marketing coup, Kenner's promotional tie-in with the General Mills Food Group meant that free bionic stickers and toy rebates could be found in boxes of Cheerios and Lucky Charms. Children the world over rushed to join the "Bionic Action Club" — a fan kit mailer that included a diploma-like certificate, membership card, logo decal, and a handsome photo of either Steve or Jaime (depending on which club they joined).

Long before the *Bionic* boom, however, toy companies had been capital-
izing on the popularity of small-screen programming by mass marketing
everything from *Davy Crockett* coonskin caps to *Lost in Space* figurines. So
when Kenner introduced the first *Six Million Dollar Man* items to coincide
with Christmas of 1975, it was simply expanding on proven ground.

Unfortunately, for Loomis, a lot of those knickknacks were missing the
Kenner seal of approval. "The deal that we struck was for games and toys
and anything that fit that description," he said. "[Steve] Adler and I were
constantly fighting over things that I felt were over the edge or infringed
on our agreement. Incidentally, we used to bring Lee Majors to toy fairs for
several years. He would pose for pictures and of course got paid for it. I was
always amazed at the interest that grownups would have in getting their
picture taken with Lee."

Kenner's licensing fee (i.e., the amount of money diverted to Universal
on every bionic sale) was roughly 6%, and was coupled with a modest roy-
alty advance. In a magnanimous gesture, Loomis voluntarily cut Majors in
on the action. "For no reason that I can explain, I said we better give Lee
Majors some part of it so he can't sell himself in any other form. We did
the same thing when we went to *Bionic Woman*, and I don't know if Lindsay
Wagner ever knew it or not, but she [or her agent] *did* try to sell a version
of herself to a rival marketer. This, despite the fact that she had a contract
that said she couldn't."

Initially, SM and BW products were simple spin-offs that remained
true to the characters while spawning a glut of appropriate accessories. As
both series continued, the toys themselves grew somewhat more extravagant (i.e. the drag-racing Bigfoot), a development of which BW producer
Ken Johnson did not approve. He remembers when a representative from
Kenner brought the *Woman* doll into his office. It had a make-up kit, and
Ken said, "What is this? This woman is a powerful, action-adventure heroine. She's like a Viking, for Pete's sake. And you're giving me lipstick?
Don't you see what you're doing in terms of stereotyping and how what
you're trying to say is terrible?"

The rep looked at him and said, "I think we're all pretty comfortable with
those stereotypes."

Johnson "couldn't believe he said that," and "hit the roof."

Bernard Loomis had a different take. "I don't even recall hearing that
story," he protested. "I will say this: Ken Johnson was wrong. We weren't
about to try to make an action figure for girls. They [girls] weren't buying
it and they haven't yet. The only chance we had at the girls' market was to
make sure that she [the doll] stayed feminine. Nobody has successfully created an 'Action Barbie.' We came the closest, but we definitely slanted it
toward girls and their preferences. It sounds like [Johnson] wanted to make
her into a dyke."

Not so, said Johnson, who takes offense to Loomis' narrow dissertation on female empowerment.

"The outrageous and infuriating notion that I had a desire to present Jaime as anything other that what she was — an action heroine who was also as feminine as any other woman — is wrong," said Johnson. "I suppose that [Loomis] would therefore consider that Jennifer Garner's character on *Alias* is a 'dyke.' His comment is so sexist, rude and ignorant as to defy description. It never ceases to amaze me how so many big corporate operatives are always more interested in making a fast buck than in elevating the taste, intelligence and tolerance of the public they supposedly serve. I wonder how such people can look at themselves in the mirror. I fear for the future of American honor and integrity."

Clearly, at Kenner Toys, profit took precedence over broad social statements. "*The Six Million Dollar Man* was a huge success," Loomis stated. "For its time, it was a great success. By contrast, *The Bionic Woman* was only a modest success. We did well with it and we were happy, but no question the category is basically a boys' market. I mean, the least important character in the world of *Star Wars* was Princess Leia."

Today, some of the most sought after bionic collectibles include the Venus Space Probe (preferably mint-in-box), Steve Austin's third-edition "Biosonic" doll, the ultra-rare Six Mill test card set by Topps, and an 18-inch Jaime Sommers doll issued exclusively in the UK. Similarly, boxed versions of the Fembot and Maskatron dolls continue to fetch a pretty penny.

"My creative people were in touch with the producers of the shows," said Loomis, who prolifically oversaw the launch of such popular toys as *Strawberry Shortcake*, *Play-Doh*, *Care Bears*, *Baby Alive*, and the *Star Wars* line. "We even worked a little bit on product placement with them. After the first year, we kinda knew what was coming and we were able to get out in front of it and create some stuff based on popular characters like Fembot, Maskatron, Bigfoot, and OSI Headquarters."

By 1978, the bionic toy universe was beginning to wane. Left on the drawing board (and never put into production) were such concepts as the SMDM Bigfoot Time Capsule, SMDM Lunar Lander, Steve Austin Sports Car, Beautiful Jaime Display, Bionic Desk Set, Bionic Boy Side-Car Cycle, Bionic Arm Tester, Bionic Super Table, Bionic Jewelry, Maskatron II, and an action figure based on Max, the bionic dog.

Michael F. Van Plew, at one time the top *Bionic* collector in the world, is passionately protective of the *Six Million Dollar Man* and *Bionic Woman* toy lines, which have developed into a hot property on the collectibles market. "Mint and boxed versions," he said, "are today becoming increasingly scarce."

Van Plew, known in certain collectible circuits as Bionic Mike, does have a favorite SM/BW toy. Namely, in the figure of Steve, who is outfitted with his Critical Assignment arm and legs. This particular Austin actioneer is wearing a white shirt and shorts. His right arm is showcased in clear plastic with printed circuitry. His lower limbs are forged in a fashion that displays a few systematic sections of his bionic reconstruction. "The likeness to Lee Majors as Steve Austin is keen," Van Plew said, "and to me that familiarity is of key importance. That's the one reason I collect *Six Million Dollar Man* toys."

As a child, he admits to not watching too many episodes of *The Bionic Woman*, but still owns a most cherished toy from the *Woman* collection: the Jaime Sommers action figure itself, which had two editions. The initial doll was readied with a white, jogging suit top and blue denim jeans. The second was designed with a blue jumpsuit and a red mission purse (the same one Ken Johnson passionately objected to). "The first," Van Plew said, "is one of my favorites because it best resembled the character. I also liked the bionic modules in both legs and the right arm, which really set it apart from other Barbie-like dolls."

Yet Lindsay points out that her Jaime miniature "had the face of Farrah," as in Fawcett, whose own *Charlie's Angels*/Jill Munroe toy-likeness was initiated much later. And even though Lee's Steve action figure was not marketed as a "doll," he sold equally well, with more rugged manly clothing, while his female counterpart was guised in more fashionable garb. The bionic franchise was so lucrative for Kenner Toys that Steve and Jaime graced the cover of the company's 1976 catalog.

As Van Plew assessed, the *Six/Woman* toy lines have surpassed their original financial value, due to sentiment, based on their popularity in the 1970s. "Most of them," he said, "were bionically ripped from their boxes and sent on secret missions."

Not only were the likes of Steve Austin and Jaime Sommers caricatured for the collectible market, sometimes the *Bionic* actors themselves would do a takeoff on the parts they played. As in the fall of 1974, when Lee Majors and Richard Anderson spoofed their cybernetic screen personas during a bit on ABC's *Funshine Sunshine Saturday* cartoon preview special.

In the segment, a videotape of animated beings was stolen by a dastardly organization called PSST! (Public School on Saturday and Sunday Too!). It was up to *The Six Million Dollar Man* (in a Superman-like costume with a money-signed S) to track it down and save the day.

If self-imitation is the sincerest form of flattery, then these good-natured jokes at their own expense only served to increase SM/BW's popularity. Two years after the PSST! spot, *The Six Million Dollar Man* became the #1 rated show in Australia, a feat never accomplished in America. Twenty years later, and despite critic Cleveland Amory's early low-blow-down on the *Bionic* universe, his former employer, *TV Guide,* ranked the program as third out of seven in a reader's poll of *All-Time Favorite Sci-Fi/Fantasy Shows* (one notch ahead of *Star Trek: The Next Generation*). In 2004, Steve

TOP: LINDSAY WAGNER IS REUNITED WITH RICHARD ANDERSON,
JENNIFER DARLING, AND RITA EGLESTON, LINDSAY'S *BW* STUNT-
DOUBLE, WHO MADE SURPRISE APPEARANCES AT LINDSAY'S 2003
OFFICIAL FAN CLUB GATHERING IN LOS ANGELES. *BOTTOM LEFT:*
LINDSAY, RICHARD, AND KENNETH JOHNSON APPEARED AT 2006'S
BIONICON, THE FIRST FAN CONVENTION DEDICATED TO THE BIONIC
SHOWS (SHOWN HERE WITH BIONIC FAN AND BOOK CONTRIBUTOR
MATT HANKINSON). *BOTTOM RIGHT:* LINDSAY WAS GIVEN A SURPRISE
BIRTHDAY CELEBRATION THE NIGHT OF THE BANQUET, AS HER
BIRTHDAY WAS JUNE 22, THE DAY BEFORE THE CONVENTION.

and Jaime shared the 19TH slot in *TV Guide's* "25 Greatest Sci-Fi Legends" series. That same year, Rittenhouse Archives issued a commemorative set of trading cards in honor of SM's 30TH anniversary.

Today, the *Bionic* reunion-movies are continually rerun on cable's Family Channel, USA and Lifetime networks, while the original shows enjoyed a mid-1990s resurgence in fame on the Sci-Fi Channel. There are numerous *Bionic* fan sites (foreign and domestic) on the Internet, where several robust discussion forums and message boards are dedicated to the shows—foremost among them *Bionicfans* (Yahoo!) and *The Bionic Wiki* (Wikipedia). In 2006, the world's first bionic fan convention, *Bionicon*, convened in Tampa, Florida. One year later, *Bionicon 2.0* was conducted in Los Angeles. Lindsay Wagner's annual fan club meetings, dating back to the early 1980s, are reliably well-attended affairs. As a testament to their devotion and adoration, loyal fans pooled their resources to finance Lee and Lindsay's respective stars on the Hollywood Walk of Fame in 1984.

Entertainment Tonight continues to cover *Bionic* developments. *Lois and Clark: The New Adventures of Superman* frequently made *Bionic* references. *The Washington Post, The Los Angeles Times, Entertainment Weekly, People Magazine, Starlog, Sci-Fi Universe, Scientific America, Maclean's, The Star* and *The National Enquirer* have all recently published *Bionic* articles.

Saturday Night Live has showcased *Bionic* skits in decades past, one of which featured 1996 *Twister* star Helen Hunt, who guest-starred on *The Bionic Woman* when she was 12 years old. In 1997, beloved TV comic Bob Newhart got in on the act with a sketch called "The Six Million Dollar Bob."

Bionic parodies have also been seen on *The Benny Hill Show, Sesame Street* (*The Six DOLLAR Man*), *The Electric Company* (*The Six Dollar and Thirty-Nine Cent Man,* featuring *Steve AWESOME*), and *The Simpsons.* In the latter, while Montgomery Burns chooses Bart as his heir, Marge has a daydream/fantasy about Majors, who picks her up and does a bionic leap in the air. In an earlier episode, the Steve Austin "action figure" was tributed.

In 1994, *bionic* staying power was evident when Coors Light Beer initiated TV and radio commercials referring to *The Six Million Dollar CAN.* "I was walking into the room when it was on TV," Lee Majors said. "I heard the title music and I saw this beer can running alongside a fence. 'The Six Million Dollar Can.' That just cracked me up."

Lee satirized himself in the feature film, *Scrooged,* released in 1988, and starring Bill Murray. He would do so again in *National Lampoon's TV: The Movie* (2006), where he played doddering Steve Boston, The Six Million Year Old Man, among other characters. In 1998, Majors donned his old red tracksuit when he visited Mary Cunningham, a real-life winner of $1.8 million from the Colorado Lottery. In the ad, Majors notes that although Cunningham may now have the means to buy a new home and a new car, she can't buy her own sound effects like Majors has from his bionic-man days. He demonstrates the sound effects while lifting a teacup to his lips. Years later, Majors filmed a similar ad for Canada's "Lotto 649."

In 2003, Lee freelanced for ING Financial Group (US), where he was spotted in an arm-wrestling contest with elderly ladies and little girls (effortlessly defeating all challengers, naturally). That same year, Majors was honored as TV's all-time "Superest Super Hero" at the first annual TV Land Awards, besting such competitors as Wonder Woman, Superman, and The Incredible Hulk. Lindsay Wagner herself snagged TV Land's "Greatest Gear or Admirable Apparatus" award in 2007, and was humble enough to perform some crowd-pleasing *bionic* stunts.

Also on the big screen: *Caddyshack* (1980), features a *bionic sound* scene, courtesy star Chevy Chase and his trusted putter, while *Austin Powers* (1997), not only makes an obvious word-play with its title, but appropriates BW's "Fembots In Vegas" episode, by placing the same-named fembots in the *city that never sleeps* (in an underground lair). *The Cable Guy* (1996) gave us a brief glimpse of Steve and Jaime's iconic fence run scene. *Dogma* (1999) cribbed the "better, stronger, faster" line. *Bio-Dome* (1996), *Mystery Men* (1999), *Zoolander* (2001), *Anchorman* (2004) and *Shrek the Third* (2007) also made use of the *bionic sound*, while the main protagonist in *The 40 Year-Old Virgin* (2005) was hung up on bionic-themed playthings.

Steve Austin, meanwhile, was the precursor for the *RoboCop* films (1987, 1990, 1993) and TV show (1994), and the classic 1989 *Cyborg* movie (which made a motion picture star of Jean-Claude Van Damme); the actual terms *cyborg* and *bionic* were introduced to the science-fiction mainstream by a trail-blazing *Six Million Dollar Man*.

Moreover, the CD-ROM game, *Frogger*, also appropriated SM's opening credits as a spoof. Other TV shows/products/commercials that have borrowed bionic themes include the following: *Footaction*, *Tetley Tea Bags* (Ireland), *Hyundai* (Belgium), *Ford & Mercury Auto Dealers Association* (British Columbia), *Hotel!* (Great Britain; guest-starring Lee Majors), *ING Financial Group* (China), *The Edge*, *King of the Hill*, *Just Shoot Me*, *Scrubs*, *South Park*, *Nintendo's BattleTanx*, *Capital One*, *MCI*, *Freaks and Geeks*, *Friends*, *Family Guy*, *Viva Pinata*, *Duck Dodgers*, *Robot Chicken*, *Are You Being Served?* (Great Britain), *The Goodies* (Great Britain), *The Carol Burnett Show*, *The Jenny McCarthy Show*, *Wayne and Shuster* (Canada), *Dr. Croc*, *Jake 2.0* (guest-starring Lee Majors), *Goodness Gracious Me* (Great Britain), *The Office* (US), *Son of the Beach* (guest-starring Lee Majors), *Veronica Mars*, *That '70s Show*, *Quicken Insurance*, *Chevy TrailBlazer*, *Chrysler PT Turbo*, *Taco Bell*, *IBM ThinkPad* (w/ Lee Majors), *Black and Decker*, *Eurosport*, *America Online* (with new voiceovers from Richard Anderson), *Lingo* (Game Show Network), *Who Wants to be a Millionaire?* and *Techno Turtle*.

What's at the core of the undying *Bionic* appeal?

For Harve Bennett, it dates back to an early stage viewing of *The Elephant Man*. The main character's classic line, "I'm not a freak, I'm a human being" continues to haunt him.

"That's the cry of Steve Austin," he said. "That's what subconsciously drew me to *The Six Million Dollar Man*. In Steve's mind, he was compensating for being a freak…an accident. In the first few [weekly] episodes, in particular, that quality of his aloneness was addressed."

SM/BW writer Wilton Denmark was at the very same screening Harve Bennett attended in late 1973. "One of the things Harve said about Lee Majors was, 'He sure knows how to wear a pair of jeans,'" he recalls.

From the get-go, Denmark was intrigued.

"It was very interesting," he said. "I liked the idea of a bionic man; the idea that medical knowledge had advanced that far. It was a little farfetched, but it was believable that something like that could happen. I often wondered what it would be like for a man to become bionic. I liked the idea of good vs. evil as well."

In the 1970s, the decade of the *Me Generation*, there were mass feelings of withdrawal. Bennett believes everyone felt alone, and set out to *find themselves*. "That's what Steve was doing," he said. "If you don't count *Superman*, he was the first modern television superhero. He displayed emotion, was not all-powerful, but flawed. People identified with that."

They still do.

Richard Anderson, Oscar Goldman's alter ego, believes that many minorities, in particular, have reckoned with Steve and Jaime over the years. "They adhere to the same tactility of isolation and ostracization," he said. Like Bennett, Anderson also frequently hears cries, if of a different nature, in the form of complaints from *Bionic* fans of every race and creed as to why Steve and Jaime ever left the airwaves. As he detects, the protests go something like this: "Steve and Jaime should have never gone off the air!" [And] "They were clean, family programs, with strong values."

In an expanded sense, *The Six Million Dollar Man* and *The Bionic Woman* paved the way for the *Terminator* (1984, 1991, 2003) films, as well as TV's wildly popular Marvel Comics' animated *X-Men* superhero series and franchise of live-action feature films, which deals with *mutant* humans who feel discriminated against in contemporary times.

Bionic producer/director/writer Ken Johnson turned down the opportunity to direct *RoboCop*, due to its violent content. And though he directed big-screen movies, including *Steel* (in 1997, with Shaquille O'Neal), *Short Circuit II* (1988), as well as foreign releases of *The Incredible Hulk* (the top-grossing film in Europe for two months in 1977) and *The Bride of the Incredible Hulk* (1979), he made certain the theme of intolerance ran rampant throughout SM and BW, as well as his other small-screen shows (*Hulk, V, Alien Nation*).

Johnson was born and raised in a virulently anti-Semitic, anti-black household in the American South. His stepfather, who was from Massachusetts, was "the biggest bigot of them all," he said. Today, "astonished" at the kind of hate language and words that he grew up with, Johnson doesn't know where it came from but, somehow, he instinctively knew "that it was all bullshit and that it was wrong."

Johnson then promised himself that, with his work, he would lash out against discrimination, prejudice and isolation, whenever he could, particularly in the area of sci-fi and fantasy. When producing *V*, he went out of his way to ensure that it wouldn't be "just about a bunch of lizard people coming from outer space." "It was about power," he explained, "and how it corrupts; how it takes some people into collaboration with the enemy, and others into the heroism against it."

As far as he's concerned, "if it's not on the page, it ain't on the stage." Whenever he begins to write, he questions his creative motives, as if to say, "Okay, what is this episode about?" Not, "What's the premise?" Or, "What's the story?" But, "What is the thematic underpinning? What emotional lines are we going to touch on here?"

Johnson fabricated the plot and the story around such ideas; a strategy, he said, added to the allure of SM and BW, and many of the other sci-fi/fantasy shows that he's produced, including *The Incredible Hulk*. "There's a surface appeal to each of them," he ascertains, "a kind of glossiness that gets people into the store to say, *Wow, take a look at that*. But once inside, they realize there's something else going on."

As with the *Hulk*, *V* and *Alien Nation*, SM and BW were, in Johnson's eyes, stories of isolation, which coincides with Harve Bennett's *Elephant Man* assessment. "Certainly," Ken said of Jaime's show, in particular, "one of the things that we were always faced with, from the beginning, was that she was *different*. In one of the very first emotional scenes that we did with Jaime [from the first two-part episode of *The Six Million Dollar Man* which introduced her], she said things like, *Why didn't you let me die? I don't want to be a freak.*"

Jaime's brother/lover show, meanwhile, introduced the first TV character to bring back the multi-dimensional, mood-swinging, true-to-life-hero in the white hat. By 1973, and soon after the Vietnam War, viewers were ready for something uplifting. The ideas introduced with SM were lifted right out of the headlines. According to Richard Anderson, such concepts were "played absolutely straight, but with a positive message, mainly because of their medical aspects."

The memorandum of *Man* and *Woman* also traveled beyond the medicinal realm into the psychological, as both Steve and Jaime stressed the importance of self-control over the control of others. They believed it was more important to have inner-strength than outer-strength. (David Carradine's

Kwai Chang Caine on TV's *Kung Fu* would call that inside power, the *chi*.) Steve didn't like guns. Jaime retained both femininity and independence. The appeal of both programs is sustained in these cynical, frequently mean-spirited times.

"There definitely is something unhealthy in the air," comments Anderson, who portrayed Oscar with a balanced amount of austerity and compassion. "There's an unhappiness about the way things are being communicated through the various [media]. TV, radio, movies, even the new electronic computer capabilities have not even begun to brush the surface of how they may truly be employed. Television, in particular, holds incredible potential for positive influence in society. To some extent, I believe *The Six Million Dollar Man* and *The Bionic Woman* parlayed into that arena very well."

Lee Majors and Lindsay Wagner portrayed positive characters that were heroic, and yet remained identifiable to viewers. Steve Austin was not merely defined as a *bionic man*, but rather as *a man who happens to be bionic*. Jaime was not solely a *bionic woman* by definition, but *a woman who happens to be bionic*; a trait which held substantial weight for Lindsay in her decision to portray the super female every week.

"As much as our Western culture professes to empower us as individuals," she explained, "it fails. Instead, we are empowered to buy things that other people want to sell. We are usually conditioned to emphasize our sexual prowess, or our ability to *beat the other guy* and *be first* in business or personal relationships. All these external developments. When, in fact, whatever real power we have, comes from within." [Another nod to the *chi*.]

Wagner perceived that, if children in particular, could view this super woman named Jaime Sommers, who defined herself irrespective of her spectacular prowess (abilities upon which she didn't concentrate), "then that would be a good thing." "Jaime's real power," she insists, "rested with her humanity."

Lindsay should know.

Beyond winning a coveted Emmy for playing Jaime (as Lead Actress in a Drama, the first such honor bestowed upon a regular TV sci-fi dramatic performer, male or female, before Gillian Anderson's 1997 win for *The X-Files*), she's starred in more than thirty-five highly-rated, socially-conscious TV-movies: *Four Extraordinary Women* (2006), *Thicker Than Water* (2005), *Contagious* (1997), *Fighting for My Daughter* (1995), *Once in a Lifetime* (1994), *Nurses on the Line* (1993), *A Message From Holly* (1992), *Shattered Dreams* (1990), *The Taking of Flight 847: The Uli Derickson Story* (1988), *Child's Cry* (1986), and *The Incredible Journey of Dr. Meg Laurel* (1979).

She creates little distinction between her life as an actress, social advocate, mother (of two sons, with former husband/BW stuntman, Henry Kingi),

TOP LEFT: LINDSAY WAGNER ACCEPTS HER WELL-DESERVED 1977 EMMY AWARD FOR LEAD ACTRESS IN A DRAMATIC ROLE FOR THE *BW* EPISODE "DEADLY RINGER." *TOP RIGHT:* IN 2007, SHE WON *TV LAND'S* FAN FAVORITE AWARD IN THE "GREATEST GEAR AND ADMIRABLE APPARATUS" CATEGORY. *BOTTOM LEFT:* LEE MAJORS ACCEPTS HIS "SUPEREST SUPER HERO" AWARD DURING *TV LAND'S* 2003 AWARD SHOW. *BOTTOM RIGHT:* LEE AND LINDSAY EACH RECEIVED THEIR STARS ON THE HOLLYWOOD WALK OF FAME IN 1984.

humanitarian and author (*Lindsay Wagner's New Beauty: The Acupressure Facelift*, Simon & Schuster, 1987; *The High Road to Health*, S&S, 1993).

What unites these various roles is a commitment to the advancement of human potential.

So from Lindsay's standpoint, Jaime's lasting appeal doesn't rest in her arm, or in her legs. "It's in her heart," the actress explained. "As individuals, we have little concept of how truly powerful we are. When there's a joint effort with others to make a difference, whether it's with a TV series, or some other form of communication, the possibilities are endless."

Communicating what true power is and the importance of inner-strength, or showcasing discretion with one's special abilities, were certainly key factors in Lee Majors' view of *The Six Million Dollar Man*. "Here was a guy," he opines, "who could break through concrete, jump extremely high and run *almost* faster than a speeding bullet. He didn't set out to prove that, not to strangers, and certainly not to those closest to him. He *went bionic* only when he had to, and the audience respected that."

The audience found equal appeal with Steve's ability to "clobber someone who deserved it," Majors adds. "But he was pretty cool about it. He never let the fact that he was bionic go to his head. He never intentionally used his powers to hurt anyone. To escape an otherwise inescapable situation, yes. He would break out with the bionics, as he would to defend or rescue himself or someone else who might be in trouble. But it was his ability to keep his head, and make the right decisions on *when* to use his powers that made him a hero."

Brendan Slattery, an entertainment writer based in the nation's capital, has this to say about one particularly patriotic *Bionic* objective:

"Although Martin Caidin's *Cyborg* made reference to Steve's tour of duty in Southeast Asia — he was injured as a chopper pilot in Vietnam — the television series wisely omitted this bit of trivia. ABC had an authentic American hero on its hands. Why ruin a good thing by reminding your core audience of the ugliness and rancor from America's recent past? Besides, any downside inferred by Steve's military credentials was offset by his connection to the highly popular US space program. To that end, Austin fit perfectly into the lore of American exceptionalism: handsome, brooding, confident (sometimes overly so), mixed with a palpable sense of vulnerability that belied his extraordinary skills. John Wayne meets John Glenn."

Slattery believes that the "oldest living Boy Scout" angle worked to the show's advantage. "It tapped into something America was hungry for, and still is," he said. "Courage, integrity, duty, love of country: these were very counter-cultural values in 1973. To appropriate a term from that era, Steve Austin was television's biggest 'square' — he loved his mother, would stick his neck out for a friend, and faithfully arrived for work on time every week. He was true-blue, decent, and endowed with a character as strong as his atomic-powered limbs."

Above all else, the Bond/Austin dichotomy had to be scuttled. "James Bond *loves* his job," Slattery observes. "He thrives on confrontation and willingly invites danger. Austin, on the other hand, is very much the reluctant hero. He is a pilot, not a soldier. His spying is motivated by a sense of debt or gratitude. Like TV's Jim Rockford, if there's an easy or sensible way out, he'll take it."

If Slattery saw a lonesome cowboy, *Six* scribe Judy Burns fancied Clark Kent. "Well, he's kinda like Superman, right? And I had always liked Superman," she said. "This fellow had a lot of superhuman qualities, with a lot of very human foibles. It allowed a writer to have some conflict within the character himself, let alone with the nemeses he might meet. I felt Lee Majors carried off a hard role. It's not easy to play that kind of part and make us love him."

After a few years, because *Man* and *Woman* were on-going shows, the programs and their characters experienced growth, contributing to an everlasting appeal. Or as Harve Bennett puts it, "The sleighs were pulled in different directions."

Steve Austin transformed tremendously when he first met Jaime Sommers, and *The Six Million Dollar Man* was pulled into one of Bennett's said "other directions." In turn, she experienced some reconstruction when she was granted her own series. For example, when the regular Sommers seasons began to air in January 1976 (following Lindsay's initial guest segments on *Man*), Jaime led more of a double life.

As the show continued into its second year (1976 to 1977), Jaime's career as a teacher diminished, altogether disappearing in the third season (1977 to 1978; on NBC).

Here, as Harve Bennett explained, the reasons for change were fiscal in nature:

"It came down to budget. When you work with children under 14 years of age, by law, you're only allowed four hours a day. Six hours in the summertime. Child labor laws make it so. That's one third of a day's shoot, which began to complicate your time. You have to drop everything, and schedule the kids around that central event. It becomes a delaying factor in completing shows on time, and on budget. It's a lot easier to be able to have the flexibility of not using kids, especially more than one or two."

Other times, Bennett said a more moderate pattern of thought was exercised on both shows, as when Steve and Jaime were injured so severely in their pre-bionic accidents. Through recovery, their personalities changed drastically from *control freak* to *underdog* to *hero* — a transposition that further advanced their attraction with the home viewers, after Steve and Jaime's excruciating physical, psychological and emotional pain and loss.

Though they may have been kind and compassionate human beings before their metamorphoses, the super pair did indeed become *better* and *stronger* people. They gained a more solid sense of self-awareness and self-esteem, through detriment.

"If a man sets a pole-vault score that breaks the world's record," Bennett proposes, "but the pole is really a hydraulic pogo stick, does he really feel that he's accomplished anything? Probably not. Steve and Jaime were forced to confront such feelings on a daily basis. What are heroes, anyway, but people in extraordinary circumstances? I was always trying to get to the essence of Steve's estrangement, which I myself, felt as a kid. How does a little Jewish kid, growing up, loving America, find a way to be an American hero? It's hard. I came to accept that if you abided by certain Jeffersonian principles, if you really believed that all men are created equal, then, you were an American hero. You belonged. That was my human solution to the dilemma of *how do you belong*, one which every human being has to confront. Everything I do is sort of an expression of that."

SM producer Lionel Siegel echoes Bennett's "alienation" argument. "*Six Mill* was the forerunner of using disabled people in contemporary drama," he said. "Steve Austin had various prosthetics attached to his body which enabled him to be normal. The fact that this gave him super strength was a bonus. For me, if the action didn't keep you tuned in, if the humor didn't work, if you didn't get a lump in your throat, and if you couldn't follow the plot, we failed. If most of the above did work, we succeeded."

The reasons for the success of *The Six Million Dollar Man* and *The Bionic Woman*, in hindsight, had more to do with Steve and Jaime's humanistic approach to living and personal interaction, as opposed to their super-humanistic powers which they were to employ mainly for professional reasons — an analysis which was light years from the assumptions that were made when *Man*, as a series, was merely a rumor. They were action adventures shows with a very deeply human content. The trick was to not let the humanity overwhelm their active-energy nature of the programs. Then they would have become sappy.

Those in charge had to inject humanity at every possible turn, without cutting down on the running and the jumping. The action was just as important to the show as was the character's development and personal interaction. One was equal to the other, and weakened without the other.

Lee Majors was akin to this perspective during SM's transformation from monthly movies to weekly episodes. "Look," he told the decision makers, "I will only do this as a series if we play down the bionics, and make sure that we retain Steve's humanity. And have him use his bionics only when necessary."

Then, later, upon Majors' suggestion that his *Man* be given a *Woman*. This *womanity* aspect of superdom transmuted into an issue for ABC, who

eventually sharpened a double-edged sword with two colossal-female programs. There was a moment in the network's history when programming
chief Fred Silverman was forced to decide between two superhero shows for
a mid-season replacement. Both properties happened to be female-super-
hero series: *The Bionic Woman* and *Wonder Woman*.

Up until the last moment before *The Bionic Woman* premiered, Silverman
wondered what to do with the other *Woman*, though he perceived *Bionic*
and *Wonder* as interchangeable. "He just saw two superheroes that were
female," Harve Bennett said, "and that was their slug [appeal]. But the differences between *Wonder Woman* and *The Bionic Woman* are the differences
between work of which I am proud, and lots of other television. This isn't to
knock *Wonder Woman*, because it had its own success. But it was just a very
different show from *The Bionic Woman*. It was a cartoon."

While Carter's supergirl eventually appeared periodically in Jaime's timeslot (and then moved to a regular spot on CBS in the same year that Jaime
moved to NBC), *Time* magazine's Richard Schickel felt compelled to draw a
then-comparison between Jaime's love, Steve Austin, and Wonder Woman's
male counterpart, the other so-called Man of Steel, Superman.

"Like Krypton's favorite son," Schickel wrote, "[Steve] can run fast,
leap far and has a reasonable approximation of x-ray vision. Better still,
when he gets wounded (at least once a week), it is always an occasion to
haul out the old screwdriver and rewire him. These scenes are bound to
appeal to every child who every got his own computer-construction kit for
Christmas."

SM/BW scribe Steven de Souza ("Death Probe," "On the Run") contends that the primary market for science-fiction shows is adolescent males.
"They are the only people that tune in every week," he said. "They'll stay with
it no matter what. The problem is trying to attract a *larger* audience."

Success of a sci-fi TV series, according to de Souza, comes when the central core market spreads to a larger one, as with *The Six Million Dollar Man*
and *The Bionic Woman*.

"You have to get the sisters, girlfriends and parents to say, 'What is it that
you're watching? How come all your friends are coming over Wednesday
night?' Then, the parents watch and suddenly you have a phenomenon."

Concerned by the program's overwhelming popularity with the kiddy
set, one parents' group in particular — The National Association for Better
Broadcasting's Comprehensive Guide to Family Viewing — excoriated *Six*
with this uproariously inaccurate appraisal of the show: "*The Six Million
Dollar Man* is a perfect illustration of the *Superman* concept, plus all the gore
and brutality that go with a program manufactured to emphasize all facets
of gratuitous violence. The hero, who claims to be *more than the sum of his
parts,* **is a monstrosity constructed from recycled parts of other humans**
after he himself was ripped to pieces in an explosive crash. This show is

rebuilt from pure rubbish, and it is no way superior to any part of its accumulated junk." [Emphasis added.]

Arthur Asa Berger, once an associate professor at San Francisco State University, coined another side of the Kent/Austin connection. "Unlike a hero such as *Superman*," Berger wrote in *Society* magazine in 1976, "The *Six Million Dollar Man* is an ordinary human being who was made powerful by doctors and scientists. In many respects he is a figure from the comics, and he represents a dream we all have: that new developments in science will help *us* become powerful and, ultimately, immortal."

Berger also stated: "Austin's power emphasizes the weakness and powerlessness of the ordinary man. The more *The Six Million Dollar Man* performs prodigies — the more he uproots trees, carries enormous weights, rips open boxcars as if they were cereal boxes — the more we recognize our pettiness and weakness. *The Six Million Dollar Man* is a humanly created superhuman figure, and his strength makes us conscious of our frailty and deals our already weakened psyches yet another blow."

More denizens of the Ivory Tower took time out from their lecterns to cast a glance at our bionic heroes. Dr. Herbert Thomas, a one-time professor of psychiatry at the University of Pittsburgh, attributed the global popularity of Steve and Jaime to childish impulses that resonate well into adulthood. For Thomas, *Bionic* infatuation gratified a childish wish to be indestructible, while constituting a form of worry-free escapism.

SM/BW producer/writer/director Ken Johnson admits the shows offered super-heroic characters and entertainment escapism for the audience. But Steve and Jaime were far from worry-free; a trait of which endeared them to the viewer, who identified more easily with their human flaws, as opposed to their cybernetic perfections.

With yet another nod to DC Comics' top two heroes, Johnson explained: "Steve and Jaime were not Superman or Wonder Woman. That was the whole point. They were regular human beings who had these additional parts that certainly made them *stronger, better, faster*, but they too, had limitations. I mean, you heat up titanium high enough, and it melts. You hit something the wrong way, even if it's stainless steel, and it dents or bends." He examples the BW outing, "Doomsday is Tomorrow," in which, at one point, an electronic door slams down on one of Jaime's bionic legs, and disables her. "Her wires got screwed up," Ken said. "And that added more reality to the piece, and made it seem more logical."

Martin Caidin expanded on the "limitations" theme: "[Steve Austin] is as vulnerable as anyone else," he said. "He's not a Superman. Put a bullet in his head and he's dead. You can drown him. He's as vulnerable as you and I. He does have more capabilities in certain areas, but he has one heart like you and I. Let's say you are a bionic soldier. You can never eat normal meals. Your systems, mechanical and electronic, had better work all the time without failure from too much heat, or cold, or humidity. The normal ability of the human form to adapt to emergency situations is lost. What replaces it is clumsy and not always available. For example, where does the cyborg get spare parts? Who adjusts those spare parts? There is far more involved than simply taking a smashed arm or leg and replacing it with an artificial implant. It has to adapt to any temperature. It must be a system that enables it to work under any situation that one can imagine."

In fact, Ken Johnson made sure that strict adherence to specific realistic rules were observed within the cybernetic realm. Writers would come in and pitch a story to him and say, "In this episode, Jaime turns over a truck," to which Ken would reply, "She can't do that."

"What do you mean?" the atomic-aspiring writer would wonder. "She's bionic, isn't she?"

"Yes, that's right," Johnson would return. "She can turn over a car, but not a truck. She can jump two floors, but not three. She can jump down three, but not four. If she jumps down four, her legs will break. Even the expanded reality of the bionic world had to have its own internal truth. By carefully adhering to those truths and limitations the audiences were helped to thoroughly believe in Jaime's character and in her world."

Though these types of laws were followed more on BW than SM, Johnson said, they helped to create the reality of both shows. It's like what comedian George Burns once relayed to him, "If you're going to tell a lie [i.e., write a science-fiction story], then put as much truth into it as you possibly can."

Ken followed suit when he produced, directed and wrote the very *Bionic*-like series, *The Incredible Hulk*. With the transformation of the late Bill Bixby's average-sized David Banner into Lou Ferrigno's massive Hulk, Johnson reveals he did an enormous amount of microbiological research into metamorphosis and into the various possibilities in order to make it as real as possible.

As will be detailed later in the book, Johnson said "all the ideas that we created with bionics are now beginning to happen. *Six Mill* and *BW* could be equally viable today because the science of bionics has advanced so much that it's even closer to reality now than it was 30 years ago." By the time BW began its third season, Ken left the series, and producer Arthur Rowe stepped in. The bionic rules began to bend and, as Johnson said, "There were too many *buys* in that final year." In other words, there were too many sci-fi/fantasy/metaphysical abstractions that the audience was asked to *buy into*, as with episodes like "The Pyramid," "The Martians Are Coming," "Sanctuary Earth" and "Out of Body."

"Lindsay's love/hate relationship with Ken was turning to hate," Jim Parriott recalls. "There was much drama. I think pushed a little by Art Rowe, who was a father figure to her, and her husband, Michael Brandon. It was ugly. The 'Motorcycle Boogie' show was the peak of the craziness, with Lindsay pulling a four-day sick-out until Ken was removed from the show. This is why I had to baby-sit Evel Knievel at the Sheraton Universal every evening. I had to reassure him that everything was OK, and that it wasn't him, and that shooting would resume soon, etc." Ken Johnson's sudden departure resulted in a temporary power vacuum at the top. To make matters worse, Harve Bennett also was MIA—the result of a lawsuit against Universal for his fair share of the bionic profits. Into the breach stepped Art Rowe, who was working on Lindsay to take over the show — a scenario that didn't appeal to Parriott.

"I was called into Frank Price's office and asked if I thought that was a good idea," he said. "I thought not. I was asked if I was ready to take over the show. I thought I was too green. Next thing I knew, Lee Siegel was walking into the BW offices declaring, 'I'm in charge now!' He really did that. I really like Lee, but I thought that was bizarre. I also don't mean to trash Art here. We had a great relationship and were great friends. But Art's relationship with Lindsay definitely didn't help her relationship with Ken."

When Johnson did the show, he tried to keep it as down-to-earth as possible. Even his bionic Bigfoot episodes of *The Six Million Dollar Man* were about as far as you could push the envelope. But no further, or else it would have become fatuous, and Johnson claims to be "a great disbeliever in silly." The emotional lines and the characters of *The Six Million Dollar Man* and *The Bionic Woman* were the keys to their success, Johnson allows. He believes that many of those in charge of creating good fantasy/science fiction don't understand that. They figure if they throw in some shots of spacecraft, a lot of good special effects and great make-up, that it will carry the day."

"Well, wrong," Johnson states. "If you can't attach yourself to a story emotionally, then all the greatest special effects in the world won't help you."

Exhibit A: *The Last Action Hero*, the F/X-laden theatrical bomb of 1993. Johnson remembers reading the script for this film and saying, "Why do they want to make this? There's nobody in it that I care about." Conversely, Ken said we cared for Steve and Jaime, because we came to know their personalities, through "good human stories, with less concentration on way-out concepts."

With *Invasion America*, a ground-breaking, Steven-Spielberg-executive-produced animated sci-fi drama (from 1998), Harve Bennett continued with worthy creative work, holding dialogue with himself, and asking several Johnson-similar queries such as: "What are the characters in this series all about? How do I relate to them? Would I like them as roommates?" "All kinds of crazy, personal, weird questions" that Bennett believes television audiences ask themselves, subconsciously, when they are deciding about inviting certain TV characters into their living rooms.

For Lee Majors, the key to the appeal of SM and BW is far simpler. "They were ethical shows," he said. "There was action, but not much violence."

After the monthly *Six* editions, Majors said, "We didn't kill people. If Steve and Jaime knocked anyone down, they were only stunned or dazed, and they always got right up again. We weren't just blasting people away. I've never minded my kids watching any of the series I did. That's important to me." The recognition of righteousness became stronger because the "temptation was greater," adds Lindsay Wagner, who expands upon her previous analysis with this conclusion on the continued success of both shows: "Steve and Jaime had to fight provocations. They succeeded because they were spiritually sound. That was their real strength. The bionics were adjunct to that."

CHAPTER 4

ASSIMILATION

"I'M SURE THERE ARE REAL-LIFE PHYSICIANS WALKING AROUND TODAY WHO WERE INSPIRED BY RUDY WELLS."

MARTIN E. BROOKS

The Six Million Dollar Man and *The Bionic Woman* have played scientific and inspirational roles in the lives of thousands of people of all ages, through the years. Take Todd A. Langenfeld. He's a special government agent who was enlivened to work for the legitimate Office of Special Investigations (the real-life OSI), an offshoot of the United States Air Force, which assists the FBI on special military cases. [In the book, *Cyborg*, there was no OSI, but rather the OSO — the Office of Special Operations.] *This* OSI is strictly a military operation, investigative by nature, and deals with crimes that are committed against the Air Force and/or by an Air Force individual. As Langenfeld explained, "We collect the facts, and then turn them over to the legal commanders."

Years following his initial view of the *Bionic* universe, Langenfeld showed up in a bit part as a commando in the third *Bionic* TV-reunion, *Bionic Ever After?*, which was shot near his factual OSI office (Detachment 310) in Charleston, South Carolina. He placed a few calls to the production company, and asked if they needed assistance. Richard Anderson then found time to visit, which the agents appreciated, and, as Langenfeld reveals, "I think Mr. Anderson got a kick out of it too."

All the agents knew that the film was being shot in town, but it was Langenfeld who was motivated to make contact. "You have the badge, the responsibility, and you carry a lot of authority," he said, "but we have lives outside of work. We are human beings. We have feelings. And we like to have fun, too." On *Six Million* and *Woman*, Langenfeld assessed, the initials, *OSI*, stand for the Office of *Scientific* Intelligence, instead of the real-life *Special* tag. Though the *Scientific* term was used in the initial *Six* pilot, it had to be changed later on, and certain legalities didn't allow the *Ever*

After? producers to employ the exact Air Force phrase.

Though Langenfeld's life came somewhat full circle as an extra in *Bionic Ever After?*, the operative said he wasn't attracted to the original shows because of the Hollywood glamour, but "because Steve and Jaime were set on doing good." Their strong sense of loyalty, he surmises, "tied in with the Air Force, and the real OSI." Two decades later, on the *After?* set, he was impressed with the producers, more specifically, how they went out of their way to ensure that the film retained a non-violent content, and remained responsible to the new, younger generation that is watching the reruns. "They were just as responsible as the producers of the original shows," he said. "They didn't confuse action with violence. They produced a quality product, with attention to detail and authenticity, with a lot of hard work. We all have our inspirations, and I've had some excellent teachers in school, and what not, but Steve and Jaime have had a profound effect on me in many ways, as well."

Paradoxically, Langenfeld grew up without a TV in the house. The only time he could watch *Six Mill* or *Woman*, would be when he was at a friend's house. "You can draw the parallels," he said. "Just as Steve and Jaime have inspired me or offered some positive instruction, negative images on TV may also do the opposite for someone else. *The Six Million Dollar Man* and *The Bionic Woman* are perfect examples of what good TV can do. And having me say that, as a person who grew up without a TV, makes it all rather ironic."

Talking with a reporter in the 1970s, Lee Majors referenced the possibility of a human being one day being able to lift an enormous amount of weight (an idea which would be used for the mid-1990s FOX TV series, *Mantis*). "At the moment, there are things called exo-skeletons," the actor said. "Structures that fit on over the human body and amplify muscular actions. Sure, they enable someone to hoist up fantastic loads, but they're hardly mobile. However, who knows what scientists will do with the current trends in miniaturization? It may be possible, fairly soon, to implant scaled-down exo-skeletons actually within a man's body. Then, well, your guess is as good as mine."

"And how about this," added Lindsay Wagner. "My bionic hearing is just a gimmick, right? But labs are developing sort of super-hearing aids, admittedly for the use of deaf persons, but which will be able to pick up and amplify sounds from great distances. Now isn't *that* like something for Jaime Sommers?"

Though these Majors/Wagner true-bionic comments are over 30 years old, they ring timely, as the medical technology that has developed due to inspiration from SM and BW is astounding.

In the mid-1970s, then LA-Dodgers pitcher Tommy John was facing premature retirement due to a problem in his pitching elbow. Dr. Frank

Jobe (the athletic world's Rudy Wells) intervened, transplanting a liga-
ment from John's leg to his elbow, allowing John to resume his spectacular
career. From that point forward, he was referred to as "the man with the
bionic arm." Before 1970 (when hip surgery began to be performed on a
wide scale), and the ensuing inspiration granted by SM and BW, those who
needed new hips, or experienced tragic, paralyzing falls (as with *Superman's*
courageous real-life counterpart, Christopher Reeve), would have most
likely faced far diminished lives, with walking becoming a serious problem.
But not anymore.

A few years back, a college football game of the week between Syracuse
and Miami, could have been considered a salute to modern medicine, as
two fifth-year seniors, Miami defensive-end Rusty Medearis and Syracuse
linebacker Dan Conley, played on rebuilt knees. Today, more than 1 million
Americans have artificial hips, and approximately 120,000 more receive one
each year, according to the National Arthritis Clearing House. Little over
one decade ago, heart and liver transplants were only envisioned. Now, they
are actually in operation, as are contemporary computerized devices that
enable the blind to see and the deaf to hear (or at least to sufficiently navigate certain sights and sounds).

In 1994, super-singer Liza Minnelli, then 48 years old, underwent hip-
replacement surgery. Retired football and baseball great Bo Jackson probably has one of the country's most famous metal-and-plastic hips. Meanwhile,
synthetic bones and joints haven't seemed to affect the lives of people like
former US Labor Secretary Robert Reich or renowned football player, coach
and TV commentator, Mike Ditka. Hip replacements may only last ten to
15 years, but the technology is improving all the time.

The year 1998 witnessed the arrival of devices such as the UCS100, marketed by companies like New Abilities, based in Palo Alto, California, and
the freedom it allows its quadriplegic operator. Sandra Bullock's Bionic Girl
character from the 1989 reunion flick, *Bionic Showdown*, mastered a similar system.

The TTK device is commanded by an inimitable tongue-touch key-
pad, which adjusts into the mouth like an orthodontic retainer. Its controls
are initiated with the end of the tongue opposite a conduit forged from
within. It grants the operator dominion over several electrical instruments
(e.g., wheelchair, power chair and bed, computer, appliances). The entire system draws its capability from the wheelchair capacity reserve. It's self-con-
tained, and its services remain transit on the wheelchair with the operator.
The results are amazing, as the user is allowed the freedoms and flexibilities
of a non-user.

"There is no reason on Earth that a person who is quadriplegic cannot
operate anything that's run by electricity," said Bob Jangovich, president
and CEO of New Abilities. "Fundamentally, that's what a wheelchair is.

In a way, the wheelchair is simply a robotic extension to our system which, essentially, is a total environment control device."

Even Steve Austin's bionic eye no longer seems farfetched. In 2002, US scientists began development on an electronic eye implant that they believe could help millions of people to see again. Made possible by $9 million dollars in funding by the US Department of Energy, the microchip works by stimulating cells around the retina. This in turn stimulates cells in the brain, helping people to see once more. The prototype implants contain 16 electrodes, allowing patients to detect the presence or absence of light. The artificial retina project's "next generation" device would accommodate 1,000 electrodes, and hopes to allow the user to see images. The microchip, which acts as an artificial retina, would be surgically implanted into the eye.

More progress was made in 2005, when US and German scientists developed a bionic eye comprised of a computer chip that sits in the back of the individual's eye, linked up to a mini-video camera built into a typical pair of glasses. Images captured by the camera are relayed to the chip, which translates them into impulses that the brain can interpret.

At the 2006 Experimental Biology Conference in San Francisco, leading scientists discussed just how close we've come to repairing shattered bodies at a symposium called "The $6 Billion (Hu) Man." Computer-controlled strap-on robotic legs, developed at Cal-Berkeley, could conceivably make the elderly and frail more mobile, while the military envisions soldiers with superhuman strength and endurance over long distances. Elsewhere, the American Yobotics laboratory has developed a powered orthotic brace that it hopes will give mobility to people who suffer from post-polio syndrome, multiple sclerosis and muscular dystrophy, as well as people whose limbs have deteriorated through age. Tiny motors drive the legs, giving wearers the strength to climb stairs and walk.

The hard of hearing also have reasons for optimism. Prof. Werner Nachtigall of the University of Saarland, Germany, and Dr. Stefan Launer, director of research at the company Phonak, have developed what they call *digital bionics*, after studying how the brain and ear interact and how the inner ear processes sounds. They have replicated the process using a tiny chip for a new generation of hearing aids.

In the mid-1990s, the North Atlantic Treaty Organization (otherwise known as NATO) conducted a conference on the feasibility of building a bionic man. As Dr. Donald Humphrey stated on The Learning Channel special, *Future Fantastic*, "We have the technology for building devices that will allow a crude bionic man. *The Six Million Dollar Man* program *was* an inspiration to some of us, I believe, to pursue this area. And specifically, what might have come from that? Well, our attempts, which we'll be making in the next few months, to have an animal control a robotic arm directly with his brain. It won't be as sophisticated as the science fiction that we saw on television, but it's the same kind of thing."

Several years have passed since Dr. Humphrey's bold prediction, but perhaps he wasn't bold *enough*. Instead of mere animals, thought-controlled limbs are presently being attached to real live human beings. Electronic artificial limbs, like those belonging to Steve and Jaime (though not nearly as strong) are now commonplace. With apologies to Ms. Sommers, the title of "world's first bionic woman" probably goes to Claudia Mitchell, a former U.S. Marine who lost her left arm in a motorcycle crash. Mitchell is the first woman to be fitted with a new prosthetic arm controlled solely by her own nerves. What is special about the new arm is the interface between body and machine.

Dr. Todd Kuiken, the arm's inventor, worked with Gregory Dumanian, a plastic surgeon, at Northwestern Memorial Hospital in Chicago to relocate the five nerves that once controlled Ms. Mitchell's flesh-and-blood arm. Dr. Dumanian then placed the ends of the nerves in her chest, where they regenerated close to the skin. Electrodes placed on the surface of Mitchell's chest then send signals that control the arm. The signals are received by the electrodes on her skin, which in turn send commands to the six motors in the bionic arm.

Mitchell's older prosthetic arm was vastly inferior, allowing her to perform only one task at a time — be it opening her elbow or flexing her hand. And to do so, she had to concentrate on a particular muscle. "It was odd," she said. "I had to think, 'OK, my hand is here. Which muscle?'" She had to focus on flexing her pectoral muscle, or the triceps, to get the arms and hand to do what she wanted. "Now I just think about it."

Mitchell's arm, which affords her enough dexterity to cut her own steak, is likely to get even better now that British scientists have figured out a way to grow skin tissue around metal. This achievement will enable artificial limbs to be joined directly to the bone, making them stronger and more versatile. The advance allows prosthetic arms, legs, thumbs, and fingers to be attached directly to the human skeleton via metal implants that protrude through the skin, without the risk of infection. As a result, this man-machine fusion creates a better "feel" for patients because the limbs are no longer strapped or fixed to a stump, eliminating painful pressure sores.

A company called Touch Bionics in Scotland recently introduced the world's first bionic hand. The futuristic appendage — dubbed the "i-Limb" — features moveable fingers driven by five tiny individual "motors." Experts in the field of prosthetics have hailed the device for allowing individual finger movements, as opposed to previous artificial hands which only allowed a pinching motion between the "thumb" and an essentially fused-together group of four fingers. "I was immediately amazed at the things I could do," said Sgt. Juan Arredondo, a 27-year-old Iraqi War vet whose hand was severed by a roadside bomb in 2005. "I never thought I'd see something like

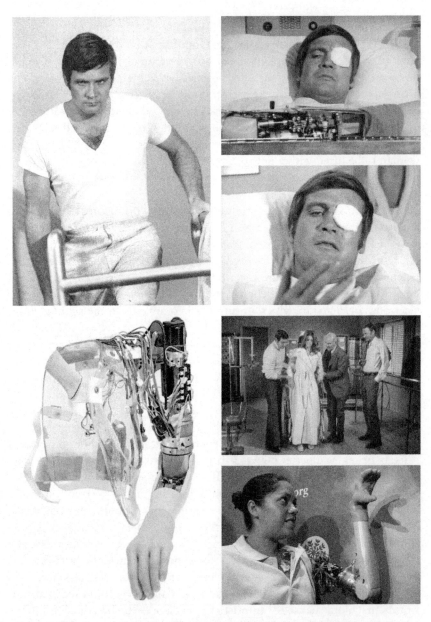

STEVE AUSTIN AND JAIME SOMMERS' REHABILITATION FROM PHYSICAL RUIN WAS LONG AND ARDUOUS, BUT PERHAPS INSPIRATIONAL TO MODERN-DAY CYBORGS LIKE CLAUDIA MITCHELL (BOTTOM RIGHT), WHOSE BIONIC LEFT ARM (PICTURED) IS CONTROLLED SOLELY BY HER THOUGHTS.

this in my lifetime," the vet said of his new hand. "My son, Diego, trips out when he sees it. We watch movies like *Star Wars*, where Luke loses his hand and they give him a new one, and Diego said, 'Look, Dad, just like you!'" The limb took approximately 15 years to develop, and costs between $60,000 and $150,000.

In the SM pilot, Steve Austin's bionic arm was patterned after an experimental prosthetic arm then being tested at the UCLA Medical Center. Though crude by today's standards, it didn't stop Lee Majors from being impressed. "The arm," he said, "had plastic skin that looked and felt like real skin. It was battery-operated; and when they hooked it up to my shoulder, I could raise and lower it, and even turn the wrist."

Not so long ago, certain children were told they would never walk again, and then did, because they watched Steve and Jaime run. Between the medical miracle of modern prosthetics and their own impulses, they were inspired by appointment television with their favorite cybernetic heroes. "These kids believed anything was possible," noted Martin Caidin, who had seen hundreds of cases where this had been documented. He said they thought, "If Steve and Jaime can do it, so can I." He observed that SM and BW became "role models for people who have been hurt, or had their limbs removed. They felt it was feasible to beat the odds because of the shows. It also encouraged a stronger following within the medical and scientific communities."

Richard Anderson agrees with Caidin's assessment, recalling one real-life rehabilitation: "About five years after *The Six Million Dollar Man* debuted, there was a man in Detroit who had lost the use of his right arm. After several months of physical therapy, and the sophisticated developments of prosthetics that came into being because of the exposure given to them on the show, this man was able to lift more than forty pounds with a newly-strengthened arm."

Continued studies into other body parts were commissioned because of *The Six Million Dollar Man*. "People who were blind were made able to see shadows and objects," Anderson adds. "There have even been experiments delving into radar-like vision that was introduced by Steve Austin's left eye. Medical research was made possible because those in control of funding were fans of the show. They believed in what *The Six Million Dollar Man* and *The Bionic Woman* were presenting on screen, in terms of hope for the disabled and other scientific possibilities."

While being interviewed for this book, Alan Oppenheimer, who, with Martin E. Brooks, shared the role of Dr. Rudy Wells, was recuperating from a medical procedure of his own: knee surgery. "It's very unusual," he begins to explain. "It's a new operation. My two parts came from a cadaver. It's called an *allograft*. I thought, this is really ironic, because a couple of years ago, I had written a letter to Michael Crichton [who directed *Westworld*,

1973, and drafted its story]. I had not been in touch with him for years. It was about the time that *Jurassic Park* [1993] was opening."

Crichton wrote Alan back, saying how nice it was to hear from him, how he had just attended a conference in the state of Washington on the recent scientific developments of parallel processors, which had once been considered only in the context of the sci-fi domain of *Westworld*. "We didn't know what we were dealing with when we made the movie," Alan said. The film introduced the concept of *parallel processors* [allowing computers to execute two functions at once] that have now been realized. "It was *pooh-poohed* a few years ago," Alan adds. "The medical community said, *Oh, it will never work*." He said the company that designed the system has recently gone out of business. "They're about to go bankrupt because no one believed in the idea. But the processors work. More and more companies will soon use them."

Like much good fiction, Oppenheimer said the *Bionic* world titillates the mind, and pushes us to wonder things like, "Which came first? The chicken or the egg? Does life imitate art? Or is it the other way around?" He promises that, if you read the science-fiction works of Isaac Asimov and HG Wells, the central ideas will be identified as fiction, which is then developed into truth. As an example, Oppenheimer points to rocketry, which was introduced in literature years before the impetus was ignited in scientists to begin real-life experiments.

Oppenheimer's Wells-compadre, Martin E. Brooks, also comments on the thin line between real and fanciful fiction, as he remembers researching his Rudy role at the UCLA medical facility and various hospitals. "They were very close to creating a bionic arm and leg," the actor said, "which they are on the verge of doing right now." Minus the extent of utilizing super powers, "they are capable of connecting the nerves in the arms, with brainwaves and thought patterns." While back on the mid-1970s sets of SM and BW, Brooks said he and his fellow actors "were very close to playing reality," which added to their performances, by way of enthusiasm.

In addition to the Detroit man who lost his arm, and was then given hope because of prosthetics, there have been several other specific instances when not only a person's biology was altered in some very positive manner, but their biography as well. When this happened, the exploits of Steve Austin, and Jaime Sommers in particular, proved that popular television could not only be entertaining, but educational, life-enhancing — and life-saving.

As with *The Bionic Woman* episode, "Biofeedback," about a high-profile scientist named Darwin (played by Granville Van Dusen) who develops a body/mind/spirit control device, via Eastern-mystic training. This unique segment happened to be one of three *Woman* outings for which Lindsay Wagner was personally responsible in getting produced.

The remaining two are "Canyon of Death," about a Native-American boy dealing with his grandfather's spirit, and "On the Run," the final segment, in which Jaime leaves the OSI to devote time to her self-discovery. "There were others that I had some influence upon," she said, "but as far as the actual conception and structure, those three episodes were my ideas and very special and, I felt, the most effective."

In fact, Lindsay continued to reject doing segments like "Fembots in Las Vegas" and "Bigfoot," until she was able to have the episodes produced to her satisfaction. "Biofeedback" initially took her about 18 months, and several conferences with the writers, to have it completed and aired. The most profound results from this segment, however, were yet to be realized.

Approximately one year after BW was canceled, a 15-year-old runaway named Mary Vincent was hitchhiking in Modesto, California, picked up by low-life Lawrence Singleton, driven to an isolated cabin, raped, and left to die, with her arms completely severed from her body. "Biofeedback" was responsible for saving this remarkable girl's life, helping her to rehabilitate her physical and emotional being. In the process, Lindsay found a new peace with Jaime Sommers. After the series ended, she believed she had not accomplished anything substantial. She was pretty much drained, emotionally. The struggles with the writers were difficult, so much so that she believed she did not attain anything meaningful. She felt like she had spent three years of her life beating herself up.

The show was successful, and she had become *famous*, but she did not "feel successful." She thought only that she had achieved so little with the amount of work that was done. She was depressed, sought to quit the business, and looked for something else to do. To find some measure of contentment, she traveled to Mount Hood in Oregon, where she remained alone for several weeks, "locked away," during a monstrous snowstorm. "I had to figure out what I was going to do with my life," she said.

On her return home to California, the horrid story of the young girl who was mangled and raped was repeatedly broadcast on her automobile's radio, something to which Lindsay "never listens." She's not fond of radio noise arriving uninvited into her car, and she was extremely strict about it back then. But for some reason, she turned the radio on that day, and heard the story. "Oh, my heavens," she thought. "What is happening in this world? Why am I listening to this?" So she changed the channel.

When a song she enjoyed ended, the same story was broadcast on that station's news spot. "I was still very upset about it," she said, "but I felt compelled to listen to the entire story this time." When she could listen no more, she turned to the station a second time, and there again was the story of the little girl. "Finally," she said, "I just turned the radio off."

Shortly after, Lindsay arrived home, walked in the door, with her phone ringing. It was her assistant. A very strange message was waiting to be relayed. A woman from the parapsychology department at USC called.

She didn't say exactly why, only that she was a member of the young girl's family, and that if Lindsay wanted to call back, that would be fine. "Nothing more," said the message.

By this time, Lindsay said her hair was "standing up on the back of my neck." She put the phone down, and called the woman from USC, who put her in contact with the young girl's mother. Before she could say more than her name, the mother cried, "Oh, my God. I can't believe you're calling. My daughter has been crying your name for two days since she's been here."

Two hours later, Lindsay chartered a jet to Modesto. Upon her arrival at the hospital, the criminal was still at large, and the authorities were very concerned. The medical facility was barricaded because, miraculously, Mary Vincent somehow managed to survive, and was able to identify her assailant. Lindsay contacted the Modesto police, who rendezvoused with her at the airport, and escorted her into the hospital through the back entrance. She was taken up a secret elevator, and placed in a private room.

Some minutes later, Mary entered, walked over to Wagner, the woman whom she had endlessly cried out for to meet, and put her head in her chest. "I hugged her," Lindsay relays, "and we both began to cry."

Still, Lindsay was "absolutely and totally confused" as to why she was there. Part of her was saying, "Okay, you're on TV, and someone admires your work and wanted to meet you." Another part of her was saying, "No. It's much more than that. Something very powerful is happening here, and I don't really understand it. But I'm going with it."

Following their near overwhelming first moments together, the star and her new special friend sat down and talked. With careful words and a gentle pace, Lindsay opened the conversation with, "I'm not quite sure why I'm here."

"Well, I do," the then-fifteen-year-old replied. "I have to thank you for saving my life."

Lindsay was more confused than before, until the courageous youth before her began to explain. "After my arms were severed," the girl said, "and I was tied up in that shack, I realized that I was going to bleed to death. Then I remembered 'Biofeedback,' and the words that Darwin said [Om, Shanti, Peace]. At one point, he was injured. He calmed himself by remembering the tree, the mountain and the water. He slowed his breathing, talked to his body, and stopped it from bleeding, until he could get to the hospital."

Lindsay was speechless.

"My uncle, who meditates," the teen continued, "once sat me down and I meditated with him. So I sort of understood what was happening in that episode, and Anatomy was one of my favorite classes in school. I knew my body very well. After that man was through with me, I started saying the words that Darwin said. I did the relaxation exercise, and started talking to my body. I instructed the particular blood vessels to close off, and then they did just that. The man who tied me up didn't know how to make a knot very well. I grew up with five brothers, and I was tied up worse than that. So I wiggled out of the rope, and walked until I finally found the highway."

Then she passed out. When she reached the hospital, she heard people saying things like, "I don't know. I think we're going to lose her." She kept thinking, "Boy, if they would just keep quiet, I could concentrate on my meditation."

Lindsay was still speechless.

"Anyway," Vincent concluded, "I just wanted to thank you for relaying the information that saved my life."

Lindsay's perspective on all that happened with and because of *The Bionic Woman* became and remains clear. "If out of those three years on the show," she said, "through every pain and doubt that I ever had about whether or not it was the right decision for me to play Jaime Sommers, and all the negativity that I felt about whether or not I was a useful human being through my work, I felt an immediate inner cleansing and healing. It didn't matter if no one else was ever again affected by *The Bionic Woman*."

That one incredible experience, about a brave little girl, who was rescued by the miracle of television, was sagacious enough for Lindsay. Her sole thought was, "Thank you, God, for letting me be your channel."

Though Lawrence Singleton was arrested once again in February of 1997 for the slaying of a woman in his Tampa, Florida home (after serving eight years and four months on mutilation and rape charges), and though Mary Vincent recently told a reporter that, "Right now," she's "not sleeping" and "can't hold any food down," and even though Vincent (today, a seldom-employed mother of two boys) is unable to collect the $2.5 million judgment against Singleton (because he is dead), there still remains a positive side to the story:

Mary has lectured and continues to speak at schools across the country, discussing the dangers of hitchhiking and running away from home. In turn, countless other lives were indirectly saved and inspirited, due to one form of communication (school seminars) that resulted from another (television); by way of a *Bionic* TV show.

As Lindsay determines, *The Bionic Woman* and *The Six Million Dollar Man* have "made a tremendous impact. They've changed the language of the world. What many people once considered impossible or miraculous [limb reconstruction], has now become reality."

So, saved by cybernetic alteration, and transformed into champions, Steve and Jaime contributed to the realities of modern medicine, inspired others to pursue patriotic careers, motivated the weak, to walk, and en*cour*-*age*d little children to not be afraid.

CHAPTER 5

ELECTRICITY

"LEE AND LINDSAY WERE BORN TO PLAY STEVE AND JAIME."

HARVE BENNETT

There was something more than pure entertainment that glued viewers to *The Six Million Dollar Man* and *The Bionic Woman*. Beyond the obvious and subliminal message of heroism, star attraction plays an undeniable role. Lee Majors and Lindsay Wagner's charisma and chemistry on screen pulled viewers in by the droves. Each performer brought a unique quality to their roles as Steve Austin and Jaime Sommers. As it turned out, Steve and Jaime played considerable roles in the lives of Lee and Lindsay. The shows brought them fame, wealth, position and respect within the Hollywood community. As previously stated, Lindsay Wagner won the Emmy for Lead Actress in a Drama Series in 1977, the first time in television history that a lead actress in a science-fiction television program attained such an award, let alone a nomination. With the adulation and the power, came the heartache and the pressure. Majors and Wagner became properties of the public domain, and it wasn't always easy.

According to director Steve Stafford, who guided *Bionic Ever After?* (as well as *The Sound of a Miracle* in 1992, and *Double Edge* in 1994, among other TV-films), and who was Majors' personal assistant on *Six* since its weekly debut in January 1974, there were several times when Lee, in particular, would find time to sneak away from the set and visit a child who was terminally ill, as he did with a youth in Denver, Colorado. "But he never wanted that publicized," Stafford said.

Majors was publicity shy, in general, due to a negative experience early on in his career. As he told *TV Guide* in 1987, "The press and I haven't had a great romance." He ventured to Hollywood as a "Kentucky boy who couldn't knot a tie." He was young and naive and explained to one journalist how his father had been killed when his mother was eight months pregnant, and how she died a few years later. He was adopted, but nobody knew that in the small town in which he was raised. He requested that this part of his life not be reported, until he gave full consent, and they agreed. Then it exploded in the headlines. That hurt him and his adoptive parents, while citizens of Middlesboro felt deceived. From that time on, he "didn't much trust the press."

There was another time when being in the public eye became less than an enlightening experience for Majors. It happened while filming *Six* on location, near a school in Utah when, suddenly, there were several young children on the set. Lee doesn't have a problem signing autographs, and he never did. But this one particular brood proved to be quite a challenge. One youth approached Lee with his mother, who said, "Mr. Majors, the boys would like to meet you." Lee replied with "Fine," and the first thing that kid did was kick him in the shins, because he thought the actor really had a bionic leg. Another young child tried to rip out Lee's eye, poked at it, and asked the actor if it was real. "They wanted to see my bionic arm," he recalls, "with the skin pulled back."

All of this proved particularly challenging because no visitors were allowed on the set when the special effects were filmed. The producers did not want to destroy the illusion for the kids. So Majors "couldn't wince or anything," because he "wanted to keep up the mystique." Though Majors was never concerned about walking into a bar, and being challenged by some inebriated fellow who may have thought he was legitimately bionic, Lee said, "Those guys had nothing on those kids."

Every now and then, however, some secrets *would* leak out. "I'd be out in the middle of a crowd, and I'd go over to pick up the car, then they'd see the guys on the other side [of the car] jacking the hell out of it," he said. "When we were revealing our secrets, yeah, I felt a little stupid. The kids were watching, and you had no choice but to disappoint them, and I felt so bad they had to see that. Like a magician uncovering a trick, it was deflating to the ego."

Added to Lee's emotional aversion to the press, and light-hearted physical encounters, were serious periodic threats to the safety of young viewers, who many times took *The Six Million Dollar Man* too seriously, with Lee feeling responsible.

While most youngsters were content to mimic Steve by running in overwrought slow motion, one seven-year-old Philadelphia boy jeopardized himself by pretending to be blind, with hopes of acquiring a bionic eye. He would also try to stop the family car by dragging his feet along the ground. Things became so out-of-hand, that *The Philadelphia Inquirer* asked Lee to pen a letter to the boy that brought him back to reality. Lee then took himself off the celebrity golf and tennis circuit because, as he told *People* magazine, "I feel I'm a terrible disappointment if I miss a shot. Arnold Palmer does, but *The Six Million Dollar Man* can't."

There was also concern for Lee's personal safety. One day, during the peak of SM's success, Harve Bennett had apparently received a telephone call from then-White House Press Secretary, Jody Powell, who said that Amy Carter, daughter to then-President Jimmy Carter, "loves Lee Majors," and wondered if there was any way for the actor to attend Amy's birthday party. "This is very exciting," Bennett told the caller. "I'll certainly find out, and call you back."

Harve contacted Lee, who thought it sounded like a great idea, and asked for the day off. Bennett granted the request, and then relayed the message to the White House. A government representative talked to Powell's secretary, who said she did not make any calls to Bennett. The White House jotted down the details of the call, and instructed Bennett to contact the Federal Bureau of Investigation (FBI) in Los Angeles. He did so, and the FBI placed a wiretap on his phone. Sure enough, about 36 hours later, the same man called. He was kept on the phone for a few minutes, while Bennett's secretary was on the other line with the FBI, who began to trace the call. The strange caller abruptly ended the conversation. "He was on to the fact that we were on to him," said Bennett. "And that was the end of that."

Still, Bennett thought several times about the motive behind the peculiar contact from this odd caller. How it all initially seemed so legitimate, so meticulously planned. Just to be safe, a special bodyguard was assigned to protect Lee Majors for the following six or seven weeks.

More pressure arrived for Majors and Lindsay Wagner, in the form of public marriages. During the pinnacle of *Million Dollar Man's* success, Lee was wedded to former Wella Balsam model-turned-top TV cherub, Farrah Fawcett (who valued her new life with Lee to the extent of hyphenating her last name with Majors). They were the *King and Queen of TV*, and considered one of the most attractive and happiest couples in town. Their career demands, however, became larger than either could endure, and their marriage ended in divorce.

During Lindsay's first year playing *The Bionic Woman* in series form, she and then-boyfriend, actor Michael Brandon (the couple did not wed until December 19, 1976), were critically injured in a frightening automobile accident, which could have easily been considered for a *Bionic* episode. Brandon almost lost an eye, and Lindsay received a severe slice in her upper-lip, which was tended to through immediate surgery.

Universal Studios, once again, went into Lindsay-panic. Production on the show had to be shut down for two weeks, making the rest of the season a flat-footed race to keep up with the schedule. Lindsay kept on working, at a time when she felt she should not have been. This happenstance, combined with her desire to appear in films, and her dissatisfaction with many of the BW scripts, left the actress with an overwhelming sense of frustration. In the studio commissary, a certain executive commented on Wagner's accident,

TOP: LEE MAJORS WITH THEN-WIFE, AND *CHARLIE'S ANGEL*, FARRAH
FAWCETT-MAJORS (1978). *BOTTOM:* LINDSAY WAGNER WITH THEN-
HUSBAND ACTOR/WRITER MICHAEL BRANDON (1977). AS WITH MOST
HOLLYWOOD MARRIAGES, LEE'S AND LINDSAY'S WERE DESTINED TO
FAIL, GIVEN THE DEMANDS AND PRESSURES OF THEIR RESPECTIVE
CAREERS.

while making sarcastic remarks about her no-bones-about-it demeanor, and said things like, "If that kid only had a bionic lip...She already has a bionic mouth."

Wagner's ambivalence was obvious to those around her. "She'd just done *The Paper Chase* and was poised to become a movie star," said SM/BW writer Jim Parriott. "Personally, I think she would've been huge. But she was pressured by the studio and her manager, Ron Samuels, to take the series. She kept saying no, until the studio offered her so much money Ron wouldn't let her turn it down. I think she regretted it. Subsequently, her attitude was not stellar that first year and a half. She liked us, and was a hard worker and did a good job, but she had an underlying resentment about having to do *The Bionic Woman*."

Somehow, someway, both Lee and Lindsay, in keeping with their on-screen personas, trudged on through it all, disappointing neither network and studio executives nor *Bionic* fans. The results of such dedication? Two classic television shows, and two real-life sound bodies, minds and spirits. Majors and Wagner prevail as confident, successful and good-hearted individuals, an image of which any true *Bionic* supporter could only hope would not be shattered. They brought a sense of personal heroism to their TV-counterparts.

A *super* part of themselves, the part that gave them strength to move onward in their personal lives, bled onto the screen. As they donned wire-laden warm-up suits and polyester jumpers to become television's first cybernetic heroes, they experienced challenging real lives.

"There was a period there when things got real tough," admits Lee on the demise of his marriage. "But I was tougher, and disappointing people is not one of my favorite things." He knew how important the show was to kids, and certainly how important it was to the network. Moreover, he was working, and making a very good living. As he puts it, "It would have been self-destructive for me to have up and left the show, and moved away to Aruba or somewhere to recoup. Maybe that would have been an easier way, but it wasn't my way." With frank honesty, he reported, "It's not like I said to myself, *Okay, what would Steve do at a time like this.* He was a character I played. A character that I cared an awful lot about. But I had my life and he had his. I was grateful for the life I was allowed because of the success he had given me."

As to his interpretation of Steve Austin, he took a down-to-earth approach to portraying the high-flying adventurer, and thought Austin was "a very Air-Force-kind-of-guy." "Steve played by the rules, and was extraordinarily military minded," he said. "He was trained to take orders, and was quintessentially American. At the same time, he was a man with feeling. It was not his choice to become bionic. He felt very isolated in the beginning, but he learned to adjust. He had to. That was his nature. No matter how

LEE MAJORS

battered he was, physically or emotionally, he wasn't about to give up on himself, even if that's what he led everyone to believe in the beginning. Or what he may have told himself."

Lee believes Austin's thinking went beyond the appreciate-what-you-have-before-it's-gone scenario. "It wasn't that simple," the actor sustains. "In fact, he was a more complicated human being *before* his accident took place. Losing his arm, his eye and his legs allowed him time to think. To realign his priorities. In the long run, it also allowed him to simplify his life, in between assignments for the OSI."

As to that James Bond version of Steve Austin that appeared in the first few monthly segments of the series? "Well, I do happen to think I looked pretty good in the tux," the actor sardonically replies. "But the character was not intended to be dashing. Steve Austin was more of a rugged type of guy."

Though, when a successful producer like Glen Larson (who produced the initial monthly Bond/Austin segments) has an idea, you give a listen. "I was also under contract," Lee states. "What was I going to say? When we did the James Bond stuff, I felt somewhat foolish. Glen is known for having more flippant kind of stuff. I'd pull out something and put it in my mouth, and breathe and swim all the way underwater to a ship. It was too gimmicky. I must say I wasn't in favor of it; it was entertaining, yes but it was a little too corny for me, and trying to be something it wasn't. When we went weekly, I believe he developed more into what Martin Caidin had in mind. He certainly became more of who I wanted him to be."

Majors also insisted that the seemingly preposterous premise be played absolutely straight. "When we went to the hour series, I wasn't sure I wanted to do it, and I didn't want it to be campy, like *Batman*," he said. "So I said we had to make this character as human as possible, let him have some feelings, keep it on that track, because if he's not human, how can human people in the audience connect with him? He had to be a guy who was in an accident and making a go of it, so people had somebody to root for, and look up to and respect."

Earlier in the book, Caidin confirmed that his version of Steve Austin came into being during the first few weekly episodes produced by Harve Bennett. As to how well Lee fit into the Austin mold in either version, [Caidin] said they "couldn't have found a better man for the job." Remember, too, that even though Caidin did not know Majors when the pilot was being cast, the studio was quite excited about retaining the actor. When the author heard about the decision, he "trusted it," due to Majors' impeccable professional reputation. "They picked Lee because he was an ex-football player and was good for action," Caidin said. "He's pretty [laconic] as an actor, but he fit the part perfectly. He appealed to that 12- to 14-year-old demographic."

Glen Larson saw beyond Majors' "strong silent type" rap. "I always liked Lee," he said. "He played some fairly thankless roles, like *Owen Marshall*. I brought him back for *The Fall Guy* because when they did *Six Mill* after I left the team, quite frankly they didn't do it with much humor. And I had felt that he had it in him to be funnier, a la James Garner. What he was, was competent for that role — he was a heroic type character; he was a great-looking guy. I think it worked for what was needed in that role."

Like millions of fans worldwide, Lionel Siegel can't fathom anyone else stepping into Steve Austin's bionic shoes. "The casting of Lee Majors eventually determined the personality and character of *The Six Million Dollar Man*," he said. "Majors is a reactor, and his responses are often cryptic and sometimes clever. He was perfect for the part. Lee had a preference for a minimum of dialogue, and that fit his southern background. He postures sometimes as a country bumpkin, but inside he's slick."

"There's one thing about Lee," said *Bionic* director Phil Bondelli, "he always knows his lines." And Bondelli is one to talk, for he knows his business.

A native of Chicago, Bondelli attended the Midwestern Conservatory of Music and American TV School. Starting in the mailroom at the ABC-TV affiliate in Chicago, he moved up to guest relations, dolly pusher and technical director. After CBS purchased the station, he did local shows and started directing repertory workshops (he was the Chicago director on the first Kennedy-Nixon debate, and he won an Emmy for *The Mikado*).

Following his move to Los Angeles in 1961, Phil produced and directed at CBS. Wanting to get into film, he worked his way up from assistant director on such TV hits as *Gunsmoke* and *I Spy*. Aaron Spelling gave him his first full-fledged directing position on *The Mod Squad*. He then went on to direct multiple episodes of *The Six Million Dollar Man* and *The Bionic Woman* (as well as *The Rookies*, *Charlie's Angels*, *CHiPS*, *T.J. Hooker*, *Vega$*, and several more shows).

As to working with Lee on SM, Bondelli said the actor was "always prepared for his scenes. I don't think he liked anyone who wasn't. He wouldn't come right out and say it, but we could feel it. His position was, *Let's try to get out of here, fellas. Come on, I have a game to go to*, or something. That would be his way of telling the actor who wasn't prepared, to get prepared. He was an unbelievable diplomat with other actors."

As well as benevolent with all his co-workers. While filming "The Bionic Boy" episode, Bondelli went to Lee's motel room. "He had all the stunt people in there with him," Bondelli said. "He hung around with those guys a lot. He was a very macho type of guy. That's why I was not surprised when he did *The Fall Guy*."

Feeling playful, Lee and the stuntmen decided to "get the director," and threw Bondelli in the motel's pool, resulting in him throwing his back out.

Bondelli said Majors was apologetic, and he didn't need to be. "He didn't even do anything," reveals the director. "It was really all the stunt guys. But I had to go to the chiropractor, and he felt bad about that. It was just a little twist of the back, and I had already had back problems, which he didn't know. But he bought me dinner that night, to make up for it."

"Not many people know this," adds Steve Stafford, "but Lee has many wonderful sides to him, including his compassion and his great sense of humor. He can play comedy very well. It was never pushed in his career. He's a very underrated actor. There are those who say, *Oh, he's a good-looking guy who just got a break.* Yet he did great work in TV-movies like *The True Story of the U-2 Spy Incident: The Francis Gary Powers Story* (1976) and *Just a Little Inconvenience* (1977)." If his career had taken him more into features, Stafford said Majors "would have been a huge film star. It's easier for today's television stars to do that. But when Lee was in his prime, it was next to impossible to make that transition."

Yet Majors hasn't done that bad on the big screen. Besides *Will Penny*, his feature films include *The Liberation of LB Jones* (1970), *The Norseman* (1978), *Steel* (1979), *Agency* (1980), *The Last Chase* (1981), *Out Cold* (2001), *Big Fat Liar* (2002), and *When I Find the Ocean* (2006), among others. In 2007, Lee played an estranged father in a music video by Bowling for Soup, an emerging pop-punk band. "We just asked him," said Soup's lead singer, Jaret Reddick. "It's funny. He was like 'I've never done it. Sure.' He was amazing, a nice guy and good to be around all day. It was a very good experience."

Ken Johnson remembers English director John Schlesinger once being interested in Majors for the lead in a motion picture, before *The Six Million Dollar Man* and during *The Big Valley*. "Lee won the part," Ken said. "But he couldn't get out of his contract with *The Big Valley*." The movie? *Midnight Cowboy*, released in 1969. The role? Joe Buck, the pathetic hustler, which went to Jon Voight.

Johnson remembers Lee's lack of bitterness, and his appreciation for success. "He was always pleasant. I enjoyed working with him. We had a lot of good times together. He would tell me and my wife about how he realized how lucky he was." Majors would say, "If I hadn't turned up this gig [playing Steve Austin], I would have been coaching football in some high school, somewhere. But as long as I'm here, I've got to try and make as much of it as I can. God only knows how long it's going to last."

Before all the controversy about the demise of Jaime Sommers, and the negotiations for Lindsay Wagner's return to the role for a second two-part *Six* — and then finally a series of her own — Ken Johnson remembers when he and Harve Bennett initially cast the Sommers part for the first SM two-parter, introducing Jaime. The two reviewed the work of several actresses. But when they saw the pilot for *The Rockford Files*, with Lindsay in the lead, the search was over.

TOP: LEE MAJORS' RUGGED GOOD LOOKS AND NATURAL ATHLETIC
ABILITY PUT HIM AT THE TOP OF ABC'S LIST WHEN CASTING STEVE
AUSTIN. LEE'S SERIOUS AND STRAIGHTFORWARD TAKE ON STEVE
AUSTIN WAS A WELL-BALANCED CONTRAST TO LINDSAY WAGNER'S
MORE LIGHT-HEARTED AND DOWN-TO-EARTH PORTRAYAL OF JAIME
SOMMERS. *BOTTOM:* AFTER CONSIDERING ACTRESSES LIKE SALLY
FIELD AND STEFANIE POWERS FOR THE ROLE, KENNETH JOHNSON
KNEW HE HAD FOUND HIS *BIONIC WOMAN* WHEN HE SAW LINDSAY
WAGNER IN THE PILOT FOR *THE ROCKFORD FILES.*

"We were so struck by the natural kind of quality that she had," Johnson said, "the real sense of spontaneity, that we decided that she was the right one. I don't think we even read her for it. We just hired her on the basis of seeing her in that episode."

Born in Los Angeles on June 22, 1949, Lindsay grew up in a primarily single-parent household (her parents having divorced when she was seven). She first greeted the public as a fresh-faced teen fashion model, but soon found the work tedious and unrewarding. After brief flirtations with dance and music, she would eventually find a home in her high school's drama department, which allowed her to channel certain feelings and emotions that she had trouble expressing in real life. A few years after graduating, Universal Studios recognized Lindsay's potential, signed her to a contract, and steadily placed her in an assortment of pre-*Bionic* shows, including *Night Gallery*, *The Bold Ones*, *Owen Marshall, Counselor at Law* (alongside Lee Majors), and a two-part guest appearance on *Marcus Welby, M.D.*, as the terminally ill love of James Brolin's Dr. Steve Kiley. If the Lindsay/ *Welby* segments are viewed today, an eerie foreshadow of Jaime's love-sick-forget-remember relationship with Steve Austin is played out each time she cries for Steve (Kiley) in several scenes. Of this odd Jaime-presage coincidence, Johnson said, "Yeah, that was funny. She got to die in a lot of shows."

Lindsay remains unfettered and admirably unapologetic about her honest approach to life, now and while filming BW. Much of what she put into Jaime and the series had to do with her personal battles. "What I wanted most," she said, "was to communicate that Jaime was someone who cared a lot about people and general fairness, with a very broad outlook. She didn't want to be a government agent. It was circumstance and karma that brought her to work for the OSI, which was very focused and relatively narrow in its goals. It wasn't really a conscious-raising organization.

"The OSI was focused on security issues for one group of people. At times, that was a real problem for Jaime. She was a person who saw unfairness in the course of her own job. She viewed human beings as a whole, as opposed to sectioned-off groups who needed protection."

Lindsay worked intensely to have such perspective incorporated into *The Bionic Woman* scripts. When she would receive a story outline, she said it was usually summarized in one way: "America is always right. Everyone else is always wrong. *We're* the good guys and *they're* the bad guys. I wanted the scripts to be more dimensional than that."

"I enjoyed greatly working with Lindsay, who is a very gifted actress," admits Kenneth Johnson. "She and I used to go over every line of each script for *The Bionic Woman*. She would read Jaime's lines and I would read everyone else's. We always joked that we should have done an episode where she played Jaime, and I played everyone else."

"*The Bionic Woman* had greater depth because of Lindsay," said unit pro-

LINDSAY WAGNER

duction manager and producer Ralph Sariego. "She was a fine actress and a sensitive, lovely person. She wanted more of a dramatic show than action-adventure. On *The Six Million Dollar Man*, Lee Majors didn't care. He just grunted, moved his eyebrow and took the money. Lindsay fought for better stories and character relationships. The producers were reluctant to do that. They were more interested in a formula show, which did seem to work better in the ratings."

Still, while Lindsay battled against certain types of scripts, she said Jaime struggled against similar attitudes within her job. "That was part of who she was," the actress contends, "and the character I was trying to create. She obviously had a great love for children, which kind of bled into that whole consciousness of seeing people-as-people, which made her job very difficult at times. The writers eventually began to express that, through the way that she interacted with the other characters. There were times when she went through great emotional struggles in having to carry out her job."

Jaime initially felt obligated and indebted to the OSI for saving her life, not once, but twice. So, as Richard Anderson adds, "she never really wanted to do that kind of work at all. She wanted to teach children peaceful things, which essentially developed out of Lindsay's personal desires."

Such words confirm for Harve Bennett how perfect Lindsay was for *Bionic* role. "There was something about Lindsay that conveyed everything I wanted Jaime to be," Bennett said. "It's a quality that's hard to describe. She had that image of everybody's girl next door. She was also extremely bright, competitive and physical." Yet, when the producer first viewed the actress in *The Rockford Files*, he said, "There goes Judy Garland. That was the child in me," he admits, "speaking about his idol." The Garland to whom he was referring, was the quintessential Dorothy character she played in the 1939 classic feature, *The Wizard of Oz*. He describes Garland's Dorothy as "a kind of wide-eyed person who said, *There really* is *no place like home*."

Bennett compares Lindsay's enormous range of talent to another charismatic actress, Meg Ryan, who has displayed extensive emotional range in films like 1993's *Sleepless in Seattle*. Like Ryan, Wagner "can make you laugh, and make you weep," he said. "Add to that, the fact that she is capable of playing a Katharine Hepburn to any Spencer Tracy, and you have the perfect package. She filled those shoes with Jaime Sommers *in spades*. All we had to do, creatively, was give Jaime an athletic background. Otherwise, you'd say she could jump high and run fast, only because she had mechanical parts."

Hence, the creation of Jaime's career in professional tennis. Billie Jean King had been victorious against Bobby Riggs in The Battle of the Sexes, and female tennis became big around the time *The Bionic Woman* first aired. Through it all, Harve said, Jaime was "fantastically feminine, and non-threatening to men. Except bad men."

In several moments, Jaime was careful to retain her quality of being female, and mindful not to bruise the ego of various male companions (besides Steve), co-workers or people in trouble. She would subtly dislodge a doorknob, and then have *the man* break down the door. She would never punch anyone. She would swipe the rug from under them, or throw a spare tire in their face.

"I didn't create those details," Lindsay explained. "That was something that the writers came up with, as a response to my request to keep her as feminine as possible. I wanted her to do fun, cute things, instead of *macho* things. As an actress, it gave me something with which to play. It was something that I wanted to continue to do as an on-going gag."

The actress, however, rarely perceived such interplay as constructive between male and female personalities. At the time, a woman was forced to hide her strength in order to make the man feel comfortable. Wagner did not want to reinforce that Old World value into young girls. Though the notion did work for the show. "Conceptually," she explained, "it would have been a little silly if Steve ever tried to hide his bionics in front of another guy. But certain feministic tactics were used as realistic ploys to keep secret Jaime's true identity."

Back at ABC, programmer Fred Silverman's visions for the show were changing week to week. *The Bionic Woman* was experiencing a bit of an identity crisis: was it a superhero vehicle, or a soft melodrama? Writer Philip DeGuere ("A Thing of the Past"), who succumbed to cancer in 1995, was at his wit's end. "Talk about network interference," he said. "Freddie Silverman used to call Universal five days a week with directives on how we were supposed to do the show. Problem was, he would flip-flop between two major directives. He wanted to make Jaime like Wonder Woman or Supergirl. His other directive was exactly the opposite: to hide her super powers and play it more natural. I developed a severe case of schizophrenia."

DeGuere, who left *The Bionic Woman* after its first season, said, "We finally decided that the non-superhero approach was the way to go. She was ladylike and operated her bionics discreetly. The conventional wisdom was that an audience wouldn't buy a real strong, aggressive female character. Lindsay did very well in the role. She was fun, and I liked her as a person."

Even better, Wagner's considerable "range" afforded producers a myriad of creative opportunities. "We picked up tremendous things with Lindsay that we didn't have with Lee Majors," said Bennett. "Lee's character was quiet and reserved. But here we had a bionic person—a woman—who could cry and tell us how she feels. So we were able to develop much more feelings in the show. She could also carry the action quotient believably. Another woman might have looked silly doing those stunts."

As Ken Johnson adds, BW debuted during the Feminist movement of the 1970s, when it was spreading to mainstream awareness. He remembers its effect while writing his first script for *The Six Million Dollar Man*, which happened to introduce Jaime. His wife, Susie, had glanced at some pages, and noticed that one of the characters was referred to as a *female doctor*. "Why do you have to *tell* us that she's a female doctor?" Mrs. Johnson wondered. "Because we expect her to be male?" Ken's own consciousness was on the rise at the time. So he replied with an "Uh oh. You're right," and subtracted the *female* modifier from the phrase, allowing it to read as just *doctor*.

Writing in the *Man/Woman* world was very tricky, he admits, with particular regards to Jaime, "Because she was obviously a character who could punch your lights out if she wanted to. We were always faced with the question of how to retain her femininity and not make her threatening."

How would Jaime become a woman that a man would feel comfortable going out with, and not feel like he's going to get his arm broken? The BW gang had to make sure that she never slugged anyone. "We always made her more clever than that," Johnson said. "She would pull the ceiling down on top of them. But there was never any fist-in-the-face direct knockout." He was inspired to present a well-rounded Jaime due to his *maternal* instincts. "I've always had very strong women in my life," he explained. "My own mother was a very active, professional woman. Yet she was always there for me when I needed her. I'll never forget that aspect of her personality."

It was intriguing for Ken to later do a show with a character like Jaime. She carried with her into the public's mind a true sense of balanced strength at a time when feminism was coming into fruition. "To be able to color and shape that into a public image was very gratifying," he admits, "especially as we were hearing about so many children being named Jaime and Lindsay in those years."

Some remained skeptical, however. According to Susan Douglas, a professor of media and American studies at Hampshire College and author of *Where the Girls Are*, Jaime has flunked more than one feminist litmus test. In a chapter entitled, *The Rise of the Bionic Bimbo*, Douglas argues that Ms. Sommers makes a less than ideal role model for impressionable young women because "she takes her orders from a man [Oscar]...while her best friend is not another woman, but rather a dog [Max]."

Ken Johnson is not persuaded. "I couldn't disagree more with that," he said. "A lot of women have spoken to me about the strength that they found in Jaime and her attitudes. We were very careful, when we created the show, that Jaime never [seriously injured] anybody. We wanted her to be a woman you could go on a date with and not be afraid of. So we tried to keep her accessible and vulnerable, so that she felt like someone that you could really be a friend with and a lover with."

Ms. Douglas is obviously oblivious to the fact that Jaime addresses the issue of feminism in the BW segment, "Road to Nashville." Here, after seeing Jaime heft a trunk for an airport skycap, Muffin Calhoun (played by for-mer *Tonight Show* band front man Doc Severinsen) said, "Doggone it! If I'd known you were that strong, I'd let you carry your own bag." To which Jaime responds, "I'm not in this revolution business."

Moreover, Douglas seems to forget that Mary Tyler Moore as Mary Richards, the 1970s icon of independent womanhood, had Ed Asner's Lou Grant jumping down her throat week after week on *The Mary Tyler Moore Show*. Nobody thought any less of *her*. And anyone with even a superficial acquaintance with Wagner's series would realize that her closest friend was not Max, but rather Oscar's secretary, Peggy Callahan (played by Jennifer Darling) who, if memory serves, is a woman.

Steve Austin, meanwhile, is a man, one in which Ken Johnson saw many feministic, albeit early politically accurate, qualities. He remembers discus-sions with Harve Bennett about the manifestation of Steve's bionic strength, how he should possess enough discretion to employ his abilities with inge-nuity, as opposed to "just handy-dandy." It was further intriguing for Ken, as a writer, to discover more unexpected, off-center, yet resourceful ways for Steve to use his bionic powers. "That made things more interesting," he said. "We were able to wink at the audience a little bit, from a stand-point of Steve saying, *Hey, you know I can do better than this, but I'm just doing this because it amuses me. And I know it amuses you, too.*"

As far as Johnson was concerned, a dash of humor was ever in the *Woman/Six* mix. It was his major contribution to the entire bionic spectrum. Before he came aboard, "they were all very earnest and straightforward about Steve Austin and all that he did," he said.   One of the first scenes he wrote for Steve (in the first two-part *Woman* script of *Man*), involved a lawn being mowed, bionically.

"No," Harve Bennett said, "we can't have him do that. He's *The Six Million Dollar Man*."

"Harve," Ken replied, "if you were bionic and you had to mow the lawn, wouldn't you do it as fast as you could?"

"You're right," Bennett returned, "I would."

Johnson created another Steve-scene, involving the hauling of a tree trunk out of the soil. The sequence, which didn't make the final cut, had Steve pulling so hard on the stump that it comes right out of the ground, as he goes flat on his rump. Johnson was instructed once more to step back, hearing, "We can't have you do that to our Steve. We can't have the audience laughing at our hero." "Of course you can," Ken argued. "What's going to make him accessible, endearing and human, is his self-deprecation. If our hero could also laugh at himself it would humanize him and make the audi-ence love him all the more."

A great fan of silent era comedians like Buster Keaton, Harold Lloyd, Charlie Chaplin and Harry Langdon, Johnson made certain his scripted sense of humor also made its way into BW, and not only when she pulled a rug from underneath a foe's footing. He began to use what became known as *pocket bionics*: throwaway tricks, like having Jaime open a can of tuna fish with her thumbnail, or cleaning the house in fast motion. Or on SM, Steve would loosen tire bolts with his bionic hand when changing to a spare. Such antics "leavened each story with truth," Johnson claims, "and made the characters more human. They suddenly became more than just superheroes. And wouldn't you peel those potatoes at bionic speed to keep up with Julia Child's cooking lesson? You bet. "

In keeping with the conscious effort to have Jaime retain her femininity, while not allowing Steve to become overly macho, there were still specific patterns of behavior that Jaime showcased and conducted as a woman, patterns that Steve, as a man, would not display. And vice versa. Beyond the obvious differences, Jaime was distinct from Steve in several ways, as was *The Six Million Dollar Man* series from *The Bionic Woman* show, and as Lee Majors' stoic performance was from Lindsay Wagner's limber technique.

"Steve was a professional test pilot," said Martin Caidin, "which meant that he was a very special breed. He was also a fighter pilot. Every fighter pilot will tell you that they're the world's greatest fighter pilot. If he doesn't, then he's not a fighter pilot. He's gonna get killed damn quick. Any fighter pilot that has a chance at success and surviving combat, must have this kind of *attack, gung-ho* attitude. It's the thing that makes them fighter pilots. A split second delay in combat could cost them their life."

Steve, in particular, became a test pilot with a tremendous engineering background. "He probably had several degrees in all the sciences," Caidin concluded, "including aerodynamics and electrical engineering. It granted him an extremely high level of status, compared to Middle America."

Still, Austin was just as human as everyone else in terms of vulnerability. In addition to the physical pain he experienced (resulting from his accident and bionic reconstruction), he suffered searing emotional problems, and felt that no woman could love him. In terms of cybernetic evolution, Caidin called Steve "a trail blazer."

Austin was the world's first bionic man, and Jaime, the world's first bionic woman. Yet by the time she came along, the media mainstream had already been introduced to the world of bionics. Both characters shared a common circumstance, and were given the same choice: Be modified or die. "Like most people in their situation," Caidin assessed, "they preferred not to cash in their chips that quickly. There was a chance they'd survive their operations." Beyond the basic male/female distinctions, he said that Jaime, more so than Steve, was eminently more involved with her personal life, and in the mainstream flux of society. "Steve was pretty well polarized into the direction of his career," he noted. "Like my own career as an author. There's a certain routine to which I adhere."

LINDSAY WAGNER'S PORTRAYAL AS JAIME SOMMERS MADE IT VERY
EASY FOR *BW*'S WRITERS TO FREQUENTLY INCORPORATE CHILDREN
AND ANIMALS INTO EPISODES, SOMETHING SHE ENCOURAGED.

Whenever Caidin penned a book about astronauts, he had a problem. A publisher may have said to him, "All these guys [characters] sound alike." To which he replied, "Well, damn it, they are alike. Some fighter-pilot types may be religious, some may not, but they all share the same hard-core developmental structure when it comes to patterns of behavior. That's what makes them who they are. That's what the case was with Steve, but was not with Jaime. She didn't have that kind of discipline. Her life was more her own. She was more of a free spirit."

Lee's more reserved *Bionic* interpretation did not safeguard the mostly conservative actor from humorous spontaneity behind the scenes. One gag, in fact, involved Lindsay during the final season of *The Bionic Woman*, when it switched networks from ABC to NBC.

To showcase no hard feelings due to their network separation (and since both shows were still filmed on the same Universal lot), Lee made a surprise visit to Lindsay on the BW set, in the studio limousine, en route to SM's side. He noticed Lindsay filming a scene, asked the driver to stop the car, got out, ran over to Lindsay, gave her a hug, ran back inside the limo, and sped off. "I don't think she even had time to react to what was happening," he recalls. "But I knew that it was going to be a shocker. We had a good laugh, and it was the perfect tension breaker."

Such *atomic* antics and good times were everyday affairs during filming of *The Bionic Woman*. Lindsay recalls birthday parties, squirt gun fights, and people skateboarding on the set. "Everyone was always getting in trouble," she said. "We were constantly doing things that we shouldn't have been doing."

One time, a male member of the BW crew accidentally ran smack into an on-location, authentic fire hydrant, exactly in the body-spot where one would most certainly not want to run into a fire hydrant. The worker was hospitalized. "The poor guy was discharged," Lindsay reveals, "and came back to the set wearing protective padding. It wasn't funny, because he was so hurt. But it was. Even though we wouldn't have dared written any of these things into our scripts, they were happening all the time in real life."

There was a method to the madness. "We had the most multi-cultural crew that you could have had then," Lindsay explained. "We were like the UN. Most crews become like family, because they spend so much time together, which we did, too. But we shared more of a common bond than usual, because we each possessed a renegade side."

Drawing on the underlying themes of isolation, prejudice and insecurity that Steve and Jaime experienced as bionic individuals, both Lindsay and Lee Majors faced a similar discrimination. Like his good friend and *Bionic Ever After?* cameo-guest Dave Thomas, president and founder of Wendy's restaurant, Lee was adopted; a happenstance which contributed to his compassion for others. He does much charitable work for adoption agencies,

AFTER *SM*, LEE MAJORS STARRED AS COLT SEAVERS, A STUNTMAN
WHO MOONLIGHTS AS A BOUNTY HUNTER, IN ABC'S *THE FALL GUY*
(1981-1986). LINDSAY WAGNER MADE A GUEST-APPEARANCE IN THE
EPISODE "DEVIL'S ISLAND." FANS WERE HAPPY TO SEE THE TWO
TOGETHER AGAIN, EVEN IN NON-BIONIC CHARACTER.

and helps to raise awareness of orphaned children and the positive options made available to them.

Many times Majors felt left out, amongst his childhood peers. "It's a feeling you don't shake," he said, "even as you move into adulthood. It really doesn't get any easier, but somehow you hang in there. The whole experience has increased my stamina as a human being, and widened my perspective on social issues. It definitely helped me in understanding Steve's feelings of isolation, and how he dealt with not knowing if his real father was alive [as in 'The Coward']."

Wagner said what she faced as a teen was preparation for her strength in character as Jaime, and as a real human being. Until her final year in junior high, she grew up in Eagle Rock, California, which was predominantly Latino. Once her parents moved to another area, it was a little different. Before that happened, however, she experienced racism. "I was the one who couldn't use the underpass at school," she recalls. "When we did *The Bionic Woman*, and worked with all these people who had experienced a similar prejudice, a communal understanding and camaraderie was established on the set. Remember, it was the 1970s. Social issues were prominent. We all shared such compassion for everything that was going on in the world, as well as within our own lives. We really felt blessed to be together."

There was also Lindsay's special bond with the youth of the world. Consequently, children and animals were inclusive in several episodes of *The Bionic Woman*. "I'm a very child- and animal-oriented person," she said. "So having children and animals in the show was a major portion of my joy in doing the show." "Lindsay is a humanist," explained Richard Anderson. "She's a dear lady, whose charm seeps through to the viewer. Her way with children is only an extension of her caring personality."

Both Lindsay and Lee employed their celebrity status for several charitable events and causes. Despite the pressures, perks and temptations that come with fame (especially overnight fame), they were very much aware that their core audience consisted of children, and careful to offer positive influence as much as possible. In many ways, Lee and Lindsay's on-screen boss, Richard Anderson, was Steve's pal and Jaime's adoptive father. Like any good parent or true friend, he rallied for the funding for their reconstruction, pursuant rehabilitation, and psychological and emotional stability. He made sure they had employment, and tended to their personal needs as much as possible. He was also proud of them.

Before Anderson's Oscar-stint, he appeared periodically on the classic *Perry Mason* series with Raymond Burr, which originally aired on CBS from 1957 to 1966. On assessing the success of any television series, Burr used to tell him, "It's all in the casting." So finding the "right" (read: "likeable") actor for a regular role on a weekly show is crucial to its success. The real-life charms of Anderson's small-screen friends and family members, Majors and Wagner, contributed to the media mastery of *The Six Million Dollar Man* and *The Bionic Woman*. "The shows worked because of the chemistry between two dynamic people," he said. "They clicked with the audience, because of their sincerity in the roles, which stemmed from their true natures."

So good was their chemistry that Lindsay agreed to guest star on a 1983 segment of *The Fall Guy*, where she once again played an ex-high-school sweetheart of Lee's. In 1995, Majors and Wagner reunited anew on the Sci-Fi Channel's four-night "Bionic Blowout" special, providing anecdotes and insight during the commercial breaks for four two-part bionic episodes.

Beyond Lee and Lindsay's personal allure, Anderson also points to the ideal story of love played out by Steve and Jaime. That remains the central key to the continued resonance of both programs. "People fell in love with the fact that Jaime and Steve fell in love," he said. "It's that simple."

CHAPTER 6

FREQUENCIES

"YOU COULDN'T HAVE FOUND A BETTER CAST OF SUPPORTING ACTORS."

KENNETH JOHNSON

Though Richard Anderson is best known to cybernetic fans as Steve and Jaime's boss, it was Darren McGavin who originated the part of Oscar Goldman (then-named Oliver Spencer) in the original *Six Million Dollar Man* pilot. McGavin left the Oliver-cum-Oscar role behind to pursue supernatural, occult and otherworldies as the tenacious Carl Kolchak in *The Night Stalker* TV-movies and series, predating by two decades a premise similar to *The X-Files*. [Anderson had the lead, opposite McGavin, in *The Night Strangler*, the second *Kolchak* television film.]

McGavin and Anderson were "great" as Steve's dean, professed Martin Caidin, "but Richard was more subtle and accepted by the audience. Darren was a bit more abrasive. And I say that in the most positive sense. They're both top actors. It's just that Richard had the element of scientific competence that entrusted him to the audience as a government official."

"It was fortuitous that I stepped in as Goldman," Anderson relays of the career-changing role that he continued in the *Bionic* reunions. "He's a good, solid-minded character with strong values. It's a pleasure to play the man." A happy experience that began when his agent called to say that there was a part for him in something called *The Six Million Dollar Man*. Anderson liked the sound of that, as in the ring of a cash register, "especially since I was talking with my agent," he laughs.

Universal consequently pegged Anderson to play the Washington man in the second *Million Dollar* movie. He read the first script, liked it, made the arrangements, and was particularly pleased to work alongside Lee Majors, with whom he had once appeared on *The Big Valley*. Anderson found Majors to be "a genuinely nice man" and, prior to production of the first *Six*, he said the two actors "agreed that we were friends."

And why wouldn't Richard and Lee be friends?

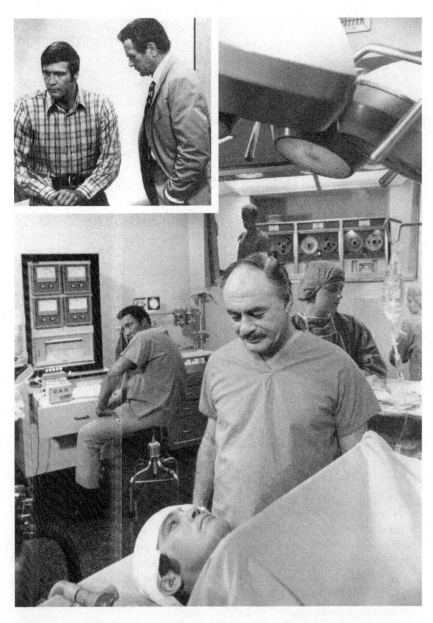

INSET: IN *SM*'S PILOT, DARREN MCGAVIN PLAYS OLIVER SPENCER —
A CHARACTER THAT WOULD BECOME OSI BOSS OSCAR GOLDMAN, AS
PLAYED BY RICHARD ANDERSON IN THE SERIES. DR. RUDY WELLS
WAS PLAYED BY VETERAN CHARACTER-ACTOR MARTIN BALSAM IN THE
PILOT.

Both are amiable fellows, who had worked together several times before *The Six Million Dollar Man* on TV shows like *The Virginian* and *Owen Marshall, Counselor at Law*. Following the demise of SM, Anderson had then acted with Majors on *The Fall Guy*.

In fact, Oscar's alter self is an extremely experienced actor who made his mark in several classic showcases for television, as well as on the big screen. Here's a little background:

Pre-*Bionics*, he was seen on programs such as *The Rifleman, The Lieutenant* (produced by Gene Roddenberry), *Perry Mason, The Fugitive* and *The Mod Squad* (produced by Harve Bennett). After *Six*, there were stints on *Simon & Simon, Cover Up, Dynasty* and *Kung Fu: The Legend Continues*.

In the halcyon days of the major movie studios, he fought for a release from his contract so he could play a role in an independent feature film that, at the time, was considered offbeat and "too different." The studio was Metro-Goldwyn-Mayer, where Anderson had appeared in over 26 films while in the process of fulfilling a six-year contract.

In 1956, Stanley Kubrick was seeking someone to play the prosecuting attorney, Major St. Auban, in his production of *Paths of Glory*. Richard read the script, was immediately intrigued by not only the character of St. Auban, but also the film in general. He thought, "Here was something different and stimulating in moviemaking."

Anderson obtained a release from the remainder of his contract and flew to Europe to act in the film. His instincts proved correct, and they paid off. *Glory* paved an important path for his career. After completing the film, Richard lived and traveled throughout Europe, returning to Los Angeles for a part in 20th Century-Fox's *The Long Hot Summer* (1958). He also found himself portraying one of the leads in *The Highest Tree* on Broadway. The production was not memorable but, as critics noted, Anderson's performance was.

Back in Hollywood, in 1960, Richard was signed for Columbia Pictures' *The Wackiest Ship in the Army*. By now, television was making its mark in the entertainment industry, and Fox beckoned again, this time for a TV series called *Bus Stop*. Richard accepted. After one season he moved on to join television's *Twelve O'Clock High* (1964 to 1967).

While fulfilling his *High* commitment, Richard also appeared in features like *Seconds* (1966) and *The Ride to Hangman's Tree* (1967). Before these, there was *The Magnificent Yankee* (1950), *It's a Dog's Life* (1955), *Forbidden Planet* (1956), *The Buster Keaton Story* (1957), and *Johnny Cool* (1963, with Elizabeth Montgomery).

Then *Along Came a Spider* (1970), *Tora! Tora! Tora!* (1970), and *Doctors' Wives* (1971). And his most recent motion pictures have been *Gettysburg* (1993), *An American in Saigon* (1994) and *The Glass Shield* (which was entered in the Cannes Film Festival of 1994).

RICHARD ANDERSON

Yet, it was in wake of *Wives* when TV producer Quinn Martin offered him a co-starring role in ABC's *Dan August* (with Burt Reynolds, *sans* mustache), which led to his most famous stint as the watcher of a computer who wore tennis shoes: Oscar Goldman on SM — a role which garnered him an Emmy nomination for Best Supporting Actor in a Dramatic Series.

Richard catered to Oscar. He loved the role, and worked feverishly to give the character sides. He modeled Goldman after Charles E. Bohlen, the American Ambassador to France and Russia in the 1960s and early 1970s. Bohlen was with the State Department and, as Richard said, "was one of the best government officials we had. He was urbane, extremely bright, and he liked to *play poker* with the press. That's how I pictured Oscar."

The actor believed that the *Gold* man had to conduct his relationship with Steve, fundamentally, on a professional level, by the book, yet with some exceptions. "He learned to treat Steve more like a comrade than an employee," Richard assessed. "When he couldn't send in the military, he would send in one special agent [and later, two] on these extremely dangerous missions. After a while, Steve would wonder, *What am I doing?*, which is a notion Jaime addressed right from the beginning."

Expanding on previously discussed *Bionic* contrasts, he said several distinctions between *Man* and *Woman* invited him to imbue dual Oscar interpretations. Even though he played the same character, the two shows were unalike for him because Steve and Jaime were two distinct individuals, whose personalities stretched into their respective shows.

"When we did *Six Mill*," he said, "we concentrated on the Washington scene. It was more of a straight adventure show. *The Bionic Woman* did more emotional stories. It was funnier, looser [than *Six*] because Lindsay has a relaxed, humorous quality. Jaime allowed me to add some colors. Oscar was firm and brotherly with Steve, and had to constantly reestablish that he, not Steve, was the boss. With Jaime, he was lenient and fatherly, almost overly protective, and only argued with her out of concern for her health and safety."

When Six was still in its infancy, Anderson would typically appear at the beginning and end of most episodes, not unlike "M" in the Bond films. Eventually, producers realized they were under-using a fine acting talent. "As time progressed, they needed storylines," Anderson said. "Consequently, they said, 'Why don't we have Oscar kidnapped?' or something like that. Also, as an actor, you bring in things. That's what actors are supposed to do; they bring in things to fill the words and so forth. When they see this chemistry between the actors and see their own personalities, they start writing for it. So, in time, the part expanded and became much more rounded."

What about the assumption by some fans that Oscar was in love with Jaime? "I won't try to hide behind that," Anderson confesses. "I think he was in love with her, and I tried to convey that in very subtle ways. He couldn't help himself." [As with the wedding scene in *Bionic Ever After?*,

TOP: RICHARD ANDERSON IN A STUDIO PORTRAIT FROM THE 1950s,
AND AS OSCAR GOLDMAN. BOTTOM: RICHARD WITH LEE MAJORS,
AND LINDSAY WAGNER. GOLDMAN AND STEVE AUSTIN WERE "PALS,"
BUT THEY ALSO HAD A RESPECTFUL PROFESSIONAL RELATIONSHIP.
GOLDMAN'S RELATIONSHIP WITH JAIME SOMMERS, WHILE ALSO
PROFESSIONAL, HAD A CARING AND PROTECTIVE EDGE TO IT,
SOMETHING RICHARD INTENTIONALLY PORTRAYED.

when a smile momentarily disappears from Oscar's face as if it finally hits him that *Steve* is the one marrying Jaime.]

While Oscar referred to Steve as *pal*, he, with extreme affection, referred to Jaime as *babe*, which today is considered politically incorrect, condescending and demeaning to women. During the time of *Bionic's* original reign, however, "Oscar was attaching it to a person for whom he cared a great deal," Anderson defends.

Ken Johnson remembers when he first saw Richard playing Oscar on the *Six* set. The actor was sunning himself with an aluminum reflector, off-stage, looking somewhat austere. "I didn't know really what he was going to be like," Johnson admits. "Then I walked past him, and he said, *You're Kenny, aren't you. I just want to tell you big guy, that you write really great love stories. Why can't you write one for me? Why can't I be in love with The Bionic Woman?*" From here on in, Johnson was on to Richard's sense of humor, and the two became "very good friends."

Anderson's general dealings on both *The Six Million Dollar Man* and *The Bionic Woman* were, in a word, "enjoyable." "It was a very happy time, and a unique experience," he adds. "I had the chance to play a very respectable character, who was involved privately and on a business level with two very special people. As Steve and Jaime grew and developed, Oscar did as well."

Bionic writer/producer Arthur Rowe has praise for Richard's *Oscar-winning* performance. Rowe liked working with Anderson, and later employed the actor on *Fantasy Island*, for which he was the supervising producer. "Richard is an extremely decent individual," Rowe sustains. "He played Oscar about as perfect as the character could be played. You had the ultimate head of this secret government organization who, despite his heady position, expressed sympathy in his dealings with Steve and Jaime."

Rowe wishes he had a dollar for every time Oscar said things like, "We have no choice, Jaime. We have to send you. I would send the bombers, the fleet, but there really is no one but you."

Rowe adds how Richard sold this melodramatic aspect of Oscar's personality extremely well, how he traveled beyond the mundane theatrical delivery of lines with which the character could have been pigeonholed. Instead, Rowe said Anderson "put more heart" into his part.

As to Oscar's fluctuating relationships with Steve and Jaime, Rowe agrees with certain fan factions. "He was definitely more of a buddy for Steve, and a romantic figure for Jaime," he said. "I never at all had any feeling that Oscar viewed Jaime as a daughter. I think he felt responsible for her, in many ways. But he was in love with her. I mean, Jaime wasn't someone that you could put in pigtails."

In one of the more historic moments of 1970s television, *The Bionic Woman* switched networks to NBC in its third (and, alas, final) season, while *The Six Million Dollar Man* remained on ABC. As a result, Anderson played the same character on two different shows, broadcast on rival networks. "And ABC," he said, "didn't like that idea at all. In fact, they tried to kill it. They were quite adamant about it, and made a big deal. They didn't want me appearing on the competition in any manner, much less one of their own born and bred characters."

Universal then wondered why ABC canceled *The Bionic Woman* in the first place.

The network was without reply, and simply wanted Anderson replaced on NBC's version of Jaime's program. Frank Price believed Richard's Oscar was intrinsically conduit to both shows, and strongly objected. ABC, on the other hand, didn't want their advertisers to move any of their accounts over to BW on NBC. In the end, the peacocky web benefited from ABC's decision to disconnect *The Bionic Woman*. And not only that, ABC itself capitalized on BW after its cancellation by employing it to market Lindsay Wagner's 1977 primetime musical special, *Lindsay Wagner: Another Side of Me*. The guest list on this show was littered with those who had also made appearances on BW, including Vincent Price ("Black Magic"), Vito Scotti ("Fly Jaime," "Assault on the Princess"), and Teddy Wilson ("Iron Ships and Dead Men"). [Note: The *TV Guide* ad for the *Another Side* special read: *The Bionic Woman* will break you up...with laughter!"]

After Oscar, next in line for friends and co-workers to Steve and Jaime was Dr. Rudy Wells, who was introduced in Martin Caidin's *Cyborg* novel, and played by three different actors on screen.

Martin Balsam, a stellar performer who appeared in several film classics like *Psycho* (1960), played Rudy in the pilot, while the also-talented Alan Oppenheimer and Martin E. Brooks shared Wells in the series.

Before delving in the various Rudy doctorings of each actor, a study of the Wells character takes precedence.

In the novel, Rudy had a thick shock of dark hair (unlike his TV counterparts) and a penetrating, hypnotic gaze. He determined what was distressing a patient just by laying his extraordinarily sensitive hands upon them, with fingertips so intuitive that they left no prints. A chain-smoker and a man who could hold a drink, this Wells had never been able to sustain a civilian practice, though he made a go of it after stints in Japan and Korea with the Fifth Air Force. He eventually returned to military service because he "missed the challenge of his former role as a flight surgeon." Though not a pilot, he had survived over a half-dozen crashes and twice had been forced to bail out of aircraft. His military buddies thought him "a little nuts." Married (to wife Jackie), he had known Steve prior to the accident, and considered him a son.

The TV Rudy Wells was educated in Austria, and was responsible for making no less than six bionic people: Steve, Jaime, Barney Miller/Hiller [The Seven Million Dollar Man, played by Monte Markham], Andy Sheffield,

The Bionic Boy [Vince Van Patten], Michael Austin, Steve's *Bionic* son [Tom Schanley in the first *Bionic* reunion movie], and Kate Mason [Sandra Bullock in the second reunion].

Wells' first bionic creation, however, was not Steve, but rather *Max, The Bionic Dog*, who was introduced in the final season of BW. In *Bionic Ever After?*, we learned that Rudy had a contemporary (or partner) named Jason Havilland, who made significant contributions to the early years of bionic research. After a falling out, Havilland launched himself on a downward spiral of booze and depression, culminating with his death in 1994. Havilland's daughter was an OSI agent seeking to avenge her father's misfortunes by "infecting" Steve and Jaime with a computer virus.

In 1976, while researching ways to help paralyzed patients regain use of their lifeless limbs, Rudy stumbled upon a putty-like substance called "adrenalizine," which, if taken internally, allowed mere mortals to mimic bionic strength and speed.

Rudy has survived a myriad of kidnapping attempts (SM's "Dr. Wells is Missing" and 1987's *Return of The Six Million Dollar Man and The Bionic Woman*), while Dr. Michael Marchetti was but one of his many protégés.

Rudy, like Oscar, was presumed to be a bachelor.

Martin E. Brooks, who played the second and better-known Rudy in the later *Bionic* years, also pulled double duty in the same role on opposing TV troupes. As the man responsible for Steve and Jaime's bionic well being, Wells was their next, closest, all-important colleague to Richard Anderson's Oscar Goldman. As mentioned, before Brooks, there were two other actors to play Rudy: the late Martin Balsam gave life to the doctor in the initial *Six* film, while Alan Oppenheimer took over when *Million* went to series. Balsam had only signed on to do the pilot, and was inaccessible to continue in the role for the series.

As Harve Bennett reported, "I would have loved to have had Marty Balsam continue the role of Rudy in the series. But I believe it was a case of simple economics. He was an expensive, well-known actor, who didn't do series-sequels to movies-of-the-week, without receiving a lot of money. Alan came on as a lower-priced alternative. I thought he was very good and wanted to keep him, but it didn't work out."

Prior to his in-step for Balsam, Oppenheimer was doing a play called *Hot L Baltimore* in downtown Los Angeles, at the Music Center. Universal casting director Joe Rich had been assigned to find a replacement for Balsam. He saw *Hot*, and suggested Alan, who then came in and read for Glen Larson, then producer of *The Six Million Dollar Man*. From there, Alan explained, "They offered me the role of Rudy."

The reasons why Oppenheimer left, and was eventually replaced by Martin E. Brooks, are little more perplexing. At the end of *Million*'s second season, Oppenheimer said, "Lindsay Wagner was the guest star who died

ALAN OPPENHEIMER WAS THE SECOND ACTOR TO PLAY DR. RUDY
WELLS, BEGINNING WITH THE SECOND *SM* MOVIE, *WINE, WOMEN AND
WAR*, THROUGH SEASON TWO. ALAN RETURNED TO THE ROLE ONE
LAST TIME FOR SEASON THREE'S "THE BIONIC CRIMINAL."

under my knife."

He then had an offer to co-star in a new CBS comedy called *Big Eddie*, featuring the legendary Sheldon Leonard and Sheree North (the latter later played Michael *Cosmo Kramer* Richards' mother on *Seinfeld*). Oppenheimer contacted Universal, and said, "Look, I don't have a contract with you people, and I have an offer to do another series." According to Rudy's second interpreter, the studio replied casually. "Don't worry about it," they told him. "We'll work around you," which Oppenheimer said, "they had always done before."

Meanwhile, the actor agreed to appear on *Eddie*, for which the first taping was August 24, 1975. He received a call from Universal, who requested his presence as Rudy for the third season debut episode of *The Six Million Dollar Man*.

"I can't do it," he told them. "I've already signed on to do *Big Eddie*."

"Well, then," the studio replied, "We'll have to replace you."

Oppenheimer tried to defend himself by reminding the studio that he had originally given them the option to employ him, exclusively. No matter.

Replacement-actor surgery was scheduled and completed. Brooks was then cast as Steve's *Bionic* doc, while Oppenheimer's courtship with *Big Eddie* turned out little ratings for CBS, and was subsequently canceled. The actor, who has appeared in over 200 commercials, and made a captain's guest shot (with toupee) on *Star Trek: The Next Generation*, takes leaving SM behind with a grain of salt. "So be it," he said. "You just go with the flow."

Don't let Oppenheimer's seemingly blasé remark be misleading. It's mere confidence, garnered over the years following an extensive body of work. He's made more than 200 guest-star and/or regular appearances in episodic television programs like *Life Goes On*, *LA Law*, *Quantum Leap*, *Star Trek: The Next Generation* and *Murphy Brown*. His TV-movie list includes the controversial (and ironically titled) *Strong Medicine* (1979), *The Two Mrs. Grenvilles* (1987), *Helter Skelter* (1976) and *Raid on Entebbe* (1977), among others. Some of his feature films are *Trancers V* (1994) and *IV* (1993), *The NeverEnding Story* (1984), *Private Benjamin* (1980), *Little Big Man* (1970), and *Star!* (1968). He's won the Drama-Logue Award for stage roles in *The Lesson*, *American Dream* and *The Collection*, completed eleven seasons of more than 60 plays at the Arena Stage in Washington, D.C., and is an accomplished voice-over artist (*The Smurfs*, *Ghostbusters*).

Like Alan Oppenheimer, Martin E. Brooks is a veteran actor of every forum.

He's appeared on TV's *Dallas*, *McMillan and Wife*, *General Hospital*, *Cagney & Lacey*, *Jessie* (with Lindsay Wagner), *Quincy*, *Combat*, *The New Perry Mason* (starring Monte Markham), *Night Gallery*, *Playhouse 90*, and more. His feature films include two with Martin Balsam (*The Man* in 1972 and *The Old Man Who Cried Wolf* in 1970). Brooks-on-Broadway roles, include Lt. Col. Chipman in *The Andersonville Trial* (replacing George C. Scott, then touring nationally), among other stage roles.

Years before *Six*, Brooks was replaced by Alan Oppenheimer as a character in Broadway's *I Am a Camera*. "So Marty and I have known each other for a very long time," he said, "and we were amused at the fact that he replaced me in *The Six Million Dollar Man*."

Harve Bennett said Brooks "is an actor of great skill, and has a very similar quality of authority to that of Alan. He was my doubles partner. We used to play tennis together. Alan, too, however, did a wonderful job in the role."

The Oppenheimer/Brooks *Six* switch transpired in a *Bewitched*-double-Darrin kind-of-way. On the classic 1960s *witchcom*, Dick Sargent was substituted for Dick York as Elizabeth Montgomery's mortal husband, with a gradual twitch-of-the-nose. Due to severe back pain, York had not appeared in several Samantha segments. In his last season, the *Bewitched* producers reran these non-Darrin segments, back-to-back. The following September, Sargent's Darrin was introduced when, for the previous four months, there had been no Darrin-presence whatsoever. The transition was almost subtle.

In a second trans-media-medic referral, Oppenheimer outlines the Wells character by comparing him to another cybernetics specialist he portrayed in the 1973 sci-fi theatrical release, *Westworld*, in which the late Yul Brenner played an android of Oppenheimer's creation. "They're very similar," he said of his twin-screen MDs. "They're both very much wrapped-up in these esoteric, exotic scientific developments." With specific regard to Rudy, Alan tried to inject as much "Oppenheimer-eccentricity" as possible to make it interesting, because he "didn't want him to do his job in an overly scientific way."

"I rely on whatever unique qualities I have as a tool for my performances," the actor goes on to say. "When I was young, I used to put on mustaches and funny noses, and speak with different accents. I learned that, over the years, the reasons we get hired as actors is because whatever it is that makes us individual human beings, hopefully, is the thing that makes us appealing as actors."

For example, when he did an NBC television show called *Eischeid* (with Joe Don Baker, in 1980, a spin-off from the 1979 movie, *To Kill a Cop*), his character's name was Captain Finnerty. "I was trying to get a handle on the role," he said, "and *Finnerty* sounded to me like *finicky*. So I played him like an old lady. Very prissy, neat and old-maidish. There's a little of all that in me, too. So I used it."

Whatever Alan brought to Rudy, then, was in him as well (or is that *as Wells?*). That is, Oppenheimer is quite fond of electronic toys and science, in general. "So I fell right into that part of his person," he said. "I didn't mind that at all." As to Rudy's relationship with Steve, Oppenheimer always felt that Wells knew much more than Steve, who would automatically do what Rudy had designed for him to do. "After all," the actor relays, "Rudy was the scientist, and though Steve was the bionic man, he couldn't function without him."

Oppenheimer is known for his comedic talents. According to Richard Anderson, he brought a sense of lightness and fun to the character of Rudy Wells, which may have not been there with Martin Balsam in the pilot. "When Marty Brooks took over the role," he explained, "the character took a different shape, but remained essentially the same." Brooks offered "a more humane, sincere interpretation of Rudy Wells," Anderson said. "He delivered more of a straightforward approach, concentrating on the fact that the character was a scientist."

When Oppenheimer left the role, Brooks was doctored up with a touch of gray, and his locks were thinned to more closely resemble Oppenheimer, who was hairless. It was later decided that Rudy should be more of a contemporary with Steve and Jaime. "So I returned to how I really looked," Brooks said. "I could run around a bit more and be more a part of the action."

Still, before he stepped into Oppenheimer's shoes, there was talk of axing the Rudy role. "Marty," Harve Bennett said, "we're only going to do one more show with Rudy. Are you interested in doing it?" "Sure, I'd be happy to," Brooks replied.

One more Wells segment turned into three more years' worth of episodes as the character, with additional appearances in the three reunion movies. Through it all, Rudy indeed became Steve and Jaime's closest friend, next to Oscar.

Commenting on this Goldman/Wells contrast, Brooks draws upon the perception some made about Oscar's relationship with Jaime. "Rudy didn't really behave any differently with Steve than with Jaime," he observes. "But in a sense, he was their father, because he created them."

As a dad tends to favor a daughter, Brooks adds, "Rudy was somewhat closer to Jaime as a parent than he was to Steve, with whom he reacted in more of like a *buddy-buddy* way" [as Austin did with Goldman].

Brooks pigeonholes the theatrical chemistry between himself, Richard Anderson, Lindsay Wagner and Lee Majors as one of the strong points on the shows. While remaining close friends with Anderson, Brooks periodically bumps into Lindsay and Lee. "We all got along on the set, and that filtered over into their performances on screen, especially with Anderson. That's because Oscar and Rudy were together more than Rudy was with Jaime or Steve. Oscar and Rudy would always talk of how to solve the problem at hand. Rudy would really only see Steve when he would break down, or when he would be in need of repairs, to install another atomic pack, telling him what to do with it or what not to do with it."

MARTIN E. BROOKS IS PROBABLY THE MOST FAMILIAR ACTOR TO PLAY
DR. RUDY WELLS. TAKING OVER THE ROLE IN *SM*'S SEASON-THREE
PREMIERE EPISODE, "THE RETURN OF THE BIONIC WOMAN," MARTIN
WOULD PORTRAY WELLS FOR THE REMAINING THREE SM SEASONS,
ALL THREE *BW* SEASONS, AND THE THREE REUNION MOVIES.

Strangely, even though Brooks and Majors worked together for years, the two did not film many scenes together. "Rudy was mostly seen in a hospital setting," Brooks explained, "while Steve did most of his stuff outside."

Yet there was an interior sequence between the two actors that Brooks said, "played particularly well." In one episode, the actor explained, "Rudy was showing Steve how to handle some technical equipment, and it became difficult to shoot the scene. It all had to be timed properly with the dialogue, and we were having trouble doing that. We did one take, and then another, and another. Well, after about ten takes, Lee is laughing his head off, and everybody is laughing their heads off, because I couldn't get it right. Finally, I do, and we get the take."

Later, the table turned. Majors, as Steve, had to show Brooks, as Rudy, that he knows how to handle the equipment. "I don't know how much of this made it on screen," Brooks reveals. "But after eight, nine or ten takes from him, we're all still laughing our heads off. I'm laughing at Lee, and everyone else is laughing at Lee. He finally gets it right."

The creation of the Rudy Wells character, however, was no laughing matter. *Bionic* scribe Martin Caidin based the character on a legitimate doctor, who remains alive and well in Cocoa Beach, Florida. In fact, the real Rudy had been Caidin's flight surgeon in the Fifth Air Force. "We were over in Japan together," he recalled. "When I was doing the book *Cyborg* [originally titled *Miracle People*], Rudy had done a great deal of experimental medical work himself. We sat down and worked out the medical aspects in excruciating details. The original book had 30,000 words and 130-140 pages of medical detail. The publisher asked me to remove that information from the book because it would have been too heavy for the public."

Caidin reluctantly agreed. "I broke my chops researching that information," he said. "I thought it was marvelous. But we still had to achieve that balance that makes a book sell. And Rudy was involved from the get-go." And he still saw the authentic Wells until the day Caidin passed away. "He's gotta be in his eighties," relayed Caidin. "I don't know if he's taking bionic pills or what, but he's in great shape. He loved being portrayed in the series. Oscar Goldman was based on a real person too, who shall go unnamed."

Brooks had the opportunity to meet the legit Wells, via Caidin. "Martin Caidin introduced us," the actor remembers, "and we had a great conversation. I remember him as a very pleasant, easy-going gentleman. He was a surgeon but, of course, he didn't worry in the same manner that the fictional Rudy Wells did."

FARRAH FAWCETT, THEN FARRAH FAWCETT-MAJORS, APPEARED IN
FOUR *SM* INSTALLMENTS AS THREE DIFFERENT CHARACTERS: "THE
RESCUE OF ATHENA ONE," "THE PEEPING BLONDE," "THE GOLDEN
PHARAOH," AND "NIGHTMARE IN THE SKY."

CHAPTER 7
AUXILIARIES

"CALLAHAN WAS A GAS."

JENNIFER DARLING

Several performers appeared in recurring roles in the *Bionic* universe, including Farrah Fawcett. Then married to Lee Majors, she showed up in four episodes of *The Six Million Dollar Man*. In "Rescue of Athena One" and "Nightmare in the Sky," she played the same character, Kelly Wood, an astronaut, and ex-girlfriend to Steve. In "The Peeping Blonde," she was Victoria Webster, while she showed up as Trish Hollander in "The Golden Pharaoh." The former-*Charlie's Angels* star, whose on again/off again relationship with Ryan O'Neal has spanned 25 years, was classified on SM as a recurring guest star.

Jennifer Darling, on the other hand, may be categorized as a recurring regular, as she portrayed Oscar Goldman's snappy secretary, Peggy Callahan, on many segments of SM and BW.

Darling, who said she's "basically an East Coast person," has appeared on TV shows like *Eight is Enough*, *The New Temperature Rising*, *LA Law*, *Cheers*, and *Hooperman* (the latter for which she received a Best Supporting Actress Emmy nomination). Her many feature films include *Up the Sandbox* (1972). On Broadway, she's played the lead in *How Now, Dow Jones?* and *Maggie Flynn*, while her off-Broadway debut was in the Village Gate for a smash-hit production of *MacBird* (which concerned the Kennedy assassinations and, as she said, "was a satire on Lyndon B. Johnson").

Following several more New York stage appearances, such as *Twelfth Night* (at the New York Shakespeare Festival), Darling, then married, was convinced by her husband to go to Los Angeles after the birth of their daughter. Shortly thereafter, she arrived on *The Six Million Dollar Man* as Callahan.

This secretary to Oscar was a single woman, who became close friends with Jaime, a development of which Lindsay Wagner was very much in favor. "There was a definite chemistry between us," Lindsay confirms. "I wanted Jennifer to be more involved with the show. It was so nice to have a woman around that both Jaime and I could relate to, and work with. We laughed an awful lot together."

"I think both of us enjoyed doing scenes together," adds Darling. "We worked well together. The egos did not get into the way. We were able to push that aside and get into the work. That was important."

Darling recalls one particular street scene, from BW's "Brainwash," in which Jaime suspects Callahan of leaking security secrets to her boyfriend: "Callahan really reamed into Jaime, and said she wasn't some mousy little secretary. We filmed it outside, and I remember people were like cheering and clapping. It was neat, almost like a stage performance, which is where I was trained. It was also neat because we really got into it."

"There was good fun between Jaime and Callahan," said Ken Johnson. "We enjoyed using Jennifer, who I always called Joannie." The producer named the actress so, because Darling's real first name is Joan. When she ventured to Hollywood, Darling had to change her moniker. There had already been an actress called Joan Darling who, ironically, once played opposite Lee Majors on *Owen Marshall, Counselor at Law*. (Today, this other Darling is a director.)

Johnson had also known Jennifer from his years at Carnegie Tech (later renamed Carnegie Mellon), his academic university. She and boyfriend-cum-husband, Paul Litkin, had shared a boarding house with Johnson. "She lived right upstairs from me," recollects Ken, who saw a spark in Jennifer from the minute he met her. "I always loved Joan's talent and abilities and sense of humor," he said, "and I was delighted to be able to get her on the series. I thought she was a wonderfully comedic actress."

When the opportunity arrived to create acting roles for Darling, Ken did just that. "I'm sort of like Bochco in that sense," he said, referring to the first-named Steven producer of *L.A. Law*, and other vintage TV classics.

Meanwhile, Darling's additional classic *Bionic* scenes transpired in the first two installments of SM/BW's "Kill Oscar" trilogy, and in BW's "Fembots in Las Vegas," Parts I and II. In each instance, Callahan was cloned as an evil fembot. "That was absolutely fabulous," Jennifer said of her time as the baneful droid. "It was so much fun to do that." During an interview with a Lindsay Wagner-admirer at the 2001 FanSource Weekend, Jennifer had this to say about filming "Fembots in Las Vegas": "The technical end of it was so interesting. Now what they do is incredible, but then, that was such a big thing to do that with the mask and everything. I had never had a mask made of my face, so that was great. And, it was real physical, and I enjoyed that. It was fun."

When asked if there was any humor on the set that day, Darling replied: "No. I was totally serious. I am fun, but I'm very serious when it comes to work."

Next-in-line for regular *Bionic* appearances is Sam Chew, Jr., who played Mark "Russ" Russell, Oscar's right-hand G-man, and appeared exclusively on BW. Since his *Bionic* days, Chew has had a steady string of work in the entertainment industry, including the portrayal of two top Kennedy family members in TV-films like *The Forgotten Kennedy* (1977, as JFK), and *Tail Gunner Joe* (1977, as Robert Kennedy).

LEFT: JENNIFER DARLING MADE HER DEBUT AS OSCAR GOLDMAN'S SECRETARY CALLAHAN IN *SM*'S SECOND-SEASON EPISODE "STEVE AUSTIN, FUGITIVE." SHE APPEARED PERIODICALLY ON BOTH *SM* AND *BW*, BUT BECAME A MORE PERMANENT FIXTURE DURING *BW*'S FINAL SEASON AS JAIME'S BEST FRIEND. *RIGHT:* SAM CHEW, JR. PLAYED OSCAR'S TRUSTWORTHY ASSISTANT MARK RUSSELL, OR "RUSS," ON *BW*. HE MADE APPEARANCES IN ALL THREE SEASONS, THE ONLY SEMI-REGULAR CAST MEMBER BESIDES FORD RAINEY TO DO SO.

"Someone once described me," he notes, "as the guy who's played every Kennedy but Rose. Who knows? I might get around to playing her one day."

More recently, Chew has voiced national commercials for such farflung corporations as Sony, American Express, AT&T, and General Motors, as well as many educational and military training films, corporate industrials, and multimedia projects. Pepsi, Xerox, Pontiac, Chevy Trucks, and Quaker Oats have also contracted his services at one time or another.

Interestingly, Chew grew up in Philadelphia, and came from a very Old Philadelphia family. His great-great grandfather drafted the Declaration of Independence, and was William Penn's lawyer and the First Chief of the

Supreme Court of Pennsylvania. Furthermore, the family's ancestral home is a landmark known as "Cliveden." So, if anyone was qualified to be playing a government agent on TV, it was Chew, a Temple University graduate who's made hundreds of small-screen appearances, as well as feature films, including 1991's *Oscar*, the latter of which ironically shares a name with Chew's former TV *Bionic* boss.

ACADEMY AWARD-NOMINEE MARTHA SCOTT *(LEFT)* AND VETERAN CHARACTER-ACTOR FORD RAINEY *(RIGHT)* PLAYED STEVE'S MOTHER AND STEPFATHER, AND JAIME'S LEGAL GUARDIAN, HELEN AND JIM ELGIN. THESE RESPECTED AND SEASONED ACTORS ADDED A TOUCH OF CLASS TO THE SHOWS, RARELY FOUND ON GENRE TELEVISION OF THE ERA.

Martha Scott and Ford Rainey portrayed Steve Austin's mother and stepfather, Helen and Jim Elgin, when their son fell back in love with Jaime. Scott, in particular, played Austin's mom in *Man* episodes prior to Jaime's debut (most notably, in SM's "The Coward"), and came to her *Six* engagement via a special invitation by Harve Bennett.

Born on September 22, 1912, in Jamesport, Missouri, Scott was educated at the University of Michigan, and had a strong stage background. Before and after SM and BW, she guested in TV-movies like *The Abduction of St. Anne* (1975) and *The Word* (1978), and on shows such as *Beulah Land* (the landmark mini-series), *Magnum P.I, Hotel, Columbo, Police Woman,* and *Murder, She Wrote* (in an artsy black-and-white sequel episode, employing classic scenes from Scott's earlier films). She first appeared on television in 1950, and subsequent credits from that decade include *Goodyear Playhouse, Kraft Theatre,* and *Matinee Theatre*. Fans of *The Bob Newhart Show* may also remember her recurring role as Bob's somewhat flaky mom, while she was also a regular on the abbreviated 1980-81 series, *The Secrets of Midland Heights*.

SM/BW producer Harve Bennett knew of Scott's talents years ago. As a child, his mother took him on an inaugural trip to New York City, to view his first Broadway production, *Our Town*, by Thornton Wilder, which became and has remained his "favorite play in the English language." This is the *Town* that had starred Scott, whom he would remember years later when the time came to flesh out Steve's family life.

Scott was "honored" that Bennett created the role specifically for her, and that Helen became a recurring role. "It was a joy to work with Lee and Lindsay," she said, and to just to be on the set. "The shows were a delight."

"Sooner or later we would have had to have a mother episode," Bennett comments. "That goes with series franchise linking. But we didn't want to do it without Martha."

The cybernetic kindred connection reaches further, as Ken Johnson's Carnegie Tech college days come into play once more. When he first arrived in Hollywood, Johnson contacted another former Tech-mate of his named Judith McConnell, who has since become a big soap star. While in school, McConnell dated a man named Scotty, who happened to be Martha's son. "So I sort of met him before I met Martha," Johnson reveals.

"By the time we started working together, we were old friends, because I had been very close to her son. She was terrific."

When working with Scott later on BW, Johnson was "in awe" of the fact that he was on the same soundstage with a woman who created the pioneering role of Emily in *Our Town*.

"She had such wonderful stories to tell about their try-outs in New Haven," he recalls, "when they weren't sure if the play was going to work. And how Thornton Wilder was in the back of the theatre, scribbling frantically, handing them pages, saying, *Here try this*. We thought, *Wait a minute. 'Our Town' is carved in stone. You mean, Thornton scrambled like the rest of us?*"

Scott also had great stories to tell about playing a leper in the caves of Italy with William Wyler, while filming the second version of *Ben-Hur* (1959; the first edition was released in 1925). Not to mention that she played the biological mother of Charlton Heston's Moses in Cecil B. DeMille's reinstatement of *The Ten Commandments*, which premiered in 1956 (the initial rendition of which hit theaters in 1923). "She was simply a remarkable, solid actress," Johnson said of Scott, who was more than up to meeting his creative needs.

When writing for Steve's parents, Johnson, as with everything he continues to pen, always found room for humor. He remembers this scene, from early on in SM's first Jaime segment, when Steve arrives home: Martha's Helen character is whipping up something in a bowl, with Steve thinking it's cake batter.

He tastes it, and said, "What is that? It's horrible."

"Wall-paper paste," she replies. "That'll teach you to stick your hand in something when you're not supposed to."

As with "any scene we threw at her," Johnson declares about Scott, "she handled it with ease."

Having Martha Scott also presented a convenient opportunity to later blend her in on a regular BW basis, along with Steve's stepdad, played by Ford Rainey. When *The Bionic Woman* became a series, Ken Johnson made certain to have Jaime move into the carriage house, which rested on the farm property of Steve's parents. This, he explained, "was a real connection that kept the integration of the two shows together, intertwining their lives. It gave Jaime a chance to talk about Steve, without Steve actually being in the show."

Meanwhile, Rainey was making connections of his own mark in the SM/BW world. He, too, had known Martha Scott from those *Our Town* auditions. According to SM producer Lionel Siegel, he's "one of the great character actors of all-time. Ford was always there with exactly what you wanted him to be."

Born in 1908, in Mountain Home, Idaho, Rainey came to Hollywood via repertory theatre (in Seattle), radio and Broadway, with time out for service in the US Coast Guard during World War II. His first film role was as a member of Jimmy Cagney's gang in *White Heat*, made in 1949. His most prestigious role on Broadway was J.B. in Archibald MacLeish's Pulitzer Prize-winning production directed by Elia Kazan. He was often cast in TV, film and various other stage roles as wise and sympathetic counselors, parents, and officials. In 1989, however, he played against type as part of a counterfeiting ring in the TV series *Wiseguy*.

Rainey, who passed away in 2005 at the age of 96, continued to perform in manifold character roles, and enjoyed his *Bionic* parental part. He recalled winning the role without having to read for it, which was something he was periodically called to do.

Once, with fellow-actor, the late Lloyd Bridges. The veteran performer, known mostly for his work on TV's *Sea Hunt*, was somewhat surprised that Rainey had to audition at all, as Bridges said with sublime, "You don't actually *read* for parts, do you?" Rainey imagined that today, however, even Lloyd must be called to audition [as with Bridges' final TV appearance on *Seinfeld* as a senior citizen health nut?). "Now, everyone reads for parts," Ford said. In the days of SM and BW, he would get calls based on previous work, and "just be cast."

And he had fond memories of playing Steve's stepdad. Like Richard Anderson, Rainey had known Lee Majors from previous *good ol' boy* work. Both were cowboys on *The Big Valley*, *The Virginian* and other TV Westerns. "Lee was a courteous fellow to work with then," Ford said, "and during *The*

Six Million Dollar Man."

Same goes for Lindsay Wagner, who Rainey met while rehearsing her first Jaime appearance on SM. "We were on location in Ojai, California," he recalled, "on some tennis court, where Lindsay was trying to learn the game. She was sort of scared to death about it. But that added to her charm. She was so unaffected by Hollywood, and a breath of fresh air. And whenever I see those Ford [car] commercials, I say, *That's the Lindsay I knew.*"

Ford believed his Elgin role interacted differently with Steve, than with Jaime, as did Richard Anderson's Oscar, mostly because he worked more on *The Bionic Woman* than he did on *The Six Million Dollar Man.* "Jim had much more contact with Jaime," Rainey relayed, "than he did with Steve. But Jim was always the same with Helen [Martha Scott]. Even though he wasn't Steve's biological father, he loved him dearly."

Rainey's scenes, specifically on BW, were filmed early in the morning. "Martha and I then had the rest of the day off," he said. "So that was nice. It was nothing but a pleasant experience to work on the show."

Like many of the characters Ford played through the years, either for television or the big screen, the role of Jim Elgin was kind and compassionate. He played many doctors, lawyers, professionals, and several presidents, including four turns as Abraham Lincoln in two different *Hallmark Hall of Fame* productions.

There were also times when the actor would appear in "shady" characters, as on TV's *Perry Mason.* "I was always cast as somebody who was under suspicion," he remembered. "I was the guy who looked like the guy who did it. I don't think I was ever found guilty. I just looked guilty. It usually turned out that I wasn't."

Rainey had missed recent reruns of his *Bionic* appearances, but he did recall viewing a classic segment of *Mason,* one night, while dining out. On the big screen, in this one particular restaurant, he noticed a huge close-up of an actor, and asked himself, *Who the hell is that?* "Quite frankly," he admitted, "I had to wait to the end credits to realize that it was me."

Ford Rainey's and Martha Scott's presence on *Man* and *Woman,* "served a dramatic function," said Arthur Rowe. "You always need contrast. If you're going into an area of relative sophistication, you take them from bucolic farm country from where they live and thrust them upon the spies and the *Mata Hari* types. The supporting characters like Steve's parents were never accidental, but were brought in for some reason. Even though Steve was bionic, he was first, a human being. Thus, he had to have parents. So you give him a Mom and Dad."

With Jaime, Rowe said, "We decided that her biological parents were to die when she was young, and that she would live with Steve's parents, her *adoptive* mother and father. She would then be pulled out of this ideal home environment and thrust into this hostile world of spies and intrigue. When it was all over, she would go back to the farm [belonging to Steve's parents] and milk Elsie, the cow."

Having parental figures on both BW and SM gave the shows "a bookend of normalcy," Rowe explained, with specific regard to Jaime. "When her missions were over, she went home to peace and quiet. You never really want to have your audience feel that his or her hero or heroine is a war-lover, who gets off on action. You're almost always better off if you have characters like Steve and Jaime approach their situation, with a certain amount of reluctance. Getting to know Steve's parents, albeit Jaime's adoptive mother and father, helped us understand and appreciate Steve and Jaime's vulnerability."

It may be pertinent to add here a few other tidbits, regarding *Bionic* lineage:

At the end of the *Our Town* production in which Harve Bennett first noticed Martha Scott, her character, Emily, died and went to heaven (in a touching umbrella scene). In Martin Caidin's *Cyborg* novel, Steve's biological father died in a Chinese prison camp during the Korean War, while his mother died four years before his accident.

The only biographical thread that remained consistent between the novel and the *Six Million* TV series was that Steve Austin was an only child.

The late Christopher Stone, who played Jaime's periodic beau, Chris Williams, on several episodes of BW's final season, was born in Manchester, New Hampshire in 1942. He would initiate a TV acting career in 1965, playing Dr. Bill Horton on the popular NBC daytime serial, *Days of Our Lives*. In 1968, he continued to work steadily on television, beginning with an episode of *The Outcasts*.

After several guest-shots on *Here Come the Brides*, he became a regular on *The Interns* (1970-1971), *Spencer's Pilots* (1976) and *Harper Valley, PTA* (1981). From 1989 to 1991, he co-starred with his wife, Dee Wallace Stone (*Close Encounters of the Third Kind*, 1977) on *The New Lassie*. He also appeared in many TV-movies, cop shows, and sci-fi outings, like *Logan's Run*, *Wonder Woman*, and *Buck Rogers*.

In the *Bionic* world, his Williams character came into Jaime's life when she switched from ABC to NBC, where Steve was not allowed to tread. By the time Stone was introduced as Jaime's new love, Lee Majors and Steve Austin were on ABC, while Jaime and Lindsay were on NBC.

Though ABC allowed appearances by Oscar and Rudy, its rival network wasn't about to permit any ABC series *lead* star to show up on one of their shows. So Steve was refused the cross-over missions he once was assigned with Jaime when she was on his network. Whether or not his appearance was a planned contrivance, Stone held a faint resemblance to Majors, and his Williams character was the next-best-thing to Steve.

"At some point," Lindsay explained, "there has to be some movement, some evolution of a character's life." With Williams, she adds, "it was time for Jaime to come alive as a woman," while switching networks "gave us the opportunity to allow her to have more of a personal life."

Yet the relationship did not last. In 1987's *Return of The Six Million Dollar Man and The Bionic Woman*, Oscar tells Steve that Williams was killed by a sniper's bullet in Budapest. To further complicate matters, it was

LEFT: RICHARD LENZ PLAYED DR. MICHAEL MARCHETTI, RUDY WELLS' ASSISTANT RESPONSIBLE FOR THE CRYOGENIC TECHNIQUE UTILIZED IN RESURRECTING JAIME SOMMERS AFTER HER "DEATH." *RIGHT:* CHRISTOPHER STONE PLAYED CHRIS WILLIAMS, AN OSI AGENT AND JAIME'S LOVE INTEREST, IN *BW*'S FINAL SEASON.

Steve who refused an assignment that could have saved Chris' life. This led to larger resentment from Jaime who, by that time, was extremely confused about her feelings for Steve.

Jaime's misplaced feelings for, and subsequent confusion about, Steve, began of course, when she was brought back to life. A central player in her rehabilitation was in the person of Richard Lenz's Dr. Michael Marchetti, assistant to Dr. Rudy Wells. In the *Six Million* segments, "Return of the Bionic Woman, Parts I and II," Dr. Marchetti falls in love with Jaime when Wells assigns him to monitor her physical and psychological rebirth and, essentially, *steals* Jaime from Steve.

Lenz (who was born in Springfield, Illinois on November 21, 1939) graduated from the University of Michigan with a degree in Theatre Arts and then went on to direct the Jackson Civic Players for two years, making his Broadway debut in 1965 (in a production of *Mating Dance*). His feature films include *The Shootist* (1976) and *Melvin and Howard* (1980). On TV, he's appeared on everything from *Hec Ramsey* to *Baywatch* to *Murder, She Wrote* to *Home Improvement*, on which he portrayed Jill Richardson's boss.

As to how viewers reacted to his *Bionic* character's rivalry with Steve Austin, Lenz said: "I gotta' tell you, I was off at Princeton doing a show at

ACTOR MONTE MARKHAM WAS CYBORG AUTHOR MARTIN CAIDIN'S ORIGINAL CHOICE TO PERSONIFY HIS STEVE AUSTIN. MARKHAM WOULD ULTIMATELY BECOME *BIONIC* AS BARNEY MILLER — A SECOND BIONIC MAN ON *SM*'S "THE SEVEN MILLION DOLLAR MAN," AND LATER "THE BIONIC CRIMINAL" (AS BARNEY *HILLER*).

the McCarter, and I received a bunch of mail sent there having to do with that very subject. A lot of it was angry in its tone. I was stunned. But it was fun. I had a good time. I was crazy about Lindsay. She was lovely. I had done an episode of *Marcus Welby* the year before [the one in which Lindsay also dies, after falling for another guy named Steve, as James Brolin's Dr. Kiley]. So we knew each other."

Unlike the mere human Dr. Marchetti, several of the other semi-regular characters on SM and BW were of the cybernetic, super-powered persuasion. Many times, as with the case of Monte Markham's Barney Miller (a.k.a. Hiller), The Seven Million Dollar Man in two *Six* episodes, they weren't even all that nice.

Markham, a TV vet (*The Second Hundred Years*) would, post-SM, make countless TV guest appearances, including stints on *Melrose Place* and

Baywatch (some of which he also directed). He also starred in the syndicated helicopter action series, *Skycrane*, while owning and managing Perpetual Motion Films (which has produced several A&E's TV shows, like *Biography*, *Masters of War*, and *Air Combat*).

On SM, he was The Seven Million Dollar Man and strong, but not nearly as respected. All four of Barney's limbs were atomic-powered, and that's why he cost more. You would think that would have given him more confidence. Instead, he freaked out, and went too far over the edge, becoming mad with power.

Markham said he was hired to play Barney after he received a *Seven Million Dollar* phone call from Harve Bennett, who was inspired to cast him upon Martin Caidin's recommendation. While Caidin thought Monte "did a fantastic job," the actor himself credits the writers with giving him a good story and character with which to work.

"It was a damn fine script," he said. "Actually, *excellent* is the word. When you usually receive a one-hour script for most television series, they're pretty unwieldy. You know that when you get it, it's going to be rewritten before you show up on the set. You hope, for whatever reason you take the part, that in the *rewrites*, the role won't be cut to pieces. With this script, it was very tight, and everything that I liked about it, remained in. It was extremely well-written."

Markham's Barney character was someone who "didn't want to live," he explained. "He felt no real value to his life. He was self-destructive, but he still had an energy and vitality. The whole point of that script was that you could make your life work, despite the obstacles." It was these aspects of the character that posed a challenge for Markham to play.

"With all the scripts I work with," he reported, "I try to find something of value in them. The old saying is that, *Television is forever*. It will be rerun through eternity. So you want to make damn sure that you're going to be proud of whatever you do; that it's something of value. Otherwise, it's going to haunt you. So never let the camera roll unless you want to see it forever. Make sure you want to do the job, and work your ass off when you do it." That's exactly what Monte feels he accomplished with the first *Seven Million Dollar* episode on *Six*. "It's as memorable as anything that I ever did," he concludes.

Following Monte Markham's more expensive, good bionic man-gone-wicked, was Vince Van Patten, as Andy Sheffield, the cheaper, good-natured-but-flustered Bionic Boy. Andy appeared in a two-hour segment of *The Six Million Dollar Man* that was created as a spin-off pilot. He injured his legs in a landslide (that also killed his father), his bottom limbs were implanted with special bionic chips, and his attitude was *bad*.

Unhappily, so were the ratings. "It's just as well," Martin Caidin commented. "Andy was a pain in the ass. All that kid did was whine. They should have sent him to reform school. I didn't buy the idea at all. The bionic boy was purely puke time. They just stretched the hell out it." To Caidin, the young Mr. Sheffield, was "a big flop," because, unlike *The Six Million Dollar Man*, *The Bionic Boy* was again, "not based in reality."

"You can't cheat your audience," he said. "They know. They have a feeling for these things. If we all knew what the audience wants, we'd all be

VINCE VAN PATTEN (SON OF *EIGHT IS ENOUGH*'S DICK VAN PATTEN) WAS CHOSEN TO PLAY ANDY SHEFFIELD IN THE *SM* EPISODE "THE BIONIC BOY." UNLIKE STEVE AND JAIME, ANDY'S BIONICS WERE NOT REPLACEMENT LIMBS, BUT RATHER IMPLANTS TO CURE THE PARALYSIS IN HIS LEGS.

rich tomorrow. But nobody knows what the public wants, so we kept taking guesses at it." Though Caidin was certain about Andy, who he "did not care for at all."

Vince Van Patten, the *Boy* interpreter, however, is a good guy, with a substantial resume. He's the son of actor Dick Van Patten (*Eight is Enough*) and nephew to actress Joyce Van Patten. Before his stint as The Bionic Boy on an SM episode of the same name, he appeared for one season on CBS' *Apple's Way* (1974-5), a then-modern-day *Waltons* (created by that same family's Earl Hamner). As an adult actor, he was doctor/boyfriend/fiancé/husband/widower to Alexandra Paul's Stephanie on *Baywatch*. Today, he is the co-host and commentator for the weekly *World Poker Tour* television program.

As Andy, he failed to have the same positive effect on the audience that Steve or Jaime influenced. So he was never reconstructed for a series. Though Martin Brooks (the third Dr. Wells) wished he was, partly because he and Van Patten got along very well. "Vince is a tennis player," explained Brooks, "and I was a tennis player. His father and I are old friends."

Brooks said the dad-image that envisioned when his character appeared opposite the Austin/Sommers duo, was also especially apparent with Andy. "From an actor's standpoint," he assessed, "Rudy was a father-figure to Andy, more so than with Steve or Jaime. Mainly because, I think, Andy was more vulnerable."

The Bionic Boy was indeed precarious and, observably, younger than Steve and Jaime. Subsequently, more pre-adult watchers readily identified with him, if a tad too much. The vulnerable Andy led some juvenile viewers to believe themselves to be invulnerable. Or as Richard Anderson reveals, a few "young children started jumping out of trees and imitating him, causing a lot of injuries. So we had to bring the entire idea of a bionic boy to a halt."

Despite the deficiency of Andy Sheffield, those in power still believed the *Bionic* franchise was worth expanding. At least for another cool million. As in Maximillian, The Bionic Dog, a with-it German Shepherd who actually pre-dated Jaime and Steve as the world's first bionic being.

Max's full name numbered how much he cost (Max-*a-million*), and Oscar gave him to Jaime for protection (as if she needed it). He lost his jaw and four legs in a frightful lab fire from which he never fully recovered, emotionally.

That's right. Emotionally. Superman had kryptonite. Max had flames. Or at least, he stayed away from them. Max failed to function anywhere near a fire (biochemically, bionics in general fail to function in extremely cold climates), and he surfaced in a double-hour segment, simply called "The Bionic Dog, Parts I and II," which opened *Woman's* third season (on NBC).

The twin-episode was a pilot for a series, as was another segment, simply called "Max," where the super dog was supplied with a supporting cast of potential regulars, including female scientist Valerie Breuer (played by Neile Adams-McQueen) and her teenage son (Christopher Knight, best known as Peter of *The Brady Bunch*).

Martin E. Brooks remains fond of the Max times. He said Rudy and Jaime had some "excellent chemistry" when the canine segments were produced, and cites one scene when Max lost control. Rudy wanted to put him to sleep, but Jaime fought against that. "He more or less created the dog, who may have become a monster," Brooks said. "Jaime made him really see the error of his ways." The actor is mostly fond of the Max segments because, as with *Bionic Boy* Vince Van Patten, there were personal ties. "I've always had a kind of shepherd dog in my life," he reveals. "I have one now.

MAXIMILLIAN, OR MAX, WAS INTRODUCED IN THE *BW* TWO-PART
SEASON-THREE OPENER, "THE BIONIC DOG," AS RUDY WELLS' FIRST
BIONIC EXPERIMENT. PROBLEMS WITH MAX'S PSYCHOLOGICAL STATE
WERE BLAMED ON HIS BIONICS, SO HE WAS KEPT SECRET FROM JAIME,
IN THE EVENT SHE DEVELOPED SIMILAR PROBLEMS. JAIME RESCUES
MAX FROM EUTHANASIA AND HE QUICKLY BECOMES *BIONIC WOMAN'S*
LOYAL COMPANION.

It's a shepherd-dobie-lab-mix."

Max was a mixture in many ways, too, as eight dogs were actually hired for the part. Brooks explained: "One could jump into fire. One could leap through hoops. One could break down doors. They used different dogs at the same time, but they all looked exactly alike. You would have needed a microscope to tell them apart. But they were all well-trained. And since I liked dogs, it all worked out."

Lindsay said seven of the canines were "stunt Maxes," with many masters, while the original Max, whose real name was Bracken, was of "a different personality," and trained, single-handedly. Bracken was the "actor Max," whom she describes as "amazing," "extraordinary," "magnificent" and "fascinating to work with."

"He was a real-people dog, who was owned by one person," she said. "It was his only dog, who was raised with love. It was like this man's child. He was trained to be a *buddy*, which was quite distinct from how the other dogs were readied [with food conditioning and other standard instructional practices]."

The original hound was used in the first *Bionic Dog* segments. When the subsequent canine BW episodes were produced ("Rodeo," "Escape to Love," "Max," "The Pyramid," "The Antidote," "The Martians are Coming," "Sanctuary Earth," "Deadly Music," "Which One is Jaime?," "Out of Body," "Long Live the King," "Rancho Outcast," "On the Run"), Bracken was replaced with the remaining seven, which proved more challenging for Lindsay.

"With the others," she said, "you kind of had to stand back, and let the trainers do the work. They would be given signals, and they just sort of did what they were supposed to do."

Here's how it worked: A particular sequence would be filmed with a particular stunt dog, who would then be returned to a kennel. Additional filming of the same scene would ensue, with only Lindsay, and she was left to speak her lines to an apple box. The original Max would have stayed put, and performed with Lindsay. "It was like working with a human actor," she said of Bracken. "He could actually act."

After the initial appearance of Max, and after it was decided to keep him as a regular, Lindsay said "there was a big political situation with the people who owned the stunt dog. They needed a dog who could run well, and one they could use for jumping."

"Because as an actor," she continues, "if something should happen, the dog is out of commission. So we got into this situation where we couldn't use that wonder-acting dog anymore." The dog's coordinator presented an ultimatum, saying, "Either use all of my dogs, or none of them." "So it was kind of sad for me," she said, "because the original dog was so easy to work with. The other dogs were nice, but they were so heavily trained with a

PROFESSIONAL WRESTLER ANDRE THE GIANT PORTRAYED THE
LEGENDARY CREATURE BIGFOOT, OR SASQUATCH, ON THE *SM*
TWO-PARTER "THE SECRET OF BIGFOOT." THE CREATURE, A HALF-
ORGANIC/HALF-CYBERNETIC BEING, WAS CONTROLLED BY A GROUP OF
EXPLORERS FROM SPACE TO KEEP HUMANS FROM DISCOVERING THEIR
SECRET BASE WITHIN THE CALIFORNIA MOUNTAINS.

TED CASSIDY (LURCH ON TV'S *THE ADDAMS FAMILY*) WOULD LATER
DON THE FUR FOR THE *SM/BW* TWO-PART CROSSOVER "THE RETURN
OF BIGFOOT." CASSIDY REPRISED THE ROLE ONE LAST TIME FOR THE
SM FINAL-SEASON EPISODE, "BIGFOOT V."

whole different mentality. It's like you couldn't really have any relationship
with them. Otherwise, they wouldn't have listened to their trainer."

According to Martin Caidin, the idea for Max stemmed from the reference to robotic dolphins in his *Cyborg* novel. Like Darwin, the affable
dolphin from TV's sunken *SeaQuest* (later named, *SeaQuest DSV, SeaQuest
2010*), Caidin's dolphins were employed by submariners.

"We've got them in real life," the author professed. "That's why I put
them in the book. But they decided not to use them in the pilot film [for
Six]. They went with the desert locations, instead of the ocean scenes, which
was obviously the better choice."

With Max on BW, the concept of a *Bionic* pet became dry-docked, more
accessible. "The dog was fun," Caidin said. "Those episodes were medically
researched. They were still stretching it, but it was fun. We all laughed at
Max. But at least we were laughing with the idea, and not at it." After Max,
Caidin "wasn't too sure what they were going to do next. *The Bionic Seal?*"

An aquatic-breathing being with bionic strength never swam its way
into one single appearance on *The Six Million Dollar Man* or *The Bionic
Woman*, but many all-too-human fictional personalities, additional atomic
heroes, and super-powered villains made frequent appearances. Pro-wres-
tler-turned-actor Andre the Giant (*The Princess Bride*, 1987), and Ted
Cassidy, better known as the deep-speaking Lurch on TV's *The Addams
Family*, shared the role of the bionic Bigfoot who was alien-programmed to
taunt Steve and Jaime in several SM/BW cross-over segments.

During the 1960s, Cassidy provided voices for Saturday morning TV
fare like *Frankenstein, Jr., The Impossibles, The Fantastic Four* and *The Godzilla
Power Hour*. He narrated the first season of Kenneth Johnson's *The Incredible
Hulk*, and did voice-work for Lou Ferrigno. In the 1970s, he supplied the
vocals for Lurch in the cartoon version of *The Addams Family*. On January
16, 1979, at age 46, he died of complications following open-heart surgery.

Like his Bigfoot successor, Andre the Giant passed away at 46, due to an
apparent heart attack, on January 27, 1993. At 7'4" and 500 pounds, he was
a professional wrestler and actor, born into a farm family in the French Alps,
as Andre Rene Rousimoff.

Andre was afflicted with Acromegaly, a disorder characterized by progressive enlargement of the head, face, hands, feet and chest, and he exploited
his enormous size to become a popular figure on the pro-wrestling circuit
in the US and elsewhere. In his early years, he would work as a furniture
mover during the day, and take wrestling lessons at night.

Though both Andre and Cassidy have passed away, they fortunately have
left their mark in the *Bionic* universe, by bringing unique personalities to
subsequent cybernetic versions of the legendary creature, also known as
Sasquatch and The Yeti.

Andre, for one, "was a real gentle soul," recalled Martin Caidin, who enjoyed watching wrestling years ago. While residing in Queens, New York, he came to know a lot of wrestlers, and appreciated their athletic ability. "I don't care what kind of show was put on," he said, "those guys really presented a tremendous athletic demonstration, which required enormous strength, dedication and great stalwart ability." Caidin also noted how well Andre got along with Lee Majors. "He simply fit into the fun of the series; he was a big, kind person who fit into the fun of the game." On *Six*, Caidin said the Giant was "good with Lee [Majors]," and "such a nice guy." Kenneth Johnson agrees, remembering Andre as a "sweet" man, who only spoke French.

The make-up used to turn this gentle man into a monster was specially designed for Andre's large features. First, a cast was made of Andre's face so a mold could be poured to change the face's basic contours. Second, extra latex molding was applied to the cheek structures. Greasepaint was then applied to this, altering the coloring of Andre's face. Last but not least, crepe hair — a special kind of false hair used to change an image — was added. In all, the make-up job took nearly three hours to apply. This had to be done every morning for all 10 days of shooting, which only added to Rousimoff's discomfort.

"It was a lot of fun doing the show," said Andre, as he relaxed on the SM set in 1976. "I had to do my own stunts. After all, how were they going to find a stand-in who is seven-foot-five inches and weighs over 400 pounds?"

Soon, the Giant's dexterity would be put to the test. "It got a little rough for me at times," he said. "There was this one scene where Steve Austin gets the upper hand and sends me rolling down this huge wooded hill. I rolled and rolled until I finally came to the bottom and almost crashed into the lighting equipment on the set.

"Because of some technical problems, we had to do that scene five times," he concluded. "By the third time, I was ready to murder the guy who kept yelling, 'We'll have to do that scene again!'"

As to why Andre was replaced by Cassidy, Ken said the Giant was out of the country, "and we couldn't afford to bring him back." Lindsay recalls Cassidy as also "very sweet," admitting that he "hated" the Bigfoot costume. "It was hot as heck for him," she said, "and very uncomfortable. But he was a real trooper, and a hard worker, who really hung in there."

Sean Cassidy, Ted's son, said his father "enjoyed the Bigfoot role [if not the costume], and was especially fond of Ms. Wagner."

With either Andre or Cassidy in the role, Bigfoot procured a huge leap in the *Six/Woman* ratings whenever he stepped into the spotlight. In fact, Harve Bennett said that the initial Sasquatch segments on SM sparked such a response, that it spawned several sequels. "Bigfoot became our staple," Bennett recalls. "If you wanted a 45-percent ratings share, pop in Bigfoot."

The foreign planeteers, who surrounded the cybernetic Yeti, also became popular with the viewers. They were variously performed by Sandy Duncan

BOTTOM RIGHT: BEFORE THE FEMBOTS, ROBOTS WERE FEATURED
ON *SM* AS CREATED BY DR. CHESTER DOLENZ (CHARACTER ACTOR
HENRY JONES) IN A TRILOGY OF EPISODES: "DAY OF THE ROBOT,"
"RUN, STEVE, RUN," AND "RETURN OF THE ROBOT MAKER." *TOP:*
IN DAY, MAJ. FRED SLOAN (JOHN SAXON), A GOOD FRIEND OF STEVE
AUSTIN'S, IS REPLACED WITH A ROBOT LOOKALIKE. *BOTTOM LEFT:* IN
RETURN, IT'S OSCAR WHO MEETS HIS DIGITAL DOPPELGANGER.

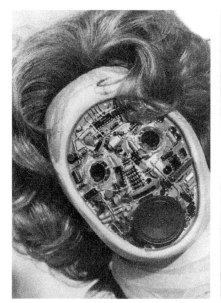

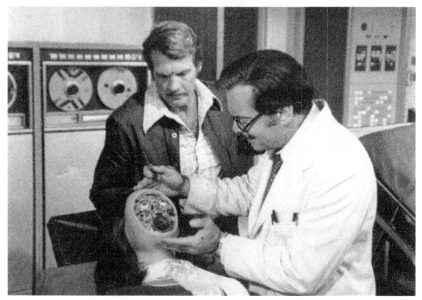

TOP RIGHT: IN THE HUGELY POPULAR THREE-PART BW/SM
CROSSOVER EPISODE, "KILL OSCAR," EX-OSI SCIENTIST DR.
FRANKLIN (ACADEMY AWARD-WINNER JOHN HOUSEMAN) CREATES AN
ARMY OF FEMALE ROBOTS – FEMBOTS – TO INFILTRATE THE OSI IN AN
ELABORATE SCHEME TO KIDNAP OSCAR GOLDMAN AND GAIN CONTROL
OF AN EXPERIMENTAL WEATHER-CONTROL DEVICE.

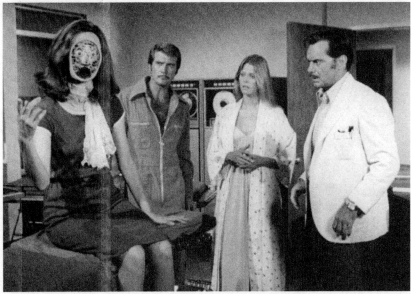

TOP: OSCAR AND CALLAHAN ARE HELD CAPTIVE BY ONE OF DR. FRANKLIN'S FEMBOTS. *BOTTOM:* STEVE, JAIME, AND RUDY LISTEN TO DR. FRANKLIN'S DIABOLICAL PLANS AS RELAYED TO THEM THROUGH A FEMBOT.

THE FEMBOTS RETURN TO MENACE JAIME IN BW'S "FEMBOTS IN
LAS VEGAS," A TWO-PART EPISODE FROM SEASON THREE. WITH
DR. FRANKLIN HAVING DIED IN PRISON, HIS SON, CARL, CARRIES ON
HIS FATHER'S ROBOT LEGACY AND VOWS REVENGE AGAINST JAIME,
OSCAR, AND RUDY.

(*The Hogan Family*), and the almost-*Bionic* woman Stefanie Powers who (along with Sally Field), was once penciled-in to portray Jaime, had Lindsay decided to erase herself out of the picture.

Bigfoot was a puppy dog compared to some of the disgruntled scientists-turned-villains who ran across Steve and Jaime's path through the years. There was the evil Dr. Franklin, played by the late John Houseman, and the menacing Chester Dolenz, interpreted by Henry Jones. A brilliant yet extremely displeased ex-OSI employee, Franklin had a falling out with the super-secret agency, which left him hell-bent on revenge. The OSI had to be made to *pay* for their fatuous gambit with Rudy Wells' bionics as opposed to Franklin's *fembots* (female androids with strength equal to bionics), who were programmed to "Kill Oscar," in the three-part *Six Million/Woman* crossover segment of the same name.

Jones' Dolenz was known to gaze upon *The Six Million Dollar Man* with scientific enchantment, if not admiration. Interestingly enough, Steve Austin had pounded to smithereens two of his creations. John Saxon played an associate of Steve's who was replaced with an evil robotic impersonator in an episode from the first *Six* season called "Day of the Robot." Months later, Steve won a fight to the death with Dolenz's Oscar Goldman lookalike in "Return of the Robot Maker." Though twice attempting to murder The Bionic Man, Dolenz's benign, stately demeanor made it almost impossible for the TV audience to muster a suitable amount of contempt or hatred. Richard Anderson said the Dolenz character was "unlikable, but it was Henry's likable interpretation that won the audience over."

Houseman's Franklin, who evil-cloned Oscar in the "Kill Oscar" trilogy, was "slightly more sinister," Richard adds. "But that added to the fun of it. I enjoyed playing a not-so-nice Oscar, alongside John's mad doctor."

As mentioned, Oscar's secretary, Callahan, was played by Jennifer Darling. Also doubled-for-trouble as a fembot in two episodes of "Kill," Darling relished playing opposite Houseman. "He was a riot to work with," she said. "The consummate professional," is how Marty Brooks describes the actor. "He had a quality about him that was very unique. He didn't talk too much on the set. He kind of kept pretty much to his own world. But he was very, very polite."

Lindsay Wagner's experience with John Houseman may also be categorized as professional, but there was an added bit of jarring flare involved. A few years before acting alongside him in BW, she had appeared as Houseman's daughter in the 1973 feature film, *The Paper Chase*. She remembers a comment the actor made when they first met, which by today's standards, may seem somewhat politically incorrect. It's all because of actor Timothy Bottoms. Two years after co-starring with the very young and inexperienced Cybil Shepherd in *The Last Picture Show* (1971), Bottoms performed with Wagner and Houseman in *Paper*.

One day on the *Paper* set, Bottoms introduced John to Lindsay, as her father, playfully referring to their fictional, big-screen relationship. Afterwards, Houseman looked at her and, as she recalls, "stuck his big, dignified hand out, and said, *My dear, incest overwhelms me.*" "So that," she jokes, "was my introduction to John Houseman. I was all of twenty-three years old. From thereon, we subsequently developed a fine friendship, and I wasn't afraid of him anymore." When Lindsay was later queried about having Houseman guest on *The Bionic Woman*, she thought it would be "great." "To have him on the set was a lot of fun," she remembers, "because I hadn't seen him in three years."

Houseman, however, would not be on the *Bionic* premises for future fembot sequences. By the time BW's "Fembots in Las Vegas" episodes went into production, the actor had been signed to reprise his *Paper Chase* role (Professor Kingsfield) in a CBS-TV version of the film. In the non-John *Bionic* world, the mean-spirited, cybernetic monsters created by Houseman's Franklin were now controlled his son Carl, played by Michael Burns. While Steve and Jaime were cyborgs with heart, these androids continued to be heartless, soulless robots, through and through. "But that's what made it interesting," said *Woman* story editor Arthur Rowe. "Jaime and Steve were confronted with the other side of themselves. What they could be, and thankfully, were not."

Singular SM/BW acting stints were performed by several celebrities. One-time *Six* spots included Olympian Cathy Lee Rigby, a Cher-less Sonny Bono, football great Larry Csonka, and comedian Flip Wilson. On *Woman*, visitors included TV king Andy Griffith, daredevil Evel Knievel, former MGM hoofer Donald O'Connor, ex-Dr. Kildare Lew Ayres, and ghoulish maestro, Vincent Price.

Price, in particular, proved to be quite an enjoyable experience for Lindsay Wagner. When she first heard Vincent's name dropped as a potential guest star, she immediately thought of "doing something *spooky* with him." The result was *price*less, as in the episode, "Black Magic," which, Lindsay recalls as "a real kick." "I really got to know him, which was great, too," she explained. "He was an avid artist, and a fine art collector."

For the Price segment, director Barry Crane set up an intricate shot, which Lindsay and the horror film legend were especially fond of filming. She explained: "It was one close up after another, after another," she reported. "We were in the library scene, where we were trying to figure out the message that Vincent's character was leaving. We'd each walk in and out, as the camera was moving. He would say a line, and then we'd wait to see how one character would react, and this would happen time and time again with each character. Ordinarily, we'd be in such a rush to film. Very rarely would the directors have any time to really do anything clever with the camera. But taking the time to set those scenes up that night was fun for everyone. It was very difficult, because if one person messed up a line, then we would have to do the whole thing over."

Harve Bennett had previously cast Price in an episode of *The Mod Squad*, and said the macabre-king was self-effacing with regards to his screen persona, and he enjoyed working with him. "He was a larger-than-life-actor, and a neat guy," Bennett concludes.

The Vincent Price episode of *The Mod Squad* more than likely originally played at 8:00 PM, on a Thursday night, when this early-version of *Jump Street* was a weekly late 1960s/early 1970s hit for ABC. Opposite *Squad* on NBC was a popular variety show starring comedian Flip Wilson, who went on to guest in the *Six* episode, "Double Trouble." Here, too, Wilson was telling jokes, but this time, it was no laughing matter: his character's head was implanted with a mind-controlling device.

Needless to say, this was the performer's dramatic debut, a milestone that did not detour his amiability off-stage. Lee Majors remembers Flip as an "absolute delight to work with. He had us all in stitches, constantly. The most hysterical thing I remember about working with him, was seeing him sitting there, on the set, between takes, with his legs wide-open, smoking a cigar. He was too much off the wall. He joked around when it was necessary to joke around, but he was dedicated to his part."

That part included a stand-up set of quips set to be delivered by Flip's comedian character, Billy Parker. Because Wilson had been known for his gender-bending, over-the-top interpretation of the wild Geraldine character on his variety show, he was not allowed to employ his own stand-up jokes for the segment. Lee Majors said ABC "wanted to make sure that we didn't do something too risqué." The network insisted on script-approval, and "Double Trouble's" writer, Jerry Devine, ended up penning Wilson's on-stage, in-character gibes.

Flip Wilson's off-stage antics were not the only guest-*jest*ures performed behind the bionic camera. In the very last shot of the BW episode "Once a Thief," which was the final scene of the season, visiting thespian Elisha Cook involved himself in an ongoing water-gag saga, portraying Lindsay Wagner as the victim. As the actress remembers, "Everyone was trying to set up the last shot, which was on me. But they really couldn't do it the way the storyboard was constructed."

Cook's shot, however, was positioned and, according to Wagner, someone on the crew said to him, "Well, you know, we just found out that there was something wrong with the camera, and we need to do your close-up. Come on, just one more shot, and we'll be out of here for the season."

After Elisha said his line, the dolly grip walked up to him, looked right into the shot, handed Lindsay a present, uttered a lengthy speech, and said things like, "I've been in this business a long time. I've never worked with anyone like you."

"He went on and on," Lindsay recalls, and then ended his quaint speech by handing her a gift, and saying, "This is just a little something from the crew." She sentimentally replied with an "Awe" and "really reacted," she said. "I figured they legitimately wanted me to have this present, and they wanted my response to it on film."

Lindsay opened the gift and, as she remembers, "inside there was this teeny, tiny squirt gun, wrapped with fifty-seven-million pieces of tape on it, so I could not possibly have unraveled it." Resting next to the itsy-bitsy gun, was a note that read, "Defend yourself." She certainly responded to that. With a down laden "Oh, no," she looked up, and everyone around her was armed with squirt guns, hoses and buckets of water. "They completely bombarded me," she recalls. "They wiped me out. People were slipping on the floor. It was just a huge free-for-all."

The levity experienced on the SM/BW attracted many guest stars. Lee Majors and Lindsay Wagner possessed welcoming personalities. Their shows were the most popular on the air at the time, and certain actors were prodded to do guest shots by their excitable offspring. According to Richard Anderson, "Everyone wanted to do the shows."

While ABC benefited from the additional attention, via highbrow guest stars, it also became fiscally feasible.

"The money was there in those days to hire whoever we wanted," said Lee Majors. "Today, you don't see too much of that. Big-name-guest stars are expensive. The budgets on contemporary action shows can barely be met, let alone be expanded to meet a guest-actor's salary."

As Lindsay sees it, the visitor performance philosophy on BW was this: "If we featured a guest star that might not necessarily appear on television, they would bring in an entirely new audience and increase the show's ratings. Someone who would have watched another show that night, may have instead tuned in to *The Bionic Woman* because of the featured guest. Mainly, it was a publicity ploy."

Of all the semi-regular or one-shot guest stars who appeared on *The Six Million Dollar Man* and/or *The Bionic Woman*, no behind-the-scenes experience is more memorable than that of what transpired with actress Sharon Farrell.

In a *Six* episode from the second season, "Stranger in Broken Fork," Farrell played a sympathetic therapist who aids Steve when he comes down with a case of amnesia due to bionic malfunction in his right arm. This episode was somewhat eerie for Farrell to play in, as this back story on the actress sustains: In August of 1970, she was in the latter stages of pregnancy when stitches from an old appendicitis operation ruptured, releasing a blood clot into her system which collapsed her lung and stopped her heart for four minutes. Besides inducing a premature birth, the lack of oxygen also rendered her a complete amnesiac. She was unaware of her fate when a fan approached her in the hospital seeking an autograph. She instinctively reached out for the pen, but discovered that she could not write, nor read for that matter.

With fierce determination, Sharon committed herself to reacquiring the life skills that most of us take for granted. Her acting career, for the moment, was on hold. But with the help of actor Steve McQueen, with whom she did a film in 1969, actress Joan Hackett and, inadvertently, Lee Majors, Farrell painstakingly reestablished a foothold in the industry. McQueen, who helped with "basic" things like hitting your mark and line memorization, even taught her how to drive again.

The rugged actor cautioned her never to reveal the fact that she had lost her memory, for that could possibly scuttle her career (a promise she kept until a few years ago on the TV talk show, *Vicki!*, when she shared her story with the general public for the first time).

Farrell did not, however, request the role in SM because of her own life experience. "*The Six Million Dollar Man*," she explained, "was my son's [who was about five] favorite program at the time. So I called one of the producers for a part and got this one out of the blue. Originally, Farrah Fawcett was slated to play this role, but decided to do a [*Cosmopolitan* magazine] cover-shoot instead. The odd thing is that I had just finished doing a *Cosmo* spread myself. Lee asked me if I was paid [well] for *Cosmo*."

Sharon said no.

"Well," Lee replied, "that'll change with Farrah."

"Lee was just wonderful," Farrell recalls, glowingly. "He was very sweet. Nice. He would take the time to explain things when I was struggling, but of course he didn't know *why* I was struggling. He also took time to play around with my son, Chance. At the time, Chance needed a strong male role model, seeing that my husband had left me. Later, when we moved to New York, Chance received a fair amount of schoolyard abuse from other kids who didn't believe that he had met The Six Million Dollar Man." Then, a few years ago, after Sharon's story became public knowledge, she happened to bump into Majors at a party. He sympathized with what she must have been going through, adding, "Don't feel as if you were lying to me [on the set]. I understand."

Today, Farrell has recently concluded a long stint on the CBS daytime soap, *The Young and the Restless*, and looks forward to a lifetime of brand *new* memories.

Bionic inspiration strikes again.

CHAPTER 8

WIRED

"GETTING THE SPECIAL EFFECTS TO WORK RIGHT WAS A CHALLENGE FOR BOTH SHOWS."

PHIL BONDELLI, DIRECTOR.

One reason why the original 90-minute movies of *The Six Million Dollar Man* were perceived as James Bond in nature, was due to the cinematic-looking backdrops crafted by the special effects artisans. Expansive matte/background shots for the longer segments were designed by Albert Whitlock, whom initial SM producer Glen Larson describes as Universal's "matte genius at the time."

The Russian and American missile miniatures constructed for segments like *Wine, Women and War,* and the caves in which they were placed, Larson said, "were pretty spectacular. Today, it's easy with CGI [computer graphic images], but back then it was an arm and a leg."

Conversely, as Ken Johnson has said, a sci-fi/fantasy show's special effects must not override the central storyline or characters. While the F/X on the weekly editions of *The Six Million Dollar Man* and then, *The Bionic Woman,* were an intricate part of each program's charm, there was no chance the backstage wizardry would outshine the plot or characterizations. The acting, writing, directing and producing talents were top-notch. When it came to producing slight-of-hand handiwork, set pieces, props, and wardrobes, there was also a lack of funds.

Six cost approximately $500,000 an episode and, later, *The Bionic Woman's* expenditures totaled approximately $600,000 a segment. "That may sound like a lot of money," Johnson relays, "until you take into account all the various expenses that we had. There was just never enough for [acting] extras or set construction. We were doing very complicated special effects, which were hard to do with the kind of money we were given."

"The shows were incredibly low-budget," continues Johnson, who remembers walking the backlot at Universal, looking for a standing set, "one that we could write into a scene, so we wouldn't have to build a new set, because we didn't have any money." For example, the interior set of the carriage house utilized as Jaime's home (on the farmland belonging to Steve's parents) was on the studio lot.

The more expansive exterior shots used were actual on-location buildings, such as with Oscar's office and OSI Headquarters, which was really the Russell Senate Office Building in Washington, D.C. The Russell facility began construction in 1906 and was completed in 1909. Prior to the early 1970s, it was simply referred to as the Old Senate Office Building, but on October 11, 1972, it was renamed after the late Senator Richard B. Russell (D-GA), who served from 1933 to 1971, and was a member of the Warren Commission's investigation into the death of President Kennedy. Oscar's second-floor window that the camera frequently panned to is located at the southwest end of the building at the corner of Constitution and Delaware. Today, that suite (which, in reality, is very cramped) is occupied by the Senate Committee on Foreign Relations, with the address SR-325C next to its door.

Despite the crude funding, *Six/Woman* opening credits, special effects, and general behind-the-scene schematics were constructed with skill. Some applications and alterations through the years were subtle. Others were not. One of the more noticeable modifications: the several changes made to the opening credit sequence for each of the three seasons of *The Bionic Woman*.

Each year, the music changed, the timing shifted. Even the scenes themselves, switched. There was no stationary opening for the entire run of the *Woman* show, while there was at least a second alteration for the closing credits (if not more for both).

It was quite different with *The Six Million Dollar Man*. Like BW, SM had approximately three distinct versions of its opening (while the closing never changed). Such variations took place over a five-year period, and were somewhat subtler than BW's opening alterations. Beginning with the 1976-1977 season, Martin Brooks made his way into the opening credits— a refection of his character's growing gravitas. More profoundly, as noted in Chapter 1, *Six's* preamble showcased the astounding real-life accident of an aircraft in trouble.

Six's opening credits sequence is instantly recognizable in look, tenor, and sound, and is so memorable that it's been parodied to death (see Chapter 3). The man responsible for the classic montage is Jack Cole, who was working as a freelance film designer in the early 1970s and devotes his time to television advertising today. Besides SM and BW, his other title sequences include *Kolchak: The Night Stalker*, *Planet of the Apes*, and *The Rockford Files* (an equally fantastic intro of its own).

In December of 1973, Cole was contacted by Universal's Frank Price, who in turn introduced the young man to Harve Bennett. Universal needed something eye-popping, and they needed it fast.

"I had a month to six weeks to complete it before its debut in January of 1974," Cole said. "They [Universal] wanted me to literally create and capsulize the story. *How do I make a two-minute movie about what happened to this guy? What are bionics all about?* I needed to capture and blend the reality of the accident with the excitement of bionics that followed."

As a filmmaker, Cole has a very simple philosophy: hook the viewers early and never let go. "I've always believed that it's imperative to seize the audience's attention within the first 20 seconds," he said. "With *Six*, we did this with seven or eight layered items to create the proper tension, such as a heartbeat monitor, warning sirens, rapidly changing altimeter readouts at the bottom of the screen to connote a loss of control, the red clockwise radar scanner, rhythmic drums, static lines, etc. All of this was designed to impart a clear sense of fear and trepidation. Oliver Nelson, who composed the familiar theme music, was then shown rough cuts of the intro and adjusted his sounds until there was a tight harmony between music and action."

A "new and improved" title sequence debuted at the beginning of the 1974-75 season. In addition to expanded dialogue from narrator Richard Anderson, fans were treated to anatomical limbs in grid-map form, with technical jargon posted opposite them (i.e., *Zoom ratio: 20.2 to 1*). This was Cole's playful imagination at work.

"These were the days before computer animation," he said, "so we created the catalog part printouts using overlapping film cells. I worked with a guy who was one of the first major computer nerds, and we created words [*upper arm assembly, feedback terminated, etc.*] as if they came from a surplus computer catalog. For the wire-frame man, we took a three-dimensional invisible model, spray-painted him white, applied graph paper, and used a still-frame camera to do stop-motion for the turns and different views of the computer-like image."

While most of the real-life images were clearly lifted from the *Six* pilot and subsequent movies, producers felt that some new footage needed to be incorporated.

"Actually, I was one of the first designers in television to shoot new, original footage for a credit sequence," Cole said. "For *Six*, it was the operating room scenes. The leg that was used came from Universal's prop house and was first seen in the 1971 Clint Eastwood Civil War pic, *The Beguiled*. We took the leg, cut a big window hole in it and inserted some circuit boards for a realistic effect. In the scene where Steve's bionic arm is being passed from one doctor to the next, that's actually me passing the arm to an extra."

Cole was also responsible for Majors' legendary "She's breaking up!" line.

"In fact, in the interests of authenticity, we had Lee come to a looping room at Universal and record the line wearing an actual pilot's helmet, complete with oxygen facemask and speaking into an actual pilot's mouthpiece that was hooked up to a miking system. The flight tower voice that you hear is authentic. We simply worked around it and inserted our own original dialogue so that it would fit and make sense."

Roughly two years later, Cole was asked to repeat his magic for a *Bionic Woman* intro.

"Harve [Bennett] called me regarding BW and said 'let's move ahead.' Ken Johnson and I reviewed stuff and screened material until he gave his final approval. Johnson was a little less involved/interested in aesthetics than Bennett was, however. The same kinds of techniques were employed, but it was not as imaginative as *Six*. Producers were simply looking to capitalize on *Six's* popularity as quickly as possible, and didn't want to stray from a winning formula."

Money, too, was a factor.

"*Six's* title sequence was produced for roughly $50,000, while BW was slightly less because there was less production value involved," he recalls. "Plus, producers didn't know if they had the same kind of hit on their hands that they had with *Six*, so they played things close to the vest cost-wise."

It's hard not to notice a stark contrast between SM and BW in terms of mood and setting. SM is mostly grim, pulse-racing, and all action, whereas BW starts out somber but is quickly replaced by images of smiling, laughing people, attentive schoolchildren and light music. All of which was quite intentional.

"We wanted to separate it from *Six's* stark masculinity," Cole said.

Today, sports broadcasters are constantly referring to modern athletes who are "bigger, stronger, and faster" than their predecessors. Is this some coy or subconscious homage to Cole's "better, stronger, faster" phrase?

"It would be very presumptuous of me to say 'yes' to that," he said. "I couldn't say for sure. What I do believe about that line is that it was the 1970s version of Superman's 'leap tall buildings in a single bound' line. Certain phrases become part of Americana as they are rhythmically strung together."

As for that *Six Million Dollar CAN* spoof?

"I thought it was cute," he said. "I wish they had called me to do it, because that's my specialty these days, but what the heck. Any parody can and should be considered a great compliment. In fact, the *Six Mill* credit sequence continues to be very popular with young filmmakers. In the late 1970s, Queens College in New York devoted an entire film course to this title sequence alone, which was quite an honor."

Though the initial moving stills of Steve's accident were taken from real life, and the *Bionic* shows themselves were based on certain realities, Martin Caidin admitted the obvious: "Even though the weekly series got within 90 percent of what I felt was the perfect kind of show, there were certain things that we did on the shows that we know are not possible. Obviously, a man cannot run 60 miles an hour without leaning into his own path of run because of the center of gravity. We all understood that. This was made to entertain."

From time to time, Austin would periodically pick up a car with his one bionic arm. "Leverage is a real hard physical thing to accomplish," Caidin went on to say. "They had to take certain liberties in the video presentation, without showing how Steve would counterbrace himself. It's like trying to turn a wrench when you are in zero-G. You'll turn it hard on the wrench to move a bolt, the bolt won't move, and you'll spin around. Because you need leverage."

To some extent, Caidin decided that the same principles could be applied to working with bionics on both SM and BW. Unequivocal creative freedoms were chosen, but the novelist/pilot pointed out that such decisions "were acceptable." "To do otherwise," he revealed, "would have just complicated the script, and compromised the logic-within-the-science-fiction-logic," on which both *Bionic* shows were based. "We allowed the super-strength to be followed through that way."

Part of this superior power involved Steve and Jaime's swift cybernetic jogs. Lindsay admitted to not being very athletic when she first started playing Jaime, but it somehow never showed. Her flowing hair and charismatic pace while in bionic speed seemed perfectly believable.

What contributed mostly to the reality of Lee's stoic Steve Austin rendition was the actor's sturdy history as a top football player, track star and all-around exceptional athlete. "We didn't have to teach him anything about athletics," Caidin said of Majors. "He knew better than anyone else, what to do when you have to run like hell. He knew that you have to lean into what you're doing; how you better handle inertia whether or not you've heard of Isaac Newton." For the *Six* pilot, and several episodes of the series, Majors found himself running in sediment in the desert. "He ran better in sand than any man I've ever seen in my life," Caidin assessed. "He was wonderful."

"They were very true to the book," Lee recalls. "All I can remember about that is going down to the desert in Yuma, Arizona, and running across those sand dunes. I didn't know the United States had sand dunes that looked like the Sahara Desert, but they do and they're huge! They had me run over there, and up here, and I'm running like crazy, it's hot and I'm thinking, *'What am I in for here?'* I had to do take after take." In the desert, Austin is soon captured and imprisoned. "Then I have to get out of a cell, and I do a drop kick," Lee said. "I did that drop kick and the guy didn't take the pins out of the door. It was a steel door, and I went *wham!* and fell to the floor. It went all up my spine. I felt like I was going to kill that special effects guy! I ran at that door and hit it hard! The crew got a good laugh. But things like that were happening all the time."

"Lee was in fantastic shape," agrees SM/BW director Phil Bondelli. "Like Lindsay, he would do most of his own running sequences. He knew that we would slow it down for the air, and that every little facial movement or grunt would be magnified. But he had it down to a science." Bondelli remembers one episode in which Lee was filmed chasing an automobile that was moving at slow-for-autos-but-fast-for-humans-speed: "We were cruising along, at 20 miles an hour, and Lee said, *Go faster*. We hit 30 miles an hour, and he said, *That's it. Hold it right there*." He said Majors "strained to catch up with that car. He knew that if it was going too slow, that he couldn't show the effort of him running." Once Majors reached the auto, "He wanted his stride to show," Bondelli determines, "and it did."

And boy did Majors run. "*The Six Million Dollar Man* may have been in slow motion, but I was running my butt off!" asserts Lee. "I can't remember in the original movie how they did the speed. I think what happened was they speeded it up and it looked too funny. It was like the Keystone Kop movies. They may have cut it, because they were embarrassed to show that running. Then they slowed it down, and it became dramatic. You could see the power in the run. And you really had to run full speed to get your face contorting."

Harve Bennett attributes Steve and Jaime's famous slow-motion effect to the astute F/X department at Universal Studios. He said the tricks first looked "nonsensical" when filmed at regular speed (for the monthly initial movie editions of *Six*). It was then decided to divert the viewer from Steve's business by shooting most of the bionic scenes in unhurried action. These "distracting" scenes worked well with the thematic music (composed by conductor Oliver Nelson), as the "slow-mo" technique became the rule on both *Six* and *BW*, rather than the exception. It had to do with maintaining the essence of that bionic buzzword, *reality,* which, according to Bennett, "is a perception."

"What you think is real," he said, "*is* real. Technically, if a human being really ran as fast as Steve and Jaime were calculated to run [60 MPH], they would be viewed as a blur. Their feet would move so fast, that it would be highly comical." The obvious way to present this effect on-screen would have been to speed up the film. From the home viewer's vantage point, however, that would have looked like clips from a silent movie, in which actors would have been perceived in fast motion, for comic relief.

The slow-motion-for-running-rapid approach was "always the biggest problem that people had when watching the shows," admits Ken Johnson, who "had a problem with it, too." He remembers watching *Six* prior to his involvement with it and thinking, "This is awkward." The only other option was to show Steve running very fast, and "that would not have looked right," Johnson said, "although we used it a couple of times when we were trying to deal cards or something like that."

While the film may have slowed down, Majors did not. "Anytime I was running, I was running as hard as I could run," Lee said. "For example, I remember many times I'd be running on an airport runway, and the focus man would get spots every 10 yards, you know, and of course when I got to the finish he'd say, *'Sorry, I missed one. Go back and do it again.'* After three or four takes, you start looking at the focus man very seriously as if to say *'If you miss it this time...'*"

The "swift" achievement was showcased in many SM's: *Wine, Women and War* (at the beginning, on a treadmill, and near the end, carrying Britt Ekland away from the nuclear blast), "Little Orphan Airplane" (when Steve transports an injured Greg Morris in a wheelbarrow, and later runs with the engine of a plane he's rebuilding), "Eyewitness to Murder" (as he leaves a park), "One of Our Running Backs is Missing" (with Steve running fast on some back roads), "Deadly Countdown" (on the treadmill again), "Nuclear Alert" (running behind a cornfield), and in the pilot, the same footage for which was used in "Burning Bright" and "The Pal-Mir Escort." Steve also exhibited some high-speed running in 1994's *Bionic Ever After?* reunion (chasing Farrah Forke's truck).

We seldom saw Jaime running fast on *Six* or her own series, save for "Deadly Ringer, Part I" and "The Bionic Dog, Part I" (both on a treadmill), but she did play a quick hand of chalk on her school room chalkboard in "Welcome Home, Jaime, Part I," in which she also cleaned her house, speedily, as she did with a convent floor in "Sister Jaime."

Harve Bennett does point out, though, that one of most intriguing parts of the 90-minute *Six* pilot, was that Steve was *rarely* shown running. "They had one marvelous shot," he said, "which took a long time to rig. It was a moving-shot of Steve, running by a [white strobe] fence." In actuality, he was moving at natural speed, and the film was simply sped up.

A different process was taken with "Nuclear Alert." Here, those in charge went to the trouble of placing a treadmill on the back of a flat-bed truck, which was traveling at sixty miles per hour, behind a cornfield, creating the illusion of super-speed. "It was very clever work by Dick Irving," said Bennett of one of *Six's* F/X mavens. "It displayed his relative speed, and the object he was passing. It took hours to shoot, for a run-by. Every once in a while, they would add something like that."

With the first *Six* 90-minute movies, Bennett said there was a special shooting schedule. At the time, Universal filmed the weekly versions in six days, when the rest of the industry was shooting in seven. "It was all the more challenging to complete those 60-minute episodes," Bennett said. And while SM adhered to its schedule (and was never more than one percent over budget), it was a different story for BW. "We sometimes had to shoot eight days," Bennett recalls, "partly because Lindsay had a little bit of bad luck. Her automobile accident made the show less budget-controllable."

LEE MAJORS PERFORMED MANY OF HIS OWN STUNTS FOR SM. TOP:
A BURIED TRAMPOLINE — USED TO GIVE LEE A *BIONIC* BOOST — IS
VISIBLE IN THIS BEHIND-THE-SCENES SHOT FROM "ONE OF OUR
RUNNING BACKS IS MISSING." *BOTTOM LEFT:* LEE IS SEEN JUMPING
FROM AN OFF-CAMERA LADDER TO SIMULATE A *BIONIC* LEAP.

As referenced earlier, budget concerns were never far from Ken Johnson's mind. "When I started producing *The Six Million Dollar Man*, with a $500,000-per-episode budget, I said, 'Wow!'" But as he soon discovered, TV money doesn't stretch too far. "In many ways, doing the bionic shows was like doing the old movie serials," he continues. "We had very little time. When we did *The Bionic Woman*, it was the first series to get seven days per episode. There was a lot of to-do from the *Six* crew about that: 'Hey, how come *The Bionic Woman* gets seven days?' I said, 'Because Lindsay's make-up takes longer than Lee's, for starters.'"

The weekly exploits of Steve Austin and Jaime Sommers featured them kicking in steel doors, jumping over electrified fences, and effortlessly moving massive boulders. "We could have gone into a more science fiction direction and thereby produced some very theatrical pieces," said Lionel Siegel, "but the cost was prohibitive. The time and expense necessary to build a robot, for instance, made that impractical."

Budget or no budget, the on-screen technicality philosophy employed specifically on *Six* changed when the show became a weekly hour series. Bennett had always been a great fan of NFL Films. Not just the game, but of the Sabol Company that immortalized Super Bowls and made millions of dollars by combining the very slow motion of powerful running with exhilarating music. That helped to create a style, which was just beginning to be explored on television (initiated by *Kung Fu*). If seeking out speed and power, Bennett today suggests viewing films of the NFL. "They're awesome," he said. "You put it on a *telephoto lens*, you play stirring music, and you make a man look like a locomotive going 60-miles an hours." A dramatic- and poetically-effective technique which, when applied to SM, was apparently an approach that pre-existed in the minds of the audience.

"I was simply tapping into something that other people had established as reality," Bennett assessed. "Here was a generation of Americans who were used to seeing Jim Brown, running like a locomotive, then saying, *God, is he fast and powerful*. One of the reasons we did 'One of Our Running Backs is Missing' [a football-premised *SM* episode with Larry Csonka], is that we were getting such a kick out of doing NFL Films with Steve Austin."

The slow-motion technique, then, allowed the *Bionic* production team to crank the camera three times faster, therefore producing three times more film than what was shot, normally. To present Steve Austin running for 30 seconds meant the series would have had one minute and 30 seconds of film with which to work. Each time Steve ran, that was a three-for-one sequence, as far as the show was concerned. Attempting to fill what Bennett and company once thought was 52 minutes of program, is now 43, mainly because the number of advertisers and promotions has eroded the program time content to be 43-46 minutes, depending upon the network.

In 1993, the playing time for Bennett's *Time Trax* series in first-run syndication was 42 minutes. "The rest was all sold-advertising and employed for news breaks," he said. "When you're trying to fill 52 minutes of action, you reach a point where you ask yourself, *Will we make it to the air this week?* When we did *Six Mill*, it was a great blessing to have two or three running sequences, which we could count on for six to seven minutes of air time, and not just three minutes. We didn't intentionally insert a lot of running sequences, but it was a gift."

Despite the slow-mo effects, scheduled filming for SM and BW was set at a hectic pace and, as Bennett explained, "Things went wrong, people got hurt, and certain things probably didn't need to happen. But at the time, Universal Studios was such a factory, with several different projects in production, simultaneously, that problems were sure to arise."

Specific mishaps were sometimes comical, as with a helicopter scene filmed at the Maxim Hotel in Las Vegas for one of BW's "Fembots in Las Vegas" segments. Here, Jaime jumps and grabs the aircraft's skid. The copter was piloted by a friend of hers, who was helping her escape from an advancing army of fembots, hot on her tail. Seemingly safe enough for a *Bionic Woman*, but another matter entirely for Lindsay Wagner, who had been shooting all day on the rooftop — which was approximately forty-five stories high.

"We were there so long that we almost forgot that we were up that high," she said. "They had completed the scene with my stunt double, who was very well secured, with belts around her, all kinds of safety devices."

As the sun declined, a close-up was needed of Lindsay, jumping up on the skid, and holding on. An airbag was positioned, and she was to be lifted approximately four feet off the airbag. Theoretically, the helicopter was going to remain stationary over the airbag.

So much for planning. When one of the special effects men yelled, "Go," Lindsay was to "just drop." But first she wondered with a yelp, "Well, what about the safety belts?" "We don't have time," she heard. "We're going to take you only four feet above in the air, anyway. You've done jumps down before that were higher than that. We just need you up off the ground a little bit so we can give that kind of shot."

Against her better judgment, Lindsay did what she was told. By this time, however, the helicopter had not been in service for hours. "The winds in Las Vegas come on very strong in the afternoon," she reveals, with a chill still in the air. "Because of the equipment we had around us, we didn't notice it that much. When the helicopter began to fly up, it struggled to stay over the airbag."

Not only did the copter find it challenging to remain hovered over the airbag, it was climbing to approximately fifteen to twenty feet in the air.

"The higher you jump onto the airbag," she explained, "the more critical your ability to control your body becomes. Your body should be positioned for the impact. That's why people are well trained to do those things. You can't just land in any old position because it's a big old balloon that you're landing on, and assume that you're going to be okay." From Lindsay's perspective, the airbag "started to look like a postage stamp" as it moved from right to left beneath her feet.

Meanwhile, the helicopter was trying to center over it. At one point, it started heading for the center of the building, and she became so frightened that her hands froze on the skid. She thought, "Oh, great. There's going to be this close-up of my face in total fear." They started yelling for her to let go, but she couldn't. "My hands wouldn't," she said.

Eventually, she did, and managed to land on one mere corner of the airbag. She rolled onto the ground, just enough to break her impact, and began to stand, almost fainting. She moved somewhat slower, and heard everyone begin to chuckle. "Gee," she thought, "that's pretty cold." With her mother by chance on the set that day, Lindsay looked at her and said, "Get me out of here." The maternal Wagner (a.k.a. Marilyn Ball) positioned her daughter in a stairwell close by. "We closed the door," Lindsay recalls, "and I burst out crying, if only to release the fear of what just happened. Finally, I asked my mom what everyone was laughing at."

"You have to admit it," Mrs. Ball replied, "what you did was pretty funny."

Lindsay was confused. "What are you talking about?" she wondered. "What was so funny about what just happened?"

"Well, when you were on your way down," Mrs. Ball responded, "you held your nose like you were diving, and stuck your other arm up in the air, just like you used to do when you were on the high board, taking swimming lessons when you were six years old. You hated that high-diving board."

"I was afraid then," Lindsay recalls, "and I reverted back to that fear when I was above the airbag."

Afterwards, when the mother-daughter tandem came out of the stairway, the crew, who labeled Lindsay, "Boss," continued their treatise. "Hey, Boss," they said, "you're pretty cool."

Lindsay's like, "Oh, there's nothing to it. Well, you know, I've got to keep you guys entertained. We just needed to end the day with a good old laugh," carrying on like a trooper, like she did it all on purpose.

As with another moment of Lindsay/*Bionic* levity behind the scenes, this time involving chip-a-way rock which, when completely drained of water, becomes brittle foam rubber. When the water is retained, it's partly clay-like. Lindsay's stunt double once became badly bruised upon whacking away at a piece of the substance, which was not completely dry. The *Bionic* budget did not allow for a luxury of time, and in this instance, there was not enough time allocated for the rock-chip to dry. "We usually did not have a lot of time or money for many of the stunts we did," recalls Lindsay, "We couldn't

WHILE NOT AS ATHLETICALLY-GIFTED AS LEE, LINDSAY STILL
HANDLED MANY OF HER OWN ACTION SCENES. *BOTTOM:* LINDSAY'S
STUNT-DOUBLE, RITA EGLESTON, IS VISIBLE IN TWO *BIONIC* SCENES.

do take after take. So we really had to give it our all when we did them."

Draining money from the budget for SM/BW special effects wasn't nearly as challenging as guessing the moves of those who handled the F/X for the shows, namely, Carl "Inky" Incorvia and Joe Goss, who were also known as *Crash* and *Burn*. When the cameras would roll, "we never quite knew what was going to happen," recalls Lee Majors, who remembers once, as Steve, having to toss a bail of hay, across a lake, to stop an escaping vehicle. "We set the cameras, and we were working with what they called an *air cannon*. The director yelled *Action*, Joe Goss hit the detonator, and we expected to see a bail of hay flying across the water. It turned out to be the air cannon. So something went wrong."

Another time, Steve Stafford, Vince Deadrick, Sr. and Steve Abrams, who hung out with Lee the most, were standing around talking. Deadrick had a jerk-away harness on, which is a leather bridle, hooked up to an air-ram. It simulates someone taking a bullet or a shotgun to the chest, and is capable of yanking someone away at extremely high speeds. The individual involved must be very well-braced for the impact, as it places a great deal of pressure on the upper-chest cavity when it goes off.

As Stafford recalls, "Vince was standing there with the harness hooked up, with a cup of coffee in his hand, and we were talking. Maybe fifty feet away, at the end of the detonator cable were Joe and Inky, sitting there wiring the whole thing up, and we hear this explosion. We look up, Vince was totally gone, and his coffee cup just floated to the ground. It knocked him out, completely. It took us about a half-hour to revive him, and for him to remember who he was."

Bionic Ever After? stuntman Vince Deadrick, Jr. practically grew up on the original SM set, as he is son to Vince, Sr. "My dad pretty much *was* The Six Million Dollar Man," he said. "Lee did all the acting, but dad did all those jumps and the big 'bionic' stuff."

In the BW segment, "Doomsday is Tomorrow, Part I," Lindsay remembers a minefield incident, which involved another special effects man with a nickname: *Oh, Shit Joe*.

"If you heard him say, *Oh, shit*," she recalls, "you would hit the deck. A lot of people say *Oh shit* on the set, but when you heard him say, *Oh, Shit*, you hit the deck. It took a quarter of the day to set up this shot, which was scheduled around a minefield. Ken [Johnson] was a little nervous, as he had rearranged the schedule for the next day. Finally, it's ready, and he asks Joe to explain the shot."

"Well, there's fifty charges up on the hill," Joe replies. "I have three men, two on the left, top and bottom, and one in the middle, behind the bushes, and each one is in charge of a section. As you run through the shot, each is cued to know when to set off their section."

Johnson then wondered if they all had walkie-talkies.

Joe said, "No."

"Well, how are you going to communicate?" Johnson inquired.

"When I'm ready," Joe answered, "and they know to designate their section when I move my handkerchief like this."

Joe waved his handkerchief. "All of a sudden," Lindsay said, "you heard, *boom, boom, boom, boom*, which was the sound of fifty charges going off as we're standing there discussing the scene. Of course, after all of these charges went off, you heard Joe say, *Oh, shit*. So we had to set it up all over again."

The two-part "Doomsday" was grueling for Lindsay in many ways. She remembers "always talking to nobody," because most of her scenes were with the computer. She even jogged in a tunnel of foam, which lessens a person's chance for oxygen. "Am I supposed to run through the foam at some point?" she asked Ken Johnson. "I should probably just take my own cue, right?"

"No, no," Johnson responded, "I'll let you know. I'll cue you."

"No," Lindsay insisted, "I think I can do this on my own. But don't forget, it's a long tunnel, and by the time I get through, it's going to be pretty full."

Johnson came back with, "Don't worry."

So Lindsay waited and waited. Suddenly, she screamed, "You better cue me!"

Johnson finally said, "Okay...now."

The tunnel filled up fast. Too fast. "All of a sudden," Lindsay recalls, "I'm running into this foam, and I'm like disappearing. You can see my head just barely bobbing in and out. I've got foam in my mouth, up my nose, everywhere. I'm swearing and swearing, and meanwhile, the cameraman is full of foam; everyone was full of foam."

Lee Majors had to navigate a pyrotechnic minefield of his own in the episode "Return of the Robot Maker." "We had two guys, who were on there for a few shows," he said. "They were like Laurel and Hardy. Nothing went right. I'd be meant to be ten feet away from an explosion. I'd cross over that explosion, and they'd blow it right up my butt. I could feel the heat. There was a lot of stuff like that. Metal bars that were meant to bend didn't. I'm just killing myself trying! It was a very physical show."

Many times, Lee's flesh-and-blood parts refused to cooperate altogether. In "The Bionic Woman, Part II," Lee and Lindsay have to leap from a window after she trips a security alarm. To "sell" the bionics, neither was supposed to brace their fall with their hands, but only Lee managed to pull it off. "You're not supposed to go to your hands, so I had to absorb it all in my knees, and all that sudden impact really killed them," he said. "It's just that with the bionics you wouldn't do that, if you had bionic knees. So they say you can't go all the way down with your hands on the ground. Try doing that even off of a three-foot box. It's very difficult."

For all the effects that did work on BW or SM, Harve Bennett said cameraman Enzo Martinelli "must be credited." Many of the *Bionic* F/X, with particular regard to *Six Mill*, he said, "were pioneering" effects that Martinelli initiated, including the "in camera" techniques. Such effects were done in-camera, without the necessity of editing to the film afterward.

"When you're under a time deadline," the producer relays, "and you're working with film as opposed to video, the post-production delay of adding effects, going through laboratory processes, etc, can be very time consuming."

At such times, Martinelli's expertise paid off handsomely. He devised a now-standard-procedure to transfer from slow-mo photography to normal. "If we could do much of our work *in camera*," Bennett said, "it was obviously very much to our benefit. It was always the standard way of doing things with video. But it was unknown at that particular moment, as commonplace practice for film."

With these break-through techniques established by Martinelli, stunt double Vince Deadrick, who filled in for Lee Majors on *Six* as well as *The Big Valley*, was allowed to create pioneering stunts of his own.

"For example," Bennett proposes, "how do you jump over a barn? You place Vince on the top of it, lock off the camera, have him jump backwards, land and run backwards out of the shot. Then we had Vince jump forward, and run naturally out of the scene. We spliced the two sequences and seamlessly, it appeared to be one shot. To do that with normal cinematic techniques, we would have required an extra two to three weeks of post-production, to coordinate a split-screen image. You think that's easy? Well, it wasn't. And no one had ever done it before."

As this procedure worked so well in the first *Six* season, the techniques were employed throughout the run of SM and BW. In short, "necessity was the mother of our invention," Bennett said.

The *daughter* of invention, on BW, anyway, was Rita Egleston, Lindsay's stunt double, whom Ken Johnson labels as "excellent." "She was constantly trying to figure out ways to make the gags better, and more interesting, by being more creative. Though they may have seemed like simple stunts, they were tricky and required an enormous amount of skill on her part."

For one *jump* stunt in "The DeJon Caper," Egleston employed a railing, a balcony, and a mini-trampoline that Ken "didn't even know was there. Rita leaped from the railing, forward onto the balcony, hit the mini-trampoline, and then came backwards over the railing, and down onto the airbag. When you reverse that film, you got a woman flying up toward the building and gliding right over the railing and into the balcony. We cut the film just before Rita hit the mini-trampoline. So it was a very subtle but smooth effect. It worked, because of Rita."

Egleston "worked her ass off for *The Bionic Woman*," Johnson adds. "She was also a dead ringer of Lindsay from ten feet away. People couldn't tell them apart. But the stunts were by no means simple to pull off. It's one

LINDSAY WAGNER WITH HER *BIONIC* STUNT-DOUBLE, RITA EGLESTON, ON THE SET OF "IN THIS CORNER, JAIME SOMMERS." *BOTTOM LEFT:* LEE MAJORS' STUNT-DOUBLE VINCE DEADRICK, SR. *BOTTOM RIGHT:* VINCE DEADRICK, JR., FOLLOWED IN HIS FATHER'S *BIONIC* FOOTSTEPS AND DOUBLED FOR LEE IN 1994'S *BIONIC EVER AFTER?* REUNION MOVIE.

thing to do a backwards fall into an airbag, and it's another thing to do a backwards fall that looks like you're jumping up. She literally had to go down feet first, until the last second when she would pull up into a *tuck*, and land on her back. Landing with your feet on an airbag is not something you would want to do very often [ankles would break]. When you're doing complicated stunt gags, even with what may be considered simple gags, you have to be really, really careful." As a lion tamer once told him, "It's the old lion that gets ya. The one that you don't worry about is the one that comes back to bite you."

Consequently, Johnson said those on *Six* and *Woman* would always measure and rehearse carefully each bionic stunt, "no matter how simple it seemed. We would always try to figure out how things might go wrong. Or how someone might have been hurt, and what we could have done to minimize those possibilities."

Usually, there were a series of coordinated lifting devices or jacks employed, when doing the larger stunts. "Sometimes," Harve Bennett said, "we would use fork lifts. The only trick was to position them just out of the camera frame. How playful we became, when we didn't get any sleep." One of the principal preoccupations of the first 13 *Million* episodes was to explore the parameters of what could be done, in fresh new ways. They needed to remind the audience, in case they'd forgotten, just how useful Steve could be.

One time, there was an episode in which nothing much happened until the middle of the First Act. Bennett suggested implanting a bionic stunt, early in the segment. "That was always one of our goals," he said. "Whenever I do a series, I always make the assumption that there is someone out there that has never seen it before. So I feel I have to, in some subtle way, restate the premise."

Lindsay Wagner's Emmy Award validated her acting abilities, but could she hit a cross-court backhand? "Rita did most of the running for Lindsay," Johnson admits. "Lindsay, bless her heart, *can* walk, act, and chew gum, but when it comes to being physical, oy! We really had to labor to make her look like a tennis pro on the show. She wasn't a sportswoman, but she was always game and was the first to say, 'Let me try that!' So she'd try it. Then we'd say, 'Ok, Rita, come on in!'"

Regardless, said writer/producer Lionel Siegel, "the physical feats Lindsay had to do were taxing. Physically, it was a tough show to do."

Some of the smaller stunts used on the shows were executed with comedic results. There were several instances where Steve or Jaime would take a bat and hit a ball, play tennis, football, or be shown in many an athletic form. Steve hits a mean golf ball in the *Man* episodes, *Wine, Women and War* and "Deadly Replay," and gives one heck-of-a-toss to a football when he meets Jaime again for the first time since college in "The Bionic Woman,

LINDSAY, IN CHARACTER AS A *BIONIC ESCORT*, POSES WITH PRODUCER
KENNETH JOHNSON ON THE SET OF "THE DEJON CAPER."
LINDSAY'S INSCRIPTION TO KENNY ON THE PHOTO IS AN EXAMPLE OF
THE SPIRIT AND HUMOR FOUND ON *BW*'S SET.

Part I" (not to mention "One of Our Running Backs is Missing," where he also does a bit of bionic bowling). We also witnessed him throwing a baseball hundreds of yards in "Task Force." Jaime herself swings quite a steady bat in the *Woman* wind-up, "A Thing of the Past." Bennett said such sequences were filmed in order to give the viewer a common image with which to bond.

During his *Apollo 14* mission, real-life astronaut Alan Shepherd was seen on the moon, hitting golf balls. Bennett and company took notice and said, "We've got to do that."

"If nothing else in the twin series," he said, "I will take entire responsibility for the sound effects of Steve's bionic eye and Jaime's bionic ear. The reason for that is, as noted, I am child of radio. Had the medium of radio continued, I'd probably still be in it. I have a very sensitive ear, and I grew up listening to sound effects. To this day, sound is critically important in all of the stuff that I do."

To properly coordinate the sound effects of Steve's eye, Bennett walked into the sound effects booth, and told the technicians that he wanted to hear a tone that would possibly accompany a bionic eye. "We listened to a variety of things," he recalls. "The one I chose was actually a kind of accelerated satellite beep. It just has a kind of feeling of grinding teeth. It sounds a little dated today, but when we did it, it was rather fresh."

Jaime's ear "was easy," he said. "I didn't have to listen to anything." He simply said to the sound technicians, "Her ear must sound sonar-like to be sonar," which he had grown up with as a boy, "watching submarine pictures." "It was a *ping*," he said, "an echo. We just speeded it up, so that it wouldn't have sounded too much like a submarine sonar, but that's what it really was."

Small props, like fake guns, were crushed or blown to smithereens by Steve and Jaime, or they were constructed by the FX/prop team to twist and bend by bionic force. Or they would implode, explode, bend or twist, all to the chagrin of evildoers. As mentioned elsewhere in this book, almost never did Steve or Jaime hold or shoot a gun in either series. At one point, however, Lindsay was holding a gun, which went off. "It was loud," she said, "and I remember disliking the sound a lot. But we had to re-shoot the scene." She was told, "You can't be doing a serious moment with a gun, and then laugh."

Lindsay was confused, like the time everyone was laughing at her after she safely landed following the helicopter incident from "Fembots in Las Vegas." Apparently, while filming the gun-scene, she smiled. The sequence had to be *shot* again. She smiled again, and they did another take. What was the problem? Why was she smiling? "I was so uncomfortable with having to pull the trigger," she replies, "and having to hear the gun-shot sound, that I was grimacing. You know, when your face kind of like goes back, and you say, *Eech!* On camera, because it wasn't a real close up, you couldn't tell that

I was really grimacing. So it looked like I was smiling."

The actress was smiling for sure when she worked with the BW set designer on how she envisioned Jaime's apartment. "I wanted very much for it to have it reflect the feel of my own home," she said. "I remember asking for the squash mortar brick for over the fireplace. From moment to moment, I was creating her. We were working so hard, so fast, so constantly."

Lindsay would view the dailies and say, "Okay, we accomplished that yesterday, here's what I think." She would give her general notes, and focus on the scenes of the present day, however many number of scenes they were to shoot, in order to make the moment as real as possible. The next day, she would do the entire process again.

"I never really had time to digest all of what I did," she said. "I would attempt to make sense, on a microcosmic level, of trying to have the story make sense. That was on Sunday, and Monday we would start on that episode. I never really got a chance to study what I was doing, and to see how I did it."

It was also hard for her to register anything during "The Return of Bigfoot" SM/BW episodes, which featured an attraction from the Universal Studios Tour in Universal City, California. During the tour, which has changed over the years, a tramcar, driven by a guide, passes through a circular tunnel. This same tunnel was disorienting for both Lindsay and Lee, while filming. In the "Bigfoot" segment, it led to the base center, which was controlled by Sasquatch's parental aliens. The man-made, rotating circular cave proved to be quite a temperamental co-star, which kept everyone off their toes, and their heads *a'spinning*. Lindsay takes a breath, and explained how challenging it was to walk from one end of the tunnel. "It moves all the way around you. Lee and I had to walk along inside it, and it threw off our equilibrium. The tours went on during the day, so we had to shoot at night. Everyone on the crew had bets going to see if anyone could actually make it to the other side of the tunnel."

The two actors had to run in sections, and state their dialogue, portion by portion, due to frequent disorientation. "We would only get about halfway through," Lindsay laughs, "and then we would literally fall down. We actually started to stumble, depending on how badly it finally overtook us. We'd walk awhile, they would film, and we would talk. We tried to look straight ahead or right at each other, so that we didn't have to use our peripheral vision more than necessary. We'd get so many lines out, fall, and then stop.

"We'd start again where we left off, and do the next section. It was like working on some weird drug. The cameraman was okay, because he was sitting down. But the dolly grip, who is the man that pushes the dolly, had some problems. So someone got down on their hands and knees and drew a line down the length of the floor. All he had to do was look straight ahead. The man holding the boom [overhead microphone] could no more walk than could Lee and I. They sat him on the back of the camera dolly, but because he had to look at us, it was kind of difficult for him to do his job. So when Lee and I were walking along, all of sudden we heard this *thud*, and the guy literally fell off the dolly. We all laughed so hard that night. And everyone lost money on the bet, because no one made it through the tunnel."

Equilibrium problems also bedeviled "The Secret of Bigfoot" set. As Lee recalls, "We rehearsed what we were going to do with the tunnel, but we had not rehearsed it with it moving. Andre the Giant, who spoke kind of broken-English, but mostly French, wasn't sure what was going to happen when we actually rolled. Enzo Martinelli [the cinematographer] was there. We were doing this hand-held shot, which was basically backing up, with me in the foreground and Andre in the background. And of course, because it was a back-up shot, we had to walk to the end of the tunnel. There was just me, Andre, the cameraman, and the camera assistant, with the crew at the other end of the tunnel.

"Well, we got inside, and the tunnel starting revolving around the bridge. All three of us started heading for the sides, and had we not the sense to lie down, which is exactly what we did, we would have been crushed by the gears that rotate that tunnel. It was quite serious."

It took Ken Johnson approximately one hour to figure out what to do. He said, "Look. No one can stand up in there when they walk." So Lee, Andre and the camera crew were placed outside the bridge. They used the revolving bridge behind them, and actually captured the shot they required. Johnson, who also wrote the "Bigfoot" segments, remembers production manager Ted Schilz's response upon reading the first draft of the script, which included an elaborate tunnel sequence.

"Kenny, Kenny," Schilz said. "What are you thinking? We can't afford this kind of thing. You have Steve walking though this big ice tunnel."

"Teddy," Johnson replied. "Go to the backlot and walk through the Universal Tour. There it is."

As stated, the tunnel is still a part of the Universal Tour and, as Steve Stafford adds, "When the tram drivers travel inside, they shut their eyes. They don't have to. But if you go through there, day after day, like they do, you could become quite ill. It's an overwhelming sense that your entire environment is turning to the left."

Also on the backlot at Universal: Jaime's coach house, which was used for her scenes with Steve parents. "It's funny how much of our *Bionic experience* may be seen on the Universal Tour," Johnson muses. "In all the time I was at Universal, I used every damn thing on the Tour. My production designer, Chuck Davis, and I would look for sets to steal. We literally wrote those sets into scripts so we wouldn't have to spend money making them. Today, there's not much of the backlot left. The place where Steve and Bigfoot had

TOP: THE RUSSELL SENATE OFFICE BUILDING IN WASHINGTON, D.C. WAS USED FOR EXTERIOR SHOTS OF OSCAR'S OFFICE AND O.S.I. HEADQUARTERS. MIDDLE: THE "COLLAPSING" BRIDGE AT UNIVERSAL STUDIOS. THE BRIDGE WAS INCORPORATED INTO EPISODES OF BOTH *SM* AND *BW,* AND WAS A POPULAR FEATURE ON THE STUDIO TOUR. *BOTTOM LEFT:* ANOTHER TOUR FAVORITE WAS THE ROTATING "ICE" TUNNEL, FEATURED IN THE "BIGFOOT" EPISODES. *BOTTOM RIGHT:* UNIVERSAL STUDIOS ALLOWED AUDIENCE MEMBERS TO EXPERIENCE BEING BIONIC AT THEIR BIONIC TESTING CENTER DURING THE LATE 1970s.

their climactic battle is now all restaurants and parking lots."

As production manager, Ted Schilz's main priority was making sure everything got done on time and on budget. "If the studio gave you x amount of dollars to do an hour show, they wanted it done at that dollar amount," he recalls. "If they gave you six days, you got it done in six days. If you didn't, they'd want to know why. None of this was easy because it was a big show. We had 30 assistant directors and 30 unit managers. It was as big as when I started at MGM in 1946. Universal [in the early '70s] was a mammoth studio; we were making 20 hours of network TV programming every week."

As to just how difficult it was, in general, to film the special effects for *The Six Million Dollar Man* and *The Bionic Woman*, Ken Johnson's colleague, Phil Bondelli, who directed segments for both, references one SM episode that he guided, "The Bionic Boy," which starred Vince Van Patten: "It was very exciting to film the bionic effects. When we made 'The Bionic Boy,' we did so mostly on location, and we had some wonderful scenery and props to work with. I remember using big rocks in scenes, which he was supposed to jump from one of them to the other. We had all these different bionic shots in that one, rather than just jumping buildings. We had great big ravines. We tried to figure out how we were going to get [Van Patten] across this ravine, to make it look like he was floating. We had a shot of him, running across a creek, stopping, and running out of frame. We had the stuntman run and jump as far as he possibly could. Then we placed a trampoline on the set, and he would go from one trampoline to the other, and right through the picture.

"The next shot, he would go from the trampoline to up in the air, and then landed on the other side of the lake. It took us like five to six shots to do just that one bionic effect. Most studios sort of frown on doing special effects-type shows, thinking that they are not real drama. *The Six Million Dollar Man* and *The Bionic Woman* were two of the most difficult, challenging shows to do, from a technical standpoint. But I loved it."

CHAPTER 9

FUSION

"AT THE TIME, WE WERE IN WHAT WAS CALLED THE
COLD WAR. AND WE COULDN'T SEND TROOPS IN
LIKE YOU DID WHEN YOU GO TO WAR. SO THIS WAS
AN OPPORTUNITY TO JUST SEND ONE PERSON IN
ON A JOB TO EITHER BRING OUT SOMEONE OR GET
INFORMATION. IT REALLY WAS CIA STUFF."

RICHARD ANDERSON

Those in charge of bringing *The Six Million Dollar Man* and *The Bionic Woman* into our living rooms understood completely the *X-Files*-like "what's out there" pulse of the times, which had developed during the 1960s (the so-called Age of Aquarius). While Leonard Nimoy's popular, pre-Discovery/Learning Channel syndicated series, *In Search of...* (strategically scheduled in several markets alongside reruns of classic *Star Trek*), investigated the strange real-life reported of Bigfoot, UFOs and ESP, Steve and Jaime did the same in reel-life. To wit: Beyond the *Bigfoot/alien/fembot* cybernetics, several SM/BW episodes addressed otherworldly topics.

In one *Million* outing, "Burning Bright" (from the first season), an astronaut (played by *Trek's* William Shatner) is affected by an electrical field while in space. His intelligence increases, and he develops the power to control the minds of those around him. In the Austin adventure, "Straight on 'Til Morning," a blue-skinned family from another planet is marooned on Earth when their space shuttle malfunctions. The aliens seek aid from a nearby town, but their radioactive touch is harmful to humans.

In a second-year Jaime jaunt, "The Night Demon," a supernatural creature that mysteriously appears and disappears causes enough havoc to disrupt The Bionic Woman's visit with a close friend. In the Sommers sojourn, "The Ghosthunter" (which was the last episode of BW's first season), Jaime goes incognito as a nanny and teams up with a psychic to investigate the strange hauntings at a home with a past of witchery. Steve, too, pairs up with a telepath in the *Man* outing, "The E.S.P. Spy," in which an unfriendly nation employs a rival psychic to steal classified information on laser weapons.

While episodes like "Spy" and "The Pyramid" allowed Steve and Jaime to contemplate and confront other dimensions, no theme was more tapped into than the Cold War strain between America and the then-ominous Soviet Union. The OSI was, after all, an intelligence agency consigned with safeguarding and advancing the USA's domestic and foreign interests. As such, several occasions for Red Menace conflict manifested.

In the late 1960s, several small-screen programs like *Mission: Impossible* and *The Man From U.N.C.L.E.* (and to some extent, the spy-com, *Get Smart*) nearly monopolized the anti-Soviet slant. But *Dollar* and *Woman* hit their stride during the historical interval of collective compromise known as *detente*. Commencing in 1973 with the initial SALT treaty, and culminating in 1978 with SALT II, the world's two predominant superpowers, compelled into cooperation by the notion of "mutually assured destruction" (or MAD), set out on a contentious course stamped with discord, distrust, and modest collaboration — specifically in the domain of space quest and arms control.

No *Man/Woman* episode addressed this uneasy alliance more forthrightly than Kenneth Johnson's two-part BW tale, "Doomsday is Tomorrow" (which also happens to feature one of Lindsay Wagner's premium Jaime performances). Here, an ingenious, terminally-ill professor named Dr. Elijah Cooper (played by the late Lew Ayres) decides, as his swan-song, that he and his vocation have done too much to hasten the collective destruction of Earth's vast peoples.

Dr. Cooper employs his considerable grey matter to construct the preeminent doomsday mechanism. Entrenched in rocky mountain terrain, and protected by space-age weaponry, the device will coat the Earth's atmosphere with a toxic substance at the first sign of war or above ground nuclear testing. Commandeering the use of a telecom satellite, he relays that we, the people of Earth, are self-destructive, and that the only devastation that will manifest is one which we ourselves will create. He proclaims to all nations that his apparatus is ready for action and cautions against ever turning to war again. Over the objections of the world's varied rulers (that it violates on their sovereign rights), peace is established. Elijah believes he has triumphed in terminating the onslaught of human savagery.

A small, yet power-hungry country then goes against the grain, executes a nuclear test, and prompts his machine to unleash devastation. The doctor succumbs to a weak heart, and the world's only hope is The Bionic Woman, who gains assistance from a Soviet accomplice named Dimitri Muskov, who goes undercover as scientist Dr. Victor Evtuhov (both played by actor Kenneth O'Brien). In her bid to reach Cooper's complex and defeat the device, Jaime dodges all forms of anti-intruder defenses (with Evtuhov in tow) until she finally reaches her destination. Successfully evading laser beams, fiery rocket blasts, suffocating foam, sinister sound effects and falling objects, she speeds toward the deepest recesses of the facility to pull the plug on the deadly machine's "brain," only to discover that she wasn't quick enough. Yet as the formidable moment approaches and the doomsday contraption is enlivened, there is no severing jar or perpetual demise. Instead, Cooper's countdown is revealed to be a bluff. In an adjoining room, a solitary granite block is impressed with this Biblical excerpt from Isaiah, 2:4:

And he shall judge among the nations, and shall rebuke many people: and they shall beat their swords into plowshares, and their spears into pruning hooks: nation shall not lift up sword against nation, neither shall they learn war anymore."

"That's what the whole premise of the piece was about," said "Tomorrow" scribe Johnson, who was motivated to write the thought-provoking episode based on his knowledge of Alfred Nobel, Enrico Fermi, Robert Oppenheimer and those involved in creating the atomic bomb. Many of these individuals became great pacifists "after the horse was out of the barn," Johnson relays.

An intriguing notion for viewers to consider, it was reflected by David Opatoshu's character from the fictional Middle East country of Satari, who goes ahead with the nuclear test after disbelieving what he's been told by the West. "There's a scene later where he's sort of *rocking his child*," Ken explained, "believing that he has signed the death warrant for his children and all future generations."

The "Tomorrow" segments also present a case of life imitating art in this and past generations. Guest star Lew Ayres was a conscientious objector during World War II and was subsequently exiled by Hollywood. Before the war, he had been a favorite leading man in motion pictures. He declared his pacifism (which had a religious foundation), was renounced by the studios and, in some cities, exhibitors declined to screen his movies. To bear arms, he said, would cause him "to live in a nightmare of hypocrisy." "I knew that Lew was a pacifist when I cast him," Johnson admits. "That was one of the reasons that he had wanted to do the episode."

A pantheist, as well, Ayres completed a documentary over the course of his whole lifetime that studied various reverent beliefs. According to Ken, "It was three or four hours long, filled with home movies that he had taken all over the world, comparing religions. Interestingly, for him, it all came down to the Golden Rule [treat others as you would like to be treated]. He was a dear, dear man, and I loved working with him."

With Ayres and BW's "Tomorrow," Johnson sought to display how the USSR and the USA could have a joint purpose and indeed work together as compatriots and comrades for a common cause. He said the episode "was a wonderful opportunity to do that and to try to increase the level of trust on both sides a bit." Johnson consciously resisted the standard stereotype where "the Soviets are the ones in the black hat all the time."

Producer Glen Larson, however, preferred conflict to conciliation. "In order to utilize Steve's tools, you gotta try to give him someone formidable to deal with," he said. "You don't pit someone with all that firepower against someone like a meter maid or a pickpocket. The Cold War always afforded us worthy adversaries. You make your hero look good by pitting him against someone competent and perhaps someone equally powerful. He had the tools, but it would look silly if you put him up against a bank robber, you know? It's all storytelling."

The very same year BW broadcast "Tomorrow," the SM venture, "Death Probe I & II," had Col. Austin confronting a nomadic Russian space explorer that had mistaken Wyoming for Venus and proceeded to threaten the countryside.

Steve's ally was the probe's architect — a radiant Russian scientist who once before aided him in "Doomsday, and Counting," where she was instrumental in thwarting a nuclear detonation at a Soviet launch site. In SM's final season, Steve teamed up with a beautiful KGB agent in "The Moving Mountain."

Yet, Steve's "communistic encounters" were not always of the Soviet mélange. As *Six* producer Lionel E. Siegel explained, "The heavies started out being Russian and Middle Easterners, and then it shifted to the Chinese, which was reflecting what Washington was dealing with. It would have been non-productive if we kept on making the Soviets the heavies, because we were trying to deal with them [in real life]."

In "The Coward," Austin races to an isolated Chinese mountaintop to retrieve decades-old diplomatic documents that outlined a compact between the Soviet Union and the old Chinese Nationalists. Even long-lost fascists were given a break on *Man*, as evident in the Steve-segment, "The Last Kamikaze," which illustrated how once-bitter enemies could come to compromise. "Kamikaze" aired approximately three decades after Imperial Japan formally surrendered on the decks of the *U.S.S. Missouri*, yet here was Steve Austin humanely brokering a unilateral treaty with a reclusive Japanese soldier who was unaware of what took place in 1945.

While Henry Kissinger could not have defused a crisis as swiftly as Steve in "Kamikaze," other *Six* installments made little pretense of a melt-down in the Cold War frost. Though conceding that progress on some fronts had been achieved, America was not quite prepared to discard time-honored grudges or deeply ingrained suspicions. This time, characters played to type.

In the *Million* episode "Divided Loyalty," Austin eludes laser security embankments and substantial opponents attempting to courier a formerly disloyal scientist and his son out of their dictatorial surroundings and back to American turf. The son's jailer/friend displays a fleeting twinge of compassion when he decides against shooting Steve and his young associate as they cling hazardously to a rope traversing a ravine. His frenzied attempt to trail the "deserters" down, however, left no question as to where his Iron Curtain sympathies rested.

Two years later, in a BW segment called "Escape to Love," Sommers penetrates an undesignated East-bloc stronghold to sneak out the son of a scientist who has defected to the West. The boy's captors threaten to kill him should his father fail to return to his post. In the comically-titled BW episode, "Motorcycle Boogie," Jaime hitches a ride from Evel Knievel (playing himself) as they unlawfully intrude Communist East Germany to obtain a stolen computer chip encoded with the names of Western agents.

While other episodes reinforced the *Better Dead Than Red* genre (including, SM's "Carnival of Spies," "Walk a Deadly Wing," "Dead Ringer," and BW's "In This Corner, Jaime Sommers"), the same glaring Red subject manner was addressed in two of the *Bionic* reunions.

In 1989's *Bionic Showdown*, the bad guys have a bionic agent of their own and renegade factions of the CIA and KGB have conspired to reverse the recent stream of good will influenced by *glastnost*.

"The network was *very* specific as to what they wanted in terms of the [TV movie's] look and storyline," said Richard Anderson. "It's no longer the commies vs. the capitalists in the world today, so we decided on the Unity Games with extreme right-wing elements in the governments of *both* sides that don't want it to happen."

In 1994's *Bionic Ever After?*, the antagonist, armed with a heavy Slavic accent, gloats to Steve that his latest bounty-hunting will earn him millions and a "dacha on the Black Sea."

When appraising the belligerent/cultural imperialistic message that was sometimes circulated by *The Six Million Dollar Man* and *The Bionic Woman*, it may be significant to bear in mind that Steve Austin and Jaime Sommers were first and foremost patriots, not pacifists. Even though they would attempt to employ their special powers only in emergency, or as a last resort (using first their human ingenuity and/or wit), and even though they abhorred violence, if a highly populated installation had to be obliterated for the sake of world peace (as it was in "Last of the Fourth of Julys"), so be it. Nobility has its limits.

"*The Six Million Dollar Man* and *The Bionic Woman* told us something about America's place in the world, without being obnoxious about it," said Brendan Slattery. "It was sort of like a televisual civics lesson every Sunday and Wednesday night. The United States was confidently portrayed as humanity's last best hope, with Steve and Jaime as roving ambassadors of bionic good will. They erred and overstepped from time to time, but their heart and integrity were never in question. Cynics might decry this as corny, but so what? They weren't the target audience anyway."

Martin Caidin, who was no stranger to clandestine operations on behalf of the CIA, elaborated on the patriotism angle. "I'm not a fanatic," he said. "This is my country. I believe in this country. [Despite] all the errors, I think we do more soul-searching than any other country in the world. I gave a college talk one time, and this was when they were anti-bomb, anti-everything. I said, *Hey, all you shitheads out there. I want to tell you something. In 1945, this country had to make a tremendous decision. We had something no one else had, the absolute weapon. We were the only people on Earth who had the atomic bomb, and we had the means to deliver it. To prevent another war, or the rise of communism, or rebirth of fascism. We had the means to take over the entire world! Really! To use what we had would have made us exactly like those we had just defeated. Instead, we gambled on the human race.* Whether we make it or not doesn't matter; to me, that was the finest moment of any nation in the course of history."

In Harve Bennett's eyes, the 1955 film, *Bad Day at Black Rock*, directed by John Sturges (who guided the 1969 film version of Martin Caidin's *Marooned*) and starring Spencer Tracy, keys into the "don't tempt me" stamina and general cybernetic connection to the central appeal and social circuitry of *The Six Million Dollar Man* and *The Bionic Woman*.

In *Day*, Tracy portrays a soldier who loses an arm during a battle in Italy, where he befriends a comrade who dies. He searches for his pal's father, traveling to a town in the middle of nowhere. He finds nothing, and the townsfolk — including Ernest Borgnine and Lee Marvin as bad guys — want him out. Tracy receives threats via automobile mishaps, falling boulders, etc. He comes to believe his friend's dad has been killed in the midst of a massive cover-up, but has no way of proving it. At one point, Borgnine starts agitations, such as placing salt in Tracy's soup, which he endures for approximately one-hour and five minutes. This instance is a lasting image for Bennett, whose original big-screen view of *Bad* took place in a Chicago movie theatre, during its initial release. As he recalls, those in the audience "were clutching their seats," especially during the *sodium* sequence in the film.

Tracy said, "I don't really like salt in my soup." Borgnine removes the cap and empties the dispenser in the soup. Tracy replies with something like, "I guess I won't have my soup," and Borgnine makes a threat, by cocking his fist. Tracy, who the audience really doesn't know anything about, then delivers with his good arm, a judo-chop to Borgnine's Adam's apple.

According to Bennett, the audience stood up and cheered at this scene, which he believes characterized "one of those indelible moments in your life, when you say, *Don't push me. If you do, watch out.*" That's how he viewed the adventures of Steve and Jaime, both of whom were balanced individuals. Yet when *pushed*, they *shoved*, and the enemy was forced to *watch out*. An aggressive reaction, this still fits with the moral message that Bennett tried to fit into SM, BW, or any project he's involved with.

"The pen *is* mightier than the sword," he said. "Steve and Jaime would always try to think their way out of a situation, before they used bionics. They obviously had to employ their powers to infiltrate a locked up area, but they would first check to see if the door was open, or leap a wall, before attempting any more physical movements."

It was Bennett's realistic influence that helped the shows become the success they remain, said Steve Stafford, who believes that SM's initial popularity, in particular, had to do with the race to the moon. "NASA was involved with various space projects, at the time," he assessed, "and since Steve Austin was an astronaut, it seemed more believable that what happened to him could actually take place."

On the other hand, Stafford said BW was one of the first shows to feature a strong female lead, one in which a woman took on a man's world. Yet, as previously relayed, one in which the capable lady retained her femininity. "If you look at the generation of women which have now become independent," Stafford explained, "they all grew up with that show. She was a great role model. She didn't take any *gup*, stood on her own, and didn't need the proverbial *man* by her side, although she wanted him emotionally."

Stafford also believes the prejudice theme was widespread in BW, as opposed to SM. "With Steve," he said, "there was more of a national security issue of not telling people about who he was. With Jaime, especially in the first episodes of *Six Mill* that she did, her vulnerability was played up, as if to say, *I'm different* or *People think I'm different*."

With SM and BW, Ken Johnson intended to help break down barriers of intolerance and mistrust. "I try and bring the world a little closer together," he said. "I know it sounds trite, but it wouldn't be a bad place to live *if we all got along*. I think what we tried to do on *Six Mill* and particularly on *The Bionic Woman* was to do good, strong entertainment shows that had a moral basis to them and a sense of integrity—both in the creation and the production, as well as in the storylines. We tried never to talk down to the audience, but always to assume that they were in fact as intelligent as we hoped that we were. And we tried to satisfy ourselves, hoping that what satisfied us would satisfy the millions of people who watched the shows. And I guess for a long time it did."

In 1987, nearly ten years after Steve Austin's final assignment on ABC in 1978 and Jaime Sommers' farewell on NBC that same year, the latter network got smart, realized the franchise potential mixture of sci-fi and nostalgia, and broadcast *Return of The Six Million Dollar Man and The Bionic Woman*. A hit, *Return* spawned the previously-mentioned sequels: *Bionic Showdown*, which the peacock web also screened (in 1989), and *Bionic Ever After?*, which CBS optioned for viewing in 1994.

The genesis of a bionic reunion began, innocently enough, in 1986, when Majors, Anderson and friends embarked on a barge holiday in the south of

RICHARD, LEE, AND LINDSAY REUNITE FOR 1987'S *RETURN OF THE
SIX MILLION DOLLAR MAN AND THE BIONIC WOMAN*, THE FIRST OF
THREE REUNION MOVIES.

RICHARD, TOM SCHANLEY, AND LEE ON THE SET OF *RETURN*.
SCHANLEY PLAYS MICHAEL AUSTIN, STEVE'S NEVER-BEFORE-
MENTIONED SON WHO, IN A LIKE-FATHER-LIKE-SON PARALLEL,
BECOMES BIONIC AFTER A SIMILAR AIRCRAFT ACCIDENT.

LINDSAY WAGNER WITH SANDRA BULLOCK FROM *SHOWDOWN*.
BULLOCK PLAYS KATE MASON, THE WORLD'S SECOND *BIONIC* WOMAN.
LIKE HER CHARACTER, BULLOCK WOULD GO ON TO BECOME A
*SUPER*WOMAN...IN THE MOVIE INDUSTRY.

France. Majors decided to go on a short jog, with Anderson and company trailing on bikes. The two of them decamped in the middle of nowhere, where they improvised a short scene.

"Hi, Steve," said Anderson.

"Hi, Oscar," replied Majors.

"How about one more mission?" queried Anderson.

To which Majors replied: "I don't think so. I'm retired now and I'm fishing."

Eventually, Lee relented.

Back in the States, Anderson approached Universal's Sidney Scheinberg and pitched the idea. "He liked it and sent me downstairs and we developed it," said Anderson. "I also had a chance meeting with Brandon Tartikoff [then head of NBC] and he loved the idea, too. So I sold it to NBC in 1987 and we did *Return*."

Return introduced Steve's bionic son, Michael Austin (played by Tom Schanley), who was a pilot like his father. Michael loses three limbs (both legs, right arm) and his right eye, in an accident eerily similar to his dad's (though Steve lost his left eye). Once fitted with bionics, Michael runs faster than both Steve and Jaime, while his new eye is not only bionic, but endowed with laser power. Written by Michael Sloan (*Kung Fu: The Legend Continues*) and directed by Ray Austin, this movie also features Martin Landau (of *Space: 1999* fame) as the villain, and Lee Majors II as an OSI operative.

The ratings for *Return* were fantastic. Emboldened, Anderson called up Tartikoff and said, "Let's do another one." NBC agreed, and made Anderson co-producer.

Showdown presents a pre-*Speed* (1994) Sandra Bullock as Kate, The Bionic Girl, whose body is implanted with a superior set of cybernetic computer chips, which grant her countless super powers. Co-written by Sloan, Robert De Laurentis and Brock Choy, this second cyber-film was directed by Alan J. Levi (another SM/BW veteran), and also featured Jeff Yagher (*V*) and the late Robert Lansing (of Sloan's *Kung Fu Legend* and classic *Trek's* non-sold pilot, *Assignment: Earth*).

Richard Anderson is particularly proud of his recruitment of Bullock. "We saw some tapes of her, and I knew we had to get a hold her," he opines. "I admired her presence, and she's a very interesting lady."

Showdown also doubled as a back-door pilot for a new series. "Brandon wanted that," observes Anderson. "Lee, Lindsay and I wanted two-hour movies. When he said he wanted to do a pilot, I didn't think any of us really wanted to do another weekly series. We all had other commitments. Out of 92 other shows that week, *Showdown* came in at number 11 under very stiff competition. We beat the odds, but for a variety of reasons, it never went to series."

FOURTEEN YEARS AFTER HIS FIRST MARRIAGE PROPOSAL TO JAIME,
STEVE STRUGGLES TO FIND THE RIGHT WORDS IN 1989'S *BIONIC
SHOWDOWN.* IT'S JAIME WHO FINALLY MUTTERS, "WHY DON'T WE
GET MARRIED?"

Ever After? culminated with Steve and Jaime's marriage. The movie was originally subtitled *The Return of The Six Million Dollar Man and The Bionic Woman, Part III*, and first main-titled, *Bionic Breakdown*, the latter of which alluded to its B-storyline: Jaime's health is in decline, caused by a computer virus programmed into her bionic structure. Farrah Forke (*Wings*) and Anne Lockhart (*Battlestar Galactica*; daughter to June *Lost in Space* Lockhart) also starred in a script scribed by Sloan, and directed by Steve Stafford, Lee Majors' assistant during the first few years of the weekly version of *Six Million*.

All three films were executive produced by Richard Anderson, who has known Sloan for years, and who also offered opening narration for *The Legend Continues*. NBC and Sloan would have passed on the first *Return* (and a $4.8 million price-tag), had it not been for Richard's forward thinking: He proposed using the TV-movie as a pilot for a spin-off series that would have featured Schanley's Michael Austin as a kind of bionic *Top Gun*, feeding off the popularity of that 1986 Tom Cruise theatrical release. Harve Bennett, who was busy with the *Star Trek* film series and developing the syndicated *Time Trax* series for TV, and Ken Johnson were nowhere in sight. "I was not really interested in getting involved," Johnson reveals. "Been there, done that. I've never seen them, but then again, I've never seen the sequel to *V*. When you have a baby and you give it over to foster parents to raise, you sort of don't want to see how things turn out."

Overall, the reunions hold up quite well, in comparison to the originals. They were not conscious of themselves, as if the characters were saying, "Oh, look, here we are doing this reunion movie." *Return*, *Showdown* and *After* were essentially three additional episodes of the series.

Majors himself enjoyed the "old home week" aspect of the reunions. "Richard is a good friend of mine," he said. "We go back a long, long way. I call him '*Old Money*,' because he just seems like he comes from old money. He's great, always has been and always will be. Lindsay and I just fall right back into our characters so easily. We've both had troubles in our personal lives. So it's fun to get back together and make the magic happen."

One of the most important developments through the *Bionic* reunion trilogy was the wrap-up of Steve and Jaime's romantic liaison. In *Return*, she still was having trouble placing her feelings for him. In *Showdown*, he attempted to pop the question when, in the end, she finally calls it. In *After*, they actually marry. "Steve was really trying to ask her in the second film," explained Sloan, "but he was too tongue tied, so she finally asked him." One movie later, with *After*, Sloan wanted to tell a love story, and to have a wedding. "The ideas of her bionics breaking down would be horrifying," he explained, "particularly in the circumstances of them getting married."

Universal liked the hitched storyline and so did the network. Sloan wrote the script, which went through various changes, and Lee Majors and

TOP: LINDSAY, RICHARD, AND LEE'S CHAIRS ON THE SET OF *BIONIC EVER AFTER? BOTTOM LEFT:* LINDSAY WITH HER PERSONAL HAIRDRESSER PEGGY SEMTOB. *BOTTOM RIGHT:* PRODUCER/WRITER MICHAEL SLOAN WAS RESPONSIBLE FOR ALL THREE *BIONIC* REUNION FILMS.

TOP LEFT: LEE ON THE WATER TOWER. *TOP RIGHT:* LINDSAY EXAMINES
THE "MANHOLE" COVER SHE'LL THROW TO STOP THE ESCAPING
VILLAINS' TRUCK. *BOTTOM LEFT:* RICHARD IN A RELAXED MOMENT ON
THE SET. *BOTTOM RIGHT:* LEE AND LINDSAY CONSULT WITH DIRECTOR
STEVE STAFFORD (BACK TO CAMERA).

AFTER NEARLY TWENTY YEARS, STEVE AND JAIME FINALLY TIED THE KNOT IN *BIONIC EVER AFTER?*

Lindsay Wagner were signed. "It all sounds very easy," the producer states, "but it took four years to get it on the air."

After is considered by many to the best of the three *Bionic* reunions, which pleases Sloan. The producer, who had also brought Dennis Weaver back to his most notable TV role in 1987's *The Return of Sam McCloud*, sought to make sure that the *After* plot and characterizations were strong. [The original *McCloud* series, remember, was produced by SM's first producer, Glen Larson.]

"Jaime was always very much at odds with the fact that she became this super person," he said. "Though the work that she performed with the OSI was heroic, eventually, she just couldn't do it anymore, which is why she left. And Steve's traits as a very charming, self-deprecating, almost shy guy had to be retained. All these footloose human elements, playing against the bionic technology are what made the original shows a success. I knew we had to repeat that formula with the reunions."

Before signing up for *After*, Wagner insisted that Steve and Jaime take the plunge. "I said I won't do it again unless they get married," she said. "You've got to give that to the public; you can't just drag them around, the two of us in wheelchairs, with people still waiting for the two of us old fogies to get married. [Our fans] have been with us, and loved us, and we've had this wonderful relationship with them, and they should have the satisfaction of that."

She continues: "Plus, what's it saying about these two who can't get off their own situation and commit to each other? Or stop having this unrequited stuff? It's a marketing game, and it was becoming painful for me. I felt bad and it was disrespectful to the audience, but they were cool. Finally, [the writers] said, 'Okay, we'll marry them,' and then we could put it to bed."

Reiterating Ken Johnson's assessment of the proper mix of sci-fi/fantasy story, character and F/X, Sloan adds, "It doesn't matter how dazzling the special effects are; if you don't care about the people, you're not going to tune in. If you think about a show like *Star Trek*, which is the most successful series in syndication history, its best episodes are morality plays [i.e., "City on the Edge of Forever"], and that's what endeared the series to its legions of fans."

As with *Kung Fu* and *McCloud*. "The audience embraces David Carradine's compassionate portrayal," he said. "They don't necessarily watch the show for the kung-fu fights. There's a very strong spiritual tone to it. As a half-Chinese/half-American monk, Caine is a very unusual action/adventure hero, whose whole thrust in life is to find goodness in the world. Like *McCloud*, Caine, Steve and Jaime are good fish out of water, with qualities that are quite transcendental. Their stories are camouflaged morality plays."

Austin and Sommers, in particular, Sloan adds, were given their powers to save their lives. He said it wasn't like Steve and Jaime said, "Gee, it really is fun to have a bionic arm. Let me just drive down to the hospital, and get that arm fixed." It's the fact that they were interesting and benevolent. "The audience wanted to come back and see them again," he explained. [With Jaime, they literally cried for Lindsay Wagner to return to the role.]

Like the original SM and BW episodes, and the two other reunions, *Bionic Ever After?* concentrated on storyline and characterizations, and lacked an extensive amount of violence. That's why Wendy's restaurant president, media watchdog, TV commercial star and Christian-based Dave Thomas not only purchased two ad-spaces of air time to be run during *After?*, but made a cameo appearance in the film.

Martin E. Brooks, who reprised his role as Dr. Rudy Wells in all three updated films, said the non-violent content allowed parents to more easily allow their children to watch. "I don't think the moms and dads of the world would have been so ready to have their kids sit and watch the shows if they were excessively violent."

Brooks categorizes the appeal of the *Bionic* programs as "phenomenal." After performing in several series, including, *General Hospital, Dallas* and *Knots Landing*, he said none have had the influence of the *Bionic* shows, from which he's usually recognized. He finds it difficult to assess how many times, even after all these years, that people see him on the street, and still say, "Hey, Rudy!" or "Dr. Wells, when are they going to do more *Bionics*?"

It all comes down, once again, to chemistry. "We all got along so well," the actor said of his performance association with Majors, Wagner and Richard Anderson. "Lee was charismatic, athletic, and believable. As Steve Austin, everyone at home was rooting for him to win. He made himself accessible to them, instead of playing it *super macho*. Lindsay's such a stunning actress. She has that vulnerability as a performer, which plays so invitingly well with the viewers. Richard was ever-so-slightly genial as Oscar when giving orders. He was demanding when he had to be, but not too much so that the audience would have shied away."

Clearly, with shows like SM and BW, viewers are allowed easy access to characters, and a series itself (sci-fi-premised or otherwise), via lack of intimidation, with a concentration on human or *real* stories. Central keys, all, to a program's success, and certainly for *The Six Million Dollar Man* and *The Bionic Woman*.

But success can invite typecasting. Richard Anderson, for one, doesn't seem to mind. Anderson, who attempted (in vain) to bring a theatrical version of *Six* to the big screen, notes that he, Lee and Lindsay are destined to be remembered as Oscar, Steve and Jaime — whether they like it or not. "The bionic concept is very identifiable," he said. "Our shows have tremendous legs."

In Anderson's opinion, if you could figure out the opening credits sequence, you could understand SM and BW. "This was a visual, high-adventure show which I think is why it became so successful in 60 countries," he said. "The dialogue was clear and simple and you could watch it without needing to know what was being said, as long as you understood the opening."

And wherever Richard roams, Oscar is never far behind. "I've done a lot of traveling since and it's been extraordinary," he remarks. "You're standing at the Great Wall of China and a Chinese man comes up and [recognizes] you! It's been unbelievable. Egypt, up river — anywhere. It's really quite satisfying. It made us all known in a different way than ever before, and from it came a period of other opportunities."

While most fans couldn't have picked Martin Caidin out of a lineup, he found that fame preceded him on a trip to South America. "A few years ago, my wife and I went to Caracas, Venezuela," he said. "We were front page news. I was known as the creator of *The Six Million Dollar Man*. At the airport were these big mobs of kids. I felt like the Pied Piper of Hamelin. The series is now showing in 72 countries."

The reunions were a chance for the principals to tie up loose strings and an opportunity for viewers to meet up with old friends. "Somebody 9 or 10 years old when we were first on is much older now, but has fond memories of us," Majors said. "I used to run home and watch *The Fugitive*. And if David Janssen was still alive and he played the role again, I would certainly watch. People remain loyal to their heroes."

He adds (with much amusement): "Everywhere I go, down in South America, all over Europe, I can't walk anywhere without people saying, 'El Hombre Nuclear!' or going '*do-do-do-do-do-do*' when I pass by."

Lindsay Wagner shares a similar experience. "The shows are popular everywhere," she said. "I was in a little village in Mexico to do a movie and I was dumbfounded. They had two TV sets in that town. But when I walked down the street, people would say, 'Oh, La Bionica!' I can't tell you how many women in their 30s and 40s still tell me that *The Bionic Woman* was a role model."

As to future cybernetic connections? "I hope there is a new *Bionic* TV show one day and a feature film," said Martin Caidin, "if not for just the fun of doing them, but for the further inspiration that they may encourage. Basically, because most of what we predicted 25 years ago has come true. I can't wait to see what the next 25 years will bring because of another *Bionic* TV show or movie."

Caidin's words proved prescient in 2006 when NBC announced plans for a new *Bionic Woman* series, starring British soap actress Michelle Ryan, to be produced by the creative minds behind yet another resurrected television show, *Battlestar Galactica*.

Ryan, a mere 22 years old when she landed the part, was not overly familiar with the original series. "I remember seeing clips of Lindsay Wagner and thinking that she looked like a very pretty, very nice lady," she said. "I was so young, and that's all I really remember. I sort of saw it as a very new piece. I didn't watch the original, apart from a few clips, and I just saw this really empowered, young female character. And I thought, this is just the sort of challenge that I've been looking for."

Aside from the atomic-powered limbs, will the new, "reimagined" Jaime in any way resemble her predecessor? "I would say she's feisty and smart and loyal, and also warm and vulnerable," said Ryan. "She's a young woman who's trying to find her way in life; she's dealing with these incredible things that are being thrown at her. But yes, she's kicking ass, and yeah, she is kind of taking on the world. But she's also feeling very vulnerable, and she has a boyfriend who isn't entirely honest with her. And you know, who can't identify with that?"

Richard Anderson is enthused about the 21st-Century Jaime Sommers. "*The Bionic Woman* is a platinum [brand] name," he said. "Wherever I go, I hear about bionics and the thing is, it's probably the perfect time for this show — people have been asking for it and my sense is that [NBC] has a golden opportunity to bring it back. If they should need a Washington man, I'll leave my phone number."

A substantial part of Martin Caidin's vision included new bionic heroes and their conjunction with telekinesis, which some term as *psycho kinesis*. "I'm not talking about that psychic crap," Caidin stressed. "I mean really being able to actually move something with your mind only. [As Kristy McNichol's character did in 'The Ghosthunter' segment of BW.] This is not just something that science is trying to do, but *has* been doing for the last 12 years. If anyone would like to learn how to do it, it will take me 48 hours to teach them. This is the truth. Why would I paint a bullseye on my damn forehead? It's real."

In terms of sci-fi and eventual real-life bionics, Caidin added, "We'll be able to affect the switches, drives, turbo-mechanisms, and solenoids within the body, by mentally controlling them. I could have some new version of Steve Austin walking down the street right now, with a combination of this new science. He could talk to any station, any agent, any control base, anywhere, anytime, day or night, in the world, just by walking. You wouldn't know that he would be in full control. He could have a holographic image in his eye, talking to the director of OSI while he's in a rowboat in Michigan or in China. We would know his location, within ten feet, by equipment that would be built right into his body." He professed that such technology has been available for years. Approximately twenty years ago, he gathered with a few scientific associates, and began working with Ken Rowley, a young boy whose lower limbs were afflicted with polio. "His legs were like two soft carrots, all his life," the author assessed. "He was never able to stand upright."

Caidin conferred with his colleagues, and said, "Wait a minute. Why don't we employ some of the ideas we used on *Six Mill?*" There were a total of four individuals, and none of them "even went to high school." They just got together. He designed a set of legs, which weighed about 60 pounds, and which they helped him to build with spare parts pirated from various automobile junkyards. They modified their creation with hacksaws, glue, wires and masking tape.

After the legs were constructed, Caidin said, "We gave them to Ken and, on his first try, he walked 36 feet. Best of all, the March of Dimes foundation came down and videotaped the entire experience, with a ¾-inch machine. Even though we got the whole damn thing on video, we never went anywhere with it. We made the terrible mistake of offering it free to our government. The Veterans Administration said, *Stop what you're doing, immediately. Cease and desist. If the word gets out that you can do this and we can't, we're liable to lose our $40-billion-dollar-a-year budget for this kind of research.* We didn't even use any power boosters. The secret was a parachute harness."

Not only that, but the system they were showcasing was similar to what was seen on *Six Mill*, back in 1976. "What we did with Ken," Caidin added, "with spare parts from junkyards, is a hundred times better than the multi-million-dollar things we're seeing now."

As to telekinesis, Caidin recalled an *experimental* meeting with John Kasher, Ph.D., a skeptical professor of physics at the University of Nebraska. "I had a sealed bell jar and a needle, balanced on a mound, with a 3x3-square piece of aluminum foil," Martin said of the test. "The idea was to try and turn it just by looking at it." He told Kasher not to worry about shaking the table, and even invited him to bang his fist on the table, promising that it would not turn. Caidin asked him if he was completely satisfied that there was no interference, looking through the room at the microwave, etc.

Kasher said it was sterile, without a doubt. Caidin told him, "We're gonna do something, and I don't want no shit from you later, like you overlooked something." At this point, Martin said those in the room became "a little upset," because he was speaking so casually with the head of the University's Physics Department.

Still, the *Cyborg* creator instructed the professor to place his hands against the jar, "because I'm gonna go *through* your hands." Martin then advised the educator to "count backwards, out loud, from 20 to 0." "By the time you reach zero," Martin promised, "your mind is going to get that target to turn." "No way," Kasher replied.

With approximately fifty people in the room, Caidin said Kasher put his hands on the bell jar, which was about one-foot-tall and six inches in diameter. "I wasn't touching him or the table," Martin claimed. By the time Kasher reached 17, Caidin told him to take his hands away from the jar, and place them in his lap. The professor was then instructed to step back about a foot-and-a-half to two feet. Caidin then said, "Now, look at the jar, and tell me what's happening?"

The target was spinning.

"Tell me which way?" Caidin asked.

"Counter-clockwise," Kasher responded.

"I told him we would bring it to a complete stop," Caidin reported. "Sure enough, the jar stood there, and the target started to slow down and reversed its direction."

"Dr. Kasher," Caidin went on to say, "you're either a cheat, a fake, a charlatan, a plain son-of-a-bitch, or you have just turned telekinetic."

According to Martin, Kasher "just freaked out, completely," and said, "You're making me go home and re-think everything I know about Physics."

Caidin returned with, "Welcome to the club, Doc."

"He was stunned," Caidin said of the prof. "The second law of thermodynamics is that you can't transmit a heat source, over a distance, without having a medium, a bead or a wire."

Kasher still wondered if Caidin was doing the turning.

"What the hell's the difference?" the author retorted.

Martin said "It wasn't a case of our saying we can do it. We don't expect anyone to believe it, no more than they believed the bionics 25 years ago. I just told him to keep practicing on his own for a while, and to call me when he has problems."

Kasher then asked about a special report on the finding.

"Doc," Martin replied, "I don't give a shit who knows it, and I don't care who believes me or who doesn't. That's not important. It's like an airplane; the damn thing flies, or it doesn't fly. I came from a life where I can bullshit all the people I want to about flying in the things I do. The records I set, the things I've done as a stunt pilot and air show pilot. If I lied to my airplane, doctor, it would kill me. We just dismissed lying from the way we do things; it's not worth it. We're not going to live that long. What other people think and don't think, it doesn't mean a thing. If you deny it [what you just did], you'll be lying to yourself, and that's the worst kind of lie there is."

On hearing this, Caidin said, "Kasher packed up all his scientific gear and left the area, shaking his head."

There may have been those network executives or TV viewers who initially felt like chucking it all and leaving *The Six Million Dollar Man* behind, during its transformation from pilot, to monthly, then weekly formats. Instead, everyone associated with the show, as well as loyal fans, stuck by it. Subsequently, a television classic, and its top-notch sequel, was born. Those involved in bringing any particularly worthy program to the air must be patient, in their execution of the given series, allowing it to find its niche and audience (and vice versa), specifically when dealing with a sci-fi premise.

Six Mill, said initial producer Glen Larson, is "not the type of show that becomes the darling of the critics. It's the type of show that becomes a hit and generates millions and millions of dollars worth of merchandising and fan devotion. It was a pretty big smash around the world, and it was an important stepping-stone for sci-fi, in terms of the audience accepting science fiction at all. Science fiction has never been very successful on television, with all due respect to *Star Trek*, which didn't make it on network TV. It's a cumulative thing — the audience today has grown up with science fiction. Years ago, when you were going for a network share, the devotees of science fiction would not get you the numbers you needed.

"So you'd have to look at *Six Mill* as a show that really sort of helped [sci-fi] break out into the general population, because it contained special elements and the audience didn't say 'nonsense' and turn it off. *Six* was a stepping stone upon which other shows have benefited since." [Ironically, it was Larson's lavish *Battlestar Galactica* that replaced *Six* in ABC's primetime schedule during the fall of 1978.]

When producing episodic television, Ken Johnson said there's a tendency to work fast. "We don't want it good," the networks or studios will say, "We want it Thursday." "That's not a positive thing," Johnson comments, "and that's why I've always tried to insert in my work a little bit of something extra, when it comes to substance. I know there's a lot of people out there who will be watching. First and foremost, they should be entertained, and enjoy what they're watching. They must be touched and moved by it, as well, and possibly, dare I say the *e-word*, even educated."

He said it's so easy for those in the entertainment industry to forget the kind of influence that they have on audiences. There's also a tendency to think that those on the soundstage are alone, thinking that it's just the actors, directors, writers, production team, because they don't get that immediate feedback, as one might receive if doing a play in front of a live audience. "There are millions and millions of people who we are reaching on a daily or weekly basis," Ken assessed. "That's a huge responsibility that should never be taken lightly."

To further illustrate his point, Johnson recalls train rides he used to take, while attending Carnegie Tech: "I would go throughout the small towns of Maryland and Pennsylvania, very late at night, and get momentary glimpses into the windows of various homes. It used to make me cry, and I never could figure out why. Finally, I realized it was because I felt there was all this humanity out there that I was never going to know, or never going to reach, because the train was moving so fast, which really turned out to be a metaphor for the pace of life.

"Now I get fan letters from places like Lima, Peru, Tokyo, Buenos Aires, and all over the United States. I've come to realize the huge responsibility that I have as someone in the entertainment industry. I have to care about what I do, and to keep a social awareness or consciousness about my work. I would rather not make television shows or movies, unless they imbue some kind of social virtue. To this day, when I recall those lonely nights peering out the window of that moving train, the feelings all flow back into me. But now instead of finding tears in my eyes, I realize that I'm smiling."

Whether he knows it or not, Johnson has soul mates in esteemed sci-fi thinker Issac Asimov and TV producer Kim Friedman, who returned super-females to the small screen with the syndicated smash, *Xena*.

Asimov, for one, once linked *The Six Million Dollar Man*, and its potential for positive influence on humankind, with an article he wrote for *TV Guide*, saying: "The ultimate cyborg will consist of a man's brain, spinal cord, and as much of his nerves as are necessary, placed within an utterly mechanical body which it controls. Such a cyborg can be visualized as a superman indeed, if the parts are properly designed. He can be incredibly strong by ordinary human standards, incredibly quick, incredibly versatile. As long as the brain is protected, he would be able to endure hard environments. He could explore other worlds with little in the way of life-supporting equipment. With nuclear energy for power, such a cyborg would have to supply oxygen only for the brain, and could remain in outer space far more easily than he could now."

"And then," he concluded, "...we may finally be allowed to join the great Universal Brotherhood of Mind that [for all we know] represents the peak and acme of what life has striven for since creation."

Meanwhile, Friedman's *Xena* infused a social consciousness of its own, with strong characterizations and morality plays, almost concealed by an action/adventure/fantasy premise. As she told *Entertainment Weekly* in early 1997, "I've always been a big believer in the power of popular culture. The best way to convey more challenging ideas is to make something that functions on a mainstream level but that has subtext that people can pick up on."

Like the morality that contributed so profoundly to *Xena's* appeal, or to that of *Star Trek* (in any of its forms), Steve and Jaime exuded integrity, and eventually arrived at a similarly important conclusion: true self-worth is internal. External differences may be obstacles or stumbling blocks, but they may also be stepping-stones to a higher level of understanding and growth in *character*. Steve and Jaime's respective accidents temporarily lead them off-track. Blessings in disguise, their *A-Type* personalities gifted them with the internal strength to deal with unfortunate circumstances.

Only after their super-powered transformations, and experience of loss, did they realize the futility of being over-driven. In their pre-bionic days, their motivation for achievement was indeed, super-human. In their post-bionic lives, however, they strived to retain their humanity, which they treasured as their most important component, thus connecting with the *great link* of television viewers around the world. Their super-human drive to *be the best* (pilot or tennis player) reached a subconscious peak with their bionic reconstruction, while their mutual love eventually blossomed, because and in spite of their bionic similarities.

Periodically, they may have felt isolated by society due to their uniquely mechanical body parts. Yet, it was these same parts that allowed them to become and comprehend what it really means to be human and whole. They were *complete* individuals, in the truest sense of the word. Complete within themselves, and as a couple.

Of the general sci-fi/pop-culture influence of *The Six Million Dollar Man* and *The Bionic Woman*, Lindsay Wagner hits the nail on the head, concluding, "Science fiction can really be a wonderful thing. It can take you beyond the mundane existence of life. If you can imagine it, you can feel it. When you feel it, some part of you knows that it's possible."

TOP LEFT, RIGHT: THE SIX MILLION DOLLAR MAN PILOT. MIDDLE
LEFT: WINE, WOMEN AND WAR (W/ BRITT EKLAND). BOTTOM LEFT:
THE SOLID GOLD KIDNAPPING.

CHAPTER 10

AUSTIN'S ADVENTURES

"AN EPISODIC SERIES IS LIKE A SONNET. A SONNET
HAS FOURTEEN LINES. NO MORE, NO LESS. IF IT
HAS MORE, IT'S NOT A SONNET."

FRANK PRICE

There are 157 produced episodes of *The Six Million Dollar Man* and *The Bionic Woman* combined: 100 segments for SM, 57 for BW. Addressed separately are the three 90-minute SM telefilms, as well as the three bionic reunion movies. This chapter, along with the following two, breaks down each segment, beginning with the episode number, title, and original airdate. A plot summary then follows, while concluding singular or various anecdotes for each are denoted by a bullet symbol (•).

The original episode guides for SM and BW begin with cast and crew lists, along with some familiar narrative remarks heard or seen during the opening credit sequences for both shows.

First up, the adventures of Steve Austin, otherwise known as — *The Six Million Dollar Man.*

Cast

Col. Steve Austin	Lee Majors
Oscar Goldman	Richard Anderson
Dr. Rudy Wells	Alan Oppenheimer (years 1-2)
	Martin E. Brooks (years 3-5)

Production

Executive Producer	Harve Bennett
Producer(s)	Kenneth Johnson
	Lionel E. Siegel
	Allan Balter
	Arnold F. Turner
	Michael Gleason

Fred Freiberger
Richard Landau

Based on a novel by . . . . Martin Caidin
Theme . . . . Oliver Nelson

Broadcast History

Between September 1973 and December 1973, there were two *Six Million Dollar Man* 90-minute television episodes that aired on Saturday night at 8:30 PM. The competition on NBC was the last half of *Emergency!* and the first hour of the *NBC Saturday Night Movie*. Over at CBS, there was *M*A*S*H*, *The Mary Tyler Moore Show*, and *The Bob Newhart Show*.

From January 1974 to August 1974, SM aired as a weekly 60-minute series on Friday nights, from 8:30 PM to 9:30 PM. Its competition on NBC was *Lotsa Luck* and *The Girl with Something Extra* (starring would-be *Bionic Woman* Sally Field). On CBS: *Good Times*, and the first half of the *CBS Friday Night Movie*.

From September 1974 to November 1974, SM continues on Fridays, 8:30 PM to 9:30 PM. Its competition on NBC: *Chico and the Man*, and the first half of *The Rockford Files*. On CBS, the last half of *Planet of the Apes*, the first half-hour of the *CBS Friday Night Movie*.

In January 1975, SM settled into its familiar Sunday night timeslot, 8:00 PM to 9:00 PM. There, it competed with such shows as *Emergency!* (NBC), *The Family Holvak* (NBC), *Rhoda* (CBS), *The Sonny and Cher Show* (CBS), and *The Wonderful World of Disney* (NBC). It would remain there until January 1978, when it moved for the last time to Monday nights as a lead-in for *Monday Night Football*, 8:00 PM to 9:00 PM.

Opening Narrative
(rough translation)

Flight Commander (lookout tower)
"Looks good at NASA One."

NASA One (trailer)
"Roger."

B-52 Pilot (Victor)
"BCS Arm switch is on."

Flight Commander
"Okay, Victor."

B-52 Pilot
"Lining Rocket Arm switch is on."

B-52 Pilot
"Here comes the throttle."

B-52 Pilot
"Circuit breakers in."

Steve
"We have separation."

Flight Commander
"Roger."

NASA One
"Inboards and outboards are on."

B-52 Pilot
"I'm comin' forward with the side-stick."

B-52 Pilot
"All looks good."

Flight Commander
"Ah, Roger."

Steve
"I've got a blow-out in damper three."

NASA One
"Get your pitch to zero."

Steve
"Pitch is out! I can't hold altitude!"

NASA One
"Correction. Alpha Hold is off...Prep selectors...
Emergency!"

Steve
"Flight Com! I can't hold it! She's breaking up, she's
break..."

Narrator (Harve Bennett)
"Steve Austin...
"Astronaut...
"A man barely alive."

Narrator (Richard Anderson as *Oscar Goldman*)*

"Gentlemen, we can rebuild him. We have the technology.
We have the capability to make the world's first bionic
man. Steve Austin will be that man. Better than he was
before. Better...stronger...faster."

* *An abbreviated version was used during the first season only.*

ABC Pilot and Suspense Telefilms
1973

Pilot Film: *The Six Million Dollar Man* .... [3-7-73]
*Written by Howard Rodman (a.k.a. Henri Simoun), Steven Bochco. Based on
the novel* Cyborg *by Martin Caidin. Directed by Richard Irving. Featuring:
Darren McGavin* (Kolchak: The Night Stalker), *Barbara Anderson* (Ironside), *
Martin Balsam, Ivor Barry, Robert Cornthwaite, Olan Soule, Charles Knox
Robinson, George Wallace, Dorothy Green, Maurice Sherbanee, Anne Whitfield,
Norma Storch, Richard Webb*

Rudy Wells has been Steve Austin's healing guardian for years. Suddenly,
Austin's experimental aircraft malfunctions and crashes, leaving him without a right arm, two legs and a left eye. The stakes are high. Oliver Spencer
(an early kingpin of the Office of Strategic Operations) orders Wells to save
Austin's life, whatever the cost (six million dollars).

Spencer's agenda and objective, however, involves a new cybernetic technology called *bionics*. He expects Steve to make a full and *stronger* recovery. Rudy foretells of his patient's possible psychological struggle. Sixteen
weeks later, the good doctor's prediction comes true. Upon awakening
from an "electro sleep" coma (and not yet bionic), Steve learns of his condition, and attempts suicide. With few options available, he okays the revolutionary procedure. His emotional stability returns, with the assistance of
Nurse Manners. On a picnic, he saves a trapped boy in a car, ripping open
his atomic arm. The mother reacts with intense revulsion. Steve is again
thrown into emotional disarray.

An OSO assignment in the Middle East may hold the cure. Rudy thinks
it may help him cope with his new psychophysical position. The now *Six
Million Dollar Man* travels to free an Arab-Israeli leader, is captured (by rev-

olutionaries), and escapes, completing his first tour of duty.

• First seen in a 90-minute format as part of ABC's very popular *Movie-of-the-Week* package, this episode is now broadcast in syndication as two one-hour segments, with 30 extra minutes of filler lifted from other episodes, new voice-overs from Martin Balsam, and a new title: "The Moon and the Desert (Parts I and II)."

• The pilot beat a Bob Hope special in the ratings — a first for ABC.

• Richard Irving, who directed the *Six* pilot, also directed the pilot for *Columbo*.

• Steven Bochco: "Dick Irving called me and said, 'I want you to re-write a pilot that we have here. It just needs work.' It was written by a wonderful, wonderful writer by the name of Howard Rodman, long since deceased. I read the script and I thought, 'Wow! This is terrific. This is a great script.' So I called Dick Irving and I said, 'I can't re-write this. This is terrific. I mean, what could I do to make this better than it is?' He said, 'Well, it needs this and it needs that. And Howard doesn't want to work on it anymore.' I said, 'I don't want to do it. I wouldn't want to offend Howard,' who was a very well-known writer. The next thing I know my phone rings, and it's Howard Rodman, who was so sweet, saying, 'I'm very flattered, but please with my blessings go ahead and do whatever you feel is [necessary].' So I did. Howard was famous for his volatile nature and his temper tantrums, but I never saw a trace of that. Years later, I worked with Harve Bennett on The Invisible Man pilot, which was fun."

• Pilot filmed at Edwards Air Force Base, California, and Yuma, Arizona.

• Many of the operating theatre scenes previously surfaced in a 1972 *Columbo* episode entitled "A Stitch in Crime."

• Although Steve was an Air Force colonel in both *Cyborg* and the weekly series, he had no such rank in the pilot. Instead, he was a civilian member of NASA.

• Oliver Spencer is introduced as Austin's superior. This character did not exist in *Cyborg*, though Oscar Goldman *did*.

• The manual that accompanies Steve's bionic arm is an exhausting 840 pages.

• In contrast to *Cyborg*, the pilot (and subsequent series) took many liberties with Steve's new anatomical features. In the book, Steve's eye is merely a camera. In the telefilm, his sight has been restored and enhanced. More extravagant abilities like fingers that shoot darts and legs that conceal small oxygen tanks were dropped altogether. He was also stronger and faster on TV as compared to the book.

• Curiously, the word "bionic" is never uttered in the pilot. Caidin first used the term in a pre-*Cyborg* novel entitled *The God Machine*, published in 1968.

• Martin Caidin's *Cyborg* was initially rejected by 12 publishers. "Nobody could understand it," he said. "In fact, NBC had an option on it for one year. One guy at NBC desperately wanted to do it, but he couldn't convince the NBC brass. They dropped it, and Dick Irving at Universal snapped it up just like that. Dick produced it himself and made sure I was there all the time as technical director. They said, *Look, we need to take certain license, but don't let us get away with anything.*"

• You may have (briefly) heard the name "Steve Austin" on primetime television *before* Six Mill's debut. In the classic *Honeymooners* episode entitled "A Matter of Record" (which first aired on January 7, 1956), Ed Norton has his hands full managing a neighborhood youth stickball team. Trouble ensues when his second baseman comes down with a case of the measles. The little boy's name? You guessed it: Steve Austin.

• *Daily Variety*: "To the pilot's credit, this farfetched science fiction concept was developed with much sincerity and sensitivity, while somehow avoiding the grisly side of Majors' initial tragedy. Considerable footage was given to how the prosthetics and other rebuilding increments would work, and it played off persuasively [whatever the factual merits may be]."

Telefilm 2: *Wine, Women and War* .... **[10-20-73]**
Written by Glen A. Larson. Directed by Russ Mayberry. Featuring: Britt Ekland, Eric Braeden (The Young and the Restless), *Earl Holliman* (Police Story), *Michele Carey, David McCallum* (The Man from U.N.C.L.E., The Invisible Man), *Lee Bergere, Simon Scott, Robert F. Simon* (Bewitched), *Dennis Rucker, George Keymas*

Steve hops on a stationary yacht to retrieve documents housed in a safe, which he finds bare. As he exits, watchmen commence fire, miss and damage the ship's fuel tank. He's disabled when Spanish militia release a depth charge, and a nuclear sub retrieves him.

Rehabilitated, he seeks out a nuclear weapons black market ring, hooking up with Alexi and Katrina. He also finds Cynthia, who invites him on a fishing trip where he is captured and again attacked. Unharmed, he swims to the beach, and hides in the trunk of the ringleader's limo.

While Steve is transported to the complex where the stolen missiles are stored, Alexi is killed trying to help him and Cynthia. After trapping two thugs and releasing a missile, he and Cynthia are then rescued by the nuclear sub.

• Richard Anderson and Alan Oppenheimer arrive in their respective roles.

• Glen Larson: "I cast Richard Anderson because when you're doing what I call a bullshit premise, you need to surround it with as much honesty and reality as you can. Richard brought us that credibility. It was less likely that the series was going to end up as a cartoon."

• Anderson's famous "Gentlemen, we can rebuild him" line can be traced to *War's* intro. In it, he issues this directive to doctors: "What if he could be *more* than the man he was? We have the technology to rebuild him. I want it done no matter what the cost."

• The first and only time Steve is seen in a bed with a woman (Britt Ekland as Katrina). We also later see his struggle with intimacy, when Cynthia (Michele Carey) asks him if he likes girls. "What you're really wondering is why I haven't made a pass at you," Steve replies. "Well, I read some place that you shouldn't be in too much of a hurry to be rid of a hurt. It's good for people to feel. That's what separates us from machines, and some institutions."

• In the weekly SM and all through BW, Steve and Jaime rarely kill anyone. Here, he intentionally sets off a nuclear explosion at an enemy complex, killing all inside and anyone within close proximity.

• Steve wears his trademark belt-buckle for the first time.

• Short scenes in *Wine, Women and War*, as well as *The Solid Gold Kidnapping*, feature large mainframe computers. The footage was borrowed from the 1970 Universal film *Colossus: The Forbin Project*. Coincidentally, bionic doc Martin E. Brooks and Eric Braeden appeared in the film.

• We witness Steve using his bionic eye for the first time, when he needs to see in the dark. A green filter is used on the camera, instead of the more familiar infrared.

• ABC's publicity department described this movie thusly: "James Bond, Superman and Batman rolled into one. That's Steve Austin, a badly injured former astronaut whose body has been replaced with super-human parts. Now a government agent, Austin, played by Lee Majors, uses his finely tooled prowess to apprehend top criminals who are, alas, only human."

Telefilm 3: *The Solid Gold Kidnapping.* . . . . [11-17-73]
Written by Larry Alexander. Story by Alan Caillou, Michael Gleason, Larry Alexander. Directed by Russ Mayberry. Featuring: Leif Erickson, Elizabeth Ashley, John Vernon (Animal House)*, Luciana Paluzzi, Maurice Evans* (Bewitched)*, Terry Carter, Craig Huebing, David White* (Bewitched)*, Polly Middleton*

American Ambassador Scott is captured and held for ransom by an international band of kidnappers. From their freighter base, the extortionists devise the seizure of other significant officials from around the globe.

Steve rescues the Ambassador from an isolated ancient Yucatan temple, returns to Washington, and sets out to rescue worldly statesman William

Henry Cameron. On his way to China (for an upper-brass Asian government mediation), Cameron had been faking an illness in a Paris hospital. He was kidnapped before he could complete his task. His costly redemption? One billion dollars in gold bullion, to be delivered within 48 hours.

On the President's consent, Fort Knox readies the order. Yet the precious metal is lifted from its concealed path prior to its rendezvous with the kidnappers. Steve's sole piece of evidence rests with the gang member who was killed during Cameron's capture.

Dr. Erica Bergner, who has cultivated a process of human brain cell transference, is called upon for assistance. The brain cells of the dead kidnapper are obtained, and Dr. Bergner delivers to Steve enough information from the cells for him to acquire the gold and free Cameron.

• Originally aired as a 90-minute movie, this episode, like *Wine, Women and War,* is shown in syndication in two separate segments with 30 minutes of extra material.

• Lionel Siegel: "I was brought into the 90-minute series by my friend, Michael Gleason. I functioned as story editor and rewriter. Gleason and I worked together on *Peyton Place* and *It's a Man's World.* I had never done action-adventure before — it was a challenge." As for the *Six Mill* premise? "I had always been interested in 'machines and the man,'" he said. "I personally felt that this guy, with parts of his body missing, was a positive model for anyone who was handicapped [as we all are one way or another]. If he could make it, if he could overpower evil, then, maybe, we might have a chance, too."

• When Dr. Bergner, played by Elizabeth Ashley, asks Steve, "What are you trying to prove?" he replies with the memorable line, "That I'm more than the sum of my parts."

• After Steve is told that he's "a slave to modern technology," he replies, "Uh-huh. You'll never know how much."

• Shares some similarities with the Martin Caidin novel *Cyborg III: High Crystal,* in which Steve is dispatched to investigate a pyramid in Mexico.

• In Mexico, *Six Mill* was called *El Hombre Nuclear. The Bionic Woman* was *La Mujer Bionica.*

• Original working titles: "The Billion Dollar Snatch" and "The Billion Dollar Diplomat."

"POPULATION: ZERO" (W/ PENNY FULLER), "SURVIVAL OF THE FITTEST," "OPERATION FIREFLY," "DAY OF THE ROBOT," "LITTLE ORPHAN AIRPLANE" (W/ GREG MORRIS), "EYEWITNESS TO MURDER," "THE LAST OF THE FOURTH OF JULYS," "THE COWARD" (W/ GEORGE MONTGOMERY)

The First Season
January 1974 to April 1974

Episode 1: *Population: Zero* . . . . **[1-18-74]**
Written by Elroy Schwartz. Directed by Jeannot Szwarc. Featuring: Don Porter (Gidget), Penny Fuller, Colby Chester, Walter Brooke, Paul Fix, Paul Carr, Virginia Gregg, John Elerick, Morgan Jones, Mike Santiago, Stuart Nisbet, Bob Delegall, David Valentine

The small town of Norris, California has a problem: Its population is apparently dead. In reality, an ear-shattering high-frequency device has temporarily immobilized the townspeople. Steve, Oscar, and a small army investigate. Dr. Stanley Bacon, a rancorous scientist who once worked for the government, is the culprit, mandating ten million dollars. If not, another town will be destroyed. Yet The Six Million Dollar Man is not about to let that happen.

• Steve and Jaime were not prone to killing, but he kills three evildoers here.

• In reality, Norris had a population of 23.

• One of the few episodes to address Vietnam (where Steve's childhood friend dies).

• Steve is locked in a freezer, and there's the first mention of how bionics don't function properly in the cold. (The frigid-aspect was mentioned again in "Bigfoot V," "Dark Side of the Moon," "Hocus-Pocus," and the BW segment, "The Martians Are Coming.")

• Establishes the "fact" that bionic limbs emit trace amounts of radiation — something also referenced in "Run, Steve, Run," "Kill Oscar Part II," and "Sharks! Part I."

• Marks the initiation of *Six* as a weekly series. Barry Diller was the head of ABC programming. "It was he who commissioned the weekly series," recalls Harve Bennett. "Steve Gantry was his *Number Two* man and, to me, was the most helpful outside force in getting *Six Mill* on the air."

• Gantry was also the man Bennett most respected at any network, "at any time." Extremely gifted, Gantry was a former naval aviator, who died tragically in a plane crash. Bruce Geller and Gantry owned the plane together, and went down in the fog in Santa Barbara. The final irony? Bennett's longtime secretary, Sylvia Rubenstein, passed away about the same time. His current secretary, Charlene Bergman, was Gantry's secretary. About one year after Steve died, Bennett relays, "we each lost our favorite person in the business." So Bennett asked Charlene to work for him, and they've been together ever since.

• Writer Elroy Schwartz is the brother of super-producer Sherwood Schwartz (*Gilligan's Island, Brady Bunch*).

• Richard Anderson's "Better, stronger, faster" voiceover makes its debut. Anderson: "I got a call one morning from the producers saying, 'Please come in. We've got some material for the title.' I was working hard all day; I was in every shot. When we wrapped, I got in my car, got to the front gate and said *My God. I forgot.* So I dashed back, walked in, and they're sitting there, waiting. And with that kind of energy I just dug in and did it. They said, 'We're gonna use some of this stuff. It's good.' To the best of my recollection, one of the producers [Bennett] had been using his own voice. But the word got out and SAG [Screen Actors Guild] got on it. SAG said he couldn't [legally] do that, so they took it out and made him stop. That's when they called me in to complete the rest of the opening narrative."

Episode 2: *Survival of the Fittest* .... **[1-25-74]**
Written by Mann Rubin. Story by Lionel E. Siegel, Harve Bennett. Directed by Leslie Martinson. Featuring: James McEachin, William Smith, Christine Belford, Randy Carver, W.T. Zacha, Laurette Spang (Battlestar Galactica, Happy Days), *Joanne Worley* (Laugh-In), *Reid Smith, Dale Johnson, Dick Valentine, Jim Raymond*

Prior to momentous conversations with Russian officials, Oscar is nearly struck by an automobile. Apparently, several nations are plotting to prevent the historic diplomatic dialogue from taking place. Still, the meetings convene. Steve and Oscar's chartered plane crashes near a Pacific island. They survive, along with Nurse Lt. Colby, Pfc. Barris, Navy commander Ted Maxwell and Air Force Lt. Ralph Cromwell, the latter of whom plans to do away with Oscar. Before Steve can stop them, they strive to bait the OSI head into a ravine for the final kill. Col. Austin intervenes, saves his wounded boss, and proves that Cromwell and Maxwell are not model citizens.

• Remade as "Fly Jaime" for *The Bionic Woman*. Both share a similar plot, location, and even dialogue, including: "Is this seat taken?" "You look like a regular *Bionic Santa Claus!*" "You're awfully chipper this morning, considering the circumstances," and "Why not? We're alive and safe."

• Steve employs two hot wires from his bionic finger to cauterize Oscar's bleeding vein after being shot (thereby launching a very special friendship); Jaime does the same for Rudy in "Fly Jaime."

• Steve's bionic eye switches from green to infrared for nighttime vision.

Episode 3: *Operation Firefly* .... [2-1-74]
Written by Sy Salkowitz. Story by Ric Hardman. Directed by Reza Badiyi. Featuring: Pamela Franklin (Buck Rogers in the 25th Century), *Simon Scott, Jack Hogan, Joseph Ruskin, Vic Mohica, Erik Holland, Joe Kapp, Bill Conklin*

Dr. Samuel Abbott, the inventor of the first portable laser projector (similar to the chemical energy used by fireflies), is abducted by a syndicate. Steve begins a rescue, with the assistance of the scientist's daughter, Susan, who's psychic. The syndicate heads, Charlie LeDuc and John Belson (an associate of Abbott's), take the artificer to the Florida Everglades. Susan's extra-sensory powers reveal her father's location. She and Steve are hunted down by henchmen who destroy their boat, and kill their guide. Steve creates a canoe from a log; a simple chore, as opposed to guiding Dr. Abbott and daughter out from the treacherous Everglades and into safety.
• Steve's "cross-hairs" eye effect (and accompanying trademark sound) is employed here for the first time.
• We learn that OSI stands for "Office of Scientific Intelligence"—the earliest explanation of what the acronym means.

Episode 4: *Day of the Robot* .... [2-8-74]
Written by Del Reisman. Story by Harold Livingston, Lionel Siegel. Directed by Leslie Martinson. Featuring: John Saxon (Planet: Earth), *Henry Jones* (Phyllis), *Lloyd Bochner, Charles W. Bateman, Noah Keen, Robert Rothwell, Lou Elias, Marc Alaimo* (Star Trek: The Next Generation, Star Trek: Deep Space Nine)

As a result of information gleaned from someone working on the inside, a group of men learn of plans for testing an anti-missile missile device. In an effort to pilfer the system (and market it to the topmost foreign buyer), they replace Steve's associate and longtime friend, Major Sloan, with an android. The tests of the missile system prove successful; the robot steals the device. Steve is forced to confront Sloan's duplicate, which has been programmed to kill the bionic astronaut.
• At the beginning of this episode, guest actor Lloyd Bochner is seen quizzing the robot, whose back is turned to the camera and is donning a hooded sweat suit. The camera proceeds to show us that Bochner is feeding questions to an automaton without its life-like face mask. One problem: a glass window directly opposite him catches the robot's reflection, and a human face can be seen fairly clearly.
• Steve knocks off the facial section of the android played by John Saxon. "That was the first time we ever did a ring mechanical effect," said Lee Majors. "It was fairly pioneering for the time. John was great. He was

diabolically perfect in the role."

• Steve is on the ground and uses his legs to turn over the car (to flatten the guy who's about to shoot him). At first we see his feet several inches away from the car. The film *jumps* and his feet are on the bumper. Worse yet, shadows cast by the chains used to topple the car can clearly be seen.

• The first time we hear the instantly recognizable bionic sound (*ch-ch-ch-shing*), it is employed not by Steve, but rather the android.

• The robot's distinctive "angry attack" sound can be traced to Universal's 1971 film, *How to Frame a Figg*.

• John Saxon reminisces about "Day of the Robot": "You know, I really liked doing that episode of *The Six Million Dollar Man*, and a lot of other people enjoyed watching it. It's rare that viewers recognize an actor from a single episode of television, but I'm recognized often from that one because it was so unusual to play a robot, which is a separate character as well. That episode is twenty-plus years old, but I find that it has stuck in the memory of many young TV fans to a considerable extent. I haven't seen Lee Majors in many years. I hope he remembers the series and that particular episode fondly, also."

• Director Les Martinson: "There's an eight-minute fight in slow motion at the end. The episode got the highest rating of that season. Some months later, I was in a theater and there was a tap on my shoulder. It was John Saxon. 'Thank you, Leslie,' he said, 'for destroying my career. Here I've done all of this theater and for the last two months, everyone refers to me as being the robot on *The Six Million Dollar Man*!'"

• Original working title: "Duel of Giants."

Episode 5: Little Orphan Airplane .... **[2-22-74]**
Written by Elroy Schwartz. Directed by Reza Badiyi. Featuring: Greg Morris (Mission: Impossible), Scoey Mitchell, Marge Redmond (The Flying Nun), Lincoln Kilpatrick, Susan Powell, Arnold Turner, Tierre Turner, Dave Turner, Ji-Tu Cumbuka, Paul Bryar, Stack Pierce, Dale Robertson

Steve journeys to Africa, discovers pilot John Perkins at a mission run by nuns, and finds film that contains evidence of UN treaty tampering. Col. Austin also learns that Perkins was injured in a crash-landing. Major Chooka and his men are closing in on the mission to collect the film, which displays weapons and soldiers being supplied at the Kataras station. Steve needs to get it out of the country. He repairs the plane's damaged landing gear before Chooka and his mercenaries show up.

• A guest star's name is misspelled in the opening credits as Scoey Mitch*lll*.

• On his government ID card, Steve's address is listed as: 13537 Federal

Street, Washington D.C. Telephone: 555-7892.

• Steve is offered a gun for protection but declines, noting that they're too "dangerous."

• Elroy Schwartz on Harve Bennett: "We had our run-ins. The first thing that he did was he hired another writer, Lee Siegel, and gave us each the same job--story editor. You're not supposed to do that. So I went over and complained about that. I said, 'My contract said story editor, and you gave Siegel the same job. How can you do that?' Harve replied, 'I'll tell you what. If you'd rather write the show, we'll turn your deal into scripts.' So I said, 'Okay, I'll do four scripts.'"

Episode 6: Doomsday, and Counting . . . .[3-1-74]
Written by Larry Brody. Story by Larry Brody, Jimmy Sangster. Directed by Jerry Jameson. Featuring: Gary Collins (The Sixth Sense, Home), *William Smithers, Jane Merrow, Bruce Glover, Walker Edmiston, William Boyett, James Gavin, Rico Cattani, Anne Newman*

Colonel Vasily Zhukov visits America to attenuate a request for a space partnership with his Soviet Union. An earthquake activates a self-destruct weapon at an island spacecraft installation. Steve suggests that he accompany Zhukov to the Arctic isle where Zhukov's fiancée, Irena Leonova, waits under the ruins. Steve doesn't have much time: He has to rescue Irena and the entire island before an atomic annihilation.

• "I was very fond of Gary Collins," said Harve Bennett of the guest star who had previously worked for him at ABC. "I always thought he was a gifted actor. He had also done a *Movie-of-the-Week* for me called *Houston, We've Got a Problem.*" Bennett said Collins was cast because he had a wonderful Slavic, high-cheek-boned look for the sympathetic Russian character he played. "I didn't think of it at the time," Bennett admits, "but that episode was relevant to two events in world history. One was the subsequent docking of *Apollo-Soyuz* and the other was Chernobyl. As I recall, that story took place in Russian territory. It required the defusing of something nuclear on Soviet soil. Only Austin can do it with the help of a fellow Russian astronaut. So it had all that *juice* going for it."

• Blooper: While attempting to remove an obstruction, a sizable chunk of concrete hits Steve in the head, but he emerges unscathed.

• Steve manages to detect the triggering device for a nuclear bomb by using a Geiger counter built into his arm.

Episode 7: *Eyewitness to Murder*........................... [3-8-74]
Written by William Driskill. Directed by Alf Kjellin. Featuring: Gary Lockwood (Star Trek, 2001: A Space Odyssey), *William Schallert* (The Patty Duke Show), *Ivor Barry, Leonard Stone, Regis Cordic, Lew Palter, Al Dunlap, Donna Mantoan, Allen Joseph, Sal Ponti, Richard Webb, Nicky Blair*

Special prosecutor Lorin Sandusky submits evidence to the grand jury on racketeer Victor Ritchie, and a sniper threatens his life. Steve bionically views the culprit, and from police mug shots, nails him as John Hopper. Hopper, however, was broadcasting live on television at the exact moment that Lorin was fired upon. Undaunted, Steve keeps a watchful eye on Lorin (his life may once again be threatened) and Hopper (who's in his hotel). The Austin instinct then proves correct. He makes a keen observation regarding Hopper's face, prompting a new course of action.
 • Gary Lockwood appeared in *Return of The Six Million Dollar Man and The Bionic Woman.*

Episode 8: *The Rescue of Athena One*...................... [3-15-74]
Written by D.C. Fontana (Star Trek). *Directed by Larry Doheny. Featuring: Farrah Fawcett-Majors* (Charlie's Angels), *Paul Kent, Dean Smith, Jules Bergman (as himself), Quinn Redeker, John S. Ragin, Doug Collins*

Major Kelly Wood is the USA's first female astronaut. In orbit, a blast injures her fellow crew member and damages the ship. With the assistance of Skylab, she anticipates the appearance of a rescue squad and medical aid, but the accident has blocked the entrance. Steve is launched into space to dislodge the obstruction. Celestial conditions weaken his bionic abilities. There is little time for him to salvage his powers: additional obstacles are appearing before all can see themselves clear.
 • The one time we see Oscar smoke (Richard Anderson is health conscious). No other main character did, except on an undercover assignment.
 • Caidin's movie, *Marooned,* was the major factor in the collaborative space effort leading to the *Apollo-Soyuz* joint U.S./Soviet space mission. To this day, all Soviet and American spacecraft have "common docking mechanisms" to allow for the possibility of future rescues.
 • Written by *Trek* vet DC Fontana, this episode initiates the substantial *Trek/Bionic* alliance: Fontana went on to write another *Six* segment ("Straight On 'Til Morning"). The first few *Trek* films were executive produced by Harve Bennett. SM's "Eyewitness to Murder" and "Steve Austin, Fugitive" featured *Trek* vet Gary Lockwood (Lt. Gary Mitchell in *Star's* second pilot, "Where No Man Has Gone Before"). George *Sulu* Takei was in SM's "The Coward," William Shatner shows up in "Burning Bright," Marc

Alaimo appears in "Day of the Robot" and "Sharks!," John DeLancie has cameos in "Death Probe" and "Just a Matter of Time," and *Deep Space Nine* producer Peter Allan Fields penned several *Bionic* episodes. Other SM/BW guest stars with *Trek* experience include William Schallert, Ted Cassidy, Malachi Throne, Arlene Martell, Paul Carr, Barbara Anderson, Robert Walker, Rene Auberjonois, Robert Lansing, Ray Walston, Bibi Besch, Alan Oppenheimer, and John Colicos.

• D.C. Fontana: "Another writer had worked on the concept, which was basically a woman astronaut, and the producers said 'Forget about it. Just give us a new story.' At that time, Air Force nurses were in training to be astronauts, be it as members of Apollo crews or working on the Space Shuttle. That never happened, at least not with the Apollo program. But I decided this would be a good place to start. The nice thing about it is was that NASA was so desperate for any kind of publicity at all, that when asked if there was any chance of pulling some footage, they said, 'Here's the library. Have whatever you want.' It was wonderful, because we ran barefoot through their stock. It was stuff that astronauts had actually shot, like space walks or linkups with Skylab. They also let us use their facility in Downey, California, where they developed and produced the Apollo command module, so we actually shot in the training capsule. And then they said 'Do you want to come to Houston and shoot in the Skylab mockup?' We couldn't afford that, so we made our own. But they were just bending over backwards to let us have anything we wanted, and in fact we used the first footage of a night launch that had ever been used in a dramatic program."

• Marks Steve's return to space since his accident. Out space-walking (to repair a solar panel on Skylab), he feels uneasy. His bionic eye blurs, while his cybernetic limbs weaken. Oscar informs him of a "new extra layer," which will be placed upon his super plastiskin — a procedure that will allow *The Six Million Dollar Man* to more easily pace in space.

• Martin Caidin: "In *Cyborg*, Steve Austin is based on two astronauts: David Scott, who flew *Apollo 15*, and Gene Cernan, of *Apollo 17*. Steve is based on them physically, how they would act, how they talk, the things they do and are capable of doing. They are two brilliant cats, engineers, pilots, who are in superb physical shape." For the record, astronaut Gene Cernan was the last man to walk on the moon.

• Oversight: Director Larry Doheny is not mentioned in the opening credits.

• Jules Bergman, who appears as himself in this episode, served as Science Editor for ABC News from 1961 until his death in 1987. His area of expertise was the American space program.

• DC Fontana's small homage to *Star Trek* in "The Rescue of Athena One"? Steve: "Space. It really is the final frontier."

Episode 9: *Dr. Wells is Missing* .... **[3-29-74]**
Written by Elroy Schwartz. Story by Lionel E. Siegel, Bill Keenan, Krishna Shah.
Directed by Virgil Vogel. Featuring: John van Dreelan, Than Wyenn, Jim Shane,
Michael Dante, Cynthia Lynn, Norbert Schiller, Curt Lowens, Ynes Van Holt,
Terry Leonard, Dave Cass

Rudy's abducted by Alfredo and Julio Tucelli, both of whom want him to
create a bionic criminal. Steve's quest for his doctor stretches into Innsbruck,
Austria, where the bionic medicine man was to accept an honorary degree
from his alma mater. Steve arrives at Rudy's inn. Apparently, Wells is out
socializing with friends, but he's really being held captive in an isolated
castle.
 • Alan Oppenheimer tried to "stretch" a lab scene, to "make a big deal."
"What the hell are you doing?" screamed director Virgil Vogel. "Just say the
line, and get through the scene."
 • Martin Caidin: "What are the odds of the real Dr. Wells and Lee Majors
growing up next door to each other in a town in Kentucky? I wouldn't even
write that in fiction. That series of circumstances is too incredible even for
a novel."
 • Major glitch: A man fighting Steve rips out a lamppost from the ground,
and we hear the *bionic* sound (also heard with Steve for the first time).
 • Repeated footage (same stuntman slides through snow twice, in the
exact same way).

Episode 10: *The Last of the Fourth of Julys* .... **[4-5-74]**
Written by Richard Landau. Directed by Reza Badiyi. Featuring: Steve Forrest
(S.W.A.T.), *Arlene Martell, Tom Reese, Hank Stohl, H. Alan Deglin, Kevin*
Tighe (Emergency), *Ben Wright, Tom Hayden, Barry Cahill*

The sinister Quail tries to eliminate prime ministers gathered in Paris.
With a laser (via satellite) set to destroy, he's cloaked in the Norwegian
mountains, protected by every modern device. The OSI finds the laser. To
evade radar, Steve is torpedoed from a submarine to the shores of Quail's
lair. His bionics are detected by radiation sensors, but with Interpol agent
Violette's assistance, he reaches the laser control room just as the satellite
comes into position. Disaster is averted.
 • Guest Steve Forrest and Harve Bennett attended UCLA, where Harve
acted "for the first and only time," as the lead in *Ah, Wilderness.* Forrest
played his big brother.
 • Forrest's real name is Bill Andrews, but changed it as not to be compared to real sibling, actor Dana Andrews.

Episode 11: *Burning Bright* . . . .[4-12-74]
Written by Del Reisman. Directed by Jerry London. Featuring: William Shatner
(Star Trek, TJ Hooker, Tek War), *Warren Kemmerling, Quinn Redeker, Rodolfo*
Hoyos, Anne Schedeen, Mary Rings, Ron Stokes, Chas. Floyd Johnson

During a space jaunt, Josh Lang, astronaut, meets with an unearthly electrical field. He now communicates with dolphins, influences the thoughts
of others, and rallies for dolphins in the space program. Despite his bril-
liance, his psychological stability is disputed. Steve remembers a comparable
celestial encounter, while Josh discovers a computer glitch, becomes violent
and is taken for medical observation. His condition deteriorates, he escapes,
becoming beset with a childhood friend's demise at a power plant. Returning
to his hometown, he kills a deputy, ascends from the top of that same power
plant, and begins to relive his friend's accident. Steve runs to the rescue.
   • Lee Majors and Bill Shatner kept breaking into laughter. "There'd be
a twinkle in either his eye or mine," Lee said, "and we knew we were going
to screw it up."
   • A "very personal show" for Harve Bennett, who has a high I.Q. A
winning-child-contestant on radio's once-popular *Quiz Kids*, he said, "In a
strange way, 'Burning Bright' was about burnout, which is what I thought
I was at 16. Sometimes you reach a certain peak in life, and you feel it's
all over, that you have nothing left to contribute." It's a syndrome he's discussed with several actors ("because they understand it"), including, child-
star-turned-director Jackie Cooper, whom Bennett respects "enormously."
"We spent three hours talking about the mechanics of how to recover from
being nationally famous in your late teens," Bennett recalls. "Jackie, of
course, was much more famous than I, but we still wondered, *Okay, now*
that we've been in the hall of fame for kids, what do we do as adults?"
   • Poignant conversation early in the episode. Oscar: "You know pal, they
say Josh Lang is, well, unstable." Steve: "Well *they* said I'd never run again."
   • Years earlier, Shatner and Majors crossed paths in a 1966 *Big Valley* episode entitled "A Time to Kill."
   • Steve hits the top speed of 66 MPH on a treadmill.

Episode 12: *The Coward* . . . .[4-19-74]
Written by Elroy Schwartz. Directed by Reza Badiyi. Featuring: George
Montgomery, Ron Soble, France Nuyen, George Takei (Star Trek), *Ken Endosa,*
Kim Kahana, Fuji

A Himalayan earthquake exposes a DC-3, downed during World War
II, which was ferrying secret documents. A post-war inquiry revealed that
the plane's pilot, Capt. Carl Austin, Steve's father, bailed out, leaving the rest

of the crew to perish in the crash. Steve's mother insists that her ex-husband never would have done such a thing. Steve journeys to the Orient to recover the papers and to solve the mystery of the missing pilot. Garth, an American ex-pat, then offers to help Steve clear his dad's name.

• An "intense, extraordinarily emotional, and very real episode," for Martin Caidin, who telegrammed those involved, a rare occurrence. "I'd rather give them hell," he said. "But it was too good. It deserved plaudits, wrenching at the heart and the soul. It was superb."

• "George Takei was wonderful," said Harve Bennett, with whom Takei later worked in the *Trek* films. "He brought a classic, as well as classy aspect to the segment."

• This was the last *Six* episode penned by Elroy Schwartz, who grew disenchanted with Harve Bennett's imperious editing style. Schwartz: "With Harve, I would turn in a script which I thought was good, only to find that he had re-written 90% of it. At the end of my four scripts, he said, 'We're picking up your contract. We want you to write four or six more.' I said 'Why? You're doing all the writing.' He wasn't trying to share credit or get money, no. But he had his concept of how the storyline should go, and he would get locked into it. I don't think he could accept another writer's viewpoint."

• The DC-3 was *My Little Girl*, a pet name Steve's dad gave to his wife, Helen.

• Introduces Martha Scott as Steve's mother.

• Steve's stepfather, Jim Elgin, is referred to as "Tim" in this episode.

• Filmed on location in Lake Arrowhead, California.

• On a somber note, "Carl Austin" is one of the thousands of names etched on the Vietnam War Memorial in Washington, D.C.

• Actor George Montgomery died on Dec. 12, 2000, after suffering a heart attack at his home in Rancho Mirage, California. He was 84.

• Original working title: "The Search."

Episode 13: *Run, Steve, Run* . . . .[4-26-74]
Written by Lionel E. Siegel. Directed by Jerry Jameson. Featuring: Noah Berry (The Rockford Files), Henry Jones, George Murdock, Melissa Greene, Bill Conklin, Fred Lerner, Victor Millan

Mr. Rossi, the leader of a criminal syndicate, and Dr. Jeffrey Dolenz, an android entrepreneur, are teamed-up to no-good. They seek to build a squad of robots to knock over Fort Knox. To do so, they must eliminate Steve Austin, but first analyze his physiology. Rossi wants Steve killed, but Dr. Dolenz is intrigued by Steve's extraordinary skills and wants to study him alive. For the moment, Steve is enjoying some time off in Utah, but then senses that he's being clocked. And he's right. He's felled by tranquil-izer darts, and Rossi wants to finish the job. Steve soon finds his patience intensely tried, when he's shackled and trapped in mortar.

• Steve remarks that cybernetic body parts have radiation shields. If so, why may radioactivity be detected at close proximity by a Geiger counter? It would seem that any amount of radiation released, via the limbs, is det-rimental to those in the surrounding area, particularly for The Six Million Dollar Man and The Bionic Woman, both of whom would have experi-enced a considerable amount of continued exposure.

• In what would become a running joke between the two, Steve tweaks Dolenz's craftsmanship, noting that his robots tend to "squeak."

• Ironically, Henry Jones played a robot supplier in the 1972 *Night Gallery* episode, "You Can't Get Help Like That Anymore."

• By the time this episode aired, *Six* had amassed a loyal youth following. Richard Anderson: "I got a call from my daughters, who were at school, and they said 'Dad, everybody's running around in slow motion!' That's when I thought we might be on to something."

• Lionel Siegel: "The robot episodes were fun. Henry Jones was a very good guy. The whole point of these episodes was: who was the better machine? Them, or Steve?"

• Original working title: "Revenge."

"THE PIONEERS" (W/ JOAN DARLING), "PILOT ERROR," "THE CROSS-
COUNTRY KIDNAP" (W/ DONNA MILLS), "RETURN OF THE ROBOT
MAKER," "TANEHA," "LOOK ALIKE" (W/ GEORGE FOREMAN), "THE
BIONIC WOMAN, PART I," "STEVE AUSTIN, FUGITIVE" (W/JENNIFER
DARLING)

The Second Season
1974 to 1975

Episode 14: *Nuclear Alert* ....[9-13-74]
Written by William Driskill. Directed by Jerry London. Featuring: Carol Lawrence, Fred Beir, George Gaynes, Felice Orlandi, Thomas Bellin, Stewart Moss, Charles Wagenheim, Irene Tedrow, Gabriel Walsh, John Stephenson, Phillip Adams, Savannah Bentley, Stuart Nisbet, Michael Kane, Ben Frommer, Sig Haig, Noel DeSouza

A disloyal government team creates an A-bomb from illegal components and plans to market the explosive to a small foreign nation. Steve and Dr. Clea Broder, a scientist, learn of the scheme, are abducted and brought aboard the plane transporting the bomb. General Wiley, of the Air Force, gives the word to interceptor planes and sets out to demolish the bomb-conveying aircraft over an isolated stretch of land. Ted Swenson, team leader of the crooks, warns the General to retreat. If not, Swenson will drop the bomb. In the interlude, Steve is devising his own strategy to halt the planes and prevent transferal of the explosive.

• Steve is seen running ridiculously fast in a cornfield (via the treadmill on a flatbed truck).

• Production manager Ralph Sariego: "Lee, during the first season, was a very affable, warm and open fellow. By the second year, he became kinda distant and kept to himself. He developed a small circle of friends. That's a very common thing to happen to a leading actor when his show becomes a hit."

Episode 15: *The Pioneers* ....[9-20-74]
Written by Bill Svanoe. Story by Katey Barrett. Directed by Christian I. Nyby II Featuring: Mike Farrell (M*A*S*H), Joan Darling, Milt Kogan, Bill Sorrells, Robert F. Simon, Angelo De Meo, Justin Wilde, Vince Howard

David Tate and Nicole Simmons, both scientific professors, have created a cell-regeneration serum that they feel will eliminate the problems of returning from a suspended state. Unfortunately, the space capsule, in which they are conducting their cryogenic experiments, crashes. Tate inadvertently receives an excessive dose of the serum and experiences a tremendous increase in physical vigor, accompanied with extreme seizures. Steve is forced to track the now-strong-man Tate and prevent him from wreaking havoc.

• Another instance when a non-bionic being (David Tate) uses the bionic sound.

• There is some very emotional dialogue between Oscar and Steve, when Austin essentially said, "Where would I be without you?"

• Joan Darling worked with Lee Majors on *Owen Marshall, Counselor at Law.*

• Darling's husband, writer Bill Svanoe, has won awards as a playwright, screenwriter, painter, songwriter and photographer. He was the co-founder of The Rooftop Singers, a musical group that recorded the million-seller, number-one record, "Walk Right In."

• Director Christian I. Nyby II died on September 17, 1993.

Episode 16: *Pilot Error* . . . . **[9-27-74]**
Written by Edward J. Lakso. Directed by Jerry Jameson. Featuring: Pat Hingle, Alfred Ryder, Stephen Nathan, Suzanne Zenor, Jill Denby, Chet Douglas, Hank Brandt, Hank Stohl, Dennis McCarthy

Col. Austin is blinded in mid-air after an oil line on his aircraft, ruptures. Senator Hill (who had approved funding for Steve's bionic reconstruction) has no choice but to make an emergency landing in inhospitable territory. Once on the ground, The Six Million Dollar Man employs his powers and makes the essential mechanical adjustments. Guided by the other passengers, he clears a pathway for the craft. Optimism remains high until the Senator, who is under investigation for incompetence, passes out, in-flight. Visually-impaired Austin is the only one capable of securely escorting the plane.

• Martin Caidin said this episode was "excellent. It involved some really well-done flying sequences. It was tremendously slavish to reality." As was Caidin, Harve Bennett is a pilot. "Pilot Error," he said, "was the traditional Bennett flying picture. It was important because, I always hated the way flying pictures were done, which was inaccurately."

• In the early 1990s, Bennett wrote the script for *Crash Landing: The Rescue of Flight 232*, with Charlton Heston, for which the FAA gave the stamp of approval. It was ABC's highest-rated movie of the week for that decade.

• Steve's bionic rebirth was approved by Senator Hill, played by Pat Hingle, here, while Jaime's reconstruction was sanctioned by Bill Conklin's General Fuller, as stated in BW's "Canyon of Death."

• Actor Pat Hingle carved out a long career on stage and screen despite a missing left pinky. In 1959, Hingle fell down a Manhattan elevator shaft, cracking his skull, leg, hip and wrist and severing the finger. Besides nearly killing him, the accident cost him the title role in the 1960 film *Elmer Gantry*. The role went instead to Burt Lancaster, who won the Academy Award.

Episode 17: *The Pal–Mir Escort* . . . .[10-4-74]
Written by Margaret, Paul Schneider. Directed by Larry Dobkin. Featuring: Anne Revere, Leo Fuchs, Denny Miller (Tarzan), John Landis (now a director), Jamie Donnelly, Don Pulford, Virginia Gregg, Robert Rothwell, Nate Esformes, Everett Creach

Prime Minister Madame Salka Pal-Mir of Eretz, a small country, faints during peace negotiations with bordering countries. Her heart is severely impaired and she's a prime candidate for the world's first bionic blood pump. It's only fitting that The Six Million Dollar Man ushers her to the classified hospital in which the procedure will commence. There are particular individuals, however, who would prefer that the prime minister not recover and, thus, discontinue the negotiations. Assassins are hired to eliminate her chances and anyone (read: Steve Austin) who becomes an obstacle.
• One of the rare instances when Steve holds and actually fires a gun. He would do so again in "The Wolf Boy" and "The Bionic Criminal."
• Guest Jaime Donnelly spells her name the same way Jaime Sommers does.

Episode 18: *The Seven Million Dollar Man* . . . .[11-1-74]
Written by Peter Allan Fields. Directed by Richard Moder. Featuring: Monte Markham (The New Perry Mason), Maggie Sullivan, Fred Lerner, Marshall Reed

What would happen if Steve became incapable of working for the OSI? Would they hire another bionic man? Auto race hero Barney Miller becomes that man. Following a serious accident, he's cybernetically refitted. He's more expensive (seven million) and substantially stronger than Steve, who's awestruck by the situation. As was first with Col. Austin, Barney is emotionally incapable of dealing with his new life. To a more dangerous degree, *he* seeks to be the only bionic being alive, and sets out to destroy Steve.
• Barney's fight with Steve was like "two bulls going against each other," said Martin Caidin. "It was head-butting time, and gave a real energy to the episode. Barney was the dark side of bionics, the evil force. But it was portrayed as though it could happen."
• Monte Markham played *The Astronaut*, a 1970 TV-movie produced by Harve Bennett, who always considered the actor "a favorite." Years ago, Bennett happened to catch a segment of *Melrose Place*, because his older children "wanted me to." There was Monte, playing a "heavy."
• In Chapter 1, we learned that Markham was an early dark-horse candidate to play Steve Austin — a development that would have displeased Lionel Siegel. "Markham, who did guest spots each year, was much too

intellectual an actor, much too much nervous energy," he said. "Lee Majors' calmness and Gary Cooper quietness works much better for a man who is part machine and occasionally needs a tune up like your Mercedes."

• Lee Majors: "When I first read the script, I was very curious to know how the writers were going to get me out of the situation. Obviously, it had to take something more than brute strength to subdue someone supposedly stronger than myself. The character that Monte played brought a whole new element to the series."

• As *Six* and *Seven* battle in the vault, Steve, with his unbionic left arm, inconceivably pushes away both of Barney's cybernetic upper limbs.

• Director Richard Moder died on April 17, 1994 (heart attack).

• Original working title: "Line of Duty."

Episode 19: *Straight On 'Til Morning* . . . . [11-8-74]
Written by D.C. Fontana. Directed by Lawrence Doheny. Featuring: Meg Foster (Cagney & Lacey), *Cliff Osmond, Donald Billett, Kurt Grayson, Lucas White, Jimmy Lydon, Robert Bruce Lang, John Calvin, Al Dunlap, Christopher Mears, Frances Osborne, Vincent Chase*

A peaceful alien family is stranded on Earth after their spaceship malfunctions. They are unaware that because of their inherent radioactivity, their touch can do great physical harm to Earth people. Steve, realizing that the interplanetary visitors have no hostile intentions, goes to their aid—even though the sheriff and his posse are trying to hunt them down. With Oscar's consent, he arranges for the adult female alien to return to her mother spacecraft in an American lunar probe. But time is running out: the sheriff and his men remain close behind.

• "This episode was my attempt to raise our literary merit," said Harve Bennett. "It was not very literary, but literate."

• Both of Fontana's *Six Mill* scripts, "The Rescue of Athena One" and "Straight On 'Til Morning," were nominated for Filmcon Awards. Furthermore, Universal Studios selected both scripts for novelization by Warner Books under the title "The Rescue of Athena One."

• Actress Meg Foster (Minonee) played "Hera" in episodes of: *Xena: Warrior Princess* and *Hercules: The Legendary Journeys*. She also portrayed Christine Cagney in the pilot episode of *Cagney & Lacey*.

Episode 20: *The Midas Touch* . . . .**[11-15-74]**
Written by Donald L. Gold, Lester William Berke, Peter Allan Fields. Story by
Donald L. Gold, Lester William Berke. Directed by Bruce Bilson. Featuring:
Farley Granger, Noam Pitlik, Dave Morick, Gary Cashdollar, Jim Connors,
Richard D. Hurst, Woodrow Chambliss, Catherine McKeown, Louis Elias,
Marcus Smith

Oscar is gone. He was last seen in Las Vegas. The rumor: he's involved
in an illegal scheme to heist gold from a government mine. Intent on seeking out the truth, Steve travels to the mine. Bert Carrington, Oscar's close
friend (who's also associated with the Mining and Research Bureau), has
plans to smuggle the gold. The pal-gone-bad needs exclusive government
transportation that only may be approved by Oscar who, despite a com-
pelling offer (and with great assistance from Steve), will prevent such a
development.
  • Oscar's personal life is explored.
  • "Julie Farrell" is the name of his secretary.
  • In a closing scene, Steve runs bionically across an Air Force tarmac, to
the amazement of security personnel. When the guards ask for an explanation, he replies, "It's all those Air Force exercises, Lieutenant. Every
morning."
  • Director Bruce Bilson also guided episodes of *Lois and Clark: The New*
Adventures of Superman.

Episode 21: *The Deadly Replay* . . . . [11-22-74]
Written by Wilton Denmark. Directed by Christian I. Nyby II. Featuring: Clifton
James, Robert Symonds, Jack L. Ging, Lara Parker, Jack Manning, William
Scherer, Regis J. Cordic

The experimental plane in which Steve Austin was critically injured has
been reconstructed and he's ready to "get right back on that horse" and try
again. Yet Oscar uncovers new information: the initial crash may have been
intentional. Questionable events occur with the new testing. Steve believes
the drills should continue; the aircraft deserves to be an important part of
NASA's agenda. In turn, those responsible will be tricked into revealing
themselves.
  • An extraordinarily poignant episode in which Steve proves once and for
all that the HL-10 was not a jinx.
  • In *Cyborg*, sabotage is never mentioned nor suspected.
  • Today, the HL-10 is mounted on a pedestal in front of the Dryden Test
Flight Center's main gate.
  • Wilton Denmark: "I went to Edwards Air Force Base and they [basi-

cally] gave me the keys to the kingdom, which I found to be most helpful. They said 'you can see this, you can show that, but there are some things you won't be able to see.' The guys at Edwards were so friendly that they let us shoot an eight-foot scale model airplane, but then we found out the model was Top Secret, so they had to confiscate the film and all that good stuff. The director [Christian Nyby II] and I had both been in the Air Force, and he knew about planes, so that's why they asked him to direct it. I was allowed to fly the simulator for the HL-10 [lifting body], and I had access to the B-52 mothership to see how it felt sitting in the thing. NASA also gave me their flight checklist so that I could get the terminology right. We got several million dollars worth of free production out of doing that episode there. I mean, just look at what we had in the background. Of course, it was good publicity for them too."

• Denmark: "This episode is what got me the job [as a regular staff writer]," he said. "It was the first time, I think, that ABC's Broadcast Standards and Practices department had sent back a script that said 'shoot it as is.' Harve Bennett, to his credit, didn't rewrite any of my stuff. He had input, sure, but he didn't bang out the words. He would say things like, 'Give me a delicious moment,' whatever that means. I guess I delivered to a degree."

• At the episode's conclusion, Steve pauses for a touching communal moment with the plane. Denmark: "When Christian, Jr. yelled 'cut,' Lee kicked the front tire and said, 'You son of a bitch! You did this to me.' Of course it never made it to air but it was in the dailies."

• Denmark: "When I first met Lee on the set at Edwards AFB, he gave me a half-cocked smile and said, 'Anybody who writes in a character named Shadetree has gotta be from the South.' It was refreshing to meet someone who was as popular as Lee and discover how down-home he was. We had some great times on and off the set."

• Denmark: "People ask me, 'How do you come up with ideas?' And I tell them, 'R&R: research or recall. If you haven't lived it, then research it.'"

• While on the set at Edwards, Denmark bumped into the real Steve Austin: "I actually talked to Bruce Peterson, the man who flew the M2-F2 that crashed in 1967. He was glad he was alive. He showed me the scrapes on his head and how many bones he had broken. He didn't walk too well and he was assigned to a desk job by that point—which he resented because he liked to fly." Bruce Peterson passed away on May 1, 2006. He was 72.

• Martin Caidin did not have Peterson's crash in mind when he wrote Cyborg. "I didn't know him, or about him," he said. "I knew there was a crash, but I had been writing about vehicles called lifting bodies for 15 years. I knew Neil Armstrong when he flew the X-1, for Chrissake."

Episode 22: *Act of Piracy* ....[11-29-74]
Written by Peter Allan Fields. Story by Dave Ketchum, Bruce Shelley. Directed by Christian I. Nyby II. Featuring: Stephan McNally, Lenore Kasdorf, Carlos Romero, Frank Ramirez, Joe LaDue, Jorge Cervera, Jr., Hagan Beggs, David Dominiquez

Dr. Louis Craig and Sharon Ellis are measuring earthquake activity in the ocean. Col. Austin is there to lend a hand. Suddenly, Santa Ventura, which is close by, abruptly halts negotiations with the United States. Craig and Ellis are advised to evacuate, but it's too late: their ship is captured; Steve's diving bell is cut apart, as could be the mounting tension.
  • The one and only time Steve wears a non-US military uniform.
  • Original working titles: "Aquanaut" and "Three if by Sea."

Episode 23: *Stranger in Broken Fork* ....[12-13-74]
Written by Bill Svanoe, Wilton Denmark. Story by Bill Svanoe. Directed by Christian Nyby, Sr. Featuring: Sharon Farrell, Robert Donner, Arthur Franz, Kristine Ritzke, Sally Yarnell, Bill Henry, Troy Melton, Eric Mason, Paul LeClair

Steve is suffering from amnesia thanks to a short in the power pack of his bionic arm. His plane crashes in the Colorado mountains. Psychologist Angie Walker finds him walking on a desolate road. Dr. Walker heads an experimental home for mental patients who are severely tormented by the locals. Ring leader/grocer Horace Milsner trumps up the charges against her. Arrest attempts fail. Sympathizers, armed with axe handles, join his cause and leave her with a choice: exit or die. Memory or not, Steve's loyalty and integrity shine through; he's obligated to protect this woman who has treated him with extensive kindness.
  • During a confrontation with local ruffians, Steve's bionic arm is injured and exposed. Still amnesiatic, he's appalled and speculates that he's simply a "machine." Probing the "wound" with his real left hand, he cuts his finger, which begins to bleed, prompting Dr. Walker to say with compassion, "Machines *don't* bleed."
  • Wilton Denmark: "This episode had a great premise: a man with those powers who didn't know who he was or what he was. The government's top secret item running around free. Harve Bennett had the idea about the little girl character who never spoke a word."
  • Robert Donner, who played the heavy in this episode, passed away on June 8, 2006. He was 75.

Episode 24: *The Peeping Blonde* . . . .[12-20-74]
Written by William T. Zacha, Wilton Denmark. Story by William T. Zacha.
Directed by Herschel Daugherty. Featuring: Farrah Fawcett-Majors, Roger
Perry (husband to Joanne Worley), Hari Rhodes, W.T. Zacha, Chris Nelson,
Martin Speer

Victoria Webster, a reporter, accidentally films Steve leaping twelve feet
to repair a space capsule. Knowing a good thing when she sees it, Webster
strikes out for more footage of this fantastic human being and follows him
on vacation in the Californian desert of Baja. Her crafty boss has other
ideas: after seeing Steve's *foot*age, he decides to abduct the superman and
market him to a foreign country.

• The only time we see Oscar shirtless.

• Wilton Denmark knew that Fawcett would be cast as the "blonde"
before he wrote the episode. "Farrah and I had lunch several times. I had to
ask her things like what does she do, what kind of language does she use to
make Lee mad, and things like that. I wanted to get her natural way of talking down so I could write the proper dialogue for her. I was amazed with
how casual and friendly she was. Not at all what I had expected from one of
the most desirable women of the century."

• One of four episodes that featured Lee Majors' assistant and *Bionic Ever
After?* director Steve Stafford, who at the time, had long, hippie-like hair. "I
had just gotten out of the Marine Corps," he explained, "and I decided that
after having my hair cut short, for so long, it was time to grow it really long.
The style was really kind of average for the time."

• Farrah Fawcett makes the second of four appearances on the show.

• Semi-remade as the BW's "Once a Thief."

• Wilton Denmark: "Lee was a trip. A funny guy. He was always joking around. He reminded me a lot of Elvis. Just a good ol' country boy who
made good. Harve Bennett's secretary told me that one of the reasons Lee
was successful as Austin was because his acting 'corridor' was very narrow.
We didn't want to get into anything that made him get too emotional or
anything more than a man living with the fact that he's half human, half
machine. The fame and fortune that Lee reaped, however, did not affect
him."

• Original working titles: "Target for Blackmail" and "Double Exposure."

Episode 25: *The Cross-Country Kidnap*. [1-10-75]
Written by Ray Brenner, Stephen Kandel. Story by Ray Brenner. Directed by
Christian Nyby, Sr. Featuring: Donna Mills (Knots Landing), *Tab Hunter,*
Frank Aletter, Robert Forward, John Gabriel, Ben Wright, Jerome Guardino

Lisa Leitman has an incredible mind. She's developed a cryptography procedure that links computer communications around the globe. She also loves to ride horses and has dreams of entering the Olympics. Ross Borden, and his team of criminals, seeks to kidnap Lisa and have her reprogram the computer so they can control a network of international secret agents. Steve is employed as Lisa's guardian, which is not an easy job considering her bad attitude and her vulnerability while horseback riding in open country.

• Harve Bennett's ex-wife has a bit part here, playing one of the riders with Donna Mills. A one-time Olympic hopeful, and cross-country horsewoman, Bennett's then-spouse coached Mills on riding. "Everyone told me we couldn't do a show about equestrians," he said, "but I said we could. So this episode ended up having a certain personal flavor to it."

• Bennett said that Tab Hunter made an appearance because he was an expert equestrian rider, "who almost made the Olympic team."

• Original working title: "Ciphers and Charades."

Episode 26: *Lost Love* . . . . **[1-17-75]**
Written by Richard Carr. Story by Mel Levy, Tom Levy. Directed by Arnold Laven. Featuring: Linda Marsh, Jeff Corey, Than Wyenn, Joseph Ruskin, Wesley Lau

Following her husband's death in-flight to Lisbon, Barbara Thatcher, Steve's ex-love, comes back into his life. The romance begins anew and Steve is on hand to thwart a kidnap attempt on Barbara by unknown assailants. Then her thought-to-be-deceased spouse makes contact. She and Steve then travel to Europe, where they encounter the dead-man-walking at a foreign embassy.

• Barbara is apparently the love of Steve's life. Two months later, however, Jaime arrives.

• Writer Richard Carr passed away in 1988.

Episode 27: *The Last Kamikaze* . . . . **[1-19-75]**
Written by Judy Burns. Directed by Richard Moder. Featuring: John Fujioka, Robert Ito (Quincy, Kung Fu), *Edmund Gilbert, Jimmy Joyce, Paul Vaughn, Jane Goodnow Gillet*

There's been an accident. An aircraft (with an atomic warhead aboard) has crash-landed on an island in the South Pacific. Steve Austin is assigned to bring it back. One problem: a reclusive Japanese Zero pilot named Kuroda has arrived there first. The Bionic Man must brave a small guerrilla army and a booby-trapped terrain to reach the warhead beforehand.

• A superior episode.

• SM moves to Sunday night for the first time.

• Judy Burns: "I went in to pitch several stories. And I pitched my heart out ... about two pages of ideas. And nothing was hitting. Strikeouts all over the place. And then I remembered a book I had seen in a bookstore window a couple days before, and pitched a story off the top of my head ... which became 'The Last Kamikaze.' It was about a Japanese soldier called Hiroo Onoda, who had been on an island in the South Pacific for 30 years. And he thought the war was still on. I said, 'What if Steve Austin had to go retrieve an atomic weapon or some such, where it had fallen on an island, and then he ran into the Japanese guy who found it first and would like to use it to 'end the war.' You could see the cherries roll on the slot machines of their eyes. They all sat up ... considered it ... and said, 'Well, let us think about it.' And the next day I had a job."

• The circuitry in Steve's bionic leg is exposed, which he uses to prove to Kuroda, played by John Fujioka, that technology has progressed significantly since the end of the war, in the hopes that Kuroda will see the futility of his one-man resistance.

• The first of two episodes to feature guest actor Fujioka, who played the Chief Priest in 1995's *Mortal Kombat* feature, and who also appeared semi-regularly on TV's *Kung Fu*.

• In a moving scene, Kuroda presents Steve with his treasured "thou-sand-stitch belt"— a piece of cloth into which 1,000 women had sewn one stitch as a symbolic uniting with the pilot. Judy Burns: "I had made a friend a few years before who loved Japanese films. She introduced me to Mifune, Kurosawa, and a lot of other films, including some war movies. I became an avid Nipon-o-phile. And I had read a lot about the Japanese soldier in the war, as well as the Samurai Code of Bushido. So all of that got laced into the stew. A year or two later I went to live in Japan for about nine months, just to live there with a family, so I became even more of a Japanese nut. Harve Bennett shared that love of the culture, as did Gene Roddenberry, who was married there. But it was the Onoda book that gave us the storyline."

• Before her script was filmed, however, Burns' ego took a bit of a tumble. "When I got the script back, it had been rewritten by the story editor, Lee Siegel, and I was royally angered and hurt," she recalls. "I thought I had fallen in with honorable men, and yet they had gutted my script. I walked right by Siegel on the Universal lot and wouldn't talk to him. Boy, was I young then. You have to realize that when you are *not* on staff, your show becomes their show. The only way to protect your writing was to be on staff. The problem was that I still really didn't know how to write. Anyway, I went home, and about a day later, I got a big basket of flowers and fruit and candy from Harve Bennett. He had sent a note, telling me 'not to worry... we're putting it back the way you wrote it.' And they did. But then he called me into his office and gave me a book, *The Art of Dramatic Writing*. I still have it today. And he and Lee proceeded to teach me how to write a *Six Million Dollar Man*. I learned, and they shot it pretty much as I wrote it."

• The tactical atomic bomb in Kuroda's possession was named Peregrine. Burns: "I suspect it came from my love of mythology and nature--the idea of naming weapons for birds or animals."

• Original working title: "The Midnight Wind." "It was taken from the idea of 'Divine Wind' Kamikaze," said Burns. "A man at midnight ... the lowest of the nights ... long after the 'heyday' of the Kamikaze. I thought it was more elegant than 'Last Kamikaze.' They [Universal] wanted to get right to the punch, so it was changed."

Episode 28: *Return of the Robot Maker* .... [1-26-75]
Written by Mark Frost. Story by Del Reisman, Mark Frost. Directed by Phil Bondelli. Featuring: Henry Jones (Phyllis), *Ben Hammer, Troy Melton, Judd Laurance, Iris Edwards, Sarah Simmons, Jean Lee Brooks*

Evil scientist Dr. Chester Dolenz has developed an android replica of Oscar. His plan: abduct the OSI head and lure Col. Steve Austin into a high-security installation laden with booby traps and gun nests. If The Six Million Dollar Man fails, the Oscar-android will have the opportunity to heist the equation for a new form of energy. Goldman's mechanical evil twin doesn't have a chance, and Dr. Dolenz's plan goes sourly awry.

• For some unknown reason, *Jeffrey* Dolenz suddenly becomes *Chester* Dolenz.

• Dolenz uses the alias "Arnold Seaton" when he pays a visit to Oscar's office. Stationed outside his door is a blonde secretary named Sally Simmons.

• We hear Steve's famous line, "Robots don't sweat when they're nervous," in reply to Oscar's question, "How did you know which one of us ... was *me*?"

• Head scratchers: What are the odds that top-secret blueprints would be kept in an unlocked vault? And if Steve tripped all of the security defenses going *in*, why did he not trip them going *out*?

• Lee Majors drove a Mercedes in this episode, as he did in real life. Its license plate number? "6ML MAN."

• Another instance when a non-bionic being (the Oscar robot) uses the bionic "sound."

• Henry Jones, the very epitome of the "gentleman" villain, died on May 17, 1999, from injuries sustained after a bad fall at his home.

• This is Richard Anderson's favorite episode.

Episode 29: *Taneha*. . . . .[2-2-75]
Written by Margaret Armen (Star Trek). Directed by Earl Bellamy. Featuring: James Griffith, Jess Walton (The Young and the Restless), Bill Fletcher, Paul Brinegar, Jim B. Smith, Trent Dolan

The world's last remaining golden cougar is about to become extinct. Livestock have been preyed upon, a rancher has been killed, and gun-toting citizens have joined forces against the animal. A ranger, who's been attacked by the animal several times, calls on his old friend Steve Austin for aid. E. J. Haskell, a local guide, faces a tough decision: should she lead Steve to the cougar's domain or watch the creature be destroyed by the band of rangers?
• Similar to BW's "Claws."
• Writer Margaret Armen died on November 10, 2003 (heart failure).

Episode 30: *Look Alike* . . . . [2-23-75]
Written by Richard Carr. Story by Gustave Field. Directed by Jerry London. Featuring: George Foreman, Robert Do Qui, Robert Salvio, Eddie Fontaine, Mary Rings, Jack Colvin, Arthur Space, Susan Keller

Unbeknownst to Steve, Oscar hires Marcus C. Garvey to botch a syndicate's scheme to pilfer the OSI's classified laser technology. A syndicate member is surgically altered to resemble Steve and copy Oscar's documents. Steve is wise to the game, hot on Garvey's trail, following him to a gym, which is a front for the syndicate. He thinks Garvey is party to the syndicate, and they're soon pitted against each other in the ring.
• George Foreman later would appear in his own 1993 ABC sitcom, *George*, produced by Tony (*Who's the Boss?*) Danza. "Someday," promises Harve Bennett, "I'm going to do *The George Foreman Story*. He's one of the world's sweetest, nicest people."

Episode 31: *The E.S.P. Spy* . . . . [3-2-75]
Written by Lionel E. Siegel. Directed by Jerry London. Featuring: Philip Bruns, Dick Van Patten (Eight is Enough), Alan Bergmann, Paul Cavonis, Robbie Lee, George Patton, Bert Kramer

Harry Green, laser maven, is assembling a classified subterranean laser weapon installation. Oscar learns that a similar facility is being built in a foreign country almost simultaneously. Coincidence? Or, as Oscar suspects, is Green a traitor? Steve thinks Green is under the control of a progressive psychic procedure and seeks the assistance of teenager Audrey Moss, a gifted telepath. Together, they endanger their existence to brandish the security break and preserve the anonymity of the laser project.

• The Moss character returns in "Hocus-Pocus."

• One of the few episodes to show Oscar at his home (in a bathrobe, no less).

• Lionel Siegel: "As producer under Harve Bennett's executive producership, my job was to 1) make the script affordable, and 2) make Lee Majors happy. Majors did not like to speak, preferring instead to nod, say yes and smile, raise an eyebrow, etc. That required a lot of clever rewriting and revising to get around that stuff."

Episode 32: *The Bionic Woman (Part I)* . . . . **[3-16-75]**
Written by Kenneth Johnson. Directed by Richard Moder. Featuring: Malachi Throne, Harry Hickox, Paul Carr, Dana Plato (Diff'rent Strokes)

Steve returns to Ojai, California, sees former sweetheart Jaime Sommers, and sparks reignite. But tragedy strikes: she critically injures herself in a sky-diving mishap. Steve begs Oscar to give her new life. Rudy is called. Jaime becomes the world's first *Bionic Woman*, with legs and right arm, super-powered, and her right ear, bionically acoustic. Jaime learns of Steve's bionic secret and the two become engaged, but a nefarious counterfeiter in Europe threatens their newfound happiness.

• Lindsay agreed to appear here as a birthday present to her little half-sister, Randi Ball, whose favorite show was *The Six Million Dollar Man*. Wagner: "My sister at the time was 13, and the start date of the show was her birthday. Talk about karma."

• Jaime wrote in Steve's yearbook: "Dear Steve, if I had a brother, he would be you. Affectionately, *Jamie*." Her name is spelled incorrectly. In at least two other instances, it's spelled the right way (*Jaime*).

• Wagner: "Before shooting, I went to a tennis pro and said, 'Look. I don't care where the ball goes; I just want you to make me look good.' So I took lessons for three days, and I was surprised at how good the film looked." Richard Anderson, a gifted tennis player in his own right, gave athletically-challenged Lindsay Wagner some tips on how to serve a tennis ball while shooting on location in Ojai, California.

• We learn that Steve first kissed Jaime at his senior year New Year's Eve dance, which makes him at last three years older than her. Or does it? In "Welcome Home Jaime Part I," Steve and Jaime reminisce about being in the third grade together, meaning they're roughly the *same* age. Since Lee was 10 years older than Lindsay in real life, writers and producers needed to "de-age" Majors to make more credible the "former high-school sweetheart" storyline in the form of Jaime Sommers.

• Original working title: "Mrs. Steve Austin."

• Ken Johnson modeled the Jaime Sommers character after an ideal date he had in mind, someone "truthful, witty and eminently attractive."

• Why a bionic ear? "It was very simple," said Johnson. "I didn't want Jaime to be exactly like Steve. He had the eye, so I decided that it would make more sense to give her the ear, and it would give us something fresh to work with that we hadn't had before."

• And that skydiving accident? "It came from a desire to have her doing something very dramatic and out of the ordinary, and which the audience would expect Steve Austin to be involved in," he adds. "More unusual, sexier [in the dramatic sense], etc."

• Jim Parriott: "I remember pitching Harve a similar story for *The Six Million Dollar Man* and being told that there was already a script in the works [being written by Ken] based on the same subject [girlfriend who becomes bionic]. I even think I pitched a skydiving accident."

• Steve and Jaime's makeout session beside a fallen tree stump was filmed at the Lake Casitas Recreation Area, just outside of Ojai.

Episode 33: *The Bionic Woman (Part II)* . . . .**[3-23-75]**
Written by Kenneth Johnson. Directed by Richard Moder. Featuring: Elisabeth Brooks, Margaret Impert, Richard Jannone, Sidney Clute

Steve and Jaime's wedding is scheduled, but is suddenly postponed. Oscar employs her to crack a safe operated by a counterfeit syndicate. Steve fears for her life. Jaime's the only one who can crack the safe and attain the pilfered counterfeit plate. Steve accompanies her on the dangerous mission. She must determine the combination within five minutes. A bionic muscular spasm trips the alarm, forcing her and Steve to flee prematurely, dodging bullets along the way. Back in the States, Jaime's behavior becomes increasingly erratic. Steve, gravely concerned, checks her into the hospital, where Rudy Wells determines that her body is rejecting her bionics. Overcome with neural pain, Jaime bolts from the hospital into the rainy night. Steve pursues, tracks her down, and races her back to the hospital in his arms— where she subsequently dies on the operating table.

• Steve's mom learns of his and Jaime's bionic reconstruction, and said, "I guess you two really *were* made for each other."

• It was Lindsay's "ear-brain pain" theatricalities that contributed to the believability of the Jaime character.

• Steve's tear-soaked parting words: "I love you, Jaime. I've always loved you."

• The heavy in this episode, Joseph Wrona, was named after Ken Johnson's American History teacher in high school.

• This emotional two-parter was the 4th highest-rated program in 1975 and the highest-rated *Six Mill* ever.

• Lee Majors on the song, "Sweet Jaime": "It might not have been any good, but at least it was personal."

• Why Ojai? "I can't remember, exactly," said Ken Johnson. "I know we wanted to get her out of Los Angeles and have a more *countrified* feeling to the thing, and it may have been that Steve Austin's family had been set up at some point as having lived out that way."

• For the record, Siegel insists that he came up with the Ojai angle. "My mother-in-law worked for the Krishnamurti organization, which was head-quartered in Ojai, California," he said. "I attended many talks given by Krishnamurti, who was an East Indian philosopher. I'd been there often; I knew the place."

• Jaime as tennis pro? Johnson: "We wanted her to have been physical [sort of a joke, since Lindsay wasn't], and have been traveling in international circles, etc., before settling down to be a teacher [to connect with our young audience]. It also gave her a reason for not having seen Steve over the years."

Episode 34: *Outrage in Balinderry* .... **[4-20-75]**
Written by Paul Schneider. Story by Paul and Margaret Schneider. Directed by Earl Bellamy. Featuring: Martine Beswick, Richard Erdman, David Frankham, Alan Caillou, William Sylvester, Margaret Fairchild, Richard O'Brien, Diana Chesney, Gavan O'Herlihy, Michael Regen

Revolutionaries abduct the spouse of the American Ambassador to Balinderry. The captors' demands: fellow revolutionaries must be released from prison. If not, the Ambassador's wife will die. Steve Austin travels to Balinderry. He enlists the assistance of Julia Flood, a stewardess who becomes his liaison with the kidnappers. En route to their hideout, Steve and Julia are captured following a raid on a secret meeting. Steve must use his bionic powers to free himself and make his way to the hideout before the radical group can carry out the threat to execute the Ambassador's wife.

• This episode was banned on all British television stations, save for Southern, because the protagonists, the IBA, were loosely based on the Irish Republican Army.

• A familiar face in B horror movies, Martine Beswick sports a number of 007 credits as well, appearing in such favorites as *Dr. No*, *From Russia with Love*, and *Thunderball*.

• Guest star Gavan O'Herlihy was one of two actors to play Richie Cunningham's long-lost brother "Chuck" on *Happy Days*. He also appeared in the BW episode, "The Pyramid." His father, veteran actor Dan O'Herlihy, had a lead role in "Rancho Outcast."

• Prolific director Earl Bellamy, who directed more than 1,600 television episodes, died on November 30, 2003 (heart attack).

Episode 35: *Steve Austin, Fugitive* .... [4-27-75]
Written by Mark Frost, Richard Carr. Story by Wilton Denmark, William Gordon, James Doherty. Directed by Russ Mayberry. Featuring: Gary Lockwood, Jennifer Darling, Andy Romano, Bernie Hamilton, Jesse Nichols, Reb Brown, Marco Lopez, Amzie Strickland

A strange telephone call beckons Steve, and leads him to an apartment, where he finds a dead man. He's tranquilized by a masked man, who frames him for the murder. The masqueraded stranger is out for revenge; Steve had previously sent him to prison. The police appear; Steve is arrested, and breaks free on the way to jail and sets out to find the real killer.

• "I cast Gary Lockwood, not because of that wonderful *Star Trek* episode," said Harve Bennett, referring to the original *Trek's* second pilot ("Where No Man Has Gone Before"), "but because of *2001: A Space Odyssey.*" Lockwood was also *Trek* creator Gene Roddenberry's first star on *The Lieutenant.*

• Wilton Denmark: "For some reason, Lee Siegel wanted Rudy snuffed in this episode. I wrote him gone. Harve had a [bleeping] fit. I rewrote. Siegel had a [bleeping] fit. I was in the middle. Harve won. Perhaps because I agreed with Harve on that one, Siegel got miffed. But Siegel was the producer and Harve was the executive producer and it was his company, Silverton, doing the show for Universal and ABC."

• Jennifer Darling debuts as Peggy Callahan (although her first name isn't mentioned). Since Oscar requires a new secretary every three months (per his security orders), she ended up replacing "Miss Johnson."

• A police radio dispatcher describes Steve as 6'2" tall and 185lbs.

• Lee Majors, heavily disguised, plays a crusty shopkeeper in this episode. He is credited as "L. Majors."

• This segment is basically a sequel to "Eyewitness to Murder."

"THE RETURN OF THE BIONIC WOMAN, PART I," "THE SONG AND
DANCE SPY" (W/ SONNY BONO), "THE WOLF BOY," "ONE OF OUR
RUNNING BACKS IS MISSING" (W/ LARRY CSONKA), "THE BIONIC
CRIMINAL" (W/ MONTE MARKHAM), "CLARK TEMPLETON O'FLAHERTY"
(W/ LOU GOSSETT JR.), "HOCUS-POCUS" (W/ ROBBIE LEE), "THE
SECRET OF BIGFOOT, PART II" (W/ STEFANIE POWERS)

The Third Season
1975 to 1976

Episode 36: *The Return of the Bionic Woman (Part I)* . . . . [9-14-75]
Written by Kenneth Johnson. Directed by Richard Moder. Featuring: Tony Giorgio, Al Ruscio (Life Goes On), *Richard Lenz*

Has Jaime come back from the dead? Does Steve see her ghost? Does someone look like his bionic soul mate? At first, he's elated to see anyone who resembles her. To his surprise, it is Jaime. But not the Jaime he knew before. She doesn't recognize him. She "died," but Rudy's assistant, Dr. Marchetti, kept her alive with cryogenics. She owes her life to him and they are falling in love. Meanwhile, Steve is heartbroken.

• The third year was transitional, mostly due to Ken Johnson. Upon completion of his work at the end of the second season, Harve Bennett said, "Kenny's exuberance and imagination were immediately felt. He thinks big."

• An agent later introduced Bennett to writer Jim Parriott, who first joined the staff on *Mill*, then *Woman*. "He's mellow, and was the perfect complement to Kenny," Bennett said of Parriott (who also created the acclaimed 1989 *Elvis* series, which Bennett calls "a work of sheer imagination and wonder"). Bennett, Steven Bochco, Johnson and Parriott, remain, "if not close, highly respectful of each other's talent," Bennett said.

• After *Man's* second year, Bennett was involved with each script-draft, but didn't perform any writing, which took him "out of the intensity loop." He viewed dailies, only when "time became hectic."

• Still, Bennett found time to produce *Rich Man, Poor Man* and *The Invisible Man*. The demise of the latter was pinned on star David McCallum (*The Man from U.N.C.L.E.*). "Everyone said it failed, because David spoke with an English accent," Bennett said. "We hired Ben Murphy and did *Gemini Man*, which became more of a superhero like Steve, and everyone was happy." (Though *that* show failed miserably, as well.)

• Martin E. Brooks formally replaces Alan Oppenheimer as Rudy Wells. Lionel Siegel: "ABC wanted a younger, more vigorous guy. It was the early wave of the network's apathy for older actors in TV series."

• Filmed on location in Ojai, California, and Pepperdine University.

Episode 37: *The Return of the Bionic Woman (Part II)* . . . . [9-21-75]
Written by Kenneth Johnson. Directed by Richard Moder. Featuring: Dennis Patrick (Dark Shadows), *Ford Rainey, George Keymas, Virginia Gregg, Richard Lenz*

Steve returns with Jaime to Ojai in hopes of restoring their life together. The result: painful recollections trigger headaches and frustration. Oscar believes he has the answer: the bionic duo travels to the Caribbean, where a rogue American businessman has been supplying a band of terrorists with arms.

• Jaime convinces Steve that she should be the one to approach Carlton Harris, in hopes of gaining his trust and entry into his fortress. "You're cute," she tells Steve, "but he's not gonna' look twice at *your* legs."

• A two-part episode of ABC's *Lois and Clark* from the 1995-1996 season, in which Teri Hatcher's Lois gets amnesia and falls in love with her attending physician, is very similar to this episode.

• Actor Dennis Patrick (Carlton Harris) died on October 13, 2002, from smoke inhalation at his home. He was 84. Ken Johnson: "You might be interested to know that the bad guy Dennis Patrick played, Carlton Harris, was named for an old friend of my father's, who was the Chief Justice of the Arkansas Supreme Court at the time. Well, the judge called me and said, 'Couldn't you have made him a great barrister instead of a crook?'"

• Speaking of Carlton Harris, the industrial facility that Steve and Jaime infiltrate is in fact the Valley Steam Plant in the North East San Fernando Valley. Ken Johnson: "If you stand atop Mulholland Drive--or fly in from the west toward Burbank Airport--looking north you can clearly see the four big smokestacks. They always make me smile when I see them out there in the distance."

• Ken Johnson: "Ojai was particularly nice because it's a very sort of quiet, intellectual community and we had a nice time. The Ojai residents were very pleasant to us and seemed to enjoy the spotlight. I also sat with Lee Majors one night and watched him drink two bottles of wine, 17 straight shots of tequila, and a six-pack of Dos Equis. He then drove himself to the set the next day and knew all his lines. It was amazing."

• Jaime's cryogenic rebirth: "I always try to do an adequate amount of research to help support my fiction," said Johnson. "As it turned out, I had written a long screenplay on cryogenics a few years earlier, so I had a lot of that research already in my head."

Episode 38: *The Price of Liberty* . . . . **[9-28-75]**
Written by Kenneth Johnson. Story by Kenneth Johnson, Justin Edgerton. Directed by Richard Moder. Featuring: Chuck Connors (The Rifleman, Geronimo), *Henry Beckman, Sandy Ward, Bill Quinn, George Jordan, Joe Brooks, Scott B. Wells*

Funding for the space program has decreased. Scientist/explosives specialist Robert Meyer has been out of work since. He thinks America owes him about five million dollars, and believes the Bicentennial is as good a time as any to collect his "due." So he purloins and sabotages the Liberty Bell to explode on its national tour, unless he gets the money. He also wants guaranteed safe passage out of the country. In a race against time, Steve and Oscar turn to Neils Lindstrom, Meyer's protégé (and prison inmate), to defuse the complicated mechanism fastened to the gigantic chime.

• Ken Johnson originally intended this for the big screen, but things didn't pan out, so he adapted it for *Six* instead.

• He recalls a *sock*-it-to-me story about one sequence that was filmed at the Fox Ranch: "Oscar had to come in and land by helicopter to deliver the ransom money. Richard [Anderson] gets out of the helicopter without any socks on, which is how he dressed all the time." "Richard," Ken said, "I don't care if *you* don't like socks, but Oscar Goldman wears socks!"

• Steve leaves Independence Hall and chases the crooks' truck through what appears to be a lush park or forest. That's impossible. Independence Hall is in downtown Philadelphia. "I've gotten a lot of grief over this," laughs Johnson. "At Knott's Berry Farm, they have an actual full-scale replica of Independence Hall, which is what I wanted to use. Walter Knott, who was then about 85, was a little bit to the right of Attila the Hun. *Six Mill* was a little too left-wing for him, if you can imagine that. We had to piece it together from stock footage, which we got to be pretty good at. Most of it was shot out at the Fox Ranch in Malibu. I always grimaced when I saw that, but I was still very pleased with the tension that we were able to achieve, which made it work."

• Lindstrom said he shouldn't risk his neck to save the Bell because his ancestors were Swedish. His fellow bomb-technician reminds him that when the Bell was first cracked in 1752, it was recast in Philadelphia by a Swede who had just arrived from Stockholm.

• Johnson on guest star Chuck Connors: "We were lucky to have him. It was terrific." Lee Majors adds: "He was an intense guy, and a great story teller. I remember sitting around the set, and listening about his days on *The Rifleman*."

Episode 39: *The Song and Dance Spy* . . . .[10-5-75]
*Written by Jerry Devine. Directed by Richard Moder. Featuring: Sonny Bono
(The Sonny & Cher Comedy Hour; once a US Congressman), Victor Mohica,
Bruce Glover, Robin Clarke, Fred Holliday, Jayne Kennedy, Susan McIver, Susie
Coelho (then-married to Sonny Bono)*

Notable celebrity John Perry is a good friend of Steve's. In fact, they
were college roommates. Oscar, however, has his suspicions. Could Perry
be involved with an international spy syndicate? Could he be privy to classified government information? Could he be sharing this data with foreign
parties? Steve is assigned to find the answers.
   • Lee said Sonny Bono "was a lot of fun to work with, always joking, and
laughing."
   • Steve Stafford said Bono had "always been a very bright man; you
could have won a lot of money on the odds that he was going to make it to
Congress, because that was about as far from anyone's mind at the time than
you could imagine."
   • Producer Lionel Siegel, who wrote the lyrics for "Gotta Get Loose"
and "Sweet Jaime" (both of which were accompanied by music written by
Oliver Nelson) wrote the words to the ballad sung by Bono, known as the
Hippopotamus song.
   • Guest Jayne Kennedy was to be spun-off as the black *Wonder Woman*,
on the latter series, which featured Lynda Carter. Yet the deal fell through.

Episode 40: *The Wolf Boy* . . . .[10-12-75]
*Written by Judy Burns. Directed by Jerry London. Featuring: John Fujioka,
Buddy Foster, Quinn Redeker, Teru Shimada, Bill Saito*

Kuroda, the World War II Kamikaze pilot rescued from the wilderness
by Col. Austin, once again needs his friend's assistance. Are the reported
true of a young boy living with wolves? Oscar's disapproval notwithstanding, Steve journeys to Japan in search of the boy, whose existence may
prove enlightening. The "wild youth" may be the missing offspring of an
American ambassador who strangely perished with his wife in the barrens.
   • Guest Buddy Foster played the son in *Mayberry, R.F.D.*, and has
recently written a tell-all about his sister, Oscar-winning actress/director
Jodie Foster. Name of the book: *Foster Child*. Buddy's new name: Lucius
Fisher Foster.
   • Judy Burns: "Harve or Lee Siegel called me and said, 'We love the
Kuroda character, and we want you to bring him back.' I actually really liked
John Fujioka, who played the Japanese man, and I never thought of pitch-
ing him again, but he was thrilled when we brought him back. The wolf boy

storyline came, of all things, from another book about feral children [raised in the wild]. My next-door neighbors were Japanese second generation, and they had lots of Japanese folks over for dinner all the time. I was a pest, asking how to say things, asking for names, anything I needed to write that episode."

• A continuity error: In commencing to chase Wolf Boy, Steve wears a huge, orange backpack. In the middle of the chase, the bag vanishes. Upon catching the boy, the bag reappears.

• Kuroda's name? "You know, I think I pulled it from the phone book," said Burns.

• Trivia: A missing six-year-old Indian child named Ramu became known as the Lucknow Wolf Boy when he was found in 1954. His parents testified that a wolf had snatched him as a baby. When reunited with his parents, he lapped milk, chewed on bones, tore his food apart, and showed particular interest in wolves at the zoo. He died in 1968 at Lucknow hospital.

• Original working title: "Way of the Wolf."

Episode 41: *The Deadly Test* . . . .[10-19-75]
Written by James D. Parriott. Directed by Christian I. Nyby II. Featuring: Tim O'Connor (Buck Rogers in the 25th Century), *Frank Marth, Martin Speer, Erik Estrada* (CHiPS), *Leigh Christian, Harry Pugh, Bill Scherer*

A subversive electronics system is set up outside Edwards Air Force Base aimed at destroying student pilot Prince Sakari's plane, but mistakenly fells a jet piloted by student David Levy, who is from a hostile neighboring country. To avert a possible conflict between the two countries, Steve, anticipating another attack on the youth, disguises himself as the prince and takes off in the jet trainer to determine the origin of the electronics system. Lt. Jan Simmons, a high-spirited pilot and the first woman to graduate from the test school, insists on going up with Steve.

• Scribe Jim Parriott, who also went on to create the popular *Forever Knight* sci-fi drama and NBC's short-lived *Dark Skies* sci-fi drama, was just out of college when he wrote this episode. It produced his first paycheck, with which he purchased a used Volkswagen convertible, "the kind that used to be made in Mexico," he said. Parriott remembers pulling down the top, and driving with his wife to Edwards Air Force Base, where this segment was shot, in mid-summer: "It was the hottest drive I ever had in my life. And nobody really wanted me on the set. I said, *Hi, I'm Jim Parriott, and I wrote this episode.* Everyone was like, *Oh, get out of here.*"

• Shortly after Erik Estrada appeared here, he won the role of Ponch on *CHiPS.*

• When an airborne missile is launched by Steve's right arm, the attached

wires (for F/X) are clearly visible.
- Original working title: "An Eye for an Eye."

Episode 42: *Target in the Sky* ....[10-26-75]
Written by Larry Alexander. Directed by Jerry London. Featuring: Rafer Johnson,
Skeeter Vaughan, Barbara Rhoades, Denny Miller, Ivor Francis, Hank Stohl

An OSI agent has uncovered a missile installation plant near the Wixted
Lumber Camp. After he disappears, Steve dons lumberjack duds, and dis-
covers a plot to destroy passing aircraft with key Presidential cabinet figures
aboard — and foreman Jeremy Burke is involved.
- Jerry London marveled at how Ken Johnson spliced this episode with
Sometimes a Great Notion, a 1971 feature from Universal. Granted use of any
close-ups of the movie's actors (including Paul Newman), Ken fashioned a
Six script with *Great* bits and pieces. "We got a six-foot-tall tree and placed
Lee on top," he explained, "and cut into a shot of a lumberjack guy sitting
on an identical tree, 200 feet in the air. There were gags, with logs rolling
down a hill, and great swathes of barren land. It looked like we had gone on
location to Oregon for two months." London learned of Ken's plans, but
hadn't (seen) *A Great Notion.* Calling Johnson a "magician," he wondered
how he did it. "He got *Shogun* out of it," Johnson laughs. "What can I tell
you? A lot of shows were created in the editing room by using stock footage
of rocket launches and stuff."
- The first time Ken worked with guest Denny Miller, whom he later cast
in *V.* "I tend to do that," he explained. "I find actors I like and cast them
again."
- We learn that Steve flew during the Cuban Missile Crisis.
- Original working title: "Steve Austin, Lumberjack."

Episode 43: *One of Our Running Backs is Missing* ....[11-2-75]
Written by Kenneth Johnson. Story by Elroy Schwartz. Directed by Lee Majors.
Featuring: Larry Csonka, Pamela Csonka, Lee Josephson, Dick Butkus, Mike
Henry, Al Checco, Earl Faison, Carl Weathers (Rocky, In the Heat of the
Night), *Tom Mack, George Clifton*

An ex-football player is very unhappy and a star running back suffers the
brunt of the former performer's discontent. As such, celebrity athlete Larry
Bronco is drugged and kidnapped by washed up participant Bob Laport
before the big game. Now the "score" will be in Laport's favor; he and his
henchmen-turned-kidnappers/illegal gamblers stand to make a killing on
the pre-game point spread. Steve Austin, a former college football player,

comes to the rescue, locates Bronco, and together they combat the mis-guided band of gridiron lawbreakers.

• Since he played football when he was younger, Lee said, he asked if he could "do an episode about the game. We had Larry Csonka and Dick Butkus, which was not a bad bunch of Hall-of-Famers. The man who cho-reographed all of the football sequences was a very young assistant coach named Terry Donahue [the former coach at UCLA and one-time San Francisco 49ers GM]. He has more old-wins to his credit that any living coach. He was the youngest coach [at 34] to take over a college football team."

• We learn that Oscar was once a prosecutor in LA's District Attorney's office (his nickname was Goldy).

• At the end of the episode, directed by Lee Majors, Csonka's charac-ter, Larry Bronco, has been rescued by Steve. Butkus' character, Bob Laport, the head of the kidnap ring who is expecting to receive the ransom money, places himself atop a car to get a better view of the getaway.

As Steve Stafford goes on to say, "The script called for him to be dis-traught, because he doesn't get the money, and that's what was filmed. But Lee wanted another take. So Dick got up on the car again, with a couple of the other guys, and they actually dropped their pants, and mooned the cam-era." Frank Price, head of Universal, had come by with his family for a visit, "and they got a pretty good view of the dailies," Stafford laughs. "Lee got a phone call the next day."

• Ken Johnson: "We wanted to call it '*One of Our Csonkas is Missing*' but the network would have none of it. Lee said to me, 'Kenny, I think it's time I directed something,' and he did a fine job."

Episode 44: *The Bionic Criminal.* . . . .[11-9-75]
Written by Richard Carr. Story by Peter Allan Fields, Ron Bishop. Directed by Leslie Martinson. Featuring: Monte Markham, Maggie Sullivan, John Milford, Don Moffat

It's no secret that Barney Hiller, The Seven Million Dollar Man, is psycho-logically unstable. Yet against Steve's better judgment, Barney is reactivated. Then an important automobile figure named Shatley disqualifies Barney (a race car driver) from a pivotal automotive event. Following a bionic rage, Barney assumes he's murdered Shatley and turns criminal, as he agrees to perform thefts because evildoers are holding his wife hostage. Steve must once again prevent the blackmailed cyborg from creating any more havoc.

• Monte Markham said this sequel to "The Seven Million Dollar Man" "was not as very well written." "I took the job without seeing the script," he adds. "But it was kind of weak, and Harve [Bennett] knew it, but we just

didn't talk too much about it. You take your shots. It's always a gamble."
• In the interests of continuity, Alan Oppenheimer briefly reappears in the role of Rudy.
• Barney Miller's surname was changed to *Hiller.*

Episode 45: *The Blue Flash* ....[11-16-75]
Written by Sheridan Gibney, Sidney Field. Directed by Cliff Bole. Featuring: Rodney Allen Rippy (young commercial star), Janet MacLachlan, Michael Conrad (Hill Street Blues), Eddie Fontaine, Jason Wingreen, Barry Cahill, Benny Nickelberry, Virgil Charles Frye, Garrison True

An OSI agent vanishes on the threshold of divulging a criminal ring (who smuggle detecting devices). To locate the missing man, Steve adopts the guise of a longshoreman and takes up residence at a boarding house where the G-man last appeared. In the meantime, Ernie Cook, the owner's young son, wrecks his bicycle, and Steve lends a bionic hand. Consequently, he's deluged with an excessive amount of damaged toys to repair. Then a much bigger problem arises: Ernie's mother vanishes.
• Forced to tell Ernie that his toys didn't just fix themselves, Steve explained that they were repaired via the magic of science (i.e., The Six Million Dollar Man).

Episode 46: *The White Lightning War* ....[11-23-75]
Written by Wilton Denmark. Directed by Phil Bondelli. Featuring: Austin Stoker, Ben Hammer, Hugh Gillin, Robert Donner, Red West, Randy Kirby, Katherine Helmond (Soap, Who's The Boss?)

Steve Austin travels to a small Georgia town where he finds Bo Willis running a distillery, with crooked Sheriff Weems in on the take. He also learns that the network of payoffs includes Charles Quinten, a high-powered lawyer representing factions all the way to Washington. Steve's only ally is a kindly woman, Middy, whose husband has also been killed by "snake bite," and whose store has been confiscated by Willis. Undaunted, he takes on the *snake bit* gang.
• There is a bit of humor when Steve simulates the sound of a rattlesnake by colliding two pebbles in his hand at super-speed, paralyzing his kidnappers with fear.
• One of the rare times when any character legitimately close to Steve is killed.
• Original working title: "The Moonshine Wars."
• Wilton Denmark: "That was drawn from a portion of my younger life

in Georgia. I knew a man who was very wealthy, knew all the oil companies, had trucks with fake fuel in them and the rest of it moonshine, etc. I told Harve about that and he thought it was a hilarious idea, and so we went for it. The actors became so much in character on the set that they were calling each other by their characters' names. Years later I met the guy who played the Sheriff. He still had the script."

Episode 47: *Divided Loyalty* . . . .**[11-30-75]**
Written by Jim Carlson, Terry McDonnell. Directed by Alan Crosland, Jr. Featuring: Radames Pera (Kung Fu), *Michael McGuire, Curt Lowens, Larry Levine, Rod Haase, Ralph Taeger, Ned Romero, Johana De Winter*

Scientist Leon Jackson defected to the Soviet Union for love. He seeks a return to the States, and Steve must help. A problem arises when Jackson's son, Alex, refuses to accompany them. The boy has made friends with the soldiers where his father has been working. He finally agrees to leave, but it may be too late: Military men get wind of the trio's intentions and blockade a hidden pathway, leaving them no way out. Or so it would seem.

• This was reconstructed for *The Bionic Woman* as "Escape to Love," and features guest Ned Romero, who played Steve's adversary, and who would later appear as Austin's rebel friend in "The Thunderbird Connection."

• Director Alan Crosland, Jr. died on December 18, 2001 (natural causes).

Episode 48: *Clark Templeton O'Flaherty* . . . .**[12-14-75]**
Written by Frank Dandridge. Story by Dennis Pryor. Directed by Ernest Pintoff. Featuring: Lou Gossett, Jr. (The Powers of Matthew Star), *Ryan MacDonald, H.M. Wynant, Louis Latham, Lillian Randolph, Susan Quick, Linda Nesbit*

All government reported coated with a classified substance (that only Steve can see) are scheduled for destruction. But that's not what's happening. Steve trails the chemical to an exclusive apartment complex, where O'Flaherty (an OSI janitor and friend) said he works for a top-secret government agency, marketing the data to an underground alliance, hoping to find the group's leader. Steve then helps O'Flaherty reclaim his reputation.

• Harve Bennett "had to write something for Lou Gossett," who played O'Flaherty. "Lou Gossett," he told himself, "is my talisman." "When you're a writer," he explained, "you write with a vision, with actors in mind for your character. He was perfect for the character."

• Bennett later cast Gossett as Peter Barton's mentor in *The Powers of Matthew Star* (on NBC, 1982-1983); a program for which Tom Cruise had auditioned. *Powers* was beset by many tragedies, including the sudden death of *Bionic* alumnus Allan Balter, and an accident involving Barton himself (when he fell backwards onto a series of road flares, and received severe burns). The show was taken off the air. "We came back," Bennett recalls, "but we lost our momentum." [Barton survived his injuries and later worked on Aaron Spelling's NBC daytime soap, *Sunset Beach.*]

Episode 49: *The Winning Smile* . . . . [12-21-75]
Written by Gustave Field, Richard Carr. Story by Gustave Field. Directed by Arnold Laven. Featuring: Stewart Moss, Robert Delegall, Milton Selzer, Harry Lewis, Ben Andrews, James Ingersoll, Rick Podell

Is Callahan to blame for leaking exclusive hydrogen fusion data to a subversive coalition? A lie detector test holds the answer, and she's insistent on taking it. Meanwhile, Steve learns that her boyfriend, Dr. Gene Finney (a dentist), is the sole individual who is party to Callahan's classified position with the OSI.
• Callahan's not-so-wonderful luck with men began.
• In a scene often cut in syndication, Steve sneaks into Callahan's apartment through a window, where he is welcomed by a loud bark. When Callahan's new dog, Peter, sinks his fangs into Steve's bionic leg, he receives a few electric shocks and quickly scurries back to his basket, where he cowers in shame. Steve grins and said to the little guy, "You did your best."
• A slight glitch: Oscar and Steve roam the streets of Washington to look for Callahan, and we see palm trees in DC.
• Somewhat similar to BW's "Brain Wash," where Callahan was *again* suspected of treason.

Episode 50: *Welcome Home, Jaime (Part I)* . . . . [1-11-76]
Written by Kenneth Johnson. Directed by Alan Crosland, Jr. Featuring: Dennis Patrick (Dark Shadows), *Roger Davis (also from* Shadows, *and ex-husband of Jaclyn* Charlie's Angels *Smith), Dee Timberlake, Alexa Kenin, Kraig Metzinger*

Jaime partly regains her memory, returns to Ojai, and moves into a carriage house owned by Steve's parents. Browsing through old photos, she begins to understand her relationship with Steve, but has no sound recollection of her feelings. Oscar lands her a teaching assignment at the Ventura Air Force Base, where she has more control over her students than most educators (employing her powers to freak them out). Her double life begins.
• "Welcome Home, Jaime (Part II)" was BW's series premiere.

• We learn that Jaime went to Carnegie Tech. She received a degree in Education.

• Her California license plate number is 826 OPP.

• Ken Johnson: "It was my idea, along with Harve's counseling, to make her a schoolteacher. It was an effort to make her ever more accessible and closer to the truth of the everyday life which audiences young and older were leading. Few of us have ever known tennis stars, but we've all had teachers."

• Did you know that Lindsay was a teacher in real life? She taught drama to sixth, seventh, and eighth graders at the Church of Religious Science. "We used the teaching-in-the-round arrangement that you see in Jaime's classroom in the series," she said. "When everyone's a part of a circle, including me, the teacher, all the energy is focused inward and all becomes one unit, with no self-consciousness and no one hiding in the back seats."

• Her parents died in a car crash when she was 16.

• While dictating remarks to a tape recorder, Oscar said "Office of Scientific Investigation." As the series progressed, it was more commonly known as the "Office of Scientific Intelligence."

• Lionel Siegel: "When they did the first two-parter, Lee and Lindsay were pretty tight. But when she had her own series that really became a problem. Lee still considered himself to be 'the boss,' but she had her own show, so she was the boss of that show. And I think, he being a Southern gentleman, women have their place, but that wasn't the place he figured her to be. Call it a power struggle. Lee's concern was eventually tempered by the fact that Majors was given a financial piece of Wagner's series."

• Ken Johnson: "I think Lee Siegel's assessment is pretty accurate. In 'The Bionic Woman, I and II' they were fine. There was never any sexual attraction between them off screen. After *Bionic Woman* spun off and they had to bring Lindsay back, she was making almost as much as Lee had been making when he was doing *Six Mill*, and he felt a little miffed and frustrated by that situation and it was always sort of a thorn in his side. And there were times when he'd get a little pissy on the set about attention that was being paid to her for anything at all. But ultimately he apologized for that behavior and behaved like a professional."

• ABC chieftain Fred Silverman: "They created a crossover episode which was only meant to be a one-time shot. But Lindsay Wagner was so good in it that I said to Michael Eisner, 'Let's make a series out of this thing.' There was no series deal or anything. We got raped in the process, but he got the damn thing on the air in two months. It was a big hit on Wednesday night, just an enormous hit. It pulled a 38 share going in."

Episode 51: *Hocus-Pocus* ....[1-18-76]
Written by Richard Carr. Story by Richard Carr, James Schmerer. Directed by

Barry Crane. Featuring: Robbie Lee, Chris Nelson, Jack Colvin, Pernell Roberts (Bonanza, Trapper John, M.D.), W.T. Zacha, Mark Wilson, Richard Geary

Crooked nightclub proprietor Mark Wharton receives more than money for his most recent job: He heists $100,000 from an armored car - and also obtains the Navy's confidential code book. Now crime-shoppers can make a real steal on the international market. To thwart Wharton's plans, Steve once again teams up with psychic Audrey Moss, as they set out to retrieve the special code tome - and the stolen loot.
   • Guest Jack Colvin later portrayed John Houseman's underworld contact in BW's "Kill Oscar," and Steve's adversary in SM's "Dark Side of the Moon." He would also star as the intrepid reporter on Ken Johnson's *Incredible Hulk*.
   • When Steve is doing a card trick for Oscar Goldman in an early scene (where the Aces seemingly poke out on their own), a wire can be seen along Steve's arm.
   • Many SM/BW's featured psychics.

Episode 52: *The Secret of Bigfoot (Part I)* . . . . [2-1-76]
Written by Kenneth Johnson. Directed by Alan Crosland, Jr. Featuring: Andre the Giant (The Princess Bride), Donn Whyte, Stefanie Powers (The Girl from U.N.C.L.E., Hart to Hart), Ford Lile, Charles Cyphers, Penelope Windust

Scientists Ivan and Marlene Beckey disappear while placing earthquake sensors near a Northern Californian fault line, where Steve discovers huge footprints. He eventually finds a gargantuan animal with which he battles. Could this be the legendary Bigfoot? Steve's not sure, but he pursues the creature, which flees into a cave, where there's an electronic hum. He collapses, awakens, and is examined by aliens, including the very attractive Shalon.
   • Jaime makes a cameo, sitting in her classroom, making a call of concern to Oscar, regarding Steve. Lindsay Wagner's name, however, does not appear in the credits.
   • This episode sparked such a response, that it spawned many sequels. "Bigfoot became our staple," Lee said. "If we wanted a 45% share [of the ratings], all we would have to do is pop in Bigfoot."
   • "I was always fascinated by the Bigfoot myth," explained Ken Johnson, who wrote this two-parter. "I thought, '*Suppose Bigfoot isn't what we think he is? What if he's a robotic entity created by extra-terrestrials?*' Once I got into it, and began to play with it, I sort of had a fertile imagination. It was fun, and the first time that I did something overtly imaginative on the show." Though intriguing to write, he wanted to direct it, as well. But he was too

busy with other scripts. Yet he was quite fond of the "surprising elements" of this segment, as when "Bigfoot's arm gets pulled off, and you go, *What the f...?*" He still has the ceramic cast of the *Big* footprint on his living room hearth, which he later used for *The Incredible Hulk*.

• Johnson said the name *Shalon* (given to the character played by Stefanie Powers), was inspired by "the road about halfway through the Sepulveda Pass in California's San Fernando Valley. It used to be Shalon Drive." He thought, "That's a great name for somebody. It's a little off-beat." Some years later, the road was re-named Getty Center Drive in honor of The Getty Museum. "Somehow, I don't think the alien's name would have sounded as good if she was *Getty Center*," Johnson said.

• A continuity error: Steve is shown on the aliens' examining table, bare-chested, then with his shirt on, and then bare-chested again when the camera returns.

• *Entertainment Weekly* rated "Secret of Bigfoot's" Austin-Sasquatch battle as the 100th greatest moment in U.S. television history. "That's the episode everybody always brings up," laughs Majors, who ultimately prevailed over the cybernetic beast. "Maybe because the ugly fella was so big, you couldn't forget him."

Episode 53: *The Secret of Bigfoot (Part II)* . . . . [2-4-76]
Written by Ken Johnson. Directed by Alan Crosland, Jr. See Part I for Cast Credits.

Bigfoot is a creation of the aliens, who seem friendly. Trouble stirs when Earth scientists surmise that a seismic quake will soon rock the world. Oscar Goldman is faced with the decision of exploding a nuclear device to relieve the pressure and thwart the quake, knowing that Steve (who has gone missing) may be killed in the blast. The aliens seem intent on sacrificing the West Coast of the United States in order to preserve their hidden lair. But Steve has other ideas.

• Ken Johnson: "Stefanie Powers was my first choice for the role of Shalon. A lot of people had major crushes on her at the time."

• Steve and Jaime would many times lift heavy objects, which were beyond the capabilities of their human skeletal structure, particularly the spine. Here, Steve prevents a mammoth boulder from descending upon a group inside the alien base. The rock could be measured in thousands of pounds. That seems impossible even for him.

• The aliens erase Steve's memory of them. In the novelization of this segment, *The Secret of Bigfoot Pass* (by Mike Jahn), the metal plate in Steve's head preserves his recollection of all events.

• Ken Johnson: "Lee was a terrific guy. When I first started doing the show, he was holding out for more money. He was very whimsical about it. He said to me, 'Kenny, don't think I don't know how lucky I am. If I hadn't lucked into this show, I'd be coaching high school football somewhere.' He was a solid pro and very easy to work with. He always knew his lines. He also knew his limitations. Lee could play that strong, silent type very well."

• In an effort to reclaim some of the fans that defected to Lindsay Wagner's show, this episode aired in *The Bionic Woman's* Wednesday night timeslot.

• The following technical personnel were Emmy-nominated here for Outstanding Achievement in Film/Sound Editing: Jerry Christian, Ken Sweet, Thomas M. Patchett, Jack Jackson, David A. Schonleber, John W. Singleton, Dale Johnson, George Luckenbacher, Walter Jenevein, and Dennis Diltz.

Episode 54: *The Golden Pharaoh* . . . . **[2-8-76]**
Written by Margaret and Paul Schneider. Directed by Cliff Bole. Featuring: Farrah Fawcett-Majors, Gordon Connell, Michael Lane, Joe Maross, Rudy Challenger, Gary Vinson, Lyndel Stuart, Joseph LaCava, Peter Ashton

A valuable foreign statue display in America disappears and is substituted with an imitation. International peace is at stake. Steve must locate the figure and concludes that Gustav Tokar, the Vice-Counsel of a neighboring nation, has stolen the artifact. Steve baits Trish Hollander, Tokar's fiancée (who's also a fanatic gambler), into offering her assistance. In return, Steve will make her debt free. She agrees, but has grand designs of her own.

• Farrah Fawcett-Majors makes the third of her four *Six* appearances.

• Ken Johnson: "Indirectly I worked with Farrah. I met her a few times, and I never saw so many teeth in one mouth in my life. This was before *Charlie's Angels*, and she wasn't much of an actress then, but has developed remarkably since then."

• This episode was clearly inspired by the King Tutankhamen Exhibit that toured the United States in 1976.

Episode 55: *Love Song for Tanya* . . . . **[2-15-76]**
Written by David H. Balkan, Alan Folsom. Directed by Phil Bondelli. Featuring:

Cathy Rigby, Terry Kiser, Kurt Grayson, Alan Manson, Elizabeth Treadwell, Walker Edmiston, Curtis Credel, Sheila Wills, Michael Cartel

Steve plays guardian to Tanya Breski, a gymnast from the USSR who's on an American tour. While embarrassed that she has a crush on him, Steve tries to convince her not to defect and to prevent her from being killed by a subversive organization. America will be blamed if she dies, and our relationship with the Soviets will be no more.

• This episode marked Cathy Rigby's acting debut, and stands out in Lee's mind, because of the Olympic athlete. "The thing I remember about Cathy," he said, "and what surprised me the most, was how tiny she is, and how great an athlete she was. When we were at the Bell Gardens Gym on location, in Orange County [California], she walked the beam and did all those things that an Olympic gymnast can do. She was amazing."

• Jaime makes a cameo appearance.

Episode 56: *The Bionic Badge* . . . . [2-22-76]
Written by Wilton Denmark. Directed by Cliff Bole. Featuring: Noah Berry, Alan Bergmann, Thomas Bellin, Susan Gay Powell, Mike Santiago, Stack Pierce

Officer Greg Banner is under scrutiny: several small atomic elements have been stolen from under his nose. As a result, a foreign power may soon have a substantial amount of components to construct their own bomb. Steve investigates, incognito, as a partner to Banner, who behaves in a rather odd manner -- and Steve doesn't have too much time to figure out why.

• Remade as the "Jaime's Shield" two-parter for BW, employing similar set locations, including the exact warehouse scene (for "Jaime's Shield, Part II").

• Wilton Denmark: "Steve played a cop with a conscience who didn't want to shoot anybody. He relied on his bionic powers instead."

• Denmark: "Richard Anderson was a delightful man. I liked him a lot--a perfect Oscar Goldman, but not like Goldman in real life at all. He was amazed with the speed with which I wrote and re-wrote episodes for SM and BW. Many times he invited me over to his home for breakfast and he would ask me how I thought Oscar Goldman would react to particular situations, mostly regarding scripts written by other writers. He never questioned any of my dialogue--neither did Lee. Perhaps my gift was I wrote dialogue the way people talk. Richard is one of the unsung heroes of the acting world."

Episode 57: *Big Brother* . . . . [3-7-76]
Written by Kenneth Johnson, Richard Carr. Directed by Cliff Bole. Featuring:

Michael Salcido, Carl Crudup, Ralph Wilcox, John Hesley, David Yanez, Jorge Cervera III, Renie Radich, Maria Elena Cordero

Steve reaches out to the Big Brother program and decides to take troubled Carlos Delgado under his wing. Carlos is a truant who has little respect for the law. As such, Steve is bent on setting him straight. For a change of scenery, Col. Austin allows Carlos to fly with him. Back on the street, The Bionic Man helps the lost boy pay off an illegal debt (set by a local gang) with a friendly game of bionic basketball.

• This episode exemplifies the type of story that writer Ken Johnson was striving for, the kind he said, "That were away from the Oscar-Goldman-coming-to-Steve-and-telling-him-that-somebody-had-been-kidnapped-by-Arabs-and-had-to-be-saved storylines. I was always trying to look for the ones with more heart."

Johnson said the intent was also to give the young kids of America the chance to think, "Gee, Steve Austin could be my big brother, too," which was partly the reason that he later made Jaime a schoolteacher. He wanted her to have that connection with young people, to display the thought of, "Oh, wow. I wish my teacher was bionic."

• Johnson: "There was a time when I was writing and producing both bionic shows simultaneously, doing the David Kelley number, and it was not fun. Too hard, even though I had the #1 and the #3 show in the country. Plus, I didn't have time to direct, which is what I really enjoyed doing the most. So I eventually let go of *Six Mill* and stayed with *BW*."

• Proving that white men *can* jump (at least when they're bionic), Steve wins the basketball game with a thunderous slam-dunk. The pick-up game is supposedly being played in a mean, impoverished neighborhood in Washington, D.C. In the background, we see the lush California hills.

• If the *Bionic* faithful were wondering why Lee Majors' hair was cut so short from "Welcome Home, Jaime" to now (in which Jaime makes a cameo), it's because Lee was required to get a crewcut for the TV-movie, *The Francis Gary Powers Story*.

"THE RETURN OF BIGFOOT, PART I" (W/ TED CASSIDY), "NIGHTMARE IN THE SKY," "VULTURE OF THE ANDES," "THE MOST DANGEROUS ENEMY" (W/ INA BALIN), "H+2+0 = DEATH," "KILL OSCAR, PART II," "THE BIONIC BOY," "U-509"

The Fourth Season
1976 to 1977

Episode 58: *The Return of Bigfoot (Part I)*.................. [9-19-76]
Written by Kenneth Johnson. Directed by Barry Crane. Featuring: Ted Cassidy (The Addams Family), *John Saxon, Sandy Duncan* (The Hogan Family), *Stefanie Powers, Stephen Young, Severn Darden, Charles Cyphers*

Bigfoot is back, reautomated, now steals jewels and gold, and Shalon no longer controls him. His otherworldly creators set out to construct a weapon (made of the goods that Bigfoot obtains) to obliterate Earth. All evidence points to Austin, who's arrested, but escapes, confronts Bigfoot in a dramatic battle, and clings to life when the atomic power packs in his legs explode, inflicting severe radiation sickness. Only Jaime Sommers can save him now.

• "The Return of Bigfoot (Part II)" was BW's second season premier.
• Lee's mustache makes its first appearance.
• Marty Brooks appears for the first time in the *Six* credit sequence.
• Ken Johnson: "My son, incidentally, ran into a young woman in Ashland, Oregon recently whose name was Shalon, and he asked her where she had gotten that name. She told him that her parents had seen a *Six Mill* episode and had liked the name of that character. And she knew someone else who had been named that also, for the same reason."
• Another list of production people here were Emmy-nominated for Outstanding Achievement in Film/Sound Editing for a Series: Dale Johnston, James A. Bean, Carl J. Brandon, Joe Divitale, Don Tomlinson, Don Weinman, Gene Craig.
• In an interview granted shortly before his death in 1979, Ted Cassidy was less than enamored with his Bigfoot legacy. "Oh, it was awful, just bloody awful," he said. "That was the most uncomfortable outfit any man could wear. There were times when I actually fell to my knees from the heat. I thought I was going to pass out, because we filmed the first show in a heat wave, and I was wearing that suit and had hair all over my face, contact lenses, a huge wig on my head, heavy high-heeled boots — I had no mobility in those things — and those awful looking teeth that clamp onto your mouth. There was hardly an orifice that wasn't plugged up. It must have been 200 degrees at all times inside that hair suit! I'm *glad* that show was canceled, at least on my behalf, because I would have had to do Bigfoot again."
• Continuity error: Steve is shown on the Elgin living room set, but an exterior shot of a different house on the Universal lot is depicted.

Episode 59: *Nightmare in the Sky* .... [9-26-76]
Written by Jim Carlson, Terence McDonnell. Directed by Alan Crosland, Jr. Featuring: Farrah Fawcett-Majors, Hank Stohl, Donald Moffat, Dana Elcar

Pilot Kelly Wood is battered by a World War II Japanese Zero while testing a multi-million-dollar aircraft. She reported the phenomenon to Oscar Goldman and Steve, who are in the control tower, but the men can only see Kelly's plane on the radar screen. Kelly is discovered after the crash-landing, but her parachute has not been ejected, and the 15-million-dollar aircraft she was flying is gone. Everyone except Steve and Oscar believe she's party to a conspiracy. They are steadfast at finding out the truth, which somehow involves a fantastic plot to simulate Bermuda Triangle-like disappearances of top-secret aircraft.

• Farrah Fawcett's Kelly Wood first appeared in "The Rescue of Athena One."

• Kenner Toys bigwig Bernard Loomis: "*Six Mill* was a big hit in Australia. My wife and I traveled there one year, and coincidentally, Lee and Farrah were there at the same time. I was playing golf with Lee one day, and he said to me, 'How much money am I gonna make out of this [merchandising] thing?' The guess at that point was $35,000, but I gotta tell you something, that was a lot of money to Lee. He also got mildly upset with me when I turned to Farrah at one point and said, 'Farrah, you're gonna be a bigger star than he is.' In my defense, this turned out to be true, but he didn't like my telling it to her." Mr. Loomis passed away in 2006 at the age of 82.

• Original working title: "The Edstrom Triangle."

Episode 60: *Double Trouble* .... [10-3-76]
Written by Jerry Devine. Directed by Phil Bondelli. Featuring: Flip Wilson, Simon Scott, Rick Podell, Mira L. Waters, Jerome Guardino

Billy Parker, a second-rate comedian, is acting funny (as in *weird*). He does not know that an electronic instrument has been implanted in his brain. The mechanism, which is remote-controlled, is endemic to a foreign authority. Steve steps in as Billy's protection, and ascertains the true identity of the real funny business culprit who controls the device.

• SM's pilot debuted opposite *The Flip Wilson Show*, which it bested in the ratings.

• Not exactly a fan favorite.

• The first and final time Steve ventured into The Big Apple.

Episode 61: *The Most Dangerous Enemy* . . . . [10-17-76]
Written by Judy Burns. Directed by Richard Moder. Featuring: Ina Balin

Steve and Rudy fly to a desolate island where Cheryl Osborne, a beautiful young scientist, has been working in total isolation for two years. Cheryl has been trying to perfect a drug which might turn an average person into a genius, using a chimpanzee as her subject. But when Steve and Rudy reach the island, Cheryl is nowhere in sight and her laboratory is in ruins. As the two men search through the rubble, Rudy's bitten by a mighty mad chimp, which flees before Steve has a chance to capture it. Rudy's strength increases, his mind, severely altered. Steve defends himself without harming the man who literally put him back together.

• "This is when Rudy youthened up, so to speak," said Marty Brooks, who plays tennis and is an ex-handball champ for the New York Four-Wall Singles. "There was running and jumping and I enjoyed it. It gave me a chance to get out there and move."

• Judy Burns: "I didn't really pitch it. They came to me and said, 'We want to do some kind of story with Rudy.' My college degree was in anthropology. Actually, I was more of a paleoanthropologist, but I had enough knowledge of Louis Leakey and of Jane Goodall to know about chimps and some such. I was going to Africa to dig bones when I broke in, and so I took that knowledge and put it to use in the show."

• Burns, who wrote a seminal *Star Trek* episode entitled "The Tholian Web," had the good fortune of working for two giants in the field: Gene Roddenberry and Harve Bennett. Her verdict? "They were dissimilar," she said. "Gene was a genius of ideas. I think Harve is that ... a genius all around, but he is a great organizer. Gene was more laid back ... more like a big teddy bear. Harve was more to the point ... high maintenance. But both brilliant mentors. I have a great affection for both. They taught me more than I even knew at the time."

• The drugged-out Rudy ties Steve upside-down on a tree limb. Lee had to stay positioned as such, until the scene was over. He was disconcerted, and screamed, "Will somebody get me down from here? My bionic eyeballs are coming out!"

• When Steve performs amazing feats of strength, Dr. Osborne naturally assumes he's been bitten by a chimp, while totally oblivious to his bionics.

• Trivia: Did you know that chimpanzees are about five times stronger than humans?

• At the end of the episode, Oscar and Steve are seen flipping through a magazine that contains several gratuitous shots of Farrah Fawcett-Majors.

Episode 62: *H + 2 + O = Death* . . . . [10-24-76]
Written and directed by John Meredyth Lucas. Featuring: Elke Sommer, John van Dreelen, Linden Chiles, Robert J. Hogan, Todd Martin, Lawrence Bame, Frank Parker, Frank Farmer

Ilsa Martin, a scientist, knows how to divide oxygen and hydrogen in water, which may lead to a supreme, if not definitive, source of energy. A by-product of the discovery that is yet to be perfected may very well be an underwater breathing device that could supply its own oxygen and power. The spy ring, Omega, doesn't know that the eight-million-dollar device is not yet perfected, and steals it. Steve infiltrates the ring as "the man with all the answers." But he's instructed to demonstrate the contrivance, in order to test his knowledge.
 • Steve is evidently knowledgeable enough in bionics to repair his own badly damaged arm.
 • At this point in her professional life, guest star Elke Sommer was experiencing the downward spiral of her once-exuberant movie career.

Episode 63: *Kill Oscar (Part II)* . . . . [10-31-76]
Written by William T. Zacha. Story by Arthur Rowe, Oliver Crawford. Directed by Barry Crane. Featuring: John Houseman (The Paper Chase), *Jack L. Ging, Corrine Michaels, Janice Whitby, Jennifer Darling*

Jaime has been nearly beaten to death by two of Dr. Franklin's fembots, who are disguised as secretaries for the OSI. Steve wants to rescue Oscar, his kidnapped boss, but is warned by higher-ups not to interfere. With the help of Jaime's bionic hearing, Rudy and Steve are able to pinpoint the location of Franklin's secret lair. The disgruntled scientist, however, is wise to their plan. Steve is lured to the hideout, where he is confronted and attacked by more of the evil doctor's deadly female creations. Steve holds his own and rescues Oscar. Or did he? Unbeknownst to The Bionic Man, the real Oscar Goldman has been replaced by a mechanical replica. But Steve is only momentarily fooled. The Oscar-impostor (heavy-footed with machinery) leaves a deep imprint on the office carpeting. This leads to an all-out war outside Jaime's hospital room, where Steve prevails. But will Franklin have the last laugh?
 • In syndication, during the Part I recap, a Jaime/Steve phone scene is reviewed, which was not shown in Part I. Also in the recap, Jaime leaps from Callahan's apartment window. We see stuntwoman Rita Egleston plunging awkwardly to one side, even though Jaime somehow managed a perfect landing at the conclusion of Part I. The jump was accomplished in two jumps (one from a lower position), because three-story jumps were difficult for Rita to control.

• Appropriately enough, this scary episode aired on Halloween night.

• Marks the second time Steve had to battle a robotic Oscar Goldman ("Return of the Robot Maker," previously).

• The fake Oscar convinces feds that Steve is a Franklin creation, by persuading them to run a Geiger counter over Steve's legs.

• Like Marty Brooks, Richard Anderson welcomed those rare opportunities when he could mimic Steve and Jaime's super-powered feats. "I wish I could have done more [action sequences]," he said. "After all, I was physically fit. But it was Lee's show, so naturally he received the lion's share of those duties."

• Ken Johnson (laughing): "Richard was the luckiest guy in show business because he was the only person I knew who had two series on the air at the same time, other than me, but he didn't have to write them all like I did."

Episode 64: *The Bionic Boy* . . . . **[11-7-76]**
Written by Tom Greene. Story by Lionel Siegel, Wilton Schiller. Directed by Phil Bondelli. Featuring: Vincent Van Patten (Apple's Way), Dick Van Patten (Eight is Enough), Joan Van Ark (Knots Landing), Carol Jones, Kerry Sherman, Richard Erdman, Greg Evigan (Tek War, My Two Dads, B.J. and the Bear), George Martin, Jack Bannon, Nick David, Frank Gifford (as himself), Woodrow Chambliss

Andy Sheffield, a once-athletic youngster living in a small Utah town, is selected by an OSI computer to receive an experimental implant to restore his paralyzed legs. Andy's paralysis is the result of a landslide that killed his father, who was a controversial figure. The atomic/bionic implant, developed by Rudy Wells, gives Andy enormous physical power and the boy sets out on a dangerous mission to clear his father's name — placing himself and Steve in extreme jeopardy.

• Originally aired as a two-hour episode; syndicated as two one-hour episodes.

• The idea began "as a joke," said Harve Bennett. "What was next? *The Bionic Rabbit?*" Still, Bennett said, " 'The Bionic Boy' was extremely well-written."

• Vince Van Patten impressed him, too. He played tennis with the actor and his dad, Dick Van Patten. "Vince became so good at tennis," Bennett said, "that I couldn't play with him anymore. Then I saw him as an actor, and said, *Hey, the kid can act, too.* We were looking for someone that age, who was also an athlete. He was perfect." [Bennett played tennis only once with Richard Anderson, and said he "was splendid."]

• Vince Van Patten: "They called me out of the blue one day. I never had to audition for the role. I got the job based on my headshot and my previous work in the industry. I think I was paid around $4,000 for the two weeks of work."

• Van Patten reflects on Lee Majors: ""Lee was an athlete long before *Six Mill*, so he was perfect for the role," he said. "We were friends with Lee socially, and I used to play tennis with Richard Anderson on the celebrity circuit. Lee's best quality was his sense of humor. He was always joking and putting others at ease. One night he and the wardrobe stylist put bed sheets over their heads, broke into the room where the director was sleeping, and threw him into the hotel pool."

• After Andy's surgery, everyone in town greets him with praise and gifts. The local shoe store owner (played by Dick Van Patten) wants to give him a free pair of running shoes. Andy ruins them, by accident, in the store, and Steve said, "Maybe we'll come back for another pair some other time." Immediately following, we see Andy wearing the shoes.

• Andy, soaked with sweat, struggles to ascend the face of a rock cliff on two malfunctioning legs. Did this scene tax the young actor? "Not really," he said. "As an aspiring tennis pro, I was in very good shape. One day we spent a lot of time shooting at the base of a small mountain. Lee bet me that I couldn't run to the top and back down again in less than 15 minutes. I won."

• Lionel Siegel: "It was fun. We went on location, and Vince tried hard and he carried it off pretty well. Had it gone to series, it would have been strictly for kids."

• A series is exactly what Van Patten had in mind, but his co-star had other ideas. "One day Lee and I were sipping beers off-set," he said. "He told me that he didn't think the [Andy Sheffield] character would evolve past this two-hour episode, and he was right. I kind of got the impression that he had veto power over the whole thing. Lindsay had her own show, so maybe another bionic series would have been too much. Having my own series is something I would have been very receptive to, even if it truncated my tennis career. Actors need to act."

• Filmed on location in Kanab, Utah. Van Patten: "Did you notice how tan all of us were, or how white my hair was? That's because it was blistering hot in Kanab those two weeks. Hanging out at the pool didn't hurt either. There was also a diner where the locals couldn't have been friendlier. This was Greg Evigan's first acting gig, and he subsequently became a friend of mine. Looking back, I'm still very fond of this episode, though my own children have yet to see it. I may not have watched *Six Mill* every week, but I thought it was cool. However briefly, I was just happy being bionic."

Written by Ben Masselink. Directed by Cliff Bole. Featuring: Henry Darrow, Barbara Luna, Bernie Kopell (The Love Boat), *Zitto Kazann, Dallas Mitchell, Joe Haworth*

Glider pilot Leslie Morales, of San Lorenzo, is in America for an international competition. Byron Falco, a rich sportsman with designs to control San Lorenzo, accompanies her. Byron's plan (involving the attainment of military jets) is powerless without Leslie's assistance, which she must offer against her will. She finds herself dropping homing devices at integral points from her glider while in flight rehearsal. Steve is assigned to investigate, and ends up preventing the destruction of several power plants, and a missile attack on the United States.
• Steve casts a lengthy, hefty missile hundreds of yards, with shocking accuracy. As with "Secret of Bigfoot" and "Sharks! Part II," this may not be considered bion-logical.

Episode 66: *The Thunderbird Connection* . . . .[11-28-76]
Written by Jim Carlson, Terrence McDonnell. Directed by Christian I. Nyby II. Featuring: Robert Loggia, Ned Romero, Susanne Reed, Jim McMullan, Barry Miller, Jeff David, Martine Beswick, Joe LoPresti

Mahmud Majid, an air marshal, governs the Burdabi people by way of the teenage Prince Hassad, whose father was murdered by Majid's regiment six months earlier. When U.S. intelligence learns that Majid is planning the same fate for the young prince, the State Department offers to dispatch the Thunderbirds to Burdabi to celebrate a national holiday. Actually, the gesture is a cover for one of Steve's most dangerous missions.
• Originally broadcast as one episode; syndicated as two-parts.
• Original working title: "Flight from Burdabi."
• On July 12, 1971 in Rabat, Morocco, the Thunderbirds flew their F4-E Phantoms at a birthday celebration honoring Prince Mohamed, the eight-year-old son of King Hassan and crown prince of Morocco (now King Mohamed II). The Moroccan visit was part of a 38-day deployment by the 1971 team visiting eight nations and performing before more than three-and-a-half-million spectators.
• Episode filmed on location at Nellis Air Force Base, Nevada.
• *Cyborg* creator and real-life pilot Martin Caidin spent three months with the USAF Thunderbirds jet aerobatic team in 1960. His book *Thunderbirds!* has gone through more than 20 printings and is still acclaimed as a classic documentary on the Air Force's aerial demonstration unit. Awarded the title "Thunderbird 8" by the team, Caidin is the only civilian ever to live and fly with them.

• In 1977, Lee and Farrah spent a second honeymoon in Iran at the invitation of the soon-to-be-deposed Shah.

Episode 67: *A Bionic Christmas Carol* . . . . **[12-12-76]**
Written by Wilton Schiller. Directed by Gerald Mayer. Featuring: Ray Walston (My Favorite Martian, Star Trek: The Next Generation, Picket Fences), *Dick Sargent* (Bewitched), *Quinn Cummings* (Family), *Antoinette Bower, Sheldon Allman, Howard McGillin, Nathasha Ryan, Adam Rich* (Eight is Enough), *Noah Keen, Barry Cahill, Kin Khriner, Ann Dusenberry, June Drayton*

Steve foregoes his Christmas vacation to inspect a disruption at a main system supplier for the space program. A conspiracy could alter plans for an exploration of Mars. The supplier's president is the mean-spirited Horton Budge, who's extremely careful when it comes to money. His nephew, Bob Crandall (an employee at Budge's factory), doesn't bring home enough bacon to care for his wife and children. Oscar believes that low company morale is the result of Budge's prudent manner. Steve employs his powers to warm Budge's soul and bring some cheer to the Crandall family.
   • Harve Bennett "always wanted to work with Ray Walston, ever since I saw him in a [stage] production of *Damn Yankees.*"
   • A takeoff on Dickens' *A Christmas Carol*, which was also parodied on *Bewitched*, though not with Dick Sargent's Darrin (who guest-starred here), but Dick York's.
   • There is a substantial sight gag in this episode. When Majors and Sargent go into a toy store to pick up some gifts for Sargent's kids, Majors is seen talking to a sales clerk. Behind the clerk, in clear view on the shelves, are *The Six Million Dollar Man* dolls manufactured by Kenner Toys (see Chapter 3). Steve doesn't notice them, and doesn't buy one; that would be two worlds (fantasy and reality) colliding.
   • Budge's factory houses a chamber called "Artificial Martian atmosphere." A nod to Ray Walston's character in *My Favorite Martian*?
   • Oddity: Steve uses a magnifying glass to study a piece of metal. Why would he do that, when he could use his bionic eye?
   • Lee Majors: "I've done a lot of independent films lately, and crew people are bringing in their dolls and lunchboxes — either it's a *Fall Guy* lunch box or a *Six Million Dollar Man* doll. That's when you realize, 'A lot of people must have been watching.'"

Episode 68: *Task Force* . . . . **[12-19-76]**

Written by Robert C. Dennis, Wilton Schiller. Directed by Barry Crane. Featuring: Alex Cord, Taylor Lacher, Edmund Gilbert, Robert Forward, Gary Cashdollar, Scott B. Wells

Steve goes undercover (as a mercenary) with those preparing to heist a $30 million missile en route from San Diego to a Nevada testing site, under the supervision of Oscar Goldman. But Steve is being watched carefully and cannot warn Goldman that the officer in charge of security is actually an impersonator. Steve's only contact is with a spunky but flaky OSI secretary named Callahan, who has found a way to stay near the mercenary gang.

• Steve's cover is blown when of the one criminal masterminds remembers that he was party to a panel that court-martialed him in the 1960s.

• Guest Alex Cord starred in Gene Roddenberry's 1973 pilot, *Genesis II*, about the world's post-war, multi-divided society-filled existence. Plugged as "*Star Trek* without the Enterprise," it didn't sell. Revamped as 1974's *Planet: Earth* (with SM guest John Saxon), it failed again. And once more with Saxon in 1976, as *Strange New World*, which never made it past its pilot.

• Marks Jennifer Darling's final appearance on SM.

Episode 69: *The Ultimate Imposter . . . . [1-2-77]
Written by Lionel E. Siegel, William T. Zacha. Story by William T. Zacha. Directed by Paul Stanley. Featuring: Stephen Macht, Pamela Hensley (Buck Rogers in the 25th Century), *David Sheiner, Kim Basinger* (Dog & Cat, *Oscar winner*, LA Confidential), *Margaret Fairchild, Harry Pugh, Mark Thomas*

The OSI figures out how computer data may be transferred to humans. The experiment is first tested on Joe Patton, a close friend of Steve's, who is transformed into a superior operative for the OSI. Now a master linguist, he effortlessly adjusts to any environment or situation, and easily conquers trivial or technical pursuits.

• Years before Brent Spiner's Data appeared on *Star Trek: The Next Generation*, this unsold pilot for a series was initially called *The D.A.T.A. Man*. In 1979, it was turned into a TV movie-of-the-week, but again failed to go to series.

• Lionel Siegel: "The original idea was from Bill Zacha. Years ago I fell in love with a play called *R.U.R.* or 'Rossum's Universal Robots,' written by a Czechoslovakian writer named Karel Capek, just before WWI. He invented the word *robot* in the English language. I optioned that play, which was owned by Paramount, and I wrote a script based on the play. I've always been interested in such phenomenon. The idea of 'Ultimate Imposter' was that the Chinese had captured a US spy, and they were training him. He seems to be perfectly normal. When we get him back, we realize that he doesn't seem to know who he is, or where he's from, or what he used to do. Nothing. So it was the opportunity to reeducate him electronically. It works, but it only works for so many hours. So now he becomes a spy. You can train him to do anything you want [cut diamonds, make double-breasted suits, etc.] but after 72 hours it fades away. I guess the world wasn't ready for it."

Episode 70: *Death Probe (Part I)* . . . . **[1-9-77]**
Written by Steven de Souza. Directed by Richard Moder. Featuring: Nehemiah Persoff, Jane Merrow, Beverly Garland (My Three Sons), *Walter Brooke, Don Dubbins, Ryan MacDonald, Ross Elliott, Bill Fletcher, Austin Stoker*

A Soviet probe crashes in Wyoming and, per its original programming, deciphers that it's landed on Venus. Because it is made of a new alloy, unknown to American technology, Soviet scientists and agents situated in the United States scramble to reach it first, but fail. The probe sets out on a zigzag course of its own, putting several population centers in peril. Steve races to intercede, confronts the probe, and is injured. Russia and America join forces to help out.
 • Reunites Steve with Irena Leonova, first seen in "Doomsday, and Counting."

Episode 71: *Death Probe (Part II)* . . . .**[1-16-77]**
Written by Steven de Souza. Directed by Richard Moder. See Part I for Cast Credits, plus John DeLancie (Star Trek: The Next Generation), *Judd Laurence*

The Venus probe is out of control. Conventional and nuclear weapons are all but ruled out. Rudy Wells arrives on the scene to administer a temporary repair to Steve's damaged right arm. Steve, Rudy, and Irena put their scientific minds to work and decide to use the probe's pressurized interior as a tool in its destruction—with the help of a helicopter.
 • In this second "Probe" installment (as with the first), the machine used is swift-moving and diesel-fueled, with an intricate shell placed over it. As it motions, a trail of exhaust fumes can be seen.
 • In 1970, the Soviet Union's *Venera 7* probe parachuted into Venus' atmosphere and lasted a mere 23 minutes before being crushed by the planet's extreme pressures.

Episode 72: *Danny's Inferno* . . . . **[1-23-77]**

Written by Tom Greene. Directed by Cliff Bole. Featuring: Lanny Horn, Frank Marth, Mills Watson, David Opatoshu, E. J. Peaker

While experimenting with a new fuel propellant for his toy rocket, 14-year-old Danny Lasswell carelessly mixes small amounts of two chemicals and blows a six-foot-deep crater in the school playground. The teen has unwittingly "invented" a new form of thermochemical energy that could eliminate the need for oil. The OSI would like to reproduce his experiment, and harness its power. One problem: He didn't measure the formula exactly. An unscrupulous land developer seeks to kidnap Danny. Steve needs to save him.

• With his right (bionic) hand, Steve touches the crude bomb (fashioned from Danny's equation), and flinches in pain. The hand is also visibly perspiring, which we all know can't be, because of its synthetic construction.

• Several segments featured children or teens, to more easily connect with the young viewers at home.

Episode 73: *Fires of Hell*. . . . . **[1-30-77]**
Written by Orville Hampton. Directed by Ed Abroms. Featuring: Ken Swofford, Melinda Naud, Heather Menzies (Logan's Run, *the TV series; married to the late Robert Urich*)*, Charles Aidman, Bruce Glover, Larry Watson, Don (Red) Barry, Bob Neill, Nat Christian*

A hidden weight of uranium rests underneath an oil-drill testing-site for the OSI. Congressman Lomax, Sheriff Burgess, and Roy Palmer (a geologist) illegally set the well ablaze to thwart the government's intervention. To protect themselves, the evil trio points their fingers at a local conservation group (who is opposed to oil drillings in the Stoney Creek Reserve). Steve goes undercover to work in the oil field, and becomes a rather large obstacle for the crooked team.

• Steve thinks he can extinguish an out-of-control oil well fire by detonating a nitroglycerine bomb right above it. Oscar is naturally concerned for Steve's safety, but Austin breaks the tension by telling him, "Just pick up the pieces and have me rebuilt."

Episode 74: *The Infiltrators*. . . . . **[2-6-77]**

Written by Sam Ross, Wilton Schiller. Directed by Phil Bondelli. Featuring: Jerry Quarry, Michael Conrad (Hill Street Blues), Harold Sylvestor, Yvonne Craig (Batman), Cliff Carnell, Pervis Atkins, Joe Kapp

Steve becomes an amateur American boxer to infiltrate a group of expatriate assassins. Their target? Any foreign amateur athlete who has defected. While working out in the ring, he observes a band of foreign boxers lift and relocate more than one thousand pounds. With the help of OSI computers, the identity of the foreign target is determined. Steve is then drugged and nearly killed, but prevents the assassination.

• Lee said guest Jerry Quarry, with whom he sparred, was "in incredible shape. We did a few rounds. He could take a punch and say, *Go ahead. Hit me.*"

• Director Phil Bondelli remembers the late Michael Conrad, who guest-starred here: "He was very fastidious about his clothes. I spent an hour-and-a-half with him in wardrobe, in order for him to pick out the suit, the tie, etc. He was extremely concerned about his colors, how his jacket looked, and that it fit correctly. He would ask, *Are my colors okay?* For such a rugged-looking guy, you wouldn't think he'd care."

• In a hilarious pub scene, Steve rips the brass railing from the bar and proceeds to tie a knot around the bad guys as if it were made of rope.

• Somehow, Steve neutralizes two baddies with his non-bionic left arm.

• As in "The Winning Smile," Washington D.C.'s mysterious "palm trees" resurface.

• Original working title: "Two Falls Out of Three."

Episode 75: *Carnival of Spies* . . . . [2-13-77]
Written by Robert C. Dennis. Story by Robert C. Dennis, Richard Carr. Directed by Richard Moder. Featuring: Lloyd Bochner (Dynasty), Gloria Manon, Cheryl Miller, Bob Minor, Wes Parker, Michael Strong, Peter Weiss, H. M. Wynant

Ulrich Rau, an East German scientist credited with designing their ground-to-air weapon system, pretends to have a heart attack and slips away from a high-level scientific conference. Steve wonders why, and traces each move he makes. Curiously, Rau heads for a traveling carnival that has set up operation within a few miles of the B-1 bomber's testing site. Mystified, Steve attempts to cut through a tight web of security presented by the close-knit carnival personnel in order to learn Rau's mission. He finds that the carnival is a disguised ground-to-air missile site. But will Rau use the Tilt-a-Whirl to sabotage the B-1?

• Steve sees an old man struggling to win his granddaughter a prize at the "strong man" game, intervenes, and sends the bell whistling through the air.

• Filmed at "The Pike" amusement center in Long Beach, California.

Episode 76: *U-509* . . . . **[2-20-77]**
Written by Michael Wagner. Directed by Phil Bondelli. Featuring: Guy Doleman, Ian Abercrombie, Ted Hamilton, Bill Sylvester, Steve Sandor, Peter Canon, Morgan Jones

Henry Bulman, a retired submariner from Her Majesty's Royal Navy, locates a deserted Nazi U-boat and puts it back into action. Inside is an antiquated assemblage of lethal nerve gas. Bulman decides to extort $20 million from the United States by threatening the lives of some 30,000 Americans. Assigned to stop Bulman or call his bluff, Steve dives to the submarine, bionically resists the water pressure, and boards the craft. But he is taken prisoner and then is faced with making a horrifying decision.
• Lee remembers a frightening moment while filming this episode: "We were actually in a WWII submarine, in Long Beach. It was very tight quarters. There was some kind of explosion on deck. The refinery blew up, or a tanker went. So we had to stop shooting, in order for the situation to be checked out. A lot of us were reluctant to go into the submarine again, because we feared another explosion. When we did resume shooting, the next day, I was scheduled to go into this torpedo hatch, which involved a lot of water pouring into it, and I did the scene. As far as that explosion was concerned, I don't think anyone on the set was ever so afraid in their lives. The sub wasn't submerged; it was at the dock, and it rocked and rolled. We got everything out of there, fast. It was insanity."
• The very same sub (including the ID, U-509) shows up in "Sharks!" during the fifth season.

Episode 77: *The Privacy of the Mind* . . . . **[2-27-77]**
Written by Vanessa Boos, Wilton Schiller. Directed by Jimmy Lydon. Featuring: Suzanne Charney, Curt Lowens, Roger Perry, Bob Neill, Leslie Moonves (today, a CBS executive), Paul Mantee

The Russians offer Dr. Berman a temporary job that pays in the area of one million dollars a week. Steve Austin wonders why, disguises himself as the professor to find out, is then knocked out, brought to a secluded laboratory, and ends up working with Dr. Tamara Batalova (a Russian scientist) on a computer/mind reading experiment. Trouble brews when the Russians realize that "Dr. Berman" doesn't really have a handle on his work with Dr. Batalova.
• A blooper: Steve and the Dr. Batalova are attempting to evade their

abductors. They shimmy out a window to a balcony. Steve intentionally takes the drain pipe from the leaves trough, and cracks it. He doesn't seek to depart just yet. He angles the pipe, and it starts to fall. We then see a crew member's hand (near the bottom of the camera frame) holding the pipe.

• One of several SM/BW's in which Steve and Jaime's powers were show-cased with extensive speed. For example, here, Steve reads extremely fast. Would his normal (though highly-intelligent) brain be able to keep up with and process the amount of informative input, as when he splices together wires with stupendous swiftness in an episode of the BW outing, "Kill Oscar Part II"? Not only does his brain keep up what's going on, but so does his other hand, which isn't even bionic.

Episode 78: *To Catch the Eagle*. . . . . [3-6-77]
Written by Judy Burns. Directed by Phil Bondelli. Featuring: Gerald McRaney (Simon & Simon, Major Dad, The Promised Land), *Jim Stathis, Peter Breck (Lee Majors' co-star on* The Big Valley), *Dehl Berti, George Loros, Kathleen Beller*

Iron Fist, a medicine man, captures two OSI scientists who are seeking radioactive ore on consecrated Indian ground. Fist fears that the rest of the tribe will discover the ore's value before he can get a chance to market it. Meanwhile, the scientists must be released, or they will not survive. To set foot on the sacred soil, Steve must overpower Iron Fist and participate in a dangerous ceremony involving the capture of an eagle.

• Shot in a very cold area, during winter. "We all were absolutely freez-ing," Lee recalls, "and Kathleen Beller was magnificent. She memorized her lines, and never complained. We all admired her performance. She's really a wonderful actress. Peter Breck, of course, I had known from *The Big Valley*. We had a thing about gun-slinging a six-shooter. I had my gun in the hol-ster, didn't even move my hand, and I said, *Did you see that? That's called the bionic hand*. It's an old joke, now."

• As Lee goes on to say, this "was a tough episode to do because we worked with animals. We had this horse that had to rear-up. I had to go in there and try to get it to stand still, while we were shooting the bionic sequences. Well, when you're doing bionics, nobody could move in the background. You had to be absolutely motionless. That wasn't an easy thing to do."

• To gain the respect and trust of the Indian community, Steve wins an arm wrestling match with his *left* hand.

• As with the next episode, Lee's mustache is suddenly nowhere in sight.

• Judy Burns: "I was brought in and Allan Balter was producing the show by that time. They said, 'We want to do a story about an Indian kid, and we want the flavor of *Walkabout*,' an Australian movie about two [white] kids who are stranded in the Outback, where they are taken under the wing of an Aborigine. They wanted a story where Steve has to deal with the American Indians. They wanted a mythic flavor, so I came up with the Eagle ritual and the mystic element of it."

• Although writer Peter Brooke's name appears in the credits, Judy Burns insists that she is the sole author of this episode.

Episode 79: *The Ghostly Teletype* .... [5-15-77]
Written by Wilton Schiller. Directed by Tom Connors. Featuring: Robert H. Harris, Les Lannom, Christina Hart, Larry Anderson, Jodean Russo, Elizabeth Kerr, Linda Dano

Steve Austin is charged with theft, and may be imprisoned for espionage. While researching the possibility of prolonging the human life span, an equation he's reviewing disappears. To prove his innocence, Steve investigates and finds that a pair of twins, who age twice as rapidly as normal people do, have telepathically stolen the formula in order to extend their lives.

• Linda Dano went on to become one of the all-time favorite actresses of *Days of Our Lives*, which was responsible for launching the career of *Bionic Woman* semi-regular, the late Christopher Stone.

• Steve's birth date is identified as February 5, 1942. His address, which differs from the one cited in "Little Orphan Airplane," is listed as 2398 Fairmont Ave, Washington, D.C.

"DARK SIDE OF THE MOON, PART II" (W/SIMONE GRIFFETH), "THE
CHESHIRE PROJECT" (W/SUZANNE SOMERS), "SHARKS!," "DEADLY
COUNTDOWN"

The Fifth Season
1977 to 1978

Episode 80: *Sharks! (Part I)*................................[9-11-77]
Written by Arthur Weingarten. Directed by Alan Levi. Featuring: William Sylvester, Stephen Elliott, Greg Walcott, Marc Alaimo (Star Trek: The Next Generation), *Buster Jones, Pamela Hensley, William Whitton, Frank Whiteman*

A nuclear submarine experiences an unusual power failure. Col. Austin goes underwater to peruse the situation. He's attacked by a school of sharks, and escapes, only to be apprehended by Morgan Grayland (a former submarine captain for the U.S. Navy). In a submerged cove, Grayland informs Steve that he and his daughter, Cynthia (a marine biologist), have criminal plans for the submarine. And Grayland's skillful sharks will impede both Steve and the Navy from any plans to intervene.

• "As season five commenced," explained Harve Bennett, "we saw episodes like 'Sharks!, Parts I and II' and 'Deadly Countdown, Parts I and II.' You get some idea of the hype that was coming at us from ABC." Bennett heard the network brass say things like, "Let's do it bigger. Let's do it bolder. Let's go where we haven't gone before!" Needless to say, this was the show's final season.

• The fifth and final season of *Six* was co-produced by Richard Landau and Fred Freiberger. Hard-core Trekkies have long accused Freiberger of hastening *Star Trek's* demise on NBC.

• Landau recalls his first meeting with Lee Majors: "I went up to his trailer outside the studio," he said. "I'm post-polio, and I use a cane for walking. Getting into the trailer was like climbing Mt. Everest. A couple of Lee's bodyguards offered to help me up and I said no, I can do it myself. After a lot of struggling, I hoisted myself up into the trailer and half-collapsed on the couch. There was Lee. I introduced myself as the new producer. He looked at me with a straight face and said, 'Tell me something. If I invited you to play tennis, would you do it?' I knew he was putting me on. I said, 'Well, shit, Lee — only if I can hop back and forth over the net to warm up first.' That broke the ice. He was a friendly, down-to-earth guy. He was great with the crew."

• Steve is forced to push a submarine along the bottom of the ocean. A stretch of the imagination, as a sub's weight is hundreds of tons.

Episode 81: *Sharks! (Part II)* . . . . [9-18-77]
Written by Arthur Weingarten. Directed by Alan Levi. See Part I for Cast Credits.

Mutiny is staged by fellow hijacker Alex Parker, who overpowers Grayland. Grayland quickly contacts Admiral Prescott, who requisitions the destruction of the nuclear sub. Prescott's plans must be thwarted, or Charleston, South Carolina will be eradicated. While the Navy retreats, Steve remains closely monitored, but must find a way to foil the initiation of global depredation and coercion.

    • Lee recalls a recent encounter with a man, who ran up to him and said, "Remember me? I was one of the guys who did that show about the sharks?" Those "guys" gave Lee a crash-course in scuba diving that took no more than five minutes. "They outfitted me with all this gear, and sent me down. You know what? They gave me an empty tank." He remembered the incident well. "I'll tell you one thing," Lee jokes, "I don't go scuba diving that often, now. When I do, what do you think is the first thing that I do?" Check the tank? "You got it."

    • "Sharks! I and II" shares traits with "Deadly Music," from *The Bionic Woman.*

    • Just prior to Season Five, Lee Majors was embroiled in a contact dispute with Universal. "Lee was a holdout," said Bennett. "Universal felt it was terribly important to hold the line. There was a protracted period of negotiations. We were asked by the studio to test five actors for the part. Since I wasn't head of the studio, I did what I was asked to do. Gil Gerard (the soon-to-be Buck Rogers) was one of the actors. He got the most attention because he was a contract player at Universal and he was the most physical. We also tested Bruce Jenner. It was all for naught, because Lee eventually signed back on." Harrison Ford was another name that surfaced, only to be rejected by Universal because the future Indiana Jones wasn't "physical enough."

Episode 82: *Deadly Countdown (Part I)* . . . . [9-25-77]
Written by Gregory S. Dinallo. Directed by Cliff Bole. Featuring: Jenny Agutter, Philip Abbott, Lloyd Bochner, Sherry Hursey, Crofton Hardester, Bill Scherer, Martin Caidin (series creator), Mills Watson

A group headed by Gordon Shanks has constructed its own missile control center and plans to "kidnap" a rocket when it is launched. The rocket carries the new electronic brain of the U.S. missile defense system, which Shanks will sell to a foreign power. In a bid to gain time, Shanks hires Julian Richman to kill Steve and delay the rocket launching. Richman, with access to the Kennedy Space Center, conceives a scheme to eliminate Steve in the high altitude test chamber. Austin, meanwhile, becomes strongly attached to the beautiful Dr. Leah Russell, a scientist who is to accompany him on the mission.

• This episode, along with Part II, was originally entitled "Enemies in Space." It was filmed on location at the Kennedy Space Center in Cape Canaveral, Florida, and featured *Cyborg* creator Martin Caidin as a radio operator for those trying to hijack the launch. "Yeah," Caidin said, "I played a real bad-ass. They used my house in Cocoa Beach, too. The police closed off the street. On the other side of our house, the north side, was the Thousand Islands, which is a group of natural islands that are protected and may never be touched. My father-in-law was the Chief of Detectives, and we had no trouble in getting full police cooperation. It was in the middle of the afternoon, 200 damn boats showed up, and everyone showed up in tuxedos and climbed ashore. It was marvelous." After the segment was completed, there had been some apparent technical difficulties with the soundtrack, and Caidin was asked to do some redubbing. "Shit, no," he said. "Get someone else with a voice like mine." "They must have got some old radio Bozo, who talked with his hand to the side of his mouth," added Caidin, who later received a telegram of compliment from Harve Bennett. "He congratulated me on my first *Six Mill* acting job," Caidin recalled. "But he said, *Boy, you sure talk funny.*"

• For this two-part episode, Majors was required to wear an authentic (if cumbersome) Apollo astronaut spacesuit. Ordinarily, the 48-pound, 23-layer suit is equipped with an internal cooling device — which just happened to be on the fritz when they were filming beneath the broiling Florida sun. Unsurprisingly, Majors was not amused. "It's like having your own personal mobile sauna," he complained. "When you start moving, you can actually feel the sweat running down inside the suit. The space suit was really built for sitting or lying down. I felt like Humpty-Dumpty trying to run."

• Dr. Russell learns of Steve's bionic secret when he goes 60 MPH+ on a treadmill.

Episode 83: *Deadly Countdown (Part II)* . . . .[10-2-77]
Written by Gregory S. Dinallo. Directed by Cliff Bole. See Part I for Cast Credits.

Steve survives the attack on his life, and Shanks' band abducts Dave McGrath's daughter, Melissa. Dave, who is Steve's acquaintance and assignment supervisor of Kennedy Space Center, schedules a pre-launch missile detonation that wounds Col. Austin. Dave fesses up: Melissa will be killed if he doesn't abort the mission. Steve is convinced that the kidnappers will not allow Melissa to live, even though Dave has fulfilled his part of the bargain. He sets out to save her before it's too late.

• Martin Caidin: "There's a scene where Steve Austin is driving a car along the river and he goes out of control. Majors' stunt double was driving. I was flying a big bomber above him at 1200 feet. I took the bomber and, per instructions, dove the damn thing about three feet off the water, tearing through that TV set like a hurricane. I knocked over all of the lights and reflectors and even blew Lee Majors into the river! The crew threw a party that night, and I was made a member of the stuntman's association in California."

• Upon his death in 1997, *Florida Today* used these words in its editorial tribute to Caidin: "An old soul, a young spirit. Terminally feisty. Forever ambitious…for himself, his people, his nation, his space program." Fittingly, Caidin's ashes were scattered in the ocean off Cocoa Beach, and his name is permanently inscribed on the "Roll of Honor" at the Kennedy Space Center.

• Caidin: "I may get killed, baby, but I ain't never gonna die."

• Director Cliff Bole (in 1977): "Sometimes I simply don't know how Lee keeps the pace up. I've directed Robert Blake on *Baretta* and the two guys on *Starsky and Hutch* and they are tough [during] a lot of physical shooting. But *The Six Million Dollar Man* has to be the most grueling show on TV for any star to put together."

• Cliff Bole directed several episodes of the *Star Trek* spin-off series, including *The Next Generation*, *Deep Space Nine* and *Voyager*.

• Many SM fans will remember guest actor Lloyd Bochner from his role in the classic "Day of the Robot" episode.

Episode 84: *Bigfoot V* . . . . **[10-9-77]**
Written by Gregory S. Dinallo, Richard Landau. Directed by Rod Holcomb.
Featuring: Ted Cassidy, Geoffrey Lewis, Katherine de Hetre, Tony Young, Regis Cordic, S. Newton Anderson

Anthropologist Hope Langston views photos of Bigfoot, and Steve is confused. His old *running* buddy was to have returned to space with his alien creators. Steve then attempts to persuade Langston not to seize the mechanical Yeti. When she rejects his plea, The Bionic Man begins his own search for his unique near-soul mate. Upon finding him, Steve is battered and abruptly deserted, as Bigfoot flees. Just prior to his second encounter with Bigfoot, the bionic giant goes berserk. In the meantime, Langston's aides plan to abduct the super-powered automaton for their own personal gain.

• The aliens left Bigfoot so that he could be converted into a 100% animal being, merging somehow with the surrounding eco-system.

Episode 85: *Killer Wind* .... [10-16-77]
Written by Gregory S. Dinallo. Story by Richard Landau. Directed by Richard Moder. Featuring: Sylvia Walden, Adam Roarke, Shelia Wills, James McEachin, Fred J. Gordon

Steve rides with Rhonda Allen and a phone-man named Nash. Rhonda's child (among others) is stuck in a dysfunctional mountain tramway. Steve rushes to make a rescue before a cyclone strikes. But Nash is really a bank thief on the run who thumps The Bionic Man unconscious when his cohorts arrive. After ditching Col. Austin, they abduct Rhonda, and take her hostage. Steve awakens in the nick of time, and recovers both Rhonda and the children.
• Really the only natural disaster (outside of earthquakes) Steve had to contend with in the series' run (weather machines, not included).
• When a stuntman fell ill, Majors volunteered to perform his own (dangerous) stunts.
• Original working title: "Rescue."

Episode 86: *Rollback* .... [10-30-77]
Written by Steven de Souza. Directed by Don McDougall. Featuring: Robert Loggia, Suzanne Charney, Paul D'Amato, Rick Springfield (General Hospital)

Steve's on a roll. He links up with a roller derby team to determine the exact location of a global syndicate's next heist. Apparently, Rand Hendricks (Steve's team manager), is scheduled to obtain ten million dollars on Halloween via barter for classified government data. The OSI is aware of Rand's scheme, but is clueless as to his knowledge of Steve's true identity, or that he's leaving behind bogus evidence. Unless Steve realizes that he's being led astray, OSI documents will remain vulnerable.
• Guest Robert Loggia appeared in "The Thunderbird Connection" and BW's "Jaime and the King."
• A year earlier, Lee's ex, Farrah Fawcett, starred in a roller derby episode of her own on *Charlie's Angels*. The family that rolls together...

Episode 87: *Dark Side of the Moon (Part I)* .... [11-6-77]
Written by John Meredyth Lucas. Story by Richard Landau. Directed by Cliff Bole. Featuring: Jack Colvin, Skip Homeier, Simone Griffeth

Charles Leith, a scientist funded by the government, is supposed to be exploring an asteroid. In reality, he's positioned an antenna that will transmit information to Houston Mission Control. So Leith journeys to the moon, changes its orbit, and the results are catastrophic: severe weather conditions plummet Earth. Unaware of Leith's treachery, Steve flies to the moon to uncover the mystery.

• Features clips of Steve walking on the moon, which were added to help stretch out the 90-minute *Six* pilot for syndication.

• As with "Deadly Countdown," this two-parter was filmed at an authentic NASA facility and utilized authentic NASA spacesuits.

Episode 88: *Dark Side of the Moon (Part II)* . . . . [11-13-77]
Written by John Meredyth Lucas. Story by Richard Landau. Directed by Cliff Bole. See Part I for Cast Credits, plus Quinn Redeker, James Ingersoll, Walter Brooke

Dr. Leith and Eric Muller, his assistant, abduct Steve and coerce him into helping them mine for what they claim is dilanthium — a productive energy derivation for Earth. If Steve decides not to lend a bionic hand, Dr. Leith will cause more severe havoc on Earth, this time employing nuclear power.

• The moon scenes are realistic, as they are showcased without sound in space, while the lunar surface lacks an atmosphere. Too much gravity, however, was evident.

• In 1974, Martin Caidin was made an honorary citizen of Dallas when he presented a very unusual moon rock valued between $200,000 and $300,000 to the Dallas Museum of Health and Science. The rock had fallen to earth during volcanic activity on the moon nearly 700,000 years ago, and then was carried into orbit around the earth and later to the moon and back by the Apollo astronauts.

Episode 89: *Target: Steve Austin* . . . .[11-27-77]
Written by Donald L. Gold, Lester W. Berke. Story by Richard Landau. Directed by Ed Abroms. Featuring: Quinn Redeker, Lynette Mettey, Curt Lowens, Larry Levine, Ian Abercrombie, Tony Epper, Walter P. Robles, Boris Aplon, Paula Victor

Steve "honeymoons" with Joan, an OSI agent and, while searching for an atomic bomb, they hope to capture a band that's compromised government security. They travel through the Southwest in a recreational vehicle, specially equipped with a top-secret nuclear power unit. The crooked crew catches on to Steve and Joan's assignment, and sets out to obtain their intricate cargo. The faux newlyweds have instructions to shield the device no matter what.

• The collapsing bridge Steve has to cross is the same one Jaime had to traverse in BW's "The Ghosthunter."

Episode 90: *The Cheshire Project* . . . .[12-18-77]
Written by John Meredyth Lucas. Directed by Richard Moder. Featuring: Suzanne Somers (Three's Company, Step by Step), *John Larch, Robert Hogan, Jim Begg, Stanley Waxman, Barry Cahill, Fred Lerner, Terry Leonard*

Jenny Fraser, Steve's girlfriend, vanishes while flying a classified airplane. Steve discovers that Hal Martin, an engineer, is aware of the aircraft's new radar-avoiding mechanism, and that he's been holding conversations with Wilfred Damien. Damien, a known criminal of classified military information, may play a part in the mystery. Steve then sets out on a search mission over the desert, hoping his bionic vision will discover some clue that an extensive Air Force search had missed.
• The ideal all-around public servant, Steve prevents a drunk from driving by lifting the rear of a car onto a trash receptacle, leaving the wheels spinning harmlessly.
• Farrah Fawcett was first cast as Jenny Fraser in this episode, originally called "Into Thin Air."

Episode 91: *Walk a Deadly Wing* . . . .[1-1-78]
Written by Jim Carlson, Terrence McDonnell. Story by Richard Landau. Directed by Herb Wallerstein. Featuring: Eric Braeden (The Young and the Restless), *John Devlin, Lanna Saunders, Steve Eastin, Eddie Fontaine*

Viktor Cheraskin invents a device that harmlessly apprehends foot soldiers. He remains protective, fearing its employment as an anti-aircraft weapon. As such, the United States and the USSR are refused access to the system. Shortly after Col. Austin goes undercover as a wing walker to gain Viktor's confidence, Edmund Dimitri, a Soviet operative, contacts the scientist. In no uncertain terms, Viktor is given an ultimatum: hand over the apparatus or his wife will be killed.
• Guest Eric Braeden guest starred in SM's *Wine, Women and War.*
• Original working title: "Walk a Crooked Wing."

Episode 92: *Just a Matter of Time* .... **[1-8-78]**
Written by Neal J. Sperling, Gregory S. Dinallo. Directed by Don McDougall. Featuring: Leigh Christian, Charles Cioffi, John Milford, Paul Carr, John DeLancie

Steve is trapped in time following a test flight in space. Six years later, he returns to Earth, and is arrested for treason. Officials are convinced that he's defected to the Soviet Union. In reality, the entire escapade is an elaborate ruse designed to convince Austin that he was snared into a space/time continuum. Steve doesn't have much "time." To clear his name and gain his freedom, he must somehow prove the validity of his experience.

• Somehow, the antagonists manage to control and redirect Steve's re-entry, but forget to disable the capsule's transmitter, which Steve later used to help Oscar zero in on his location.

• One of the few episodes of both *Bionic* shows which deals with time travel. Others include the "Bigfoot" segments, in which the Yeti's alien creators were time-travelers, who invited Steve and Jaime to take quantum leaps with them.

Episode 93: *Return of Death Probe (Part I)* .... **[1-22-78]**
Written by Howard Dimsdale. Directed by Tom Connors. Featuring: Than Wyenn, Ken Swofford, David Sheiner, Robert Lussier, Jimmy Joyce, Ken Chandler

There is no question about it: Death Probe is back — stronger and deadlier than ever. This time, Steve is overwhelmed by the atomic powers of the Probe's immense claws, gyrating blades and intense laser. Unless nuclear warheads are immediately delivered to those in control of the Probe, immense destruction will result.

• Austin was no stranger to blue-collar occupations during the series' tenure, as he posed as a steelworker in this episode. He also was a crewman on an oil rig, a lumberjack, a longshoreman, and an aerial acrobat.

Episode 94: *Return of Death Probe (Part II)* .... **[1-29-78]**
Written by Howard Dimsdale. Directed by Tom Connors. See Part I for Cast Credits.

Steve attempts to overpower the Death Probe employing a bulldozer armed with a new form of alloy. At first the machine is victorious, but then Steve lures it into an abysmal hole. The enclosure will soon be filled with acid. Unfortunately, the Probe commences to tunnel its way free, and heads for the city just as quickly as before, not leaving Steve too much time for rescue procedures.

• In a scene perhaps inspired by the 1976 film *Carrie*, the Probe is dissolving in an acid bath and is pronounced dead, but makes one final lunge with a pincher-claw that emerges from the acid, but to no avail.

Episode 95: *The Lost Island* .... [1-30-78]
Written by Mel Goldberg. Story by Lou Shaw. Directed by Cliff Bole. Featuring: Jared Martin (The Invaders, Fantastic Journey, Dark Shadows *[1991]*), *Robin Mattson, Anthony Geary* (General Hospital), *Terence Burke, Alf Kjellin, Robert Symonds, Don Pulford, Paul Deadrick, Kwan Hi Lim*

Steve is assigned to retrieve a satellite that has fallen into the Pacific. He saves Da-Nay, who is drowning and being relentlessly pursued. Grateful, Da-Nay tells Steve that the satellite has banked on her island, which is safeguarded by an inviolable force field. The isle is occupied by alien descendants, who are desperate for a serum that is being developed at the University of Hawaii. An island resident named Torg is heading a rebellion. The alien offspring can't escape to another island. They have no immunity against disease.
• Filmed on location, this originally aired as two hours; it's now shown in two parts.
• Beginning with this episode, *SM* moves to Monday nights.
• Lee Majors: "Each episode of *Six* was shot over at least six days. That was kind of boring for me. We were always in like a warehouse or in a utility plant, some place that wasn't very attractive. It wasn't like shooting in Hawaii (as in 'Lost Island'). I was always breaking in and out of things. Generally, if I was outside, I was running down a pasture or down a runway, running as hard as I can run, and they were showing it in slow motion."

Episode 96: *The Madonna Caper* .... [2-6-78]
Written by Gregory S. Dinallo. Directed by Herb Wallerstein. Featuring: Bibi Besch (Star Trek II: The Wrath of Khan), *Steve Arvin, Len Birman, Mike McManus, Frank Parker, Diana Webster, Robert Hoy, Dominic Barto, Bruce Glover, Rudy Challenger*

With Steve's help, Lysandra Korischeva, a countess, must attain a microdot (with crucial military data) concealed on a five-million-dollar museum portrait. While Steve tangles with the museum's security system, Korischeva replaces the original painting with an imitation. She plans to market the artwork to Chilton Kane, a crime lord. Oscar then assigns Steve to recover the original masterpiece before an art authority arrives from the Soviet Union.

• In one of Lee's more inspiring performances, he shows his range by donning the guise of a completely over-the-top Texas art collector, complete with Southern drawl and ten-gallon hat.

• Shares a similar plot with BW's "The DeJon Caper."

Episode 97: *Dead Ringer* . . . .**[2-13-78]**
Written by Robert I. Holt. Story by Charles Mitchell. Directed by Arnold Laven. Featuring: Linda Dano, Robert Karnes, Mel Allen, Leonard Stone, George Wilbur

After Steve sees strange mirror images of himself that stare back and then vanish, Dr. Margaret Winslow, a reputable parapsychologist, is brought in to investigate. Apparently, Col. Austin was clinically dead for 32 seconds following his aircraft mishap, and he still may be in grave jeopardy. The books are filled with cases of out-of-body stories or near-death experiences (NDE's). Many incidents on record involve the spirit exiting the body at death, and its inability to find peace after the person returns to consciousness. The only way in which the spirit may be completely at rest, is if the physical body is no-more. As such, Steve's spirit will stop at nothing to achieve that end.

• Of director Arnold Laven, Martin E. Brooks recalls: "It was at Arnold's tennis court that Harve Bennett originally offered me the role of Rudy Wells."

• Steve's "ghost" turned out to be nothing more than a hologram employed by Eastern European types snooping for bionic secrets.

• Common sense conundrum: Dr. Winslow is apparently "possessed" by Steve's spirit and tries to kill him. But why? The whole spirit thing turned out to be a hoax.

• Dr. Winslow asks Steve is he's ever been married, to which he flatly replies "no." But in *Return of Six Mill and BW*, Steve concedes that he got married right out of flight school, siring a never-before-mentioned son in the process.

Episode 98: *Date with Danger (Part I)* . . . .**[2-20-78]**
Written by John Meredyth Lucas, Wilton Schiller. Story by Wilton Schiller. Directed by Rod Holcomb. Featuring: Robert Walker, Jr., Elaine Giftos, Luke Askew, Hank Brandt, Paul Tully, Robert Hackman, Raymond Davis, Eric Lawrence

Steve attempts to clear the name of his friend, Joe Canton, who is the chief of communications for OSI. The charges: embezzlement and espionage. Austin examines the central memory of the government's computer, which self-destructs. Someone, or something other than an OSI employee, may have altered the computer banks. Therefore, a mysterious party has tapped into America's economy, and its classified information. Steve is then enigmatically lured to Datamate, a dating service that's operated by a computer genius named Emily Patterson.

• Guest Robert Walker, Jr. (Charlie X from the classic *Star Trek* episode of the same name) and Lee Majors once squared off in a very moving episode of *The Big Valley*, in which Lee defended Linda Evans' honor.

• Original working title: "The Demon Machine."

Episode 99: *Date with Danger (Part II)* . . . . [2-27-78]
Written by John Meredyth Lucas, Wilton Schiller. Story by Wilton Schiller. Directed by Rod Holcomb. Featuring: See Part I for Cast Credits, plus Peter Mark Richman, Noah Keen

When the computer decides to eliminate Steve Austin, Emily sides with her new bionic friend. After evading a hit man employed by the computer, Steve is hospitalized and classified as a maniacal menace. From there, the machine sets out to destroy anyone who's aware of its existence, including its creator. Eventually, *The Six Million Dollar Man* destroys the computer before it attempts worldwide annihilation.

• Steve is able to trace a call here, just by scanning hundreds of telephone wires with his bionic eye.

• This two-parter is virtually identical to the pilot for the 1988 *Probe* series, which starred Parker *Hardy Boys* Stevenson.

Episode 100: *The Moving Mountain* . . . . [3-6-78]
Written by Stephen Kandel. Directed by Don McDougall. Featuring: John Colicos (Battlestar Galactica), *Lisa Farringer, Michael Ebert, Paul Coufos, Beverly Kushida, George Clifton, Keith Langsdale, Susan Fleming*

A Russian mobile rocket launcher and American self-guided missiles are apprehended by Santos, a militant group leader. His plan is to use them as a threat to extort huge sums of money to finance terrorist activities. Russia's General Gorbukov dispatches beautiful top agent Andrea Mestrova to collect their property - and the American missiles to boot. Oscar gets Steve to assist Mestrova, whose father was killed by The Bionic Man several years earlier. Meanwhile, Gorbukov's plan necessitates Austin's "accidental" demise.

• "I really did little or had nothing to do with the final season of *The Six Million Dollar Man*, or with *The Bionic Woman*, for that matter," Bennett explained. Yet, if he had known there would have been no sixth season for *Six*, he said, "I would have probably sent Steve to Mars." "My last episode would have been the lift-off. After five years of earth-bound adventure, it would have been God-speed to Steve Austin to another planet, and another life."

• Martin Caidin on *Six's* lasting influence: "When I wrote the novel *Cyborg*, nobody really believed in bionics. Now bionics has become a byword throughout the world. It's changed the way people think in terms of their own health, and the ability [science has] to repair their bodies. When I wrote the book, it was a dream. Now there's a whole generation growing up in a world where bionics is a reality."

• Caidin: "Two things killed the show. One, I couldn't convince the producers to update the technology. After a few years, it all became predictable. The other thing that killed it was the star. We had a clean show, with no sex, no titillation, no monstrosity. But Lee Majors' personal life was getting so public; it had a deleterious effect on the audience. I told the producers to kill him off and bring in Monte Markham, who had been our first choice for the part."

• Lee Majors: "I had no idea how big the show was at the time we were doing it because I was always working. When I was off, I didn't have time to go anywhere — I was resting. It's only been in the last 10 years or so that I've been able to look back and think, 'That show must have been pretty good.'"

"WELCOME HOME, JAIME, PART II" (w/DENNIS PATRICK), "ANGEL
OF MERCY" (w/ANDY GRIFFITH), "BIONIC BEAUTY" (w/BERT PARKS),
"JAIME'S MOTHER" (w/BARBARA RUSH), "CANYON OF DEATH," "FLY
JAIME," "THE JAILING OF JAIME," "MIRROR IMAGE"

CHAPTER 11

JAIME'S JOURNEYS

"LINDSAY AND I USED TO GO OVER EVERY LINE OF EACH SCRIPT FOR *THE BIONIC WOMAN.* SHE WOULD READ JAIME'S LINES, AND I WOULD READ EVERYONE ELSE'S. WE ALWAYS JOKED THAT WE SHOULD HAVE DONE AN EPISODE WHERE SHE PLAYED JAIME, AND I PLAYED EVERYONE ELSE."

KENNETH JOHNSON

The Bionic Woman
Cast

Jaime Sommers . . . . Lindsay Wagner
Oscar Goldman . . . . Richard Anderson
Dr. Rudy Wells . . . . Martin E. Brooks
Helen Elgin . . . . Martha Scott
Jim Elgin . . . . Ford Rainey
Peggy Callahan . . . . Jennifer Darling
Chris Williams . . . . Christopher Stone
Russ . . . . Sam Chew, Jr.

Production

Executive Producer . . . . Harve Bennett
Producer(s) . . . . Kenneth Johnson
Lionel E. Siegel
Craig Schiller
Arthur Rowe
James D. Parriott
Creator . . . . Kenneth Johnson
Based on a novel by . . . . Martin Caidin
Theme . . . . Jerry Fielding

Broadcast History
From January 1976 to May 1977, BW aired as a weekly 60–minute series on Wednesday nights, 8:00 PM to 9:00 PM. Rival shows in the same slot included *Tony Orlando and Dawn* (CBS), *Little House on the Prairie* (NBC), *and Good Times* (CBS). BW migrated to Saturday nights on NBC from September 1977 to May 1978, occupying the 8:00 PM to 9:00 PM timeslot. It battled the *Bob Newhart Show* and *We've Got Each Other* on CBS, as well as *Fish* and *Operation Petticoat* on ABC.

Opening Diction
THE FOLLOWING INFORMATION IS
CLASSIFIED:
TOP SECRET
[BIONIC REPLACEMENT CATALOG #87312/JSB]
CLEARANCE AUTHORIZATION LEVEL 6
JAIME SOMMERS
SEX: FEMALE
AGE:[27] 28
PAST PROFESSION: TENNIS PRO
[PROFESSIONAL]
PRESENT PROFESSION: SCHOOL TEACHER
[GRADE LEVEL 6 & 7]
GRADE LEVEL 7, 8, & 9
PRESENT RESIDENCE: OJAI, CALIFORNIA
CRITICAL INJURY
PARACHUTE ACCIDENT
ANATOMICAL DAMAGE
BOTH LEGS
RIGHT ARM
RIGHT EAR
OPERATIONAL PROCEDURE
BIONIC REPLACEMENT
[AUTHORIZATION: OSCAR GOLDMAN]
ESTIMATED COST: CLASSIFIED
[SECOND BIONIC REPLACEMENT
COMPLETE]

Note: The items in brackets were displayed in initial segments, and were either altered or eliminated later.

The First Season
January 1976 to May 1976

Episode 1: *Welcome Home, Jaime (Part II)*. . . . . **[1-14-76]**
Written by Kenneth Johnson. Directed by Alan Crosland, Jr. Featuring: Kip Niven, Dennis Patrick (Dark Shadows), *Gordon Jump* (WKRP in Cincinnati), *Christian Juttner, Bob Bralver, Alycia Gardner, Nick Pellegrino*

Carlton Harris, a tycoon who's marketing classified information, has detected Jaime's extraordinary abilities and captures her on film. While Oscar fears for her safety, Jaime correctly surmises that Harris wants to exploit her powers for his own ends. Oscar and Jaime stage a disagreement to lure Harris into hiring her. It works. She then pirates classified data, which will indict Harris, and bonds with his son, an aspiring lawyer who is troubled by his dad's penchant for criminal avocations.

• First seen as part of *Man*, January 11, 1976, this episode and Part I are now screened as segments of *Woman*.

• Talent agent Ron Samuels: "When I told [ABC] what we wanted — $500,000 a year for five years — there was absolute silence in the room. They simply couldn't talk."

• Jaime loses her feelings for Steve, and struggles to relocate them. "When anyone comes out of a head trauma," Lindsay Wagner explained, "they're like an infant. Many times, the memory never returns. It's like starting over, which is exactly what Jaime did. She had to develop an entirely new relationship with Steve." It was a creative decision that left producers in wonderland. How would they bring Jaime back to life? What would be the justification for having two series if she reunited with Steve? Would she continue on her own? "They couldn't have had a relationship," said Lindsay. We would see Jaime rip phone books in class, speed-write on the board, or bionically clean house. "We made an effort to keep her involved in human-istic situations," Lindsay said, "and still utilize what was perceived as the critical aspect of the franchise, which was the bionics."

• Dennis Patrick later appeared in Johnson's *The Incredible Hulk*.

• Confused by the "Jaime" vs. "Jamie" spellings? You're not alone. Wagner adds some clarification: "I'll tell you a funny story about that. We did one episode ['Return of Bionic Woman'] where, with my bionic fingernail, I had to carve my name into a tree. So they brought on a special effects tree, with some soft stuff where I was to do the 'carving,' and said 'go ahead and write your name just there, but be careful and do it neatly because that's the only one we've got.'

"So I walked up to this tree, and spelled out the name in what I thought was the logical way [i.e., J-A-M-I-E]. It never occurred to me to do it any different. And then from behind the cameras they all started shouting out

'Stop! You're ruining our tree!' and similar things. So they had to put a whole new lot of soft putty in the tree and make it up all over again and I got it right the next time.

"You can imagine the teasing they all did — The Bionic Woman who couldn't even spell her own name!

"There's a post script to that, too. After all their teasing, the first two episodes of *The Bionic Woman* had Jaime's name spelt wrongly in the credits. So I took great delight in pointing that out to them."

• During the opening credits of the show, a computer readout describes Jaime's vital statistics, but then it gets to this item: "Estimated Cost — Classified." Was Jaime a bargain-rate model? Not exactly. Ken Johnson: "We didn't want to specify and get into an inflation situation." Jack Cole remembers it a little differently: "Coming up with an amount that was higher, equal to, or below $6 million would have drawn a comparison to *Six*," he said. "Not naming an amount kept it open-ended. If we assigned her an amount that was less than Steve's reconstruction, we were afraid of flak such as, *Oh, you value a woman less than a man?*"

• In a memorable scene, Jaime rips a telephone book in two, thereby intimidating her mischievous students. The BW FX crew baked the phone book at 350 degrees for three days, which left it brittle enough for Wagner to tear apart.

• *Daily Variety*: "There is little reason not to believe that this childlike fantasy series will not do as well or better than its source, as the ingredients (as well as the basic competition) are relatively the same. Wagner has a lot more animation than Majors, although her tennis serve belies her former top tennis pro pose, and starts off with a built-in audience identification. The comic-strip hijinks are beneath critical analysis, but apparently slick hokum of this nature can rake in the numbers in 'family hour' placement."

• Continuity error: Jaime bends the plant stand on Harris' patio, but when cutting to the bionic close-up, we see that Jaime's gray sleeve has turned to blue.

Episode 2: *Angel of Mercy*. . . . . **[1-28-76]**
Written by James D. Parriott. Directed by Alan Levi. Featuring: Andy Griffith (The Andy Griffith Show, Salvage I, Matlock), *Claudio Martinez, James Karen, Jean Allison, Robbie Rist* (The Brady Bunch), *Bert Santos, Paul Berrones*

Jack Starkey, a macho helicopter pilot, accompanies Jaime on a mission to save a U.S. ambassador in Costa Bravo. Due to Jaime's gender, Starkey objects to her involvement. Then she proves to be the optimum co-pilot. However, the copter is shot down. The situation really becomes complicated when the ambassador and his wife get caught in a shattered facility, and an orphaned youth appears.

• In these first few episodes, Jaime leads a more clearly-defined double life, teaching children of Air Force personnel, while remaining on-call for Oscar. She once even placed her hair back in a ponytail, and wore glasses to help conceal her true identity (a la Wonder Woman/Diana Prince). The academic segments were then cut.

"There was no conscious attempt to distinguish between her double life," Lindsay claims. "It was simply an external expression of how, in the beginning, there were minor experiments in how we felt Jaime should have been portrayed. One at a time, they decided to leave out the children," who proved restrictive to work with. "There are far more variable factors when you're working with children," she explained. "You have to be somewhat more flexible, and it may take a little longer. You can't like just *cram it and jam it*."

She said the kids were primarily employed as "an external expression of how *homey* Jaime really was." As to Jaime's spectacles, she couldn't run 60-miles-an-hour with glasses on. "So automatically," Lindsay said, "I just had to take those off." And the hair? "On camera, it just looked pretty to see the hair flowing in the wind," Wagner relays. "That's how the dualism was created. But Jaime wasn't a *foo-foo* kind of gal. She was a teacher." Lindsay refused to present "this gorgeous educator, with *the clothes* and *the hair*." She was like, "No. She's a real person. Jaime wasn't into being terribly vain."

• The number listed on Jaime's classroom phone is 555-2368. Curiously, this is the same phone number listed on the phone in her apartment.

Episode 3: *A Thing of the Past*............................. [2-18-76]
Written by Philip DeGuere, Jr. (The New Twilight Zone). *Story by Terrence McDonnell, Jim Carlson. Directed by Alan Crosland, Jr. Featuring: Donald O'Connor, Don Gordon* (Ironside), *Roger Perry, W.T. Zacha, Christian Juttner, Alycia Gardner, Robbie Wolcott, Brian Cutler, Lori Busk*

A field trip with teacher Jaime and her school children is no picnic, when the bus they're riding in gets into an accident. To keep her true identity and feminine mystique under wraps, Jaime saves the day, but Harry Anderson, with no assistance from Jaime, enters the burning bus to retrieve a child who had been overlooked. He makes newspaper headlines, and Harry's past creeps out of the good work. Apparently, he once viewed a crime syndicate leader make a hit, and he's been on the run ever since. Due to the press, the gangster now knows Harry's location. So, as he has for many years, Harry runs. That is, until Jaime lends a hand. As a result, Harry happily remains in Ojai.

• Lee Majors has a cameo.

• First episode to correctly spell "Jaime's" name in the opening credits.

• Composer Joe Harnell: "For me, *The Bionic Woman* was a good experience, although it did have one negative effect. I was asked to write a new theme to replace Jerry's, but I sensed that wasn't really cricket. I said, 'I don't want to do this because Jerry Fielding is a dear friend.' 'If you don't want to do it, we'll get someone else.' With some reluctance, I wrote a theme for the main title and closing credits. Jerry called me in a fit of anger, 'How could you take money off my table?' I apologized and said, 'What could I do, Jerry? Should I have turned it down?' 'Yes, you should have turned it down.' Shortly after that we instituted a policy where they used his opening music and my closing music."

• Ever wonder why the BW title sequence begins in color ("The following information is classified: Top Secret ..."), switches back to black and white to recreate the accident and operating room scenes, then back to color again? Jack Cole: "We wanted to create a sense of 'past' by using black and white as a clear separation."

• Bionic scribe W. T. Zacha, who penned "Kill Oscar Part II," played the character "Raines" in this episode.

• Veteran song-and-dance man Donald O'Connor succumbed to heart failure on September 27, 2003. He was 78

Episode 4: *Claws* . . . . **[2-25-76]**
Written by Sue Milburn. Directed by Phil Bondelli. Featuring: Alicia Fleer, Tippi Hedren (The Birds), *William Schallert, Jack Kelly* (Maverick), *George Wallace, Mills Watson, Robbie Rist*

While Susan Victor, an animal instructor, adopts Neil, a timid circus lion, Katie, a student of Jaime's, works to conquer her shyness. On a visit to Jaime's class with Susan, Neil proves how animals may be conditioned with tenderness. Yet local ranchers believe Neil is responsible for the recent demise of their livestock. On ranch-watch, Jaime and Katie are approached by ranchers, bent on killing Neil. In the end, a cougar is the culprit in the livestock murders. With Neil's help, Katie comes out of her shell.

• According to Lindsay, Neil's trainer said, "Oh, yeah. My lion's great. He never hurts anyone. He works on hand signals. You won't have to worry about me screaming over the shot." "Well, this lion was so old or so drugged," Lindsay said, "that the reason the trainer didn't scream, was because his lion probably couldn't hear him. Just to get him to move and walk out of the shot was a challenge. We'd yell, 'Neil, get up. Get up,' and he would just sit there." The cameras rolled, and the actors would attempt to maintain their posture.

As soon as Neil got up, they'd speak. "So," Lindsay said, "no matter what anyone said, Neil wouldn't leave." The lion did turn his head when the trainer yelled, "Come on, Neil, you turkey," as if to say, "Hey, don't call me a turkey." Yet, the cat still would not budge. "There we'd be," Lindsay recalls, "standing there, poised, trying not to laugh." Neil was finally motivated to walk out of the scene.

Another trainer was working with chimps. He had a particular scent about him to which the lion was attracted. "Neil tried to mount him," Lindsay said. "The chimp-trainer had to stay away from the lion, who just loved the way this guy smelled. So when the lion finally got up and went to the right of the screen [from the audience's perspective], and we cut, there was this wooden, coral-type fence."

A ladder was created on that side of the fence, with a rope placed at the bottom. The chimp's trainer was positioned to stand outside the camera's view. When the cameras rolled, the co-trainer ran to that mark, called the lion, who then turned around and saw him. He jumped, ran after him, up the ladder, over the fence, and then the rope that was tied to the ladder was jerked so Neil couldn't get up over the fence.

"That's how they got this lion, who supposedly only worked on hand signals, out of the shot," Lindsay said. "The trainer just kind of kept going into his truck." "Women," she adds, "can't work with these animals during their menstrual cycles. They can get a little too friendly, and though they do not intend to hurt you, they will. They're so heavy and big, that if they try and jump on you, it's over. Of course, Neil came up to me in the course of the shoot. I was standing there talking, with him on my left. All of a sudden, he kind of leaned his head beside me, put my leg in his mouth, and started chewing."

• Timeline glitch: Jaime is talking to Bill Elgin on the phone and tells him not to worry about her. He said that he does so out of habit, dating back to when Jaime was twelve. However, Jim and Helen Elgin did not become Jaime's legal guardians until the death of her parents when she was sixteen.

• While shooting one day, a Universal tour guide tram happened to pass by. The tram's narrator announced the following: "You are now watching the filming of *The Bionic Woman* series. The lady with the lion is the star of the show — Lyle Waggoner."

Episode 5: *The Deadly Missiles* . . . . **[3-3-76]**
Written by Wilton Denmark. Directed by Alan Levi. Featuring: Forrest Tucker (F Troop), *Ben Piazza, Alicia Fleer, Christian Juttner, Gary McLarty*

Oscar asks Jaime to contact her old friend, J.T. Connors, an aerospace mogul. J.T.'s ranch may be the launch spot of a missile that landed close to

Los Angeles. The American-made armament was able to stealthily pen-
etrate L.A.'s airspace when the area's missile detection system had been
mysteriously jammed. While Jaime believes that her friend is innocent of
any wrongdoing, she's not so sure about Warren Riker, J.T.'s right-hand
man.

• Lee Majors has a cameo.

• A minor blooper, employing stock footage from SM's "Population:
Zero": Steve uses a metal pole as a javelin to blow up a communications
truck. Jaime pulls the same neat trick, but the pole she pulls has a metal sign
attached to it. When we see it flying through the air, the sign mysteriously
disappears. When the pole meets its target, it's back.

• Original working title: "Deadly Toys."

• Wilton Denmark: "Lindsay definitely had a preference for human-
interest stories. I don't think I ever saw Lindsay as a spy, but because she
worked for the OSI and that was the premise of the show, we just went
along with it. That said, I doubt they could have found a better person to
play Jaime Sommers."

• Actor Ben Piazza (who played bad guy Warren Riker) just happened to
be from Wilton Denmark's hometown. Piazza died on September 7, 1991
(cancer).

• Rita Egleston joins the series as Lindsay Wagner's stuntwoman. She is
seen sporting a helmet-like wig, which is eventually replaced by Rita's own
hair.

• It was right around this time when Wagner was involved in an off-
screen car mishap. "Lindsay's auto accident slowed us down for a week or
so," said Ken Johnson. "She was very lucky that it wasn't worse, and of course
she ended up with that nasty scar on her lip and a little emotional damage.
I remember rushing to the emergency room at UCLA that night to see her,
and we were all very concerned for her. But it worked out okay; we managed to keep going."

Episode 6: *Bionic Beauty* .... **[3-17-76]**
*Written by James D. Parriott. Directed by Alan Crosland, Jr. Featuring: Bert
Parks, Gary Crosby, Helen Craig, Charlotte Moore, Henry Polic, Lisa Parks,
Katie Hopkins, Cassie Yates*

Oscar receives notice from an agent stationed in Paris: Miss Florida
will win the Miss United States contest. To investigate a possible threat to
the nation's security, Jaime enters the competition, and performs the song
"Feelings" (which she dedicates to Steve). The event *is* fixed; Miss Florida
will courier to Europe a stolen micro-computer component which plays an
indispensable role in U.S. security.

• Jim Parriott on Lindsay's "Feelings": "You usually pre-record a song, and then the actor or singer lip-syncs to it, while filming. We did that. Then she heard the pre-recorded version, and wanted to do it live, which didn't work, and we had to redo it, backwards, with her lips moving. We had cut the vocal out of the track.""The whole recording session was a fiasco,"admits Wagner. "I cringe every time I think of it."

• Joe Harnell: "I was asked to write an arrangement of the song 'Feelings' for Lindsay Wagner. Lindsay was a nice lady but not much of a singer. We recorded all night, did 38 takes, and were saved by a brilliant editor who combined them into an acceptable performance. Over the two and a half years of *The Bionic Woman*, I did most of the episodes. In my scores I used fragments of thematic material, in addition to musical colors and combi-nations of 'odd' sounds. Since there was a new character on the show each week, I wrote a special theme for each of them."

• Parriott wrote the song performed by Bert Parks. The producers were refused use of the Miss America theme. Getting Parks "was a mil-lion laughs," said Ken Johnson. The budget didn't allow for an audience. So Johnson hired one hundred extras, huddled them at the front, and kept the rest of the theater dark. He then instructed prop-man Rick DuNarry, whom he later worked with on *Alien Nation*, to set up thirty flashbulbs, and place them around the theater. "We'll keep everything dark," Johnson told him, "and shine a couple on Lindsay." The result looked "completely spon-taneous," Ken said, "like the audience was taking photos. When Lindsay came out on stage, the flashbulbs went off, the spotlights were flashing, and we had our crowd of one hundred people. By the time the sound effects were added [for the crowd and orchestra], it looked liked the *Miss America Pageant*."

He got the idea from seeing "the Pope or the Beatles playing some huge auditorium where a thousand strobe lights went off at the same time." Later, Harve Bennett told him, "Boy, you're really good." "That meant a lot to me," he admits, "because I admire Harve a great deal. It was like the beginning of the passing of the torch."

• From 1958 to 1960, Bennett produced the Miss America Pageant, which made him "a small sum of money." A pool was started as to which woman would garner the title. He won every year. "I must have an eye for something," he jokes.

• This is the first time Lindsay did a one-story, high-jump: "It was done in one shot," she said. "Myself and Rita [Egleston, her stunt double] jumped from the window to the landing [on an air-bag] behind the bush where I was hiding."

• On guest Gary Crosby: "He was a lot of fun. We had a lot of practi-cal jokes. He was so proper. We teased him a lot." When Crosby went on stage, Lindsay whispered, "Your fly's open." "He was just shattered,"she said.

He teased Lindsay in return. If they ever got married, he said, "I would have a brother and wife with the same name." Incidentally, Lindsay appeared as Gary Crosby's girlfriend in a 1972 episode of *O'Hara, U.S. Treasury*.

• A *Wonder Woman* episode, "Beauty on Parade," which aired on October 13, 1976, was similar to this segment.

• Sandra Bullock, who played The Bionic Girl in the 1989 *Bionic Showdown* reunion movie, starred in and produced the 2000 feature film, *Miss Congeniality*, about an FBI agent who goes undercover at a beauty pageant.

Episode 7: *Jaime's Mother*. . . . . [3-24-76]
Written by Arthur Rowe. Story by Worley Thorne. Directed by Leo Penn (Sean's father). Featuring: Barbara Rush, Norma Connolly, Sam Chew, Jr., Joseph George, Dan Barton, Carlena Gower

The Bionic Woman's mother and father (ex-operatives for the Department of Defense) have been dead for years. A woman arrives and claims to be Ann Sommers, Jaime's mom. Oscar and Helen are unsettled. Jaime decides to confront this mysterious person at her mother's now-alleged gravesite. Ann claims to have extensive knowledge of Jaime. Oscar has his doubts: she may be an impostor. He's right. Ann is an actress named Chris Stuart who's up to no-good.

• "I was real impressed with Barbara Rush," said Lindsay of the guest actress. "I thought she cried, faster, longer and better than anyone I ever worked with. When it was time for her to shed tears, she was like, *Bam...* just right there with it. I remember being in awe. She had to do it over and over and over again. I was feeling so bad for her because there was one thing after another going wrong."

"You want to talk about underrated actresses," adds Harve Bennett. "I had gone to school with Barbara Rush, who, in her day, was considered the queen of television. She never quite got the recognition she deserved. She was supposed to do *Psycho* [but Janet Leigh got the lead instead, 1960]."

• According to their tombstone, Jaime's parents (victims of a car crash) died on April 16, 1966. "What happened to Jaime's parents was never fully explained," said writer Arthur Rowe. "But the more ideal Midwest backgrounds you can give them, the more identifiable to the audience, the better off you are. If it's not going to serve some dramatic purpose, then drop it."

• Actress Martha Scott (Helen Elgin) died of natural causes on May 28, 2003.

• Photos of Jaime's parents are shown in "Welcome Home, Jaime (Part I)," however, they are not the actors used in this episode.

• Continuity error: Jaime has a bad dream and bionically bends one of the bars on her brass headboard. A phone call from Oscar awakens her, but the bar shows no signs of distress.

Episode 8: *Winning is Everything* . . . . **[4-7-76]**
Written by James D. Parriott. Directed by Phil Bondelli. Featuring: John Elerick, Alejandro Rey (The Flying Nun), *Nancy Jeris, Frank Cala, Rene Assa, Stephen Coit*

Jaime enters an international auto race, with a skittish driving partner. The OSI must have entry to a city in the East-Asian country of Taftan, where a cassette with critical data has been concealed. Double agents stop at nothing to get the cassette before Jaime.

• Guest Alejandro Rey slipped in the cantina. "After that," Lindsay said, "we couldn't stop laughing. All we could do was visualize him falling. After 10 or 15 times, we became paranoid about not being able to get it right, which made it worse, and we laughed even harder. It's like if you're in church, and someone does something funny and you're not supposed to laugh, you have to be real quiet and not laugh. You try to hold it in and your whole body starts shaking."

• Anti-Semitism is addressed when Jaime wonders why her boss is using the name, Oscar Bartholomew. "I don't think the name Goldman would go over too well in this country," he said.

• Jim Parriott searched for stock film in Long Beach, "at this guy's house all day long, with him hanging over my shoulder, looking at dune buggy footage, of which he was very proud." Jim still had his Volkswagen, with the "weird," unconventional climate control. "It was a cold drive back to LA, wickedly cold," he said.

• Ken Johnson's conversation with editorial technicians —
   KJ: Okay, guys, the race is going to run right to left.
   Tech: The numbers on the cars will be backwards.
   KJ: Nobody's gonna notice. The cars will be going so fast.
   Everyone will just see the dust.

"No one did notice," Johnson said today. [Until now.] "We needed Jaime to reach the finish line, which we couldn't afford to have, along with a couple hundred extras, cheering them on." What if she never reached the finish line? Suppose they just said, "Well, it's clear sailing now. She's gonna' win the race." "That's what we did," Ken concludes, "because we literally could not afford to *finish* it."

Episode 9: *Canyon of Death* . . . . [4-14-76]
Written by Stephen Kandel. Directed by Jerry London. Featuring: Guillermo San Juan, Robbie Rist, Gary Collins, Paul Cavonis, Don McGovern, Annette Cardona, Jack Stauffer, Dee Timberlake, Jim Ingersoll, Bill Conklin, Todd London, Nina Weintraub

Jaime deals with an Indian student named Paco (who has a huge imagination), just as Oscar asks her to shield the desert testing of the OSI's latest invention: a flying suit. The head of security has lifted the drill suits, and sets out to heist the genuine apparel. Meanwhile, Paco sees the missing drill suits being used, but no one listens to him due to his inclination for storytelling.
    • General Fuller, who approved Jaime's reconstruction, makes an appearance.
    • In a magnanimous gesture, Richard Anderson spends a good part of his time with the California Indian Manpower Consortium, which concentrates on education and job training for Native Americans.
    • Robbie Rist: "*The Bionic Woman* episodes were fun because not only did I really like the show but I *still* have a huge crush on Lindsay Wagner."
    • Special effects bloopers: When Jaime leaps into the air to grab the bad guy, you can clearly spot the wires suspending him. Also, when she jumps over a security gate while chasing Paco, you can plainly see the mini-trampoline that stuntwoman Rita Egleston uses to propel herself over.

Episode 10: *Fly Jaime* . . . . [5-5-76]
Written by Arthur Rowe, Mann Rubin. Story by Mann Rubin. Directed by Barry Crane. Featuring: Spencer Milligan (Land of the Lost), *Jerry Douglas* (The Young and the Restless), *Vito Scotti, Arline Anderson, Dick Valentine, Jim Raymond*

The Bionic Woman goes undercover as a stewardess to protect Rudy Wells on a return flight from Brazil, where he memorized a scientist's important theorem. Hit men hired to eliminate Rudy, and a passenger with a crush on Jaime, are a little too much to deal with, compared to the electrical storm that forces the aircraft to ditch near an isolated island.
    • In this complete remake of SM's "Survival of the Fittest," Rudy and Jaime, bond. "It's also wonderful," Marty Brooks said, "because of the character conflict that was established, deep in the jungle." He recalls when Jaime had to capture a snake and throw it away: "They used a fake snake, of course, but Lindsay hated snakes in real life."

• This episode, along with "The Most Dangerous Enemy," is one of Marty's favorites.

• A great scene with guest Vito Scotti: Sporting a short skirt, Jaime's long, shapely legs catch the eye of Scotti's character, who can't help but admire them. "Nice legs," he said, getting the attention of Rudy Wells, who is sitting right next to him on the plane. "Oh, yes," Rudy comments. "I couldn't have asked for nicer ones if I made them myself." Jaime, who was bionically eavesdropping on the conversation, couldn't repress a chuckle.

• Rudy tells Jaime, "They're all dead," referring to the flight crew in the cockpit, after the plane crashes. Later, we find out that the pilot survived.

• Director Barry Crane was a National Bridge Champion. "One of the top players in our country," Harve Bennett clarifies, "if not the world. He would go on these tournaments. Every time he would come back to direct another show, we would be like, *Where are you going this time?*"

• Actor Vito Scotti, known as the man of a thousand faces, succumbed to cancer on June 5, 1996.

Episode 11: *The Jailing of Jaime* . . . .[5-12-76]
Written by Bruce Shelly. Directed by Alan Crosland, Jr. Featuring: Barry Sullivan, Philip Abbott, Anne Schedeen, Tom Bower, Ross Elliott, Skip Homeier, Sam Chew, Jr.

Dr. Ellis Hatch creates a vital decoder, which Jaime is assigned to transport to whom she thinks is General Partridge, at a subterranean testing area. Pilot Ted Ryan takes her there. The real Partridge never received the component. Apparently, Jaime has sold out. She is arrested, jailed, and told to stay put until Oscar can straighten things out. Impatient, she busts out and tracks down Ryan's girlfriend, just in time to bionically eavesdrop on an incriminating conversation. Dr. Hatch, it seems, is not the patriot he appears to be.

• Oscar's special relationship with Jaime is reinforced when he elects to stand outside a locked vault that's about to explode (with her inside) instead of fleeing to safety.

• Dr. Hatch's facility is the same one used for Carlton Harris' firm — "Electrodyne Inc." — that Jaime infiltrates in "Welcome Home, Jaime Part II."

Episode 12: *Mirror Image* . . . .[5-19-76]
Written by James D. Parriott. Directed by Alan Levi. Featuring: Don Porter, Herbert Jefferson (Battlestar Galactica), Terry Kiser, John Fink, Harry Wiere, Sam Chew, Jr. Fuddle Bagley, Christopher Barrett

Lisa Galloway (Jaime's physically-altered twin) is under orders from Dr. James Courtney (her plastic surgeon and enemy of the OSI) to photograph top-secret information in Oscar's office. The real Jaime's vacation in Nassau is then interrupted by Courtney's attempt on her life. Jaime survives, places a frantic phone call to Oscar, and Lisa is captured. When Galloway refuses to talk, Jaime assumes her identity in a bid to discover the name of her evil benefactor. Lisa later escapes, leading to a bionic/mortal showdown.

• Jim Parriott: "Lindsay was a terrific person and actress," he said. "She was best when she had a good character conflict [as in this episode]. I liked putting her in more emotional situations, but the network still wanted an action show. In most episodes, it was the guest stars that were in conflict. Jaime was there to console and rescue them. In the best shows, it was Jaime who had the emotional and moral dilemmas."

• Jaime is sunning on the beach in Nassau, becomes somewhat fettered with her uneven tan (caused by her artificial skin), and mutters, "Oh, Rudy. Why can't you make a bionic skin that tans?"

• The underwater sequence of Jaime breaking out of a submerged crate was filmed in a tank on the Universal lot. Lindsay's double, Rita Egleston, waited underwater before breaking out of the box to be sure to get the shot — which made the crew worry that something had gone terribly wrong.

• This episode is a mild reworking of Six Mill's "Look Alike."

• Guest Don Porter's specialty was playing suave authority figures, such as the boss in TV's Private Secretary, and Sally Field's father in Gidget. He died at the age of 84 on February 11, 1997. He also appeared in BW's "Deadly Ringer," as well as SM's "Population: Zero."

Episode 13: *The Ghosthunter* . . . . [5-26-76]
Written by Kenneth Johnson, Justin Edgerton. Directed by Kenneth Johnson. Featuring: Paul Shenar, Kristy McNichol (Family, Empty Nest), *Bo Brundin, Merry Loomis*

Dr. Alan Cory, a research scientist, has a problem: strange happenings continue to upset his household. Jaime goes undercover as a nanny for Amanda, his daughter, whose track record with nannies isn't all that hot. Emil Laslo, a parapsychologist, finds the entire situation quite fascinating. Why? One of Amanda's ancestors was accused of witchcraft, put to death, and now Laslo thinks her ghost is at the center of Dr. Cory's discontent. Jaime believes there's another answer, which may not only involve a threat to the nation, but to Amanda, as well.

• "Kristy was just a delight," said Lindsay. "We had a great time working together. When we see each other, there is such an affection."

• "It was a fun episode to shoot," she adds, "but it was also kind of scary.

The bridge we used in one scene would rope out, from underneath us. It was also as cold as heck one night, and it was real hard to stand up."

• Recycled prop alert: In the opening scene, the camera pans over a large silver box situated in Dr. Cory's lab. Inside is the "Cryptograph Analyzer" that Jaime Sommers was accused of stealing in "The Jailing of Jaime."

• Early in this first season, Lindsay was involved in an automobile accident with then-love, actor Michael Brandon. "I was on painkillers," she remembers, "and I shouldn't have even been working. I don't remember a lot of stuff from that period, because I was hardly there. After those first few shows, I was just trying to make it through until the hiatus period. I was miserable. I was still so bruised and sore. They could only shoot one side of my face, because of my lip. When I first came back to work, you could see the scar."

• This was the first one-hour episode of "anything" that Ken Johnson directed. "I wanted to do an episode that was particularly stylish and that would have some interesting camera work," he said. "I wanted a really strong young actress." He remembers reading Valerie Bertinelli (*One Day at a Time*), who was then about fourteen, for the role. "But she was too sexy," he said. "When she auditioned, and started talking about how she wanted to be close to her dad, it sounded like she really wanted to be *close* to him." Kristy McNichol, on the other hand, had only done one other role before this, Johnson said. "She was a goldmine." He also "loved the house that we used in Pasadena," where the interiors were filmed. The moving-bridge was on the lot at Universal.

New Season! The Bionic Woman and Steve Austin battle for their lives against deadly space aliens and "Bigfoot." Lindsay Wagner stars. Special guest star, Lee Majors.

BIONIC WOMAN
ⓐⓑⓒ **7:00PM** ⑨

TV GUIDE AD FOR THE ORIGINAL BROADCAST OF "THE RETURN OF BIGFOOT, PART II"

The Second Season
1976 to 1977

Episode 14: *The Return of Bigfoot (Part II)* . . . . [9-22-76]
*Written by Kenneth Johnson . Directed by Barry Crane . Featuring: John Saxon,
Stephen Young, Severn Darden, Ted Cassidy, Sandy Duncan, Stefanie Powers,
Charles Cyphers, Gavin James*

The Six Million Dollar Man is close to death. The Bionic Woman
must acquire the futuristic medication to save him. An ailing Shalon, the
alien woman who, along with her peers, created Bigfoot, offers the only
hope. During Jaime's quest, dissident aliens, Dallett and Nedlik, order the
mechanical Sasquatch to destroy her. Gillian then appears in the nick of
"time," rescues Jaime, and employs a Time Line Converter, which beams
The Bionic Woman to refuge. Fortunately, Shalon and Apploy have just
enough of the antidote to save Steve's life. But can Steve and Jaime stop the
impending eruption of a volcano?

• A continuation of the September 19, 1976 season opener of *The Six
Million Dollar Man*, which employs the hovel-like Universal set piece as the
pathway to Bigfoot's alien hideaway.

• Guest Severn Darden (Apploy), a founding cast member of the Second
City comedy troupe in Chicago, died May 26, 1995, at his Santa Fe home at
the age of 65, following a debilitating stroke in 1994.

• Guest John Saxon played the evil android in SM's "Day of the
Robot."

• *Daily Variety's* review was less than kind: "The conclusion was even
more ludicrous than the opener, relying even more on superhuman gad-
getry. The far-fetched storyline concluded with *Man's* Lee Majors stopping
a volcano that had already exploded by throwing a time-speedup gadget into
the crater. Even goggle-eyed kids must have gagged on that. The episode's
most unintentional funny scene was Bionic star Lindsay Wagner fending off
papier-mâché rocks, being thrown at her by Bigfoot, with the phony stones
bouncing away like foam rubber balls. One gets the impression that the BW
and SM producers are beginning to scrape the bottom of the barrel."

• As Steve and Jaime speed toward an erupting volcano, viewers are
treated to Joe Harnell's exceptional blending of the SM and BW theme
music.

Episode 15: *In This Corner, Jaime Sommers* .... **[9-29-76]**
Written by Robert L. McCullough, Kenneth Johnson. Story by Robert L. McCullough. Directed by Alan Crosland, Jr. Featuring: Norman Fell (Dan August, Three's Company, The Ropers), *Marcia Lewis, Marsha Shapiro, Marj Dusay, Margaret Shocklee, Lew Palter, Brett Dunham, Bill Keene, Bill Conklin, Sandy Parker, Gene LeBell*

Wayne Haley (an OSI operative) vanishes at an athletic facility. The Bionic Woman goes undercover as lady wrestler Savage Sommers. In her search for Haley, Jaime learns that the facility supervisor is entangled in an illegal scheme to smuggle satellite parts. Jaime's true identity is then revealed by an evil scientist (who's defected from Russia) with a personal agenda.

• A favorite episode of Lindsay's, who said: "They wrote a kind of human drama within the caper. Jaime was interacting with this woman on a human level. We were allowed to execute a compassionate personality, as well as execute a caper."

• Ken Johnson on Wagner's athletic limitations: "It's not uncommon for a star not to have the abilities that you need for the character, so you use stunt people. Rita Egleston was the surrogate Bionic Woman and was extraordinarily gifted. It *was* sort of amusing that Jaime was a tennis pro who could barely hit a tennis ball. It took a lot of creative effort to make it work."

• Besides Savage Sommers, she was also promoted as Joltin' Jessie Sommers.

• Killer quote from Jaime (to Oscar): "I don't suppose you'd consider putting Steve in a dress?"

• Guest Marcia Lewis was a friend of Lindsay's then-assistant, Linda Wiser.

• Guest Gene LeBell, who played the referee, is an accomplished wrestler and martial artist in his own right. He is also a veteran stuntman.

Episode 16: *Assault on the Princess* .... **[10-6-76]**
Written by Wilton Denmark. Directed by Alan Crosland, Jr. Featuring: Ed Nelson, John Durren, Steve Kanaly (Dallas), *Vito Scotti, Dick Dinman, Tony Giorgio, Ron Wilson, Abraham Alvarez, Don Maxwell*

Unstable archetype energy cells (which must remain in frigid temperatures) are lifted from the OSI. Agent Sommers then fakes it as a blackjack dealer on the *Princess* gambling sea cruiser. The ship's proprietor, Lucky Harrison (purportedly The Ice Man), may be the thief who heisted the cells. Subsequently, Jaime must find the cells before they are marketed. What's worse, they may detonate, and demolish the cruiser and every passenger on board.

• Jaime squeezes shut the pipe that is venting steam. When she's finished, the film speeds up for a couple of seconds. As she puts the push-arm back in place, she uses her left hand to hammer the bolt (her right arm is the bionic one). She then rips a rope anchor from the ship's deck, and hurls it at a rowboat. It punches a hole through the bottom, causing the boat to sink; an extremely precise toss.

• Lindsay recalls a lot of night-shooting for this episode because of the boat, and "having so much fun watching all the card sharks that were hired to lend authenticity. They would do tricks for the cast and crew in between shots."

• Vito Scotti, who was very good friends with BW scribe Arthur Rowe, reprised the character Romero that he played in "Fly Jaime." Convinced that Jaime had a twin, he dubbed her Jaime *Winters*, which was her undercover name in "Fly Jaime."

• *Princess Louise* was the ship's full name.

• Original working title: "Assault on a Golden Lady."

• This is the first episode in which we see Rita Egleston perform her "over the railing" jump, which she invented.

• Wilton Denmark: "The 'Ice Man' was a James Bondish supervillain who was a bartender on *The Princess*."

Episode 17: *Road to Nashville*. . . . .[10-20-76]
Written by James D. Parriott. Directed by Alan Levi. Featuring: Doc Severinsen, Hoyt Axton, Scott Arthur Allen, Fionnula Flanagan, Dick Haynes, Roy Daniels, Jr.

Oscar's aware that classified data is being relayed to the enemy by way of Nashville. Yet he's uncertain as to the method of transfer. Jaime goes on assignment with Muffin Calhoun, a country musician, to find answers. Calhoun confronts the amiable Big Buck Buckley and his producer Tammy Dalton. Jaime bionically tunes in to hear a message on Buck's music in the recording studio. And it looks as though Mr. Big may be party to the scheme.

• "A whole lot of laughing on this episode, mostly R-rated," said Lindsay.

• Jaime carries a good tune here with "Good to be Alive in the Country." The song, written by Ken Tobias, originally appeared on his 1973 album, *The Magic's in the Music*. Lindsay can also be heard singing a portion of this song in the 1976 feature film, *Second Wind*.

• Hoyt Axton died on October 26, 1999, of a heart attack due to complications from a stroke. He was 61.

• The song "Don't Know Why I Love You" appears on Axton's 1977 album, *Snowblind Friend*.

Episode 18: *Kill Oscar (Part I)* ....[10-27-76]
Written by Arthur Rowe. Story by Arthur Rowe, Oliver Crawford. Directed by Alan Crosland, Jr. Featuring: John Houseman (The Paper Chase), *Janice Whitby, Jack Colvin, Corrine Michaels, Jack L. Ging, John Dewey Carter, Eugene Peterson*

The acrid, though brilliant, Dr. Franklin and his Fembots (female super-powered androids) scheme to infiltrate OSI headquarters to heist a weather-control machine. To do so, Oscar Goldman must be neutralized. Two critical OSI secretaries, Callahan and Lynda Wilson (who's assigned to Rudy Wells), are kidnapped and replaced. Shortly thereafter, Goldman, too, is abducted, despite Jaime's best efforts to save him. Making matters worse, he leaves explicit instructions that he is to be killed should he ever fall into enemy hands. Callahan's shaky performance during the governmental investigation leaves Jaime suspicious, so she pays her "friend" a visit at her apartment. Franklin realizes that Jaime is getting a little too close to the truth, so he orders fake Callahan and another fembot to apprehend The Bionic Woman. An all-out melee ensues, and Jaime's only route of escape is Callahan's bedroom window, high above the street. She jumps, shatters her legs, and clings to life in a hospital bed.

• Ken Johnson: " 'Kill Oscar' was a challenging show because of the technology, the props, the ripping off of faces, wires underneath, etc. I understand a lot of kids were really freaked out. A lot of parents told me that the trilogy just terrified their kids. I had no idea it was gonna have that much of an impact, and was a little distressed to hear it at the time. John Houseman, of course, was an institution and had his own way of doing things and his own pace, which was incredibly *slow*. Trying to get him to speed up and get the scene over with in less than a day and a half was a bit of a difficulty."

• "Kill Oscar (Part II)" was broadcast as an episode of *The Six Million Dollar Man*.

• When the Callahan-fembot talks to Jaime on the phone, Jaime winces because she hears the ultrasonic whine its circuitry is transmitting. Does a telephone have enough fidelity to pick up and transmit ultrasonic sound? Also, you can clearly see the boom mike hovering over Callahan's head.

• Discerning viewers will notice that the opening credits theme music was given a creepy upgrade for the "Kill Oscar" trilogy. This was only used, however, in syndication and home video versions. The original broadcast featured the short main title with the Jerry Fielding score.

Episode 19: *Kill Oscar (Part III)* . . . . [11-3-76]
Written by Arthur Rowe. Story by Arthur Rowe, Oliver Crawford. Directed by
Alan Crosland, Jr. Featuring: John Houseman, Jack L. Ging, Corrine Michaels,
Janice Whitby, James McMullan, Sam Jaffe, Eugene Peterson, Byron Morrow,
Howard K. Smith

All military attacks on Dr. Franklin's island are useless against his now-operational employment of the weather-control system. Jaime and Steve then persuade Admiral Ricter to transport them (via submarine) close to Franklin's enclave. The bionic duo swim the rest of the way, and soon find themselves battling with Amazonian Fembots in an effort to save Oscar, the OSI, and the world.

• A blooper: While running with Jaime across the island, Steve is seen wearing tan-colored sneakers that have a habit of appearing and disappearing during the chase. Once he reaches the dam, a noticeably heavier stuntman replaces him.

• Life was pretty chaotic for Richard Anderson in the mid-1970s, shuttling back and forth between two production sets. How did he keep his sanity? "It was a full-time setup and there really wasn't much time to do anything else," he said. "The studio organized me well; they had a driver and a warm car in the winter and air conditioning in the summer. I remember one day I had to pop back and forth four times, and we had pick-up scenes we couldn't finish. I had dialogue from three or four different shows in one day!"

Episode 20: *Black Magic* . . . . [11-10-76]
Written by Arthur Rowe. Directed by Barry Crane. Featuring: Vincent Price,
William Windom (Murder, She Wrote, Wait 'Till Your Father Gets Home),
Hermione Baddeley, Julie Newmar (Batman), *Abe Vigoda* (Fish), *Alvah Stanley,*
Roger Til, George Margo

Cyrus Carstairs created a unique formula that peaked the interest of the OSI. Now he's dead, and an unfamiliar family relative is marketing the admixture for a top-dollar price. So Jaime travels to Carstairs' mysterious LaFitte Island manor in Louisiana. Her encounters with a swamp creature, Manfred (Cyrus' brother), and Warfield (the manservant) prove quite unnerving.

• By this time, Lindsay wanted Jaime "to start going undercover a lot. It was important to me that the audience was not locked into a solid image of thinking they knew exactly who I was [as an actress]. That was one of my fears about doing the series anyway, that I would get typecast. As long as I kept the character versatile, I was fine."

• Guest star Hermione Baddeley's name is misspelled in the opening credits as "Hermoine."

Episode 21: *Sister Jaime*. . . . .[11-24-76]
Written by Kenneth Johnson. Directed by Alan Levi. Featuring: Kathleen Nolan, Ellen Geer, Catherine Burns, Ron Hayes, Dran Hamilton, Cynthia Whitham, Al Hansen

The OSI apprehends a nun bearing illegal diamonds. Jaime Sommers temporarily enters the sisterhood in search of a possible convent connection. When the diamonds are pilfered, apparently by a priest, it's Jaime's job to recover them. Meanwhile, the Bishop is scheduled to visit the convent, which must be in tip-top shape to prevent it from closing. So Jaime literally has her hands full.

• On Jaime going undercover as a nun, Kenneth Johnson would sit back and say, "What venues do I want to see her in? The idea of a Bionic nun was just hysterical to me, 'cause obviously she would pull off miracles."

• Johnson: "In this one scene, a group of nuns sends a flock of sheep down a road to slow the limo in which Oscar was riding. So I gave Richard Anderson the classic line, 'Sister, you're gonna have to get the flock out of here.' Richard said, 'Kenny, they're not gonna let me say *that*.' But they did."

• Lindsay would later play a former nun-turned-rape counselor in the CBS-TV-film, *Sins of Silence*, first broadcast in 1996.

• Rita Egleston performed no stunts in this episode, but was allowed to drive the truck so that she could get paid for the week.

• Filmed at the Guasti Winery and Chapel in Guasti, California.

Episode 22: *The Vega Influence* . . . . [12-1-76]
Written by Arthur Rowe. Directed by Mel Damksi. Featuring: Richard Lenz, Philip Carey, Don Marshall (Land of the Giants), *John Lawrence, Jamie Smith Jackson, Roy Poole*

Jaime and Dr. Michael Marchetti land their transport aircraft at Dr. Boylin's biological island center to refuel. They find the place deserted, and their crew enigmatically vanishes. Dr. Boylin is somehow involved; a meteorite (which he distillated from permafrost) has apparently developed its own consciousness.

• "Oh, no," Lindsay recalls, "the one with the zombies; a dreadful show. It was so hard to keep a straight face during all that stuff."

• Adds guest Rick Lenz, "My daughter, who's in her mid-thirties, and her friend tease me about this episode. They seem to know it for some reason."

• Director Mel Damski would direct Lindsay again in *Their Second Chance*, which was first broadcast on cable's Lifetime channel, February 9, 1997.
   • The last appearance of Dr. Michael Marchetti (and his first since "Welcome Home, Jaime Part I").

Episode 23: *Jaime's Shield (Part I)* .... [12-15-76]
Written by James D. Parriott. Directed by Alan Crosland, Jr. Featuring: George Maharis, Diane Civita, Rebecca Balding, Linden Chiles, William Bryant, Arch Johnson, James McEachin, Amy Joyce, Mike Santiago

Oscar finds out that a foreign operative has joined the police academy. With Commissioner Hart's assistance, Jaime becomes a cadet to seek out the agent's identity. Initially, she has doubts about her roommate, Arlene, who seems too proficient for academy status. The Bionic Woman, however, is unaware of some important facts: A) *Arlene is Commissioner Hart's daughter*, and B) *She's become a cadet incognito because her dad is against the decision.* As a result, she feels that her performance must reach beyond exceptional to justify herself, and make a point to her father.
   • Filmed on location at the actual LAPD police academy.
   • Guest star Diane Civita also pops up in "Rancho Outcast."

Episode 24: *Jaime's Shield (Part II)* .... [12-22-76]
Written by James D. Parriott. Directed by Barry Crane. See Part I for Cast Credits, plus Amapola Del Vando

Assigned to the Fifth Precinct, Jaime and Arlene are promptly employed as Premiere Gabrin's motorcade squires. Parker, an unassuming file room worker, is really the head of a nefarious scheme to assassinate Gabrin; a plan which involves eliminating Jaime and Arlene, and replacing them — and their entire safety brigade — with bogus police.
   • This two-part episode was serviceable for Lindsay in two ways. First, it catered to the action-oriented fans of the series. Second, it allowed her to portray another character-within-a-character, as Jaime went undercover again, which Lindsay enjoyed doing. Yet, as the actress recalls, "Sometimes when Jaime went undercover, I would be that character. Other times, I would be in a different costume, and still act like Jaime."

"THE RETURN OF BIGFOOT, PART II" (W/TED CASSIDY), "ROAD TO NASHVILLE" (W/DOC SEVERINSEN), "IN THIS CORNER, JAIME SOMMERS" (W/GENE LEBELL), "KILL OSCAR, PART I," "BLACK MAGIC," "JAIME'S SHIELD, PART I," "DOOMSDAY IS TOMORROW, PART I," "THE NIGHT DEMON"

Episode 25: *Biofeedback* .... [1-12-77]
Written by Daniel Kibbie. Story by Kenneth Johnson. Directed by Alan Levi. Featuring: Granville Van Dusen, Peter Haskell, Lloyd Bochner, Jan Aaris, Inge Lindgreen

Darwin Jones is a revolutionary scholar who has created a body/mind/ spirit system that continuously receives government funding. Unfortunately, Payton (Darwin's brother) and his system of examining codes, does not secure the same support. Sour and hostile, Payton markets his invention to East Germany and Ivan Karp, a vendor in covert operations of state. Jaime Sommers is assigned to find Payton and his creation. Darwin, who follows in an effort to persuade his brother to reconsider his plans, complicates her task.

  • Lindsay's favorite episode.
  • "Yeah, they stretched the concept of biofeedback a little bit," said Martin Caidin of the plot employed in this segment. "But it was worth doing because biofeedback was coming into vogue, and it was a good, fun show to do."
  • Ken Johnson: "Biofeedback was an interesting concept, and we also saw it as a potential spin-off. I'd always been interested in the possibilities of biofeedback, and it found its way later on in the *Hulk* episode called 'Married.'"
  • Most importantly, this is the segment that saved the life of the little girl from Modesto, California, who was raped and mutilated. [See Chapter 4, "Impact," for details.]

Episode 26: *Doomsday is Tomorrow (Part I)* .... [1-19-77]
Written and directed by Kenneth Johnson. Featuring: Sam Chew, Jr., David Opatoshu, Ken O'Brien, Lew Ayres (Dr. Kildare of the movies), James Hong (Kung Fu), Guerin Barry, Ed Vasgersian

Dr. Elijah Cooper, eminent nuclear physicist and father of the Cobalt Bomb, makes a global proclamation: He will render the Earth uninhabitable if even one more thermonuclear device is detonated. Luminary scientists from the United States, Soviet Union, Japan, and France are summoned to confer with Dr. Cooper and examine the machine. Jaime poses as the French representative. Dr. Cooper programs Alex, a supercomputer with a human personality but devious tendencies, to carry out his plan for worldwide destruction. Jaime is then left to battle the maniacal machine alone.

  • "To me," surmises Harve Bennett, "Lew Ayres was not Dr. Kildare [whom the actor was first famous for in the 1940s feature film series]. He was Paul Baumer in *All Quiet on the Western Front*." Bennett studied this movie for the first time, as a student at UCLA. "It just blew me away," he said, "and it was an honor to then later to meet and work with Lew."

• When cost-conscious Ken Johnson couldn't afford an expensive set for Dr. Cooper's lair, inspiration came from an unlikely source: the morning newspaper. "In 'Doomsday is Tomorrow,' we needed to show Jaime running through a giant complex," he said. "I spent some time with my location guys searching for interesting locations around the LA area that had not been filmed too much, and then I wrote the script to fit the locations that we found. A lot of it was filmed at the Hyperion Sewage Treatment Plant in El Segundo, near the airport. That would include the sequence where the crane is dropped on top of her head and where she's running through the corridor with the foam cutting in at her. The Castaic electric power station was under construction at the time, and I saw a photo in the *L.A. Times* of a guy standing inside a huge pipe and I thought, 'Gee. That looks interesting.' So we went down there to shoot a number of scenes, including Lindsay climbing down into this huge concrete circular pit, which is where one of the turbines for the power station eventually went. I went back and shot that location again in the 'Prometheus' episode of *The Incredible Hulk* after it was completed. The central core of the complex that Lindsay drops into at the end was the Sylmar Power Switching Station, where there are gigantic circuit breakers that are like three stories high. We had to be very careful there because you can only go near those things when the power is off, because otherwise the electricity is so intense that it flies right out and electrocutes you. And the big steel door that opens at the end of 'Doomsday' to reveal the block of granite was an actual door that was there, and I thought, 'Oh Gosh, we gotta find a way to use *that*.' The exterior stuff was shot out in the West Valley. This is where she and Ken O'Brien were scaling the rocks. It was shot on the property of Rockwell's Rocketdyne Division. They had a big test facility out there. We also shot the blockhouses out there for the Arabic situation. The scene where the Arabic guy is rocking his child near the swings was shot in the front yard at Sylmar."

Episode 27: *Doomsday is Tomorrow (Part II)* .... [1-26-77]
Written and directed by Kenneth Johnson. See Part I for Cast Credits, plus Ned Wilson, George Whiteman, Stack Pierce, Steve Powers

In a battle royale, Jaime employs all her powers to gain access to Alex's central memory mechanism. But the heartless machine is programmed to protect itself, and impairs one of her super-powered legs. She trudges on against a security system created to terminate military assaults, and wins the computer's admiration. In the meantime, an aircraft is launched to obliterate Alex. Ironically, it's loaded with a type of phenomenally destructive apparatus that Dr. Cooper originally objected to.

• Ken Johnson: "There's a scene where this computer tries to suffocate Jaime by filling up a tunnel with foam (see Chapter 8). We got a big foam machine that the fire department used, and it was great. We sort of pieced it together with nickels and dimes, but the overall look of the episode — especially when we added Joe Harnell's music — was terrific."

• Johnson concedes being a tad disappointed when ABC submitted "Deadly Ringer" for Emmy consideration instead of "Doomsday." "Lindsay did a fine job in 'Deadly Ringer,'" he said. "When it comes to Emmy consideration, voters love to go for those big, obvious kinds of character displays such as playing two characters at once. Vincent Price once told me if you want to win an Academy Award, play a drunken nun. And I think that's true. Lindsay's work in 'Doomsday' I think is probably better in many ways, and not as melodramatic, but more real. There's a couple of extraordinarily powerful scenes, and I'm sorry that it didn't get more recognition than it did because it was quite a good show and still holds up remarkably well. That came out of Lindsay and I working together day in and day out to make the best drama we possibly could."

• Actor Guerin Barry supplied the creepily detached voice of Alex.

Episode 28: *Deadly Ringer (Part I)* . . . . [2-2-77]
Written by James D. Parriott. Directed by Alan Levi. Featuring: Don Porter, Warren Kemmerling, Katherine Helmond (Soap), *John Zenda*

Dr. James Courtney procures a medicinal specimen that he concludes to be at the core of Jaime's bionic abilities. He springs Lisa Galloway (Jaime's lookalike gone bad) from jail, and replaces The Bionic Woman. Lisa (as Jaime) travels to Ojai to acquire the formula (in order for it to be marketed to parties abroad). Meanwhile, Jaime tries to convince prison authorities that she's the real McCoy — before plans forge ahead to surgically reconstruct her face to match Lisa's original features.

• Early on, Jaime is seen in her carriage house, using embroidery, stitching the phrase, "To Your Own Self Be True"(from William Shakespeare's *Hamlet*). By the end, Lisa Galloway has the embroidery.

• The Lisa character and Dr. James Courtney initially appeared in the episode, "Mirror Image."

• Lindsay's sister, Randi Ball, appears in this episode as Jaime's student Karen Gilbert.

Episode 29: *Deadly Ringer (Part II)* .... [2-9-77]
Written by James D. Parriott. Directed by Alan Levi. Featuring: See Part I, plus Don (Red) Berry, Don Fenwick

Lisa is quite content with Jaime's identity, resolves to conserve the formula for herself, and decides to live indefinitely as The Bionic Woman. Meanwhile, Jaime sets herself free, but is being tracked by the police force and their specially-trained canines. She contacts Oscar, who doesn't believe she's the real Jaime. He tells the prison warden where she is. Soon ensnared at a railroad station, Jaime has only one chance, uses it, and prevails: She validates herself to Oscar with her bionic hearing. Yet Lisa is still impersonating her, and Dr. Courtney remains free.

• Lindsay won the Emmy for this episode.

• Jim Parriott: "This segment was, for me, my most rewarding work for the series."

• To this day, however, Parriott is miffed that Lindsay never thanked him for the teleplay. "Everyone was deeply offended," he said, "not just for me but because she didn't thank anyone else from the show. Everybody was going, 'Huh?' But again, Lindsay wasn't thrilled to be doing *The Bionic Woman.* That was her mind at the time. Even later, when she did the three bionic film reunions, she did them mainly as a favor to Richard Anderson, who was the producer."

• A minor glitch: When trapped at the railroad station, Jaime is seen making a phone call to Oscar, but there's a bloody scratch on her *right* hand, and we all know that can't be (because it's bionic).

• Another glitch: Jaime sinks waist deep in quicksand, soaking her prison-issued jeans. She recovers, fells a tree, precariously walks across it, jumps to the other side of the riverbank, and begins running. Her jeans? Clean as a whistle.

• Features an original song called "Time Changes."

Episode 30: *Jaime and the King* .... [2-23-77]
Written by Robert L. McCullough, C. Robert Brooks, Arthur Rowe. Directed by Alan Crosland, Jr. Featuring: Robert Loggia, Lance Kerwin (James at 15), *Joseph Ruskin, Tanya L. George, Brioni Farrell, Annette Cardona*

Shah Ali Ben Gazim conducts an oil appraisement meeting at his French dominion. Oscar believes an assault may be made on the leader's life. Jaime governs Gazim's son, Prince Ishmail, who views women as subordinate, honoring only vigor and might. The Shah's prime minister is at the center of the assassination attempt. Jaime may be declared a foreign informant. Ishmail observes her contacting the OSI.

• "I remember being absolutely mortified trying to do some of that belly dancing," said Lindsay. "Not exactly my style."

• Lance Kerwin: "Yeah, I played an Arabic prince who was a snob, had an attitude, and made his private teachers quit. He was too rough on them, but of course Lindsay was too tough to be forced around. That was a neat show; we had a lot of fun."

• Kerwin *(continued)*: "Lindsay Wagner was way cool! I went to go to work on the show the first day, but I was sick. I had a hundred and something temperature. They sent me home and said if you can be well by Monday, you'll still get the part. Otherwise, we're going to have to hire someone to replace you. So I went home and got on the garlic, man. I started rubbing on the garlic, trying to kick it and sure enough by Monday I was working on *The Bionic Woman* being kissed by Lindsay Wagner."

• Trivia: Filmed on location at the home of singer David Lee Roth's father.

• Rita Egleston did not double for Lindsay in the belly dancing or fencing scenes.

Episode 31: *Beyond the Call* . . . . **[3-9-77]**
Written by Daniel Kibbie, Arthur Rowe. Story by Daniel Kibbie. Directed by Alan Levi. Featuring: Sam Groom, Mariel Aragon, Sandy Ward, Madison Arnold, Ron McCabe

Oscar commissions Jaime to master the great outdoors with Major John Cross, a wilderness survivalist. The Major, a veteran of the Vietnam War, leaves his daughter Kim with Helen and Jim. Kim, however, begrudges her dad. The two have not truly communicated since the death of her mother (who was Vietnamese). Kim proves to be more than Jim and Helen can handle, and flees amid an imminent storm. Meanwhile, Jaime remains in the dark about the Major himself, and his plot to heist and market a missile guidance component.

• Lindsay said guest Mariel Aragon, who played Kim, "is a true, definable genius." "She entered high school at age 10. We've kind of lost contact over the years. But I know, that the last time we spoke, she was trying to get into UCLA, and she wanted to take Pre-med and Pre-law classes at the same time."

"Are you sure you want to do both at the same time," Lindsay asked.

"Oh, yes," Aragon replied. "It's very important these days, because so many people are being sued. Even though I want to be a doctor, if I'm a lawyer as well, and I come across a malpractice suit, I will be able to defend myself."

Lindsay was like, "Oh, okay. What a stupid question? Why would I even ask?"

• Aragon later appeared in the final BW episode "On the Run," as a completely different character.

• Marks the final series appearance of Martha Scott as Helen Elgin.

• Exterior "Ojai" scenes were filmed on the Universal lot.

• Original working title: "Kim."

Episode 32: *The DeJon Caper* . . . . **[3-16-77]**
Written by Arthur Rowe. Directed by Barry Crane. Featuring: Rene Auberjonois (Star Trek: Deep Space Nine, Benson), *Sydney Chaplin, Erik Holland, Roger Til, Bernard Behrens, Ben Wright, Maurice Marsac*

Artful dodger Pierre Lambert accompanies Jaime to Paris, and touches base with a merchant in stolen artwork named Beaumont, for whom he is to fabricate a canvas. Jaime is to seize the culprit when he substitutes the real painting for the fake one. Pierre imperils the assignment when he has Jaime taken into custody, and Beaumont determines her true identity.

• The facility used was a Catholic School, and Jaime went undercover as a prostitute. "Here I was,"Lindsay said, "embarrassingly out of context, with my fish-net stockings, hiked-up skirt, and bleached-blonde wig. It was intimidating for me. I'm so sensitive, that I even get upset if I find out I'm hurting someone else. So I put a robe on over my costume when I walked around the set."

• Guest Rene Auberjonois (Odo on *Star Trek: Deep Space Nine*) worked with Harve Bennett on *The Mod Squad*, playing a good twin/bad twin. "Rene can play anything," said Bennett, who caught a recent performance. "He's all actor, legs and arms, like Icabod Crane [penned by Washington Irving]. A phenomenal actor, and a very good friend."

• In France, *The Bionic Woman* was known as *Super Jaimie*. Six Mill was *L'Homme Qui Valait 3 Milliards.*

Episode 33: *The Night Demon* . . . . [3-23-77]
Written by Justin Edgerton. Directed by Alan Levi. Featuring: Jeff Corey, Howard McGillin, John Quade, Gary Lockwood, Jay Saunders

An Indian evil spirit starts to materialize following the discovery of Masauu, a cryptic sculpture. With the help of Thomas Bearclaw, Jaime views the incubus and goes after it. In the gloom of the night, she encounters Lyle Cannon, a rancher who's being scared into putting his property up for sale. Jaime soon learns, however, that Lyle is the responsible party who invented Masauu to shock intruders off his land.

• Lindsay "felt so stupid trying to pick up these foam-rubber rocks, trying to make them look heavy, and all the isometrics that go along with the special effects. The [F/X] guys could have at least made them a little heavy, so I wouldn't have had to work so hard." The crew was attempting the opposite. "Now I have to work harder," Lindsay joked. Though, she concludes, "It was a beautiful location. We shot out at a place called Bathescad Rocks."

• In the opening of this episode, we see Jaime listening to a "Big Buck Buckley" (Hoyt Axton) song on her car radio. The song originally surfaced in "Road to Nashville."

• Alternative working title (overseas): "Daemon Creature."

Episode 34: *Iron Ships and Dead Men*........................[3-30-77]
Written by James D. Parriott. Directed by Mel Damski. Featuring: Ray Young, Stephen Elliott, Edward Walsh, Theodore Wilson

Oscar's brother Sam vanished amid Japan's sneak attack on Pearl Harbor. He allegedly did so with $250,000, which he was to have transferred to a double agent aboard the *Henderson* (a destroyer). The navy has since insinuated that Sam lifted the loot. Now, his remains are found on the *Henderson*, which is being discarded. Jaime signs on as part of the extrication team. She comes upon an old bullet. Many of her shipmates conspire to eliminate her — and any chance of finding out what really happened to the money more than thirty years before.

• A touching episode, in which Oscar said goodbye to his brother at a long overdue funeral at sea.

• Oscar's age is clarified when he notes that he was just a boy in December 1941 (11, to be exact). But in *Bionic Showdown*, his date of birth is said to be March 25, 1927, which would have made him 14. Confusing the matter further is the SM segment, "Sharks!," where Oscar explained that he was part of an underwater demolitions crew in the Navy during this period.

• Oscar mentions that he was in Navy intelligence after WWII, but in real life, Richard Anderson served in the U.S. Army during the war. He also serves on the Board of Directors of Veterans Park — a hallowed ground of the Los Angeles National Cemetery.

• Trivia: Oscar's late brother's name is Sam.

• Jim Parriott recalls using stock footage of a Japanese Zero strafing the deck of a ship. The footage originally appeared in the 1970 film, *Tora! Tora! Tora!* Harve Bennett would end up borrowing the exact same footage for the 1979 TV version of *From Here to Eternity*. "It was in the Universal Stock Footage library and pretty easy to get," said Parriott. "Back then, action stock footage was fairly easy to buy from the studios. They had a loose exchange policy and the prices weren't too bad. Now — and I believe it's because big time feature directors got sick of seeing their footage on a TV show only a few years after the release of their movies — it's a much tighter situation. Thank God that CGI is becoming affordable."

• Parriott *(continued)*: "We shot our own footage and intercut the death scene where his brother gets gunned down. The planes come in and strike the battleship. ABC's then-broadcast-standards person, Mary Garber, was prim and proper. But she had a little ankle bracelet, which we all thought was a little kinky. She always gave us notes that we were too violent, which we weren't."

So tricks were played. During the first screening of this episode, subliminal cuts with blood were inserted during the attack scenes. She became pale and said, "Don't you think that was kind of bloody?"

"No, not really," Jim replied. "It must have been you're imagination."

She insisted, "No. No. No. I definitely saw blood."

"You want to look at the film again, just to make sure?" he asked.

"Oh, yes," she said. "I have to do that."

"Of course," Jim explained today, "we had the editors remove the cuts before she saw it again. When she looked at it a second time, in slow motion, there was nothing there. We got a good laugh out of that one. But we never told her."

• More backstage shenanigans: "Somehow," Lindsay said, "I got my hands on a squirt gun, and started squirting people on the crew when they weren't looking. This went on for weeks. Everyone was being zapped. No one could figure out where it was coming from. But there was this catwalk on the exterior of the ship we were using."

After a while, there were those who suspected that Lindsay was the responsible party, but no one could catch her in the act. At one point, she went up on the catwalk, while the crew remained on the dock. The wind was blowing just so. She found that if she shot at a particular angle, she could actually hit them "all the way down on the dock." They all kept looking up, as if to say, "Is it raining or what?"

Then someone figured out that it had to be Lindsay, because she was the only one not present on the dock. "Then they all tried to trap me," she said. "And this went on for months."

Later on in the series, someone got hold of a canister called a Hudson sprayer, which looked like an over-sized fire hydrant, about two-to-three feet tall, with a little hose. It was a contraption the special effects crew used to wet things down. "Eventually, I got hold of this thing," Lindsay said. "By that time, I was busted. The truth was, no one could get me back, because I was always in wardrobe for shooting. So they were really frustrated. Later, I opened this fire hose on one of the episodes we shot. I ripped around the corner, tugging and dragging this hose behind me."

She said, "I know I promised that I wouldn't use the Hudson sprayer, but…" and the room just cleared. "Everyone ran," she recalls. "By this time, they were all so paranoid that they thought for sure I was actually going to do it." She was like, "Geeze, guys. I don't even know how to turn this thing on."

Episode 35: *Once a Thief* . . . . [5-4-77]
Written by Kenneth Johnson. Directed by Alan Levi. Featuring: Elisha Cook, Ed Barth, Fuddle Bagley, Dick Balduzzi, Sonny Klein, Dick Bakalyan, Frank Cala, William Boyett

Jaime goes undercover as a bank robber in order to infiltrate and dissolve a massive crime ring. The situation seems simple enough until an amicable swindler named Inky bribes her into partaking in a theft. Unfortunately, he places both himself and Jaime in a jeopardous position.

• As a tribute to BW crew members, all the characters here carried either the first or last names of BW staffers. "That was my idea," said writer Kenneth Johnson. "I always tried to do that. And we had a great time on this episode because of it."

• The crew got their revenge on Lindsay at the wrap of this episode, when she was sprayed by a number of seltzer bottles.

• This story features a chimpanzee named Tumbellina.

• The bionic stunt where Jaime pulls the rug out form under Inky was to feature the stuntman doing a back flip, but Rita Egleston notes that they couldn't get the timing right.

• Ken Johnson: "As I recall, the original carriage house exterior was in Ojai — which is why you never saw much of it in the series. We couldn't afford to go running back up there [week to week]. I think we may have eventually built a small piece of it for a couple of shows."

"FEMBOTS IN LAS VEGAS, PART II," "RODEO" (W/ANDREW PRINE), "MOTORCYCLE BOOGIE" (W/EVEL KNIEVEL), "BRAIN WASH" (W/ JENNIFER DARLING), "ESCAPE TO LOVE" (W/MITCH LAURENCE), "ALL FOR ONE" (W/FRANKLYN AJAYE), "THE PYRAMID" (W/HENRY KINGI), "ON THE RUN"

The Third Season
1977 to 1978

Episode 36: *The Bionic Dog (Part I)* .... [9-10-77]
Written by James D. Parriott. Story by Harve Bennett, James D. Parriott.
Directed by Barry Crane. Featuring: Taylor Lacher, Carlene Watkins, Al Hansen,
David Himes

During a bionic physical at the OSI, Jaime learns about Maximillian, The Bionic Dog. Max, a German Shepherd, has become severely unpredictable. He may be rejecting his super-powered four legs and jaw. He's scheduled to be put down, and studied. But he's simply reacting to the six-year-old memory of the fire in which he nearly lost his life. If the dog *is* rejecting, Jaime fears that she may someday share his fate. She establishes a bond with Max, and takes the unique canine under her wing.

• The only time Steve's name was mentioned during the 1977-78 season (due to NBC's rivalry with ABC).

• Lindsay Wagner welcomed the 1977 summer hiatus, which gave her a chance to catch her breath: "I was very drained as far as input to the show. But I had a chance to go away and be Lindsay for awhile and when I do that, I seem to come up with a lot of ideas."

• As to why ABC canceled BW in the first place (when, for the '76-'77 season, it was in fourteenth place in the ratings), Jim Parriott said: "We were pulling a 30 share when ABC canceled us, but ratings don't reflect demographics. ABC felt that *The Bionic Woman* was slipping, and their researcher told them, 'Drop the show while it's still hot and get something else in there because *Bionic Woman* is gonna fail next season.' They may have been right, because we went over to NBC and only lasted a season."

• Wilton Denmark: "Fred Silverman had a great dislike for Lindsay and never wanted her for any series. That's why he canceled the show when he was with ABC and then canceled it again when he moved to NBC."

• On the appearance of Max, Parriott said: "NBC was looking for something strong to debut with. I think they were also looking for a franchise for another show. We almost saw *The Bionic Dog* as a series. So Max was meant to serve as a quasi-pilot."

• ABC initially tried to dissuade Richard Anderson from appearing on a rival network, noting that he was contractually obligated to them and them alone. Bad feelings were assuaged, however, when NBC secretly agreed to shift some projects to ABC as compensation — a fact unknown to Anderson until many years later.

• The building that purported to be Rudy's West Coast lab (perched on a hill) actually resides on the CalArts campus in Santa Clarita, California — 30 miles north of Los Angeles.

• Ford Rainey makes his final appearance in the series.

Episode 37: *The Bionic Dog (Part II)* . . . . [9-17-77]
Written by James D. Parriott. Story by Harve Bennett, James D. Parriott.
Directed by Barry Crane. Featuring: Dale Robinette, Lee Jones-DeBroux, Jack
Garner, Will Hare, Jason Johnson, Al Hansen

Jaime and Max are evading the authorities. In the wilderness, she meets
up with forest ranger Roger Grette, an ex-love who offers loyal refuge. A fire
in the trees ignites, and Max runs away in a frightened frenzy. Mistaking
him for a wolf, a rancher shoots Max in his bionic jaw, which sparks a forest fire. Delirious with pain, he flashes-back to six years before, and charges
Jaime. The Bionic Woman has to tend to the dog's wounds, battle a raging
inferno, and escort Roger to safer ground.

• Roger Grette is clearly still smitten with Jaime, as evidenced by the
high-schoolish doodles of heart images he scribbles around her name on
the APB.

• Ken Johnson: "The story had Max and Jaime trapped in a forest fire.
So I went to the stock footage library and raided an old Irwin Allen movie
called *Fire*. It was about a town caught in the middle of a horrific fire. There
was a great sequence of a train moving through the fire. I said, 'This is great.
We'll write our story so that Jaime travels on a train.' But the only train
Universal had was the one on the Universal Tour. Worse, it only had about
30 feet of track. So we put Lindsay on the train, and shot 12 different angles
of this train going its 30 feet. At one point, we had the train stand still and
we gave it the illusion of movement by having a half-dozen extras run beside
it, holding up burning branches. With the smoke blowing past the train, it
made it look like it was really moving past a burning forest."

• Ken Johnson on Max: "I felt that it sounded a little *jakey*. What was
next? Bionic butterflies? Although, Jim Parriott's notion that the bionic dog
had preceded bionic people, and was the test animal, was really kind of
interesting."

• Harve Bennett: "The series got a reprieve by moving to NBC. But
in moving to NBC, we lost the crossover appearances of Steve Austin on
Bionic Woman. We could only do this while both shows were on ABC. So
we couldn't perk up the shows that way. We also lost the potential that Steve
and Jaime might restart their love affair."

• Even if Max *had* landed his own series, it's doubtful his creators would
have netted a financial windfall. Jim Parriott: "In the third season of BW,
Harve came to me and said that we should create a bionic dog. He and I
came up with the idea of a German Shepherd named Max who was injured
in a fire. I wrote the script — we shot it — then Harve and I were surprised

to learn that Universal was not going to pay character payments for our creation [Max]. We appealed to the Writer's Guild, as we believed we had created a unique character [a bionic dog] and received a hearing. The Universal
lawyers showed up and produced — to our great astonishment — a book
written by a British [I think] woman several years earlier. In it, there was a
German Shepherd named Maximillian who was injured in a fire and reconstructed bionically. I kid you not. They produced the manuscript. Amazing
and humiliating — but neither one of us had ever heard of the book."

Episode 38: *Fembots in Las Vegas (Part I)* . . . . **[9-24-77]**
*Written by Arthur Rowe. Directed by Michael Preece. Featuring: James Olson,
Michael Burns, Melinda Fee, Jeannie Wilson, Nancy Bleier, Lorna Sands, Lisa
Moore, Alexander Courtney*

   Carl Franklin, the son of a deranged scientist, reactivates his father's army
of feminine robots to capture America's first directed-energy ray weapon.
While Oscar confronts Rod Kyler, inventor of the energy weapon, Jaime
discovers that Kyler's "girlfriend," Tami, is a fembot. Kyler, a virtual prisoner
in his Las Vegas penthouse and the potential victim of a fatal disease, refuses
to divulge information about the weapon to Oscar and Jaime. Suddenly,
an army of fembots, under the direction of Franklin, assaults Kyler's penthouse, renders Oscar unconscious, and battles Jaime to gain possession of
the energy ray.
   • This, along with Part II, is *not*, as Lindsay said, "one of my favorites."
Martin Caidin agreed, believing by this time that the fembot plotlines had
gotten a little out of hand. "They didn't need that shit. To me, those robots
were idiotic. Science has not yet been able to do it. So why go to something
that's only going to be a hunk of tin."
   • The helicopter incident transpired here (when Lindsay jumped, holding her nose). The noise from the helicopter was so loud, Lindsay had to
later dub her dialogue.
   • Continuity error: Robotic Callahan is seen wearing a scarf before
applying her facemask. With the face securely in place, the scarf is suddenly
missing.
   • "Fembots in Las Vegas" was filmed at Space Launch Center 6 at
Vandenberg Air Force Base in California, making *The Bionic Woman* the first
television series ever permitted to film at the missile launching site. Other
locations included the Dunes Hotel in Las Vegas.

Episode 39: *Fembots in Las Vegas (Part II)* . . . . [10-1-77]
Written by Arthur Rowe. Directed by Michael Preece. See Cast Credits for Part I, plus Paul Tinder, Ted Schliesman

Carl Franklin and his fembots take over Vandenberg Air Force Base and launch the weapon into Earth orbit. Seeking revenge for the death of his father, Franklin notifies Washington that he wants Jaime, Oscar, and Rudy — the three people he holds responsible for his father's demise. Held captive by Franklin at an abandoned missile site, Jaime must overcome the deadly fembots and prevent Franklin from using the weapon.
• Actor Michael Burns (Carl Franklin) is now an Emeritus Professor of History at Mount Holyoke College in Massachusetts.
• A hotel fire forced the cast and crew to evacuate.
• Henry Kingi (Lindsay's third husband) became the show's stunt coordinator after this story. Tony Brubaker directed the stunts on this episode.
• Some of the "Doomsday is Tomorrow" set pieces were recycled for this episode.
• Jaime jumps down (as she is fighting with the three fembots) over a fence, and we see it's stuntwoman Rita Egleston.

Episode 40: *Rodeo* . . . . [10-15-77]
Written by Herman Groves. Story by Kenneth Johnson. Directed by Larry Stewart. Featuring: Andrew Prine, Jason Evers, Thomas Bellin, Don Gentry, John Crawford

Dr. Billy Cole, a scientist, has grown weary of his work with the OSI, and opts to pursue his fantasy as rodeo master. Oscar is somewhat concerned. Cole is the sole link to the Minerva Code (an indispensable component to America's safety). Oscar's anxiety is well warranted, especially since East German operatives scheme to abduct Cole during a rodeo.
• Lindsay rode Scooter Dolly, whose owner was a rodeo barrel racer. "The horse was magnificent," she explained. "All I had to do was give a *click* sound, and Scooter would take off. She made me look so good, that I bought her. Everyone was like, 'Boy, you ride well.' Anyone would have looked good on her."
Yet at one point, Scooter failed to get up to enough speed. Her trainer said she was bored. "Well, so am I," Lindsay remarked. "What do I do?"
"Change your click sound," he replied.
She did so, and Scooter sped off. "It took very little to restimulate this horse," she said.
• Director Larry Stewart: "Lindsay worked hard and had a great sense of humor, but she didn't enjoy being the 9,000-pound gorilla. She wanted

to play it more feminine. In one show I directed, she had to chase bad guys at a rodeo. Lindsay got pissed off with the story and walked out. The producer, Arthur Rowe, said to me, 'Boy, she really hates this script.' I said, 'Let me kick it around,' because I'm also a writer. I rewrote it as a love story set in a rodeo."

• Guest Andrew Prine is Lindsay's friend, whom she met, modeling at age 12 (for *16 Magazine*) and, years later, through a friend. Prine is known for dramatic work. "People don't think he has a sense of humor," Lindsay said. "But he's a very funny person, with a great laugh."

• Another instance when Jaime uses her *left* arm and we hear the bionic sound.

• Original working title: "Jaime, Queen of the Rodeo."

• Legendary pilot Art Scholl performed the aerial stunts in this episode.

Episode 41: *African Connection* . . . . **[10-29-77]**
Written by William Schwartz. Directed by Alan Levi. Featuring: Dan O'Herlihy (The Life and Times of Grizzly Adams, A Man Called Sloan), Raymond St. Jacques, Don Pedro Colley, Joan Pringle, Kipp Whitman

The Bionic Woman travels to Africa and meets up with boozy Harry Walker, and tries to hinder the criminal efforts of Azzar, a baron who's fixing free elections. The mogul is holed up in a massively-secured complex, and possesses a computer part which will somehow declare him a sanctioned victor. Jaime and Harry are apprehended by Azzar's adversaries, who discover that she bears a substitute computer component. Is Agent Sommers Azzar's partner-in-crime?

• In the midst of this mayhem, Jaime runs into an old college classmate and recognizes her instantly, yet never remembers being smitten with Steve.

• Ken Johnson: "I left early in the final season of *BW*. Lindsay had had a lot of [personal] problems and had gotten very difficult to deal with, so I asked off of the show. One day I fired someone she was particularly fond of, and she decided that she wouldn't come out of her trailer until I was no longer the producer, and I said, 'That's great. I'm out of here.'"

Episode 42: *Motorcycle Boogie* .... **[11-5-77]**
Written by James D. Parriott, Kenneth Johnson. Directed by Ken Gilbert.
Featuring: Evel Knievel, Bernard Behrens, Spencer Milligan, Chris Anders,
Erik Holland

Jaime journeys to West Germany to collect a stolen computer tape. She
secures the involuntary assistance of a man on a motorcycle who is allegedly the famous Evel Knievel. After ending up in East Germany, the mismatched duo at long last attain the reel. One major hurdle: a quantum leap
across a cement canal is the only passage back to West Germany.

• "What *didn't* happen in this episode," Lindsay said. "Evel Knievel
hated my guts. Apparently, women don't talk back to him, and I did." The
segment took 14 days to shoot (most episodes were shot in seven), because,
"He threw a tantrum and stayed in his room for a week."

For one scene, in Franklin Canyon, all Lindsay had to do was sit on the
back of his motorcycle. He was to roll in, have Lindsay get off the bike, and
do some dialogue. During rehearsal, "He just took off with me on the back
of the bike and we flew up the canyon," she recalls. "I was screaming and
pounding on his back for him to stop. I was scared. But he just kept laughing out loud. We went all the way up the canyon and all the way back. I was
so horrified when I got back off the motorcycle, that I made this face. My
assistant was with me that day, and she happened to have her camera. She
snapped a picture the minute I got off the cycle. If you see it, you'll notice
that he's totally bombed, and I'm scared to death. I laugh about it now, but
I wasn't then."

• Jim Parriott: "Well, I'll yield to Lindsay and how she wants to portray events. But, I can assure you, it was Lindsay who was not showing up
on set. Evel may have been crazy and acting petty once the show started
shooting — but he was pissed at her for making him wait and thought he'd
make her do a little waiting as payback. I'm not, however, saying that Evel
didn't have plenty of loose screws."

• Evel Knievel was a hot property at the time, and was paid $50,000 to
guest on the episode. "For those days, that was an outrageous amount of
money," said Parriott.

• Jim and Ken Johnson wrote this episode in three days. Parriott reminisces: "Every night I'd have to go over to the Sheraton and hold Evel's
hand. He took over the bar. He would sit there, and have all these people
come up to him, and pay him homage. He was like The Godfather. So I
would be sitting at his table, and he would order Wild Turkey and Heineken
beer. He'd take a sip, throw the rest on the carpet when no one was looking,
and put the empty glass on the table. The carpet was drenched with Wild
Turkey. I think we did that for about four days in a row."

• Ken Johnson: "This was done around the time Evel Knievel was working on a stunt to bail out of a plane without a parachute and land in a bale of hay in the middle of a stadium. Evel was amazing, but he was a banana! He invited [the *Bionic Woman* producers] to dinner, but we ended up paying. He would say to the waiter, 'Bring me a bottle of Rothschilds!' So they brought him this 100-dollar bottle of wine. He autographed it and gave it to me. 'Here you go, Kenny! It's from me to you, pal. My pal, Kenny!' Who do you think ended up paying for the wine?"

• In Germany, *The Bionic Woman* was *Die Sieben Millionen Dollar Frau. Six Mill* was *Der Sechs Millionen Dollar Mann.*

• Evel's character was originally named Chuck Davis.

Episode 43: *Brain Wash.* . . . . **[11-12-77]**
Written by James D. Parriott. Directed by Michael Preece. Featuring: Michael Callan, Sam Chew, Jr., David Watson, Pepe Hern

Callahan's in love with John Bernard, a hair-stylist whose talents reach beyond the average cosmetic techniques of his boutique. He's proficient in persuading his clientele into divulging classified facts from the OSI. Jaime detects that Callahan is disclosing professional secrets that she would otherwise not do. She investigates by making an appointment with Bernard. The outcome: Oscar's life is threatened, and something is definitely amiss.

• Guest Michael Callan introduced Lindsay to Andrew Prine.

• This episode was based on a leading German spy family, "who was around just prior to the attack on Pearl Harbor," said Jim Parriott. "They ran a beauty salon for the officers' wives, and they basically *bugged* the salon, in order to hear what the women had to say, while under their hair dryers. It's how they found out about troop movements."

• This is the only time that certain characters were implied to be gay on *The Bionic Woman.*

Episode 44: *Escape to Love* . . . . **[11-26-77]**
Written by Ellen Wittman, Lionel E. Siegel. Directed by Alan Levi. Featuring: Philip Abbott, Mitch Laurence, Peter Mark Richman, John Reilly, Michael Richardson, Ed Sancho-Bonet

Jaime attempts to free Dr. Arlo Kelso and son, who falls in love with her, from behind the Iron Curtain. The boy becomes frightened, and must be left behind. When certain of his father's security, Jaime retrieves him. Dr. Kelso must abandon his escape, or die.

• This remake of the SM's "Divided Loyalty" (with an added prepubescent crush) had two previous titles: "A Matter of Love or Death" and "First Love."

• Jaime frequently penetrated hostile territory to retrieve people or information, but did you know she almost tracked down a famous female aviator? *Six* writer Judy Burns explained: "I came up with a story about Amelia Earhart, where Jaime was sent to find Amelia, much like Steve had gone to find a bomb but found Kuroda instead," she said. "In my story, she went to find Amelia after rumors came out that she was alive, still captive on an island. We went through story, and I was paid for it, but it just didn't take off."

• Lionel Siegel, who co-wrote this episode, recalls a night he'd like to forget: "When it was decided that I would executive produce the *Bionic Woman* series, I had dinner with Lindsay Wagner [and her boyfriend, Michael Brandon]. I drank too much and accepted their invitation to follow them home. I ended up on their bathroom floor, practically unable to move, and I slept there. I left them a note early in the morning before I left. That was my first day on the job with Lindsay."

• The Windsor Castle set on the Universal lot was used for the prison scenes. Stuntwoman Rita Egleston did not possess the upper body strength needed to scale a rope, so she was filmed scaling down backwards. The film was then reversed to create the illusion of her climbing up.

• As in other episodes, Jaime's *left* arm is seen performing some bionic feats.

Episode 45: *Max* . . . . **[12-3-77]**
Written by William Schwartz. Story by William Schwartz, Lionel E. Siegel. Directed by Don McDougall. Featuring: Neile Adams-McQueen, Christopher Knight (The Brady Bunch), Sam Chew, Jr., Bill Fletcher, Rudy Solari (Garrison's Gorillas), Sandy Kenyon

When Jaime Sommers enters the hospital to undergo a thorough bionic exam, an OSI scientist, whose nephew thinks the dog is cool, supervises Max. The young man takes Max for a stroll, only to have him abducted. Yet Max makes his capture difficult. So the professor is kidnapped and forced to expose the hidden truth about The Bionic Dog. If not, Bobby will be no more.

• Christopher Knight's portrayal of Bobby was one of his few post-*Brady* TV appearances in the late 1970s in this episode that was a potential spin-off vehicle.

• *Daily Variety:* "None of the cast were required to extend themselves too much, including Max — whose talents seem restricted to barking, running [in slow motion] and tugging on ropes. Even the target audience of moppets must have found Max's adventures rather tame."

• In one blooper reel from the show's archives, Jaime is hospitalized, and hooked up to an IV. "There's a shot of my face," recalls Lindsay, "that trails down to my arm to the IV, and then up the cord to the IV bottle. Instead of the IV bottle, we placed a can of Union Oil there."

Episode 46: *Over the Hill Spy*: . . . . **[12-17-77]**
Written by Joe Viola. Directed by Ken Gilbert. Featuring: Richard Erdman, Michael Thoma, Jeff David, Felice Orlandi, Rick Beckner, Whit Bissell (The Time Tunnel), *Alana Collins*

Former operative Terrence Quinn investigates a seemingly proficient master of disguise (with whom he once came to blows). Disgruntled because he was coerced into leaving his job, the mighty Quinn makes extensive contract demands. Oscar concedes, but Jaime must accompany him. All's calm, until Quinn lays Jaime unconscious, and goes solo.
  • "Those two guys who played the over-the-hill spies were so cute," said Lindsay. She also recalls shooting in the Pasadena Gardens. "It was gorgeous."

Episode 47: *All for One* . . . . **[1-7-78]**
Written by James D. Parriott. Directed by Larry Stewart. Featuring: Franklyn Ajaye, Roger Perry, Viola Kates Stimpson, Garret Pearson, Gary Barton, Henry Kingi, Joe Al Nicassio

Jaime goes back to college to uncover a computer criminal who's netting $25,000 a night from disparate banking customers. She locates the *accountable* party, and is shocked. He's not who she thought he would be. Someone else is involved.
  • Henry Kingi, BW stuntman who later married Lindsay (1981), plays a bandit in this episode, which was shot at Northridge College. In one scene with Henry and Lindsay, a food catering truck was to explode, via an FX bomb. "We were supposed to run out," Lindsay recalls, "go in this ditch, and with the truck burning in the background, we were supposed to do our dialogue. It was a little nerve-racking, and it was also a scene that ordinarily, the stunt people would have done."
  Though she trusted Henry's judgment for the scene. "He was very meticulous about safety. So we went ahead and did it." Five of the bombs were to be set off consecutively, but only four of them detonated, while they were running. "Then I started the dialogue," Lindsay said, "and the fifth one went off."
  • Director Larry Stewart: "*The Bionic Woman* was a fine series. It was action-adventure-myth, and it humanized its premise to a great degree. It

worked out well. Nobody has anything to be ashamed of with that show."

• Larry Stewart (continued): "At the time, I was president of the Academy of Arts and Sciences. Lindsay won the Emmy as best actress in 1976-1977. My job as Academy president was to be backstage as the winners came off the stage. I'd take their Emmy to have it engraved for them. Lindsay and I hadn't met before, and she didn't know that the next day I was scheduled to direct a *Bionic Woman*. So when she came off the stage with her Emmy, I congratulate her and took the statue, promising it would be back to her in a few days. She said okay and started walking away. I yelled, 'Oh, and I'll see you tomorrow at five a.m.!' She turned around with a bewildered look of, 'What does that mean?' So the next morning, as she came out of her dressing room, the producer introduced us. 'Lindsay, meet your director.' She looked at me and said, 'Oh my God. It's you.' We got a good laugh out of that. Two days later, we were filming on the lawn of a local college in front of all these college students. Lindsay's doing a scene where she's picking up some books. I had her engraved Emmy, and with the cameras rolling, I snuck up to her and said, 'Lindsay?' She turned around. I said, 'I thought I'd give this to you in person.' I handed her the Emmy in front of 1,500 students. She was extremely pleased. It was a very satisfying moment."

Episode 48: *The Pyramid* . . . . [1-14-78]
Written by Margaret Armen (Star Trek), *Alf Harris, Arthur Rowe, Lionel E. Siegel. Story by Margaret Armen, Alf Harris. Directed by Barry Crane. Featuring: Eduard Franz, Gavan O'Herlihy, June Barrett, Henry Kingi*

While investigating a strange signal, Jaime and Chris get snared in a pyramid with a newly-roused extraterrestrial. The alien acts as the structure's protector. His race will shortly settle on Earth, but an atmospheric imbalance will cause their ship to explode. So the alien's race will annihilate Earth. Jaime, with Chris incapacitated, has her hands full. She must rescue her platonic boyfriend, somehow contact the foreign planeteers, and keep Earth in one piece.

• An outtake was filmed in the days of wrap-around skirts. "The skirt I was wearing was made of a real silky material," Lindsay recalls, "and it slipped right off my body. It was hard to keep a bow tied, because of the silky material. Usually, when I would do a landing, I did so with my legs bent, and then stood up. This time, I stood up and the skirt just kept on going."

• It was frigid during filming: "We shot a lot of it at night," said Lindsay. "Poor Henry, who was running around in this loin cloth, was freezing."

• Margaret Armen: "The interesting thing in writing for a female lead was that you could use her feminine reactions. In this episode, we could show a growing attraction between Jaime and the alien. At first, I was not impressed by the *Bionic Woman* series and I didn't care for Lindsay Wagner's acting, but I got to like her work."

• Jim Parriott: "I don't know if anyone has sung Henry's praises, but I'm singing them now. Wonderful man. Calm, strong, stabilizing. Lindsay got the right guy and turned back into the incredible woman she is to this day."

• With regards to the bionic-arm-switch incongruity that periodically graced the segments of both *Man* and *Woman*: Here, Jaime hoists an enormous boulder. She places her right hand below the rock, to sustain its heavy mass. Yet she's holding it at its outmost parameter, as opposed to its median mark, and she places her left hand on top, to assist with the leverage, as she raises the stone. By not elevating the rock from the middle, it will loosen and descend out of her right hand (so her left hand must remain above). Is this plausible, minus the super powers of her left hand?

Episode 49: *The Antidote* . . . .[1-21-78]
Written by Arthur Rowe, Tom and Helen August. Story by Dan Ullman. Directed by Don McDougall. Featuring: Linda Wiser, John Myhers, Brett Halsey, John Milford, Suzanne Charny, James Blendick, Jennifer Darling, Christopher Stone

Rudy holidays in an isolated area. Jaime and Dmitiri Zhukov, a diplomat from the USSR, are poisoned. Those responsible are anticipating Oscar's arrival in order to assassinate him. Jaime struggles for her life. Chris and Max attempt to find Rudy. Zhukov does not survive, and a crooked hospital nurse schemes to make certain that Jaime meets the same fate.

• Lindsay Wagner, on the emergence of the Chris Williams character: "[On ABC], Jaime Sommers took care of a lot of kids and busted a lot of people, but she didn't really get involved with anybody. She wasn't much of a human being. They were afraid to let her have a lover of any kind or an intimate friend because they were trying to keep her relationship with Steve Austin going as the main source of her inspiration. However, that was only a couple of times out of a year, which made her relationships pretty shallow. That's an area [I tried] to work on … to show more of Jaime to the audience, more of what she thinks about, what she does, who she is, what it's like to be a bionic woman. In the beginning of the series, they did that for about three shows and that was it. All of a sudden, it was 'Well, I'm adjusted, and I'm bionic, and I can handle anything now.' It just didn't make sense to me. Jaime had a good life, but it's an adjustment to have artificial limbs. How does she handle that? My argument was that as long as she's running and jumping, why can't they show her other sides as well?"

Episode 50: *The Martians Are Coming, The Martians Are Coming* . . . [1-28-78]
Written by Robert A. Urso, Tom and Helen August. Story by Robert A. Urso.
Directed by Larry Stewart. Featuring: Jack Kelly (Get Christie Love!), *Frank*
Aletter, Frank Marth, James McMullan, Lynn Carlin, Amanda Davies

Rudy goes fishing, but not really. He's experimenting with a way to locate and track alien spacecraft. He's beamed aboard an alien ship hovering above the pier. Oscar witnessed the entire incredible sight. Jaime's the only one who can locate her Dr. Wells, and decipher how he disappeared.

• Of guest Jack Kelly (who has since passed away) and Lynn Carlin, Marty Brooks said: "They were wonderful to work with. I remember, for one scene, we were all locked in this one room. There were bouts with claustrophobia, and someone was allergic to aluminum. We couldn't stop with the jokes. We were all going a little bonkers. But the final product was excellent."

• The UFO in question turns out to be an ordinary helicopter with a cloaking device (displayed with special effects as a red blob).

• Jaime expresses shock that a UFO was spotted off the coast, but should she be all that surprised? After all, she had run-ins with otherworldly types in "The Return of Bigfoot" and "The Pyramid."

• This episode was typical of the Irwin Allen-type storylines that beset the third season, a development that displeased Ken Johnson: "After I left *The Bionic Woman*, the rules got lax. From what I heard, the shows had gotten pretty goofy and Lindsay by that point was really trying to exert her influence on it and do a lot of spacey, weird things. It got too far out to understand or care about. While I was running the show, I wrote the episodes into Lindsay's strongest suits and also we were very intent on keeping a reality base and a humor base. I think it began to get very earnest after I left."

• Jim Parriott is of like mind: "Part of all this was the desperation to get a good number and keep the show alive. The other part was that Ken and Harve were gone and the show lacked their creative direction. Oddly, at least to me, I was just working with a guy who watched BW when he was a kid. Favorite episode? Fembots. Go figure."

Episode 51: *Sanctuary Earth* . . . . [2-11-78]
Written by Rudolph Borchert. Directed by Ernest Pintoff. Featuring: Helen Hunt
(Mad About You), *Jim Hager, Jon Hager, David Matthau*

Jaime meets Aura, a young alien girl who said she's the daughter of a distant planet's leader. Apparently, her mission on Earth is somehow related to stopping a battle on her home world. Jaime doesn't accept what Aura is telling her. Yet, will alien bounty hunters abduct the young girl? One peculiar incident takes place after another, and The Bionic Woman has little choice but to consider celestial possibilities.

• Lindsay had not seen guest Helen *Mad About You* Hunt since this episode was filmed. Then she went to the Golden Globe Awards as a presenter. Hunt was seated at her table. "It was such an odd feeling," Lindsay recalls. "Here she was, this full-grown person. I was having trouble computing the experience."

"You were just so nice to me," Lindsay remembers Hunt telling her. "You made it so easy."

"It was like she almost became a little girl again talking about it," Lindsay said today. Then, "Helen had some tough scenes. She had to come out of this nasty water. She was a real good sport."

• Hunt's first name on *Mad About You* is Jamie (spelled differently than Lindsay's Jaime), and at one point changed the color of her hair from blonde to red, as did Lindsay.

• On the NBC show *Later* with Bob Costas, Helen Hunt confessed that if she could burn one piece of film from her career, this episode would be it.

Episode 52: *Deadly Music* . . . .**[2-18-78]**
Written by Conner Everts, Lionel E. Siegel. Directed by Thomas Connors. Featuring: Frank Converse, Henry Darrow, Robert Ellenstein, Roger Cruz, Chip Lucia, Greg Barnett, Darrow Igus, James Crittenden

Agent Sommers scuba-dives to investigate adverse parties vandalizing experiments with a submarine detection mechanism. The criminals soon catch on to Jaime's assignment, and attach her to an apparatus that entices deadly bionic-woman-eating sharks.

• Lindsay did all her close-ups in a water tank. "Everything else," she said, "was done with stunt-doubles. I never used scuba gear before, and I was supposed to look like I knew what I was doing."

Various experts would periodically tutor Lindsay on whatever it was that Jaime was supposed to do (i.e., belly dance in "Jaime and the King"). "This time," she said, "I didn't get any help. I was just told not to breathe too fast, or I would hyperventilate."

• *BW* unit production manager Ralph Sariego: "Universal promised Fred Silverman [head of NBC programming] a show where Jaime would fight sharks. I spent two months reading books on sharks and looking at shark footage from all over the world. We shot the episode off the coast of California. We used real sharks — a 12-foot and 9-foot nurse shark — and had a double for Lindsay. Every morning we put ropes on the tails of the sharks and filmed their run-bys. On the last day of filming, the sharks were so tired that we took the ropes off them. It was a great adventure for one episode."

Episode 53: *Which One is Jaime?* .... **[2-25-78]**
Written by Jim Carlson, Terrence McDonnell. Story by Martha Humphreys, Ted Pedersen. Directed by Jack Arnold. Featuring: Sam Chew, Jr., Brock Peters, Regis J. Cordic, James B. Sikking (Hill Street Blues, Doogie Howser, M.D.), *Robert Feero, Adrien Royce, Marcus Mukai*

Jaime's in danger and she's put into the safeguarded care of the OSI. Callahan stays at Jaime's home to watch over Maximillian, and is abducted. She's thought to be The Bionic Woman. The culprits comprehend their error, and position her as bait to reel in Jaime.

• Jaime disarms a sniper by tossing upwards a teddy bear approximately 200 yards, hitting him square in the torso.

• According to her driver's license, Callahan lives at 232 Landeraft Street, Washington, D.C.

• The sole episode where Sam Chew, Jr. (Mark Russell) gets credited during the opening credits.

• Filmed on location at Six Flags Magic Mountain in Valencia, California.

Episode 54: *Out of Body* .... **[3-4-78]**
Written by Steven de Souza. Story by Steven de Souza, Deborah Blum. Directed by Ernest Pintoff. Featuring: Charlie Hill, Nehemiah Persoff, Philip Jennings, Richard Lynch (The Phoenix, Galactica 1980), *Antony Ponzini, Allan Magicovsky*

Philip Jennings, a scientist, is determined to filch his own invention: an eminently lethal explosive. Tommy Littlehorse (his virtuous aide) is inadvertently shocked with electricity. Jaime attempts to retrieve Jennings' creation. The evil professor apprehends her and attaches her to the combustible device. Littlehorse (who has blacked-out) is having astral experiences, and his conscious soul is attempting to rescue Jaime.

• "This was one of the episodes that was very special to me," said Lindsay, who calls guest actor Charlie Hill, "an incredible person." After the series ended, she accompanied the actor to a Pow-Wow, in Colorado, which began her involvement with the Native-American community, in which, over the years, she has "become more and more active."

Yet, when she first read the script for this episode, she said, "Oh, yeah. We were able to embody some of the concepts that, to me, are very real."

Episode 55: *Long Live the King*. . . . . **[3-25-78]**
Written by Mel Goldberg, David Ketchum, Anthony DiMarco, Tom and Helen August. Directed by Gwen Arner. Featuring: Carmen Argenziano, John Reilly, Charles M. Cioffi, Rene Assa, Dov Gottesfeld, Brian Burgess, Elise Cattlin, Rachel Bard

Oscar visits New York City, and learns of a scheme to assassinate King Kusari, of the Middle East. Jaime is assigned as the leader's social secretary and bodyguard. Those who plan to kill Kusari are fellow countrymen, and know of Jaime's true identity. So she's added to their list of those scheduled to die.
• Jaime and Sam Sloan (John Reilly) are seen in an eatery, the exterior of which is the same employed for Monk's Coffee Shop on *Seinfeld*.

Episode 56: *Rancho Outcast* . . . . **[5-6-78]**
Written by Arthur Rowe. Directed by Ivan Dixon. Featuring: Donald Calfa, Keenan Wynn, Diane Civita, Dave Cass, George Cheung, Henry Kingi, Robert Easton

Jaime travels to a complex in Central America where wicked types are shielded from the authorities. Petie *The Weasel* Regan is promised exoneration on one condition: He must act as Jaime's guide, and assist in finding missing currency plates, as well as the cutthroat individual who pilfered them. The Weasel lives up to his name, ditches Jaime, leaving her to engage in a super-powered Flamingo dance to cloak her identity and guard her life.
• "So here I was flamingo dancing," Lindsay explained. "I had two days to learn how to at least look like I knew what I was doing." The same dancer who doubled for her in "Jaime and the King," did so here.
• She said there was "a big flood going down the street, with animals running all over the place. But it was fun because we were doing so much of the espionage, high-tech stuff." "It was a very active episode," she attests.
• The aforementioned flood scene was filmed on the Universal Studios backlot and is a regular tour attraction.

Episode 57: *On the Run* . . . . [5-13-78]
Written by Steven de Souza. Directed by Tom Blank. Featuring: Linda Wiser, Andrew Duggan, Skip Homeier, Juno Dawson, Kenneth O'Brien, Mariel Aragon, Johnny Timko, Bob Benedetti, Hannah Dean

Jaime Sommers, ex-tennis pro, ex-love to Steve Austin, OSI agent/ teacher/Bionic Woman, is worn out, tired, drained and uncertain of where her life is going. So she leaves the OSI. Not an easy decision. Both she and Oscar have mixed feelings about it. Nonetheless, she goes ahead with her plans. Oscar pays a personal visit to Ojai. He explained how the government fears Jaime's new life as a private citizen may lead to danger. She may be abducted and dismembered by disputant agents. He warns her that she is about to be transferred to a secluded complex where special operatives and scientists abide in safety. She's to stay there in commodious, though prison-like, conditions for the entirety of her existence. Jaime freaks out, pulls herself together, and then hits the road, leaving Max in Oscar's care. A massive manhunt ensues.

• The first and only time that Oscar tells Jaime, "I love you."
• Original working titles: "Together Again" and "The Last Mission?"
• Kenneth O'Brien, who played Jaime's adversary-turned-friend in "Doomsday is Tomorrow," has a small role here as a traveling salesman.
• Linda Wiser, who portrayed Sarah during the last season of *The Bionic Woman*, was a very close longtime friend of Lindsay's. Linda was Lindsay's personal assistant during *The Bionic Woman* and she also took many candid photos of her on the set. Wiser expired on March 7, 1984, after a courageous battle with cancer. (Seven years earlier, Lindsay made a point of thanking her in her Emmy acceptance speech.)
• Writer Steven de Souza: "Lindsay told me over lunch, 'I feel Jaime Sommers has never been comfortable as a tool of the government. She's basically a peace-loving person, and she's only doing it because she's grateful the OSI saved her life. What would happen if they called her one evening and told her she had to be airborne to Russia that night...and she doesn't want to do it anymore?' So I wrote a story that really brought that to the fore." In the end, Wagner and Sommers were virtually indistinguishable. "Lindsay, who was tired of doing a network show, played Jaime Sommers, who was tired of being a spy."
• Lionel Siegel: "The series benefited from Lindsay's warmth, charm, intelligence and sincerity."
• Harve Bennett: "The series had gotten more expensive every year because it took longer to shoot. For that reason, Universal was less anxious to continue it than *The Six Million Dollar Man*."
• Lindsay Wagner: "This was my story about how I was feeling about the

series," she concludes. "The episode starts out in a zoo, which is kind of a metaphor for the type of retirement they had in mind for Jaime. What follows is an intensely human look at the character — her hopes, her dreams, and her doubts about what she's become. I was very much involved with the creation of the story, which was pretty much a metaphor for what I was going through in real life. In reference to the series, we didn't know if we were going to be picked up. I didn't want to be picked up. Honestly, the show ceased to be fun. One-person action-adventures are *killers*, and the network wanted a Steve Austin with cleavage. On the other hand, we felt like we had finally gotten the kinks worked out, so we all kind of *did* want to be picked up. It was a very ambiguous time for everyone. As much as I loved the series, I wanted to end it, because I was so wiped out. I was completely torn."

In all, there was a real opportunity for some closure, which is something that not many shows get to do.

CHAPTER 12

REACTIVATED

"THE ORIGINAL EPISODES OF *THE SIX MILLION DOLLAR MAN* AND *THE BIONIC WOMAN* WERE REALLY MORALITY PLAYS. AND WE TRIED TO CONTINUE THAT WITH THE *BIONIC* REUNIONS."

MICHAEL SLOAN

Reunion 1: *Return of The Six Million Dollar Man and The Bionic Woman*
....[5-17-87] NBC
Written by Michael Sloan. Story by Michael Sloan, Bruce (brother to Angela) Lansbury. Directed by Ray Austin. Featuring: Tom Schanley, Martin Landau (Mission: Impossible), Lee Majors II, Gary Lockwood, Terry Kiser, Scott Kraft, Bryan Cranston, Keith Farrell, Phil Nordell, Pamela Bryant, Catherine McGoohan, Deborah White, Julie Morgan, Sandey Grinn, Leonard Kibrick

An early form of militia, named Fortress, breaks into an infantry storehouse, and steals containers of automatic arms. They seek to employ them in America, via a scheme by an old OSI enemy, Lyle Stenning.

Steve, on the high seas, playing the skipper of a fishing boat, meets up with pals of Michael, his son with a woman he briefly wed. After their divorce, she passed away. Due to Steve's responsibilities with the OSI, Michael went to live with next of kin. Though father and son have drifted apart, Michael is making his Air Force graduation, and requires his dad's counsel.

Steve complies, as Oscar asks him to confront Stenning, whom they had battled a decade before. Steve's retired, and not interested, even if Jaime is involved, which Oscar hints may be the case. With time to think, Steve meets Michael's military instructor, and discovers his son to be somewhat of a daredevil.

Michael's all-too-risky attitude may have resulted from his all-too-frequent self-comparisons to his famous father's super reputation. They meet over dinner. Unbeknownst to Steve, Oscar makes certain that Jaime makes an appearance, albeit with a dull, computer nerd for a blind date.

Upon viewing Steve, she's nearly mortified, and attempts to get away. But it's too late. Steve notices his Bionic Woman, and their remerger is anything but idyllic. A quarrel ensues; Jaime pitches her Six Million Dollar Man right through the restaurant window, landing him on the sidewalk, at Michael's feet. She makes a beeline for the exit, while father and son attempt to communicate.

Steve then promises to be present when his son graduates the Academy. Meanwhile, Stenning is out to get his hands on Steve, who is eventually chased down by a car.

Steve later hooks up with Oscar and Jim Castillian (a brash young operative), and discovers Oscar's plan to reunite the *Bionic* duo. Oscar said Jaime's memory is returning, but that she's been upset with Steve because he apparently didn't care anymore. Oscar later speaks with Jaime, who is also not too crazy about his plans to rematch her with Steve.

In the interim, Steve confronts Stenning, who discloses his evil plan to establish a new military faction in the US. Jaime is soon kidnapped by Stenning's hoods, only to be rescued by Steve, who tells her that he has a son and that he's always kept a candle burning for her. Now she's sorry that she tossed him through that window. But she explained what she was feeling. She now realizes that blaming Steve for the death of former boyfriend Chris Williams was a mistake.

Neither of them, however, will yet admit their mutual love. After Jaime's safety is secured, Steve leaves to rescue Michael from another assault from Stenning and his troupe. Michael now realizes his dad is not like other fathers. Steve said he'll clarify the situation at Michael's graduation, which Jaime and Oscar also attend.

Unfortunately, during Michael's ceremonial flight, his aircraft's hydraulic combination falters and, in an eerie replay of his father's accident, the plane collides with the Earth. Michael survives by ejecting himself at the last second. There's only one solution for saving his life: Michael must become bionic.

In the end, both his lower limbs and his right arm become bionic, as does his right eye (which is also incorporated with a laser beam, with many settings, including stun). Together, Steve, Jaime, Michael, and Oscar confront Stenning and Fortress.

• Original working title: "The Bionic Reunion."

• According to *TV Guide*, Lee Majors II was considered for the role of Michael Austin.

• Lee Majors: "There were some emotional scenes unlike anything I'd done in *Six Mill*. It's about being brought back together with my son after we've been estranged. I feel that personally. I never knew my blood father, and I never really got to raise my son. He grew up back in Kentucky, and while he was in California [with me] all summer, that wasn't day-to-day. I feel like I missed something."

• Martin Brooks explained what it was like that first day on a *Bionic* set, after so many years: "It was terrific, and it proved to be a reunion in many ways. Lee, Lindsay, myself and Richard were together again. And Lee's son, who we had all known as an infant, had grown into a man."

• As far as TV-reunions go, this first film and the two that followed were of the highest quality, meeting the expectations of *Bionic* fans. Most television regatherings remain conscious of themselves, and set out merely to present an "Oh, look how we changed" update on the characters, instead of offering an actual two-hour continued episode of a given series. The *Bionic* reunions have been just that.

• Everyone was there, except Max. "Well, think about it," Lindsay said. "It was nearly ten years since the shows went off. Max would have been pretty darn old."

• *Return* came in number four in the week's ratings, making it one of NBC's highest-rated TV movies of the year.

• Tom Schanley's Michael Austin runs on a treadmill, and manages to reach 300 MPH. Highly implausible when you factor in wind resistance.

• Steve's first wife was named Karen. Ironically, Lee's wife at the time of filming was former *Playboy* model Karen Velez.

• Co-star Terry Kiser (Santiago) appeared in SM's "Love Song for Tanya" and BW's "Mirror Image."

• *Daily Variety*: "Never mind that fans of the original may wonder why he wasn't even wed in his years as superman; that's 'explained' with some fuzzy lingo by the Austin character. Lindsay Wagner and Majors are back in action for the pilot, handed a soggy script full of holes, confusing and boring. Majors and Wagner talk about the good old days, much of it mumbo-jumbo accompanied by overloud music by Marvin Hamlisch. Rock Music is tossed into the show, and the only good thing about the mess is that NBC did not choose to put it on the fall sked. Tom Schanley is likeable and convincing as the new bionic man, but his bionic eye can't whip the script."

• Rita Egleston returned as Lindsay's stunt double. Rita performed the big jumps in this movie, but broke her ankle while landing a small jump. Stuntwoman Donna Evans completed the remaining jumps, which included crashing through a window.

ORIGINAL *TV GUIDE* ADS AND PUBLICITY PHOTOS FOR 1987's *RETURN OF THE SIX MILLION DOLLAR MAN AND THE BIONIC WOMAN* (TOP) AND 1989's *BIONIC SHOWDOWN* (BOTTOM).

Reunion 2: *Bionic Showdown* .... [4-30-89] NBC
Written by Michael Sloan, Brock Choy. Story by Michael Sloan, Robert DeLaurentis. Directed by Alan Levi. Featuring: Lee Majors II, Sandra Bullock, Jeff Yagher, Josef Sommer, Geraint Wyn Davies (Airwolf, Dracula: The Series), *Lawrence Dane, Robert Lansing, Carolyn Dunn, Jack Blum, Andrew R. Dan, David Adamson, James Kee, Marcia Levine, Robert McClure, David Nerman, Steve Pernie and Steve Morris*

The World Unity Games soon take place in Toronto; global athletes will come together in courtesy and good sportsmanship for this Olympic-type event. For varied nations to become better acquainted, a celebration is showcased at the Pentagon. The affair is littered with antagonists who have attacked Steve, Jaime and Oscar on a number of occasions.

Oscar meets up with General McAllister, who doubts Mr. Goldman's proficiency with security measures. Steve enters, and is met by the humor-ridden Jimmy, Oscar's nephew. Steve sees Jaime, and finally decides to propose. The moment to pop the question is postponed.

There's been a break-in at the Pentagon. Important data is lifted to a helicopter, gunfire ensues, and Oscar is injured - by a bionic assailant. Close by is Kate ("Katie" to her friends and family), a young friend/patient of Jaime's who is restricted to a wheelchair. Jaime speaks with Rudy about Kate's cybernetic transformation, addressing the psychological and physical adjustments.

Successful bionic surgery is completed. Steve reaches OSI Headquarters, and is refused security admittance. Oscar later tells him and Jaime that someone bionic was entangled in the recent robbery. Michael, Steve's son, is in Florida. It's either Jaime, Steve or the newly-powered Kate.

General McAllister has now named himself security chief of the Games, and believes that another organization or country has attained and created cybernetic beings. Still, Jaime and Steve are held on suspicion, but break free to do some investigating of their own.

Oscar feigns resignation from the OSI after Gen. McAllister denies his request to transform Jimmy, who's apparently been in a horrible explosion, into a bionic young man. Kate, The Bionic Girl, with whom Jimmy is in love, shares her time with OSI operative Alan Devlin who, unbeknownst to her, is a bionic double agent, scheming to kill a USSR foreign minister and destroy the World Unity Games. In the end, Steve, Jaime, and Kate save the day, Jimmy really wasn't wounded and, before Steve can say another word, Jaime asks him to marry her.

• As with the first reunion film, this was a multi-reunion for Martin E. Brooks, who had previously worked with guest Robert Lansing, who succumbed to cancer in 1994. "We went back a lot of years," Brooks said. "We did a play in New York called *The Lovers*. He was a fine actor."

• Lansing was featured in the classic *Star Trek* episode, "Gary Seven" (an unsold series pilot) and would co-star in *Kung Fu: The Legend Continues*, for which Richard Anderson would provide the opening narration (beginning in 1993).

• Regarding the marriage proposal, Lindsay: "Oh, well, we had to do that."

• As to the parking lot attendant who refused to let Steve in: "Sorry, Colonel," he said. "You're not gonna go bionic on me, are you?" *Bionics* are top secret. How would a lowly parking lot attendant know Steve is bionic?

• Continuity error: Kate looks to the audience, during the Games, and notices Alan Devlin, clothed in a trench coat. Seconds later, Devlin's in a room with Steve, Jaime and Castillian, minus the coat. Later still, he's back in the throng of people, with the garment, moving in precisely the same manner in which he had maneuvered himself when Kate had first taken notice.

• Jaime completes a run through the park with Kate and appears quite winded. Should this be the case? In the *Six Mill* pilot, Dr. Wells notes that Steve's lungs "are used to handling oxygen for the blood supply for two arms and two legs. Now they only have to take care of one." So why is she gassed? Age notwithstanding, her bionic legs should be doing all the work.

• FYI, the race scene was filmed at the Royal Botanical Gardens in Hamilton, Ontario. The scenes that took place at the World Unity Games event were filmed at Copps Coliseum, also in Hamilton.

• Steve and Jaime are jailed in an OSI cell. He paces, expediently. She tells him that he's making her nervous. He said it's payback for all the times that she made *him* nervous, noting that it probably all started "when we carved our initials into that tree ten years ago." Considering when they filmed this movie, a more common sense estimate would have been 25 years earlier.

• In an attempt to compile a list of potential suspects, Oscar Goldman notes that there are only four bionic human beings in the world: Steve, Jaime, Michael Austin, and Kate. But what about Seven Million Dollar Man Barney Hiller? Or Andy Sheffield, *the Bionic Boy*? Either Oscar forgot, or the writers didn't do their homework. Probably the latter.

• Jeff Yagher: "I loved *The Six Million Dollar Man*. I was about 14 then. I liked *The Bionic Woman* too, though I was older then. Lindsay's [good looks] probably made me watch it more than the actual science fiction."

• Cute banter closes the film when Jimmy said,

> "I think this is going to be a lot of fun."
> "What?" Kate asks.
> "Having a bionic girlfriend," he replies.
> "You think so, huh?" Kate returns.

• *Daily Variety*: "Even though stars Lee Majors and Lindsay Wagner have been true-blue for what seems like decades, and even though the new bionic spy's sound effects don't have the 'click' of Majors' and Wagner's, the bureaucrats insist on treating the heroes like the prime suspects. When the story finally gets past these theatrics (and even more ludicrous tantrums involving Anderson's character), we get around to an actual adventure, but it's just a humdrum plot to set off a bomb at a *glastnost*-themed track meet."

Reunion 3: *Bionic Ever After?* . . . . [11-29-94] CBS
Written by Michael Sloan, Norman Morrill. Story by Michael Sloan. Directed by Steve Stafford. Featuring: Farrah Forke (Wings), *Anne Lockhart, Alan Sader, Geordie Johnson, Ivan Sergei, Robert D. Raiford, James Shanta, Michael Hartson, Ann Pierce, Michael Camden Richards, Shanghai Stafford, General Fermon Judd, Jr., Michael Burgess, Dave Thomas*

Jaime's become a counselor of OSI agents, and suddenly starts having problems with her bionic systems. She may be dying, on the verge of her wedding to Steve. Oscar tracks down Rudy (suggesting that the bionic program is not a high priority anymore), and the good doctor tries to save Ms. Sommers.

Turns out someone replaced one of the computer chips in her arm with one that has a virus, which invaded her bionics, making her feel ill. That someone is OSI agent-gone-bad Kimberly Harmon who is, unknowing to all, the daughter of Rudy's former assistant, Dr. Jason Havilland.

Meanwhile, terrorist Miles Kendrick is after a tennis pro named Astaad Rashid, who wants to defect to the USA. Kendrick will detonate a nuclear warhead at the US Embassy in Nassau unless Rashid faces punishment for treachery from Rashid's uncle. The terrorist will be paid handsomely by Rashid's uncle (who is an arms dealer) if he pulls off this job as planned.

Jaime may be dying, so she pushes Steve out of her life. He decides a mission will take his mind off Jaime, and volunteers to the situation down in the Bahamas at the embassy. Oscar's against it, but gives in.

Before Steve leaves, Kimberly shows up with a dumb excuse to go along, and does the same things to Steve that she's done to Jaime, implanting a viral-infecting chip. Thanks to Rudy, Jaime recovers and figures out who nearly killed her. Newly equipped with night vision, she flies down to Nassau, saves Steve, and they both stop Kendrick. Later, they get married and live bionically ever after.

• "The original version of this script was more action-packed," said director Steve Stafford. "There were three times as many bionic gags than we actually used. But we were running low on the budget funds, so we had to

WORLD PREMIERE MOVIE

WILL THEIR LOVE SURVIVE WHEN THEIR BIONICS FAIL?

The technology that saved them twenty years ago may now destroy the happiest day of their lives.

LINDSAY WAGNER is The Bionic Woman

LEE MAJORS is The 6 Million Dollar Man

CBS 8 PM

BIONIC EVER AFTER?

ORIGINAL *TV GUIDE* AD AND PUBLICITY PHOTOS FOR 1994'S *BIONIC EVER AFTER?*

make cuts."

He wanted to use some cutting-edge camera techniques, which had not been done before. "We began a camera process called *ramping*," he explained, "which allowed us to go from 24 frames with sync-sound, and to crank up the camera to high speed, for the bionics, without having to stop the camera, and cut-away. If you look carefully at the bionics that we did do for this film, you'll notice that there's not that usual cut, and then move to slow motion.

"It just kind of becomes slow motion. Whenever Steve or Jaime are about to do bionics, they'll start out with a piece of dialogue in normal speed, and then all of sudden, the scenes become bionic, rather than the hard-cut to the high speed-cam. It's real effective, because most people don't notice it. If they do, then the director is doing something wrong."

• Like Michael Sloan, Stafford came to understand the world of cybernetic TV quite well. Years after working as personal assistant to Lee Majors, Universal was searching for a director to guide *Ever After?* Without mention of his previous SM connection, Stafford landed the appointment, and remained true to the central chemistry of the original shows. He went after the job, because he thought it would be "fun to relive the past." "But I wasn't sure how Universal was going to take it," he said, "especially because I once worked for Lee, and because I had known Richard Anderson and Lindsay."

Though he had just completed directing a well-received TV-movie (*Double Edge*, with Susan Lucci and Robert Urich, in 1993), Stafford admits his prior *Bionic* liaison was definitely an advantage on *Ever After?* "Lee, for one," he said, "did more for me, personally, than he would have done for another director."

• Original working title: "Bionic Breakdown." The first version of the script had Steve Austin jilted at the altar, unaware that Jaime had been kidnapped.

• In all three reunion movies, OSI stood for "Office of Scientific Information."

• Though it took four years to bring *Bionic Ever After?* to television screens, it took a mere 20 days to film it. The budget was approximately $3.7 million, the same cost as *Bionic Showdown. Return* ran $4.8 million.

• Lee Majors: "It's kind of shameful that she's [Wagner] the one who knocks the door down to save me. Usually, *I'm* the one who knocks down the doors. Actually, though, I was glad about it. I'm getting a little too old to be knocking down the door."

• Also, Stafford recalls: "We lost much of our location sets, because the people in Charleston did not want filming in their community. Rainy weather didn't help either."

• A minor, but important, glitch with one of the props: The manhole cover that Jaime flings at Kimberly's truck has the insignia, *CPW*, which stands for Charleston Public Works, denoting the actual filming location of the set, in Charleston, South Carolina (and not the fictional Nassau setting). Producer Michael Gallant said that Charleston was chosen over Jacksonville, Florida, and Wilmington, North Carolina, as the location that best combined elements of the Bahamas and Washington, D.C.

• Guest Farrah Forke was named after Farrah Fawcett. While growing up in Corpus Cristi, Texas, Forke was a big fan of the respective shows. "It was a show that was important to me as a child," she said. "It wasn't the bionic thing as much as it was Lindsay and Lee are so charismatic, and the characters that they play are so real and human and caring. They're not mechanical. So it's kind of a man with a machine thing instead of a man against a machine thing."

• Cameo star Dave Thomas, who passed away in January 2002, was good friends with Lee Majors. Though both were orphaned as children, they managed to retain a sense of humor. During filming, Lee ribbed Dave a little bit about his Wendy's ads and cameo, saying, "You said my show is your favorite. You flew down for an hour to visit me, and we put you in the movie. The least you can do is buy some air time." "Well," Majors now gleefully reported, "he did."

• The airing of this film on CBS sealed the fact that *The Six Million Dollar Man/Bionic Woman* television franchise has appeared on all three major television networks in one form or another, be it a series or reunion movie, which is somewhat of a rarity in the industry.

• The wedding dress that Lindsay wore was sold at auction for $643.07.

• *New York Post's* John Podhoretz: "They are a mismatched couple of gigantic proportions, since Lindsay Wagner's Jaime is brittle, neurotic and whip-smart, while Lee Majors' Steve is a dumb good-time Joe — want to bet they're playing themselves? ... The movie ends with Steve and Jaime talking about having kids, when what these two rather long-in-the-tooth newlyweds should really be talking about is signing up for membership in the American Association of Retired Persons and getting more fiber in their diet. But I know nothing I can say will deter some of you from watching. So go ahead. Let *Bionic Ever After?* bring back those exciting memories of the 1970s — memories like the fall of Saigon, Watergate, gas lines, and platform shoes."

• *Daily Variety*: "Main trouble is the comic book aspects have been jettisoned in favor of a *Mission: Impossible* urgency. It doesn't work in Bionia. Forke and Johnson overplay the villainy, and the special effects are so-so."

CONTRASTING DATA

Steve was born in Ojai, California, where a road sign reads "The Home of American Astronaut Steven Austin." Jaime, ex-tennis pro-cum-psychologist, also lived there, before she became a celebrity athlete, returning after to live with Steve's mother Helen (played by Martha Scott) and his stepfather, Jim Elgin (Ford Rainey).

When not running, he drives an automobile like everyone else. (At one time, he drove a car with the license plate 299KKL.) His automobile of choice was a Mercedes, but he was also seen driving a metallic blue Datsun 280Z (as did Jaime).

During the first few seasons of SM, he adorned an inscribed POW/MIA bracelet on his right bionic arm. Commonly worn by Air Force personnel and private citizens, it disappeared by the fourth year. Beginning with *Wine, Women and War,* the first 90-minute movie sequel, he frequently wore a particular metal belt buckle. (Apparently, it was brass.) Yet for all intents and purposes, he was no superman of steel, but a human aircraft pilot, whose life was forever changed from the moment his testing vehicle colliding with the Earth.

Through the years, as the audience came to know Steve and Jaime, there would be inconsistencies. For example, as a freshman in high school, Jaime first kissed Steve at his senior year New Year's Eve party. (His friends kidded him that he was "robbing the cradle.") Yet, as mentioned in Ken Johnson's first BW script, "Welcome Home, Jaime," he met her when they were both in the third grade, "when Jaime dared Steve to eat all that food." He did and he became very ill.

Most of the "little things," however, are clear. The Capri was Steve and Jaime's pizza haunt and, when they were troubled, the downed tree near the shore of the lake provided a refuge for sorting things out. Nearby is another tree with their initials carved into it. And while Ken Johnson may have named Jaime after a water skier, she was not known for aqua abilities, but rather her expertise with a tennis racket. Facts pertaining to her court prowess were handled with detailed care:

She was one of the top five female tennis pros in the world, with the potential to beat the very best in her business. A little girl (portrayed by Dana *Diff'rent Strokes* Plato) watching Jaime play at an Ojai tennis court said to Steve: "Boy, I just know she's gonna beat Billie Jean King at Forest Hills next time," referring to the US Open. After a brief stop in Ojai, she was scheduled to travel to Barcelona for a professional tournament.

As to the events leading up to Jaime's accident, she and Steve jumped from a single engine plane (I.D. Number N5794A) and descended to Earth. When Jaime's altimeter read 8, she and Steve pulled their respective ripcords. Both parachutes opened, but Jaime's malfunctions and sends her plunging to the ground.

We hear: "Her legs have so many breaks we still haven't counted them all. The hemorrhaging from her right ear seems to indicate interior damage to the cochlea and corti. And her right arm and shoulder are completely ... I'm sorry, Colonel. We'll try to save her but there's only so much we can do. Maybe some day we'll be able to repair broken bodies like hers."

She would later experience a complete recovery, thanks to an integral cybernetic transformation (which allowed her to run the mile in 58 seconds). She would relinquish her career as a tennis pro to become a schoolteacher (grade levels, six to nine) at the Ventura Air Force Base in California (her cover for the OSI). Her carriage house over the stable at the home of Steve's parents would even allow for her own phone (given verbally and seen on camera as 311-555-2368, but also seen on camera as 311-555-7306).

PART I
REPAIR MANUALS

Super-strong but hardly invulnerable, Steve and Jaime had their share of bionic mishaps. Many episodes from both shows, listed below, attest to this. (Segments where they received minor injuries or routine tune-ups have been omitted.)

Austin's Attacks

In *The Pilot*, Steve, while picnicking, happens upon a car accident and performs his first post-surgery act of heroism when he rescues a little boy from a burning car. The ordeal, however, comes at a price: a badly-impaired bionic arm.

In *Wine, Women and War*, while dodging depth charges, Steve's bionic arm is split open in the process of retrieving a top-secret code book.

In "Population: Zero," Dr. Bacon, familiar with bionic construction and its fallibilities, puts Steve on ice to slow down the astounding astronaut.

In "Survival of the Fittest," Steve slices open his bionic right index finger to provide the two hot hires needed to cauterize a dying Oscar's bleeding vein.

In "The Rescue of Athena One," Steve's bionic hardware malfunctions in the zero-gravity of outer-space. His astronautic career is salvaged, however, after Oscar informs him that Rudy can make the appropriate adjustments.

In "Dr. Wells is Missing," Steve's right arm is damaged in a scrimmage with the Tucelli brothers' goons.

In "Pilot Error," an in-flight oil spray renders Steve's mortal and bionic eye useless.

In "The Pal-Mir Escort," during an emergency procedure, the atomic power pack from Steve's right arm is removed so that it may be used for the world's first bionic heart transplant.

In "The Pioneers," Steve's synthetic arm requires a sling when a crazed astronaut attacks it with an iron beam.

In "Stranger in Broken Fork," Steve's bionic arm is ripped open after defending a caravan of mentally ill patients from local yokels.

In "The Cross-Country Kidnap," Steve's bionic arm takes a bullet while pursuing a sniper.

In "The Last Kamikaze," the bionic components in Steve's ankle are exposed after falling into a cleverly camouflaged pit constructed by his Kamikaze captor.

In "Steve Austin, Fugitive," Steve is shot in his left leg, but with the aid of Callahan and a folksy electronics store owner (played by Lee Majors, no less), Steve is able to do an admirable patch-up job.

In "The Return of the Bionic Woman, Part I," Steve's legs are damaged while trying to disrupt a meeting between underworld syndicates.

In "Clark Templeton O'Flaherty," hoodlums throw a knife that penetrates Steve's bionic right arm. Without flinching, he pulls the bloodless knife out, much to the hoods' amazement.

In "Hocus-Pocus," ruffians place Steve in a sub-zero freezer, sapping him of his bionic strength.

In "The Deadly Test," a device which has the power to short-out the engines of jet fighters also succeeds in shutting down Austin's bionic eye and right arm.

In "The Return of Bigfoot, Part I," the atomic power packs in Steve's legs burst when a hydraulic lift crushes them.

In "The Most Dangerous Enemy," Steve is rendered temporarily powerless when Rudy wraps his legs with a magnetic coil.

In "H+2+O = Death," Steve's bionic arm is punctured while wrestling for control of an underwater breathing device.

In "Kill Oscar, Part I," Steve's bionic arm is jolted by a laboratory-controlled bolt of electricity when doing tests on the OSI weather machine.

In "Vulture of the Andes," Steve's right arm is weakened when it is suddenly yanked by a rope attached to a tow plane.

In "Death Probe, Part II," Steve's bionic arm is damaged in a confrontation with the erstwhile Probe.

In "Danny's Inferno," Steve's right arm requires a sling after it comes into contact with super-heated chemicals.

In "To Catch the Eagle," Steve's right arm is pierced during an altercation with a Native American unhappy with Steve closing in on two missing OSI geologists.

In "Deadly Countdown, Part I and II," when outlaws attempt to hijack a space launch via electronic jamming, Steve's space-age eye begins to fail him.

In "Bigfoot V," Steve falls into an icy river and temporarily loses power in his bionics.

In "Dark Side of the Moon, Part II," a super-cooled metal beam extending from the moon's frosty surface is used to "chill out" Steve Austin.

In "Walk a Deadly Wing," Steve suffers a temporary loss of power in his left leg.

In *Bionic Ever After?*, Steve's bionic systems go haywire when the same computer virus that halted Jaime afflicts the world's first bionic man.

Jaime's Batteries

In "The Deadly Missiles," Jaime's right leg is shorted out by an electrified floor.

For "Fly Jaime," see SM's "Survival of the Fittest" (with Rudy substituted for Oscar).

In "Kill Oscar, Part I," Jaime's heroic leap from Callahan's bedroom window proves too much for her cybernetic legs, which burst into a hail of sparks upon impact - prompting Rudy to worry about renewed bionic rejection.

In "Doomsday is Tomorrow, Part II," Jaime's courageous battle with super-computer Alex is interrupted when a sliding door slams shut on one of her legs. Like Steve, she is proficient enough in bionics to do a quick fix-it job (aided by one of Alex's better-behaved computer cousins).

In "The Bionic Dog, Part II," a temporally-disoriented Max bites Jaime on her right arm, exposing some wires.

In "The Martians Are Coming, The Martians Are Coming," Jaime courts big trouble when she's thrown into a deep freeze.

In "The Pyramid," the power pack from Jaime's right arm is removed in order to power a crystal converted into an interstellar transmitter.

In "On the Run," Jaime's right arm is injured while preventing a botched kidnapping attempt at a zoo.

In *Bionic Ever After?*, a rogue OSI agent secretly implants microchips infected with a computer virus into a drugged-up Jaime's right arm.

PART II

MECHANICS ILLUSTRATED

Steve and Jaime's bionic parts were quite intricate. Following is a list for both, beginning with his —

Hardware

Bionic Visual Cortex Terminal
Catalog #075/KFB
43MM O.D. F/0.95
Zoom Ratio: 20.2 to 1
2135 Line 60HZ
Extended Chromatic Response
Class JC
Classified

*Bionic Neuro-Link Forearm/
Upper Arm Assembly (Right)*
Catalog #2821/WLV
And
Bionic Neuro-Link Hand (Right)
Catalog #2822/PJI
Neuro Feedback Terminated
Power Supply:
Atomic Type AED-4
Catalog #2821 AED-4
1550 Watt Continuous Duty
Nominal Double Gain
Overload Follower
Class MZ
Classified

Bionic Neuro-Link
Bipedal Assembly
Catalog #914 PAH
Neuro Feedback Terminated
Power Supply:
Atomic Type AED-9A
4920 Watt Continuous Duty
Nominal Double Gain
Overload Follower
2100 Watt Reserve
Intermittent Duty
Class CC
Classified

Software

Bionic Audio Micro Sensor
Catalog #6314-KMH.
.004 Micro Mill .J75
Amplification 1400 DBS
.001 Distortion Max
Class BG
Classified

Bionic Neuro-Link Forearm/
Upper Arm Assembly (Right)
Catalog #2821/WLV
And
Bionic Neuro-Link Hand (Right)
Catalog #2822/PJI
Neuro Feedback Terminated
Power Supply:
Atomic Type AED-4
Catalog #2821 AED-4
1550 Watt Continuous Duty
Nominal Double Gain
Overload Follower
Class MZ
Classified

Bionic Neuro-Link
Bipedal Assembly
Catalog #914 PAH
Neuro Feedback Terminated
Power Supply:
Atomic Type AED-9A
4920 Watt Continuous Duty
Nominal Double Gain
Overload Follower
2100 Watt Reserve
Intermittent Duty
Class CC
Classified

PART III

TECHNICAL TERMS

Adrenalizine	A putty-like substance that allows mere mortals to mimic bionic strength and speed.
Alex-7000	Dr. Elijah Cooper's Machiavellian supercomputer in charge of carrying out the dying scientist's doomsday threat (which proved to be a no-show).
Babe	A term of endearment Oscar reserves for Jaime.
Bionic	The marriage of cybernetic and human components resulting in superhuman strength.
Capri	An Ojai pizza parlor that doubled as Steve and Jaime's old haunt.
Carnegie Tech	Jaime's college. Loosely based on Carnegie Mellon University in Pittsburgh, Pennsylvania — the real-life alma mater of Ken Johnson and Jennifer Darling.
Colorado Springs	The site of Steve's bionic rebirth.
Cryogenics	A revolutionary medical procedure responsible for giving Jaime a second chance at life following her first bout with bionic rejection.
Cybernetic	Another term for bionic.
Cyborg	The term used to describe a half-human/half-machine.

Directed Energy Ray Weapon	America's first energy ray weapon, invented by Rod Kyler and stolen by renegade Fembots.
Dirty Dozen	The derisive name given to Jaime's Air Force brats, whohad notorious discipline problems.
Edwards Air Force Base	The site of Steve's near-fatal crash.
Euthenium J	A principle substance of Dr. Cooper's doomsday device.
Feelings	The title of the song Jaime sang when she entered the Miss United States Beauty Pageant; may also be used to define the character herself, her emotional ties to Steve, and life in general.
Fembots	Super-strong female androids that were the brainchild of a disgruntled ex-OSI scientist.
Fortress	Name of a xenophobic mercenary outfit, led by Lyle Stenning, that reemerges in the late 1980s, causing headaches for the OSI.
Level 6 Clearance	An OSI security code allowed to those who are knowledgeable of bionics in general, and Steve Austin and Jaime Sommers, in particular. The reference to *6*, as in *six million dollars*, may or may not be intentional.
Lisa Galloway	Jaime's surgically-altered identical twin.
Marsden Ranch	Steve's newly-acquired home in Ojai.
My Little Girl	The nickname given to Steve's mother, Helen, by her first husband, Carl Austin. Also the name given to Carl's WWII airplane, in which he perished.
Neotraxin	A miracle wonder drug (concocted by Bigfoot's alien friends) that wards off disease and cures ailments.

NSB   Short for National Security Bureau, which is a US agency that tried to put Jaime away (in BW's "On the Run").

Ojai, CA   The childhood hometown of Steve and Jaime and residence of Steve's mother and stepfather (as well as the adult Jaime Sommers).

OSI   The Office of Scientific Intelligence.

Pal   Oscar's pet name for Steve.

Peregrine   The name of the nuclear device Steve was attempting to retrieve from a wayward WWII Japanese solder.

Saint Emile Island   Dr. Franklin's home base, from which he wreaked havoc on the world with his dastardly weather machine.

San Angelo Fault Line   The secret hiding place of Bigfoot and friends.

Sasquatch   A Native-American name given to Bigfoot that evolved from a lower-life form and absconds unsuspecting humans to be studied by his alien masters.

Snow White   Oscar's top-secret priority code.

Summer Maiden   The name of Steve Austin's fishing boat in the first reunion movie.

TLC   *A Time Line Converter* time-travel device that allows Bigfoot's alien family to move faster or slower relative to the objects around them.

Unity Games   A Toronto-based international competition whose security was arranged by Col. Austin. Also the venue where a villainous cyborg met his demise.

USS Henderson   The US warship upon which Oscar's brother, Sam, died during Japan's sneak attack on Pearl Harbor.

Ventura Air Force Base   The site of Jaime's first teaching job.

Venus Space Probe   A Russian device that errantly reenters Earth's atmosphere and wreaks havoc on Wyoming; also known as Death Probe.

SIX MILLION EPISODES IN ALPHABETICAL ORDER

ABC Suspense Telefilms

Six Million Dollar Man, The (#1)
Solid Gold Kidnapping, The (#3)
Wine, Women and War (#2)

The Six Million Dollar Man

Act of Piracy (#22)
Big Brother (#57)
Bigfoot V (#84)
Bionic Badge, The (#56)
Bionic Boy, The (#64)
Bionic Christmas Carol, A (#67)
Bionic Criminal, The (#44)
Bionic Woman, The, Part I (#32)
Bionic Woman, The, Part II (#33)
Blue Flash, The (#45)
Burning Bright (#11)
Carnival of Spies (#75)
Cheshire Project, The (#90)
Clark Templeton O'Flaherty (#48)
Coward, The (#12)
Cross-Country Kidnap, The (#25)
Danny's Inferno (#72)
Dark Side of the Moon, Part I (#87)
Dark Side of the Moon, Part II (#88)
Date with Danger, Part I (#98)
Date with Danger, Part II (#99)

Day of the Robot (#4)
Deadly Countdown, Part I (#82)
Deadly Countdown, Part II (#83)
Dead Ringer (#97)
Deadly Replay, The (#21)
Deadly Test, The (#41)
Death Probe, Part I (#70)
Death Probe, Part II (#71)
Divided Loyalty (#47)
Doomsday, and Counting (#6)
Double Trouble (#60)
Dr. Wells is Missing (#9)
E.S.P. Spy, The (#31)
Eyewitness to Murder (#7)
Fires of Hell (#73)
Ghostly Teletype, The (#79)
Golden Pharaoh, The (#54)
H + 2 + 0 = Death (#62)
Hocus-Pocus (#51)
Infiltrators, The (#74)
Just a Matter of Time (#92)
Kill Oscar, Part 2 (#63)
Killer Wind (#85)
Last Kamikaze, The (#27)
Last of the Fourth of Julys, The (#10)
Little Orphan Airplane (#5)
Look Alike (#30)
Lost Island, The (#95)
Lost Love (#26)

Love Song for Tanya (#55)
Madonna Caper, The (#96)
Midas Touch, The (#20)
Most Dangerous Enemy, The (#61)
Moving Mountain, The (#100)
Nightmare in the Sky (#59)
Nuclear Alert (#14)
One of Our Running Backs is Missing
   (#43)
Operation Firefly (#3)
Outrage in Balinderry (#34)
Pal–Mir Escort, The (#17)
Peeping Blonde, The (#24)
Pilot Error (#16)
Pioneers, The (#15)
Population: Zero (#1)
Price of Liberty, The (#38)
Privacy of the Mind, The (#77)
Rescue of Athena One, The (#8)
Return of Bigfoot, The, Part I (#58)
Return of Death Probe, Part I (#93)
Return of Death Probe, Part II (#94)
Return of the Bionic Woman, The,
   Part I (#36)
Return of the Bionic Woman, The,
   Part II (#37)
Return of the Robot Maker (#28)
Rollback (#86)
Run, Steve, Run (#13)
Secret of Bigfoot, The, Part I (#52)
Secret of Bigfoot, The, Part II (#53)
Seven Million Dollar Man, The (#18)
Sharks!, Part I (#80)
Sharks!, Part II (#81)
Song and Dance Spy (#39)
Steve Austin, Fugitive (#35)
Straight on 'Til Morning (#19)
Stranger in Broken Fork (#23)
Survival of the Fittest (#2)
Taneha (#29)
Target in the Sky (#42)
Target: Steve Austin (#89)
Task Force (#68)

Thunderbird Connection, The (#66)
To Catch the Eagle (#78)
Ultimate Imposter, The (#69)
U-509 (#76)
Vulture of the Andes (#65)
Walk a Deadly Wing (#91)
Welcome Home, Jaime, Part I (#50)
White Lightning War, The (#46)
Winning Smile, The (#49)
Wolf Boy, The (#40)

The Bionic Woman

African Connection (#41)
All for One (#47)
Angel of Mercy (#32)
Antidote, The (#49)
Assault on the Princess (#16)
Beyond the Call (#31)
Biofeedback (#25)
Bionic Beauty (#6)
Bionic Dog, The, Part I (#36)
Bionic Dog, The, Part II (#37)
Black Magic (#20)
Brain Wash (#43)
Canyon of Death (#9)
Claws (#4)
Deadly Missiles, The (#5)
Deadly Music (#52)
Deadly Ringer, Part I (#28)
Deadly Ringer, Part II (#29)
DeJon Caper, The (#32)
Doomsday is Tomorrow, Part I (#26)
Doomsday is Tomorrow, Part II (#27)
Escape to Love (#44)
Fembots in Las Vegas, Part I (#38)
Fembots in Las Vegas, Part II (#39)
Fly Jaime (#10)
Ghosthunter, The (#13)
In This Corner, Jaime Sommers (#15)
Iron Ships and Dead Men (#34)
Jailing of Jaime, The (#11)
Jaime and the King (#30)

Jaime's Mother (#7)
Jaime's Shield, Part I (#23)
Jaime's Shield, Part II (#24)
Kill Oscar, Part I (#18)
Kill Oscar, Part III (#19)
Long Live the King (#55)
*Martians are Coming, The, Martians
     are Coming, The* (#50)
Max (#45)
Mirror Image (#12)
Motorcycle Boogie (#42)
Night Demon, The (#33)
Once a Thief (#35)
On the Run (#57)
Out of Body (#54)
Over the Hill Spy (#46)
Rancho Outcast (#56)
Return of Bigfoot, The, Part II (#14)
Road to Nashville (#17)
Rodeo (#40)
Sanctuary Earth (#51)
Sister Jaime (#21)
Thing of the Past, A (#3)
Vega Influence, The (#22)
Welcome Home, Jaime, Part II (#1)
Which One is Jaime? (#53)
Winning is Everything (#8)

The Reunion Movies

Bionic Ever After? (#3)
Bionic Showdown (#2)
*Return of The Six Million Dollar
     Man and The Bionic Woman* (#1)

AUTHOR HERBIE J PILATO WITH RICHARD ANDERSON, LEE MAJORS
AND LINDSAY WAGNER ON THE SET OF 1994'S *BIONIC EVER AFTER*.

ACKNOWLEDGMENTS

I am grateful to all of those who contributed to *The Bionic Book*, in the form of countless interview hours and commentary, research, editorial and graphic design, photos, moral support and encouragement.

First and foremost, I would like to thank the late, unforgettable Martin Caidin, without whom there would have been no Steve Austin or Jaime Sommers, let alone a *bionic* book. I would also like to thank: Harve Bennett, Glen Larson, Kenneth Johnson, Lionel Siegel, Arthur Rowe, James Parriott, Richard Anderson, Lee Majors, Lindsay Wagner, Martin E. Brooks, Alan Oppenheimer, Jennifer Darling, Vince Van Patten, Sam Chew, Richard Lenz, Ford Rainey, Martha Scott, Sharon Farrell, Monte Markham, John Fujioka, Jack Cole, Philip DeGuere, Wilton Denmark, Elroy Schwartz, Michael Sloan, Phil Bondelli, Sean Cassidy, Steve Stafford, Todd Langenfeld, Greg C. Jensen Sr., Bernard Loomis, Dee Wallace Stone, and the many other actors, writers, directors, producers and additional members of the *Bionic* team, behind and in front of the camera.

Sincere appreciation for those individuals who contributed to the book or "bionic fandom" in a substantial way: Rod Rehn, Jim Sherrard, Mike Van Plew, Kory Dayani, Nick Wall, John Patterson, Clive Banks, and Craig Pierce. A heartfelt thank you is extended to Rosemary Haynes and her incredibly helpful colleagues at the U.S. Library of Congress. Special thanks to Mark Phillips and Frank Garcia for their excellent tome, *Science Fiction Television Series* (1996), which proved to be a useful source of episode anecdotes and insightful quotes.

Thank you, too, to the entire family of professionals at BearManor Media, especially to publisher Ben Ohmart for his loyalty and respect for all media things classic, and his wife and executive assistant, Mayumi Ohmart, and typesetter Brian Pearce.

Thank you also to graphic designer/photo archivist Matt Hankinson, who created the brilliant, eclectic cover of this book, and to the proficient

Brendan Slattery for his fact-checking, editorial guidance, voluminous resource materials, and impeccable research assistance.

The Bionic Book would have never been properly assembled without any of you.

ABOUT THE AUTHOR

Herbie J Pilato is an award-winning writer, producer, director, TV personality and performer whose eclectic list of critically-acclaimed pop-culture/media tie-in books, includes *Connery, Sean Connery: His Life and Career Before, During and After His Most Famous Role* (BearManor Media, 2023), *Retro Active Television: An In-Depth Perspective Of Classic TV's Social Circuitry* (Headline Books, 2023, which the Los Angeles Book Festival named "Book of the Year," and which named Pilato "Author of the Year"), *The 12 Best Secrets of Christmas: A Treasure House of December Memories Revealed* (Archway, 2022), *Mary: The Mary Tyler Moore Story* (Jacobs Brown Press, 2019), *Dashing, Daring and Debonair: TV's Top Male Icons From The '50s, '60s, And '70s* (Taylor Trade, 2016), *Glamour, Gidgets and the Girl Next Door: Television's Iconic Women From The '50s, '60s, And '70s* (Taylor Trade, 2014), *The Essential Elizabeth Montgomery: A Guide To Her Magical Performances* (Taylor Trade, 2013), *Twitch Upon A Star: The Bewitched Life And Career of Elizabeth Montgomery* (Taylor Trade, 2012), *NBC & ME: My Life As A Page In A Book* (Bear Manor Media, 2008), *The Bionic Book: The Six Million Dollar Man And The Bionic Woman Reconstructed* (Bear Manor Media, 2008), *The Kung Fu Book Of Wisdom* (Tuttle, 1995), *The Kung Fu Book Of Caine* (Tuttle, 1993), and *The Bewitched Book* (Dell, 1992).

Pilato has served as executive producer, director, and writer on the TV documentary *Elizabeth Montgomery: A Bewitched Life* for the Reelz Channel, as a consultant and audio commentator for the Saturn-Award-nominated Blu-ray release of *The Six Million Dollar Man and The Bionic Woman*, and as a consultant and on-screen commentator for CNN's hit eight-part series, *History of the Sitcom*. He's also worked on various other Blu-ray and DVD releases, as well as broadcast, and cable TV documentaries such as Bravo's *100 Greatest TV Characters*, *Bewitched: The True Hollywood Story*, *David Carradine: The E! True Hollywood Story*, A&E's *Biography* of Lee Majors, TLC's *Behind the Fame* specials about *The Mary Tyler Moore Show* and *The Bob Newhart Show*, *L.A. Law* and *Hill Street Blues*, the Syfy Channel's *Sciography* series, and the TV Guide Channel's hit five-part series, *100 Moments That Changed TV*, among others.

In addition to his books, Pilato has written for the Television Academy at Emmys.com and *Emmy Magazine* and has contributed to several other media outlets, such as *Closer Magazine*, and TVWriter.com, for which he has served as Contributing Editor Emeritus for over twenty-five years. In 2010, Pilato established The Classic TV Preservation Society, a formal 501(c)3 nonprofit organization dedicated to the positive influence of classic television shows. In 2019, pioneered the classic TV talk show format, serving as a host and an executive producer (with Joel Eisenberg) on *Then Again with Herbie J Pilato*, which premiered on Amazon Prime, Amazon Prime UK, and Shout! Factory TV.

For more information, please visit www.HerbieJPilato.com.

PHOTO CONTRIBUTORS

Photos are identified by page number. For pages featuring multiple photos, individual photos are identified by number — starting from the top row, left-to-right, top-to-bottom.

Printed in Great Britain
by Amazon

34928676R00215